Android Development with Kotlin

Enhance your skills for Android development using Kotlin

Marcin Moskala
Igor Wojda

BIRMINGHAM - MUMBAI

Android Development with Kotlin

First published: August 2017

Production reference: 3081117

Published by Packt Publishing Ltd.
Livery Place
35 Livery Street
Birmingham
B3 2PB, UK.

ISBN 978-1-78712-368-7

www.packtpub.com

Credits

Authors
Marcin Moskala
Igor Wojda

Reviewers
Mikhail Glukhikh
Stepan Goncharov

Commissioning Editor
Aaron Lazar

Acquisition Editor
Chaitanya Nair

Content Development Editor
Rohit Kumar Singh

Technical Editor
Pavan Ramchandani

Copy Editor
Safis Editing

Project Coordinator
Vaidehi Sawant

Proofreader
Safis Editing

Indexer
Francy Puthiry

Graphics
Abhinash Sahu

Production Coordinator
Nilesh Mohite

About the Authors

Marcin Moskala is an experienced Android developer who is always looking for ways to improve. He has been passionate about Kotlin since its early beta release. He writes articles for trade press and speaks at programming conferences.

Marcin is quite active in the programming and open source community, and is also passionate about cognitive and data science. You can visit his website (`marcinmoskala.com`), or follow him on GitHub (`MarcinMoskala`) and on Twitter (`@marcinmoskala`).

I would like to thank my co-workers in Gamekit, Docplanner, and Apreel. I especially want to thank my supervisors, who were not only supportive, but who are also a constant source of knowledge and inspiration: Mateusz Mikulski, Krzyysztof Wolniak, Bartek Wilczynski, and Rafal Trzeciak.

I would like to thank Marek Kaminski, Gleb Smirnov, Jacek Jablonski, and Maciej Gorski for the corrections, and Dariusz Bacinski and James Shvarts for reviewing the code of the example application.

I would like to thank my family and my girlfriend - Maja Markiewicz - for their support and help. I especially want to thank them for making an environment that supports passion and self-realization.

Igor Wojda is an experienced engineer with over 11 years of experience in software development. His adventure with Android started a few years ago, and he is currently working as a senior Android developer in the healthcare industry. Igor has been deeply interested in Kotlin development since long before the 1.0 version was officially released, and he is an active member of the Kotlin community. He enjoys sharing his passion for coding with developers.

To learn more about him, you can visit him on Medium (`@igorwojda`) and follow him on Twitter (`@igorwojda`).

I would like to thank the amazing team at Babylon, who are not only professionals but also inspiring and very helpful people, especially Mikolaj Leszczynski, Sakis Kaliakoudas, Simon Attard, Balachandar Kolathur Mani, Sergio Carabantes, Joao Alves, Tomas Navickas, Mario Sanoguera, and Sebastien Rouif.

I offer thanks to all the reviewers, especially technical reviewer Stepan Goncharov, Mikhail Glukhikh, and my colleagues who gave us feedback on the drafts, especially Michał Jankowski.

I am also thankful to my family for all of their love and support. I'd like to thank my parents for allowing me to follow my ambitions throughout my childhood and for my education.

Thanks also go to JetBrains for creating this awesome language and to the Kotlin community for sharing knowledge and being helpful, open, and inspiring. This book could not have been written without you!

I offer special thanks to my friends, especially Konrad Hamela, Marcin Sobolski, Maciej Gierasimiuk, Rafal Cupial, Michal Mazur, and Edyta Skiba for their friendship, inspiration, and continuous support. I value your advice immensely.

About the Reviewers

Mikhail Glukhikh graduated from Ioffe Physical Technical School in 1995 and from Saint Petersburg State Polytechnical University in 2001 with a masters degree in information technologies. During 2001-2004, he was PhD student in the same university, and then he defended his PhD thesis in 2007. The title of his thesis is *Synthesis method development of special-purpose informational and control systems with structural redundancy.*

Mikhail worked in Kodeks Software Development Center during 1999-2000, and in Efremov Research Institute of Electrophysical Apparatus during 2001-2002. Since 2002, he has been a lead developer at Digitek Labs, in the computer system and software engineering department. He was a senior lecturer at the department from 2004 to 2007; from 2007 he has been an associate professor. In 2013, he had one-year stay at Clausthal University of Technology as an invited researcher. In 2014, he worked at SPb office of Intel corporation, since March 2015, he participates in Kotlin language development at JetBrains.

Mikhail is one of Digitek Aegis defect detection tool authors. He is also one of the Digitek RA tool's authors. Nowadays, his primary R&D areas include code analysis, code verification, code refactoring, and code reliability estimation methods. Before he had also interests in fault-tolerant system design and analysis, and also in high-productive digital signal processing complex development.

Stepan Goncharov is currently working at Grab as the engineering lead of the Driver Android app. He is an organizer of Kotlin User Group Singapore and has developed apps and games for Android since 2008. He is a Kotlin and RxJava addict, and obsessed with elegant and functional code. He mainly focus on mobile app architecture.

Stepan makes a difference by spending more and more time contributing to open source projects. He is the reviewer of *Learning RxJava,* by Thomas Nield, published by Packt.

www.PacktPub.com

For support files and downloads related to your book, please visit www.PacktPub.com.

Did you know that Packt offers eBook versions of every book published, with PDF and ePub files available? You can upgrade to the eBook version at www.PacktPub.com and as a print book customer, you are entitled to a discount on the eBook copy.

Get in touch with us at service@packtpub.com for more details.

At www.PacktPub.com, you can also read a collection of free technical articles, sign up for a range of free newsletters and receive exclusive discounts and offers on Packt books and eBooks.

Mapt

https://www.packtpub.com/mapt

Get the most in-demand software skills with Mapt. Mapt gives you full access to all Packt books and video courses, as well as industry-leading tools to help you plan your personal development and advance your career.

Why subscribe?

- Fully searchable across every book published by Packt
- Copy and paste, print, and bookmark content
- On demand and accessible via a web browser

Customer Feedback

Thanks for purchasing this Packt book. At Packt, quality is at the heart of our editorial process. To help us improve, please leave us an honest review on this book's Amazon page at `https://www.amazon.com/dp/1787123685`.

If you'd like to join our team of regular reviewers, you can e-mail us at `customerreviews@packtpub.com`. We award our regular reviewers with free eBooks and videos in exchange for their valuable feedback. Help us be relentless in improving our products!

Table of Contents

Preface

Nowadays, the Android application development process is quite extensive. Over the last few years, we have seen how various tools have evolved to make our lives easier. However, one core element of the Android application development process hasn't changed much over time, Java. The Android platform adapts to newer versions of Java, but to be able to use them, we need to wait for a very long time until new Android devices reach proper market propagation. Also, developing applications in Java comes with its own set of challenges since Java is an old language with many design issues that can't be simply resolved due to backward compatibility constraints.

Kotlin, on the other hand, is a new but stable language that can run on all Android devices and solve many issues that Java cannot. It brings lots of proven programming concepts to the Android development table. It is a great language that makes a developer's life much easier and allows them to produce more secure, expressive, and concise code.

This book is an easy-to-follow, practical guide that will help you to speed up and improve the Android development process using Kotlin. We will present many shortcuts and improvements over Java and new ways of solving common problems. By the end of this book, you will be familiar with Kotlin features and tools, and you will be able to develop an Android application entirely in Kotlin.

What this book covers

`Chapter 1`, *Beginning Your Kotlin Adventure*, discusses the Kotlin language, its features, and reasons to use it. We'll introduce the reader to the Kotlin platform and show how Kotlin fits into the Android development process.

`Chapter 2`, *Laying a Foundation*, is largely devoted to the building blocks of Kotlin. It presents various constructs, data types, and features that make Kotlin an enjoyable language to work with.

`Chapter 3`, *Playing with Functions*, explains various ways to define and call a function. We will also discuss function modifiers and look at possible locations where function can be defined.

`Chapter 4`, *Classes and Objects*, discusses Kotlin features related to object-oriented programming. You will learn about different types of class. We will also see features that improve readability: property operator overloading and infix calls.

`Chapter 5`, *Functions as First-Class Citizens*, covers Kotlin support for functional programming and functions as first-class citizens. We will take a closer look at lambdas, higher order functions, and function types.

`Chapter 6`, *Generics Are Your Friends*, explores the subjects of generic classes, interfaces, and functions. We will take a closer look at the Kotlin generic type system.

`Chapter 7`, *Extension Functions and Properties*, demonstrates how to add new behavior to an existing class without using inheritance. We will also discuss simpler ways to deal with collections and stream processing.

`Chapter 8`, *Delegates*, shows how Kotlin simplifies class delegation due to built-in language support. We will see how to use it both by using built-in property delegates and by defining custom ones.

`Chapter 9`, *Making Your Marvel Gallery Application*, utilizes most of the features discussed in the book and uses them to build a fully functional Android application in Kotlin.

What you need for this book

To test and use the code presented in this book, you need only Android Studio installed. `Chapter 1`, *Beginning Your Kotlin Adventure*, explains how a new project can be started and how the examples presented here can be checked. It also describes how most of the code presented here can be tested without any programs installed.

Who this book is for

To use this book, you should be familiar with two areas:

- You need to know Java and object-oriented programming concepts, including objects, classes, constructors, interfaces, methods, getters, setters, and generic types. So if this area does not ring a bell, it will be difficult to fully understand the rest of this book. Start instead with an introductory Java book and return to this book afterward.

- Though not mandatory, understanding the Android platform is desirable because it will help you to understand the presented examples in more detail, and you'll have a deeper understanding of the problems that are solved by Kotlin. If you are an Android developer with 6-12 months of experience, or you have created few Android applications, you'll be fine. On the other hand, if you feel comfortable with OOP concepts but your knowledge of the Android platform is limited, you will probably still be OK for most of the book.

Being open-minded and eager to learn new technologies will be very helpful. If something makes you curious or catches your attention, feel free to test it and play with it while you are reading this book

Conventions

In this book, you will find a number of text styles that distinguish between different kinds of information. Here are some examples of these styles and an explanation of their meaning.

Code words in text, database table names, folder names, filenames, file extensions, pathnames, dummy URLs, user input, and Twitter handles are shown as follows: "Let's look at the `range` data type, which allows us to define end-inclusive ranges."

A block of code is set as follows:

```
val capitol = "England" to "London"
println(capitol.first) // Prints: England
println(capitol.second) // Prints: London
```

When we wish to draw your attention to a particular part of a code block, the relevant lines or items are set in bold:

```
ext.kotlin_version = '1.1.3'
repositories {
    maven { url 'https://maven.google.com' }
    jcenter()
}
```

Any command-line input or output is written as follows:

```
sdk install kotlin
```

New terms and **important words** are shown in bold. Words that you see on the screen, for example, in menus or dialog boxes, appear in the text like this: "Set name, package, and location for the new project. Remember to tick the **Include Kotlin support** option."

Warnings or important notes appear like this.

Tips and tricks appear like this.

Reader feedback

Feedback from our readers is always welcome. Let us know what you think about this book-what you liked or disliked. Reader feedback is important for us as it helps us develop titles that you will really get the most out of.

To send us general feedback, simply e-mail `feedback@packtpub.com`, and mention the book's title in the subject of your message.

If there is a topic that you have expertise in and you are interested in either writing or contributing to a book, see our author guide at `www.packtpub.com/authors`.

Customer support

Now that you are the proud owner of a Packt book, we have a number of things to help you to get the most from your purchase.

Downloading the example code

You can download the example code files for this book from your account at `http://www.packtpub.com`. If you purchased this book elsewhere, you can visit `http://www.packtpub.com/support` and register to have the files e-mailed directly to you. You can download the code files by following these steps:

1. Log in or register to our website using your e-mail address and password.
2. Hover the mouse pointer on the **SUPPORT** tab at the top.
3. Click on **Code Downloads & Errata**.

4. Enter the name of the book in the **Search** box.
5. Select the book for which you're looking to download the code files.
6. Choose from the drop-down menu where you purchased this book from.
7. Click on **Code Download**.

Once the file is downloaded, please make sure that you unzip or extract the folder using the latest version of:

- WinRAR / 7-Zip for Windows
- Zipeg / iZip / UnRarX for Mac
- 7-Zip / PeaZip for Linux

The code bundle for the book is also hosted on GitHub at `https://github.com/PacktPublishing/Android-Development-with-Kotlin`. We also have other code bundles from our rich catalog of books and videos available at `https://github.com/PacktPublishing/`. Check them out!

Errata

Although we have taken every care to ensure the accuracy of our content, mistakes do happen. If you find a mistake in one of our books-maybe a mistake in the text or the code-we would be grateful if you could report this to us. By doing so, you can save other readers from frustration and help us improve subsequent versions of this book. If you find any errata, please report them by visiting `http://www.packtpub.com/submit-errata`, selecting your book, clicking on the **Errata Submission Form** link, and entering the details of your errata. Once your errata are verified, your submission will be accepted and the errata will be uploaded to our website or added to any list of existing errata under the Errata section of that title.

To view the previously submitted errata, go to `https://www.packtpub.com/books/content/support` and enter the name of the book in the search field. The required information will appear under the **Errata** section.

Piracy

Piracy of copyrighted material on the Internet is an ongoing problem across all media. At Packt, we take the protection of our copyright and licenses very seriously. If you come across any illegal copies of our works in any form on the Internet, please provide us with the location address or website name immediately so that we can pursue a remedy.

Please contact us at `copyright@packtpub.com` with a link to the suspected pirated material.

We appreciate your help in protecting our authors and our ability to bring you valuable content.

Questions

If you have a problem with any aspect of this book, you can contact us at `questions@packtpub.com`, and we will do our best to address the problem.

1
Beginning Your Kotlin Adventure

Kotlin is great language that makes Android development easier, faster, and much more pleasant. In this chapter, we will discuss what Kotlin really is and look at many Kotlin examples that will help us build even better Android applications. Welcome to the amazing journey of Kotlin, that will change the way you think about writing code and solving common programming problems.

In this chapter, we will cover the following topics:

- First steps with Kotlin
- Practical Kotlin examples
- Creating new Kotlin project in Android Studio
- Migrating existing Java project to Kotlin
- The Kotlin standard library (stdlib)
- Why Kotlin is a good choice to learn

Say hello to Kotlin

Kotlin is a modern, statically typed, Android-compatible language that fixes many *Java* problems, such as null pointer exceptions or excessive code verbosity. Kotlin is a language inspired by Swift, Scala, Groovy, C#, and many other languages. Kotlin was designed by JetBrains professionals, based on analysis of both developers experiences, best usage guidelines (most important are *clean code* and *effective Java*), and data about this language's usage. Deep analysis of other programming languages has been done. Kotlin tries hard to not repeat the mistakes from other languages and take advantage of their most useful features. When working with Kotlin, we can really feel that this is a mature and well-designed language.

Kotlin takes application development to a whole new level by improving code quality and safety and boosting developer performance. Official Kotlin support for the Android platform was announced by Google in 2017, but the Kotlin language has been here for some time. It has a very active community and Kotlin adoption on the Android platform is already growing quickly. We can describe Kotlin as a safe, expressive, concise, versatile, and tool-friendly language that has great interoperability with Java and JavaScript. Let's discuss these features:

- **Safety**: Kotlin offers safety features in terms of nullability and immutability. Kotlin is statically typed, so the type of every expression is known at compile time. The compiler can verify that whatever property or method we are trying to access of a particular class instance actually exists. This should be familiar from Java which is also statically typed, but unlike Java, Kotlin type system is much more strict (safe). We have to explicitly tell the compiler whether the given variable can store null values. This allows making the program fail at compile time instead of throwing a `NullPointerException` at runtime:

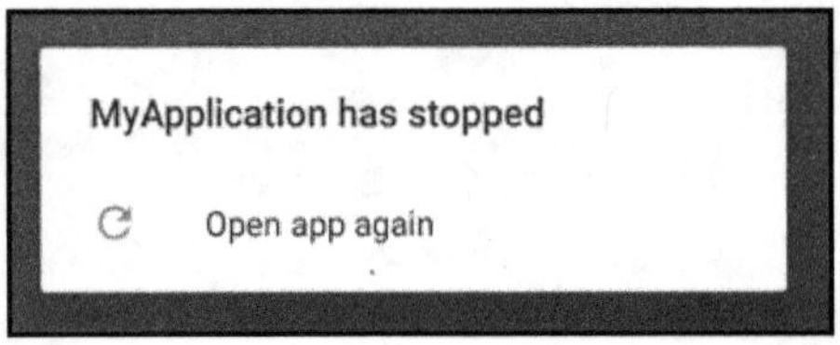

- **Easy debugging**: Bugs can be detected much faster during the development phase, instead of crashing the application after it is released and thus damaging the user experience. Kotlin offers a convenient way to work with immutable data. For example, it can distinguish mutable (read-write) and immutable (read-only) collections by providing convenient interfaces (under the hood collections are still mutable).
- **Conciseness**: Most of the Java verbosity was eliminated. We need less code to achieve common tasks and thus the amount of boilerplate code is greatly reduced, even comparing Kotlin to Java 8. As a result, the code is also easier to read and understand (expressive).
- **Interoperability**: Kotlin is designed to seamlessly work side by side with Java (cross-language project). The existing ecosystem of Java libraries and frameworks works with Kotlin without any performance penalties. Many Java libraries even Kotlin-specific versions that allow more idiomatic usage with Kotlin. Kotlin classes can also be directly instantiated and transparently referenced from Java code without any special semantics and vice versa. This allows us to incorporate Kotlin into existing Android projects and use Kotlin easily together with Java (if we want to).
- **Versatility**: We can target many platforms, including mobile applications (Android), server-side applications (backend), desktop applications, frontend code running in the browser, and even build systems (Gradle).

Any programming language is only as good as its tool support. Kotlin has outstanding support for modern IDEs such as Android Studio, IntelliJ Idea, and Eclipse. Common tasks such as code assistance or refactoring are handled properly. The Kotlin team works hard to make the Kotlin plugin better with every single release. Most of the bugs are quickly fixed and many of the features requested by the community are implemented.

> Kotlin bug tracker: `https://youtrack.jetbrains.com/issues/KT`
> Kotlin slack channel: `http://slack.kotlinlang.org/`

Android application development becomes much more efficient and pleasant with Kotlin. Kotlin is compatible with JDK 6, so applications created in Kotlin run safely even on old Android devices that precede Android 4.

Kotlin aims to bring you the best of both worlds by combining concepts and elements from both procedural and functional programming. It follows many guidelines as described in the book, *Effective Java, 2nd Edition*, by Joshua Bloch, which is considered a must-read book for every Java developer.

On top of that, Kotlin is open sourced, so we can check out the project and be actively involved in any aspect of the Kotlin project such as Kotlin plugins, compilers, documentation, or the Kotlin language itself.

Awesome Kotlin examples

Kotlin is really easy to learn for Android developers because the syntax is similar to Java and Kotlin often feels like a natural Java evolution. At the beginning, a developer usually writes Kotlin code by having in mind habits from Java, but after a while, it is very easy to move to more idiomatic Kotlin solutions. Let's look at some cool Kotlin features and see where Kotlin may provide benefits by solving common programming tasks in an easier, more concise, and more flexible way. We have tried to keep examples simple and self-explanatory, but they utilize content from various parts of this book, so it's fine if they are not fully understood at this point. The goal of this section is to focus on the possibilities and present what can be achieved by using Kotlin. This section does not necessarily need to fully describe how to achieve it. Let's start with a variable declaration:

```
var name = "Igor" // Inferred type is String
name = "Marcin"
```

Notice that Kotlin does not require semicolons. You can still use them, but they are optional. We also don't need to specify a variable type because it's inferred from the context. Each time, the compiler can figure out the type from the context; we don't have to explicitly specify it. Kotlin is a strongly typed language, so each variable has an adequate type:

```
var name = "Igor"
name = 2 // Error, because name type is String
```

The variable has an inferred `String` type, so assigning a different value (integer) will result in a compilation error. Now, let's see how Kotlin improves the way to add multiple strings using *string templates*:

```
val name = "Marcin"
println("My name is $name") // Prints: My name is Marcin
```

We need no more joining strings using the + character. In Kotlin, we can easily incorporate single variable or even whole expressions, into string literals:

```
val name = "Igor"
    println("My name is ${name.toUpperCase()}")
    // Prints: My name is IGOR
```

In Java, any variable can store null values. In Kotlin, *strict null safety* forces us to explicitly mark each variables, that can store nullable values:

```
var a: String = "abc"
a = null // compilation error

var b: String? = "abc"
b = null // It is correct
```

By adding a question mark to a data type (string versus string?), we say that the variable can be nullable (can store null references). If we don't mark the variable as nullable, we will not be able to assign a nullable reference to it. Kotlin also allows us to deal with nullable variables in proper ways. We can use the *safe call* operator to safely call methods on potentially nullable variables:

```
savedInstanceState?.doSomething
```

The method `doSomething` will be invoked only if `savedInstanceState` has a non-null value, otherwise the method call will be ignored. This is Kotlin's safe way to avoid null pointer exceptions that are so common in Java.

Kotlin also has several new data types. Let's look at the `Range` data type that allows us to define end inclusive ranges:

```
for (i in 1..10) {
    print(i)
} // 12345678910
```

Kotlin introduces the `Pair` data type that, combined with *infix notation,* allows us to hold a common pair of values:

```
val capitol = "England" to "London"
println(capitol.first) // Prints: England
println(capitol.second) // Prints: London
```

We can deconstruct it into separate variables using *destructive declarations*:

```
val (country, city) = capitol
println(country) // Prints: England
println(city) // Prints: London
```

We can even iterate through a list of pairs:

```
val capitols = listOf("England" to "London", "Poland" to "Warsaw")
for ((country, city) in capitols) {
    println("Capitol of $country is $city")
}

// Prints:
// Capitol of England is London
// Capitol of Poland is Warsaw
```

Alternatively, we can use the `forEach` function:

```
val capitols = listOf("England" to "London", "Poland" to "Warsaw")
capitols.forEach { (country, city) ->
    println("Capitol of $country is $city")
}
```

Note that Kotlin distinguishes between mutable and immutable collections by providing a set of interfaces and helper methods (`List` versus `MutableList`, `Set` versus `Set` versus `MutableSet`, `Map` versus `MutableMap`, and so on):

```
val list = listOf(1, 2, 3, 4, 5, 6) // Inferred type is List
val mutableList = mutableListOf(1, 2, 3, 4, 5, 6)
// Inferred type  is MutableList
```

Immutable collection means that the collection state can't change after initialization (we can't add/remove items). Mutable collection (quite obviously) means that the state can change.

With lambda expressions, we can use the Android framework build in a very concise way:

```
view.setOnClickListener {
    println("Click")
}
```

The Kotlin standard library (stdlib) contains many functions that allow us to perform operations on collections in a simple and concise way. We can easily perform stream processing on lists:

```
val text = capitols.map { (country, _) -> country.toUpperCase() }
                   .onEach { println(it) }
                   .filter { it.startsWith("P") }
                   .joinToString (prefix = "Countries prefix P:")
// Prints: ENGLAND POLAND
println(text) // Prints: Countries prefix P: POLAND
.joinToString (prefix = "Countries prefix P:")
```

Notice that we don't have to pass parameters to a lambda. We can also define our own lambdas that will allow us to write code in a completely new way. This lambda will allow us to run a particular piece of code only in Android Marshmallow or newer:

```
inline fun supportsMarshmallow(code: () -> Unit) {
    if(Build.VERSION.SDK_INT >= Build.VERSION_CODES.M)
    code()
}

//usage
supportsMarshmallow {
    println("This code will only run on Android Nougat and newer")
}
```

We can make asynchronous requests easily and display responses on the main thread using the `doAsync` function:

```
doAsync {
    var result = runLongTask()  // runs on background thread

    uiThread {
        toast(result)           // run on main thread
    }
}
```

Smart casts allow us to write code without performing redundant casting:

```
if (x is String) {
    print(x.length) // x is automatically casted to String
}

x.length //error, x is not casted to a String outside if block

if (x !is String)
    return

x.length // x is automatically casted to String
```

The Kotlin compiler knows that the variable `x` is of the type `String` after performing a check, so it will automatically cast it to the `String` type, allowing it to call all methods and access all properties of the `String` class without any explicit casts.

Sometimes, we have a simple function that returns the value of a single expression. In this case, we can use a function with an expression body to shorten the syntax:

```
fun sum(a: Int, b: Int) = a + b
println (sum(2 + 4)) // Prints: 6
```

Using *default argument syntax,* we can define the default value for each function argument and call it in various ways:

```
fun printMessage(product: String, amount: Int = 0,
    name: String = "Anonymous") {
    println("$name has $amount $product")
}

printMessage("oranges") // Prints: Anonymous has 0 oranges
printMessage("oranges", 10) // Prints: Anonymous has 10 oranges
printMessage("oranges", 10, "Johny")
// Prints: Johny has 10 oranges
```

The only limitation is that we need to supply all arguments without default values. We can also use *named argument syntax* to specify function arguments:

```
printMessage("oranges", name = "Bill")
```

This also increases readability when invoking the function with multiple parameters in the function call.

The data classes give a very easy way to define and operate on classes from the data model. To define a proper data class, we will use the `data` modifier before the class name:

```
data class Ball(var size:Int, val color:String)

val ball = Ball(12, "Red")
println(ball) // Prints: Ball(size=12, color=Red)
```

Notice that we have a really nice, human readable string representation of the class instance and we do not need the `new` keyword to instantiate the class. We can also easily create a custom copy of the class:

```
val ball = Ball(12, "Red")
println(ball) // prints: Ball(size=12, color=Red)
val smallBall = ball.copy(size = 3)
println(smallBall) // prints: Ball(size=3, color=Red)
smallBall.size++
println(smallBall) // prints: Ball(size=4, color=Red)
println(ball) // prints: Ball(size=12, color=Red)
```

The preceding constructs make working with *immutable* objects very easy and convenient.

One of the best features in Kotlin are *extensions*. They allow us to add new behavior (a method or property) to an existing class without changing its implementation. Sometimes when you work with a library or framework, you would like to have an extra method or property for a certain class. Extensions are a great way to add those missing members. Extensions reduce code verbosity and remove the need to use utility functions known from Java (for example, the `StringUtils` class). We can easily define extensions for custom classes, third-party libraries, or even Android framework classes. First of all, `ImageView` does not have the ability to load images from a network, so we can add the `loadImage` extension method to load images using the `Picasso` library (an image loading library for Android):

```
fun ImageView.loadUrl(url: String) {
    Picasso.with(context).load(url).into(this)
}

//usage
imageView.loadUrl("www.test.com\\image1.png")
```

We can also add a simple method displaying toasts to the `Activity` class:

```
fun Context.toast(text:String) {
    Toast.makeText(this, text, Toast.LENGTH_SHORT).show()
}

//usage (inside Activity class)
toast("Hello")
```

There are many places where usage of *extensions* will make our code simpler and more concise. Using Kotlin, we can fully take advantage of lambdas to simplify Kotlin code even more.

Interfaces in Kotlin can have default implementations as long as they don't hold any state:

```
interface BasicData {
    val email:String
    val name:String
    get() = email.substringBefore("@")
}
```

In Android, there are many applications where we want to delay object initialization until it is needed (used). To solve this problem, we can use *delegates*:

```
val retrofit by lazy {
    Retrofit.Builder()
        .baseUrl("https://www.github.com")
        .addConverterFactory(MoshiConverterFactory.create())
        .build()
}
```

Retrofit (a popular Android networking framework) property initialization will be delayed until the value is accessed for the first time. Lazy initialization may result in faster Android application startup times, since loading is deferred to when the variable is accessed. This is a great way to initialize multiple objects inside a class, especially when not all of them are always needed (for certain class usage scenarios, we may need only specific objects) or when not every one of them is needed instantly after class creation.

All the presented examples are only a glimpse of what can be accomplished with Kotlin. We will learn how to utilize the power of Kotlin throughout this book.

Dealing with Kotlin code

There are multiple ways of managing and running Kotlin code. We will mainly focus on Android Studio and Kotlin Playground.

Kotlin Playground

The fastest way to try Kotlin code without the need to install any software is Kotlin Playground (`https://try.kotlinlang.org`). We can run Kotlin code there using JavaScript or JVM Kotlin implementations and easily switch between different Kotlin versions. All the code examples from the book that does not require Android framework dependencies and can be executed using **Kotlin Playground**.

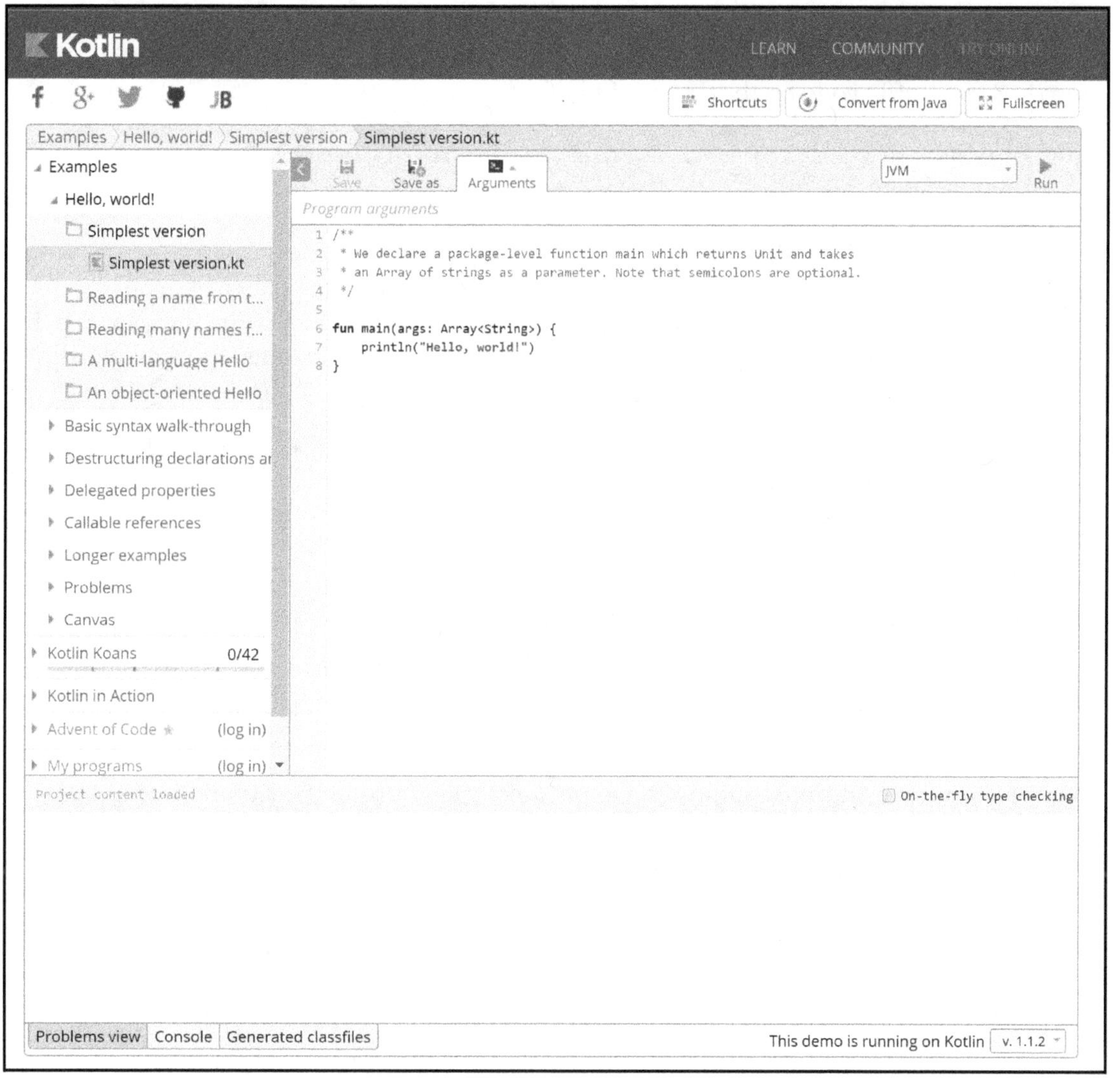

The `main` function is the entry point of every Kotlin application. This function is called when any application starts, so we must place code from the book examples in the body of this method. We can place code directly or just place a call to another function containing more Kotlin code:

```
fun main(args: Array<String>) {
    println("Hello, world!")
}
```

Android applications have multiple entry points. The `main` function is called implicitly by the Android framework, so we can't use it to run Kotlin code on the Android platform.

Android Studio

All Android Studio's existing tools work with Kotlin code. We can easily use debugging, lint checks, have proper code assistance, refactoring, and more. Most of the things work the same way as for Java, so the biggest noticeable change is the Kotlin language syntax. All we need to do is to configure Kotlin in the project.

Android applications have multiple entry points (different intents can start different components in the application) and require Android framework dependencies. To run the book examples, we need to extend the `Activity` class and place code there.

Configuring Kotlin for the project

Starting from Android Studio 3.0, full tooling support for Kotlin was added. Installation of the Kotlin plugin is not required and Kotlin is integrated even deeper into the Android development process.

To use Kotlin with Android Studio 2.x, we must manually install the Kotlin plugin. To install it, we need to go to **Android Studio** | **File** | **Settings** | **Plugins** | **Install JetBrains plugin...** | **Kotlin** and press the **Install** button:

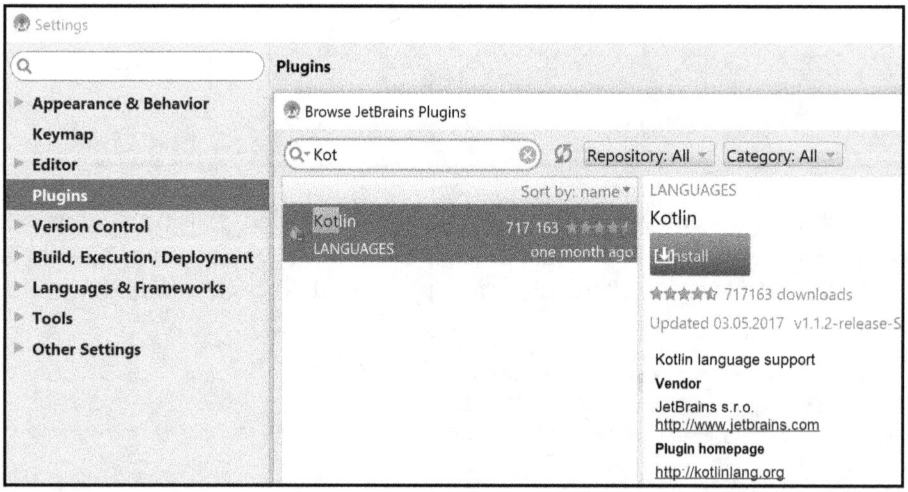

To be able to use Kotlin, we need to configure Kotlin in our project. For existing Java projects, we need to run the *Configure Kotlin in project* action (the shortcut in Windows is *Ctrl+Shift+A*, and in macOS, it is *command + shift + A*) or use the corresponding **Tools** | **Kotlin** | **Configure Kotlin in Project** menu item:

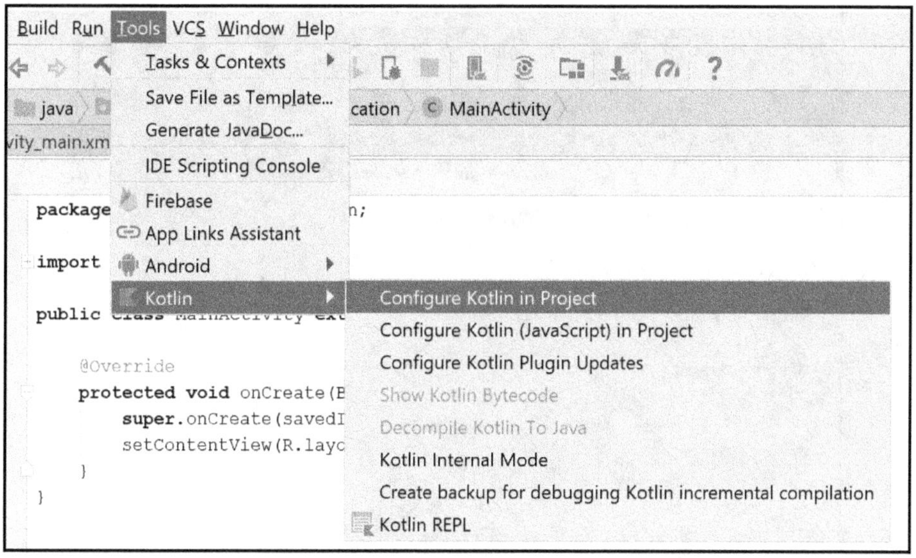

Then, select **Android with Gradle**:

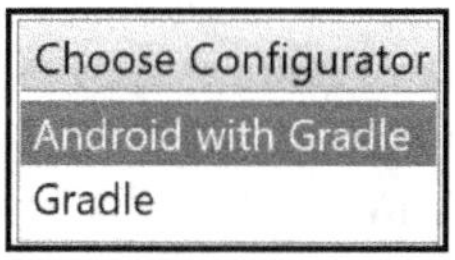

Finally, we need to select the required modules and the proper Kotlin version:

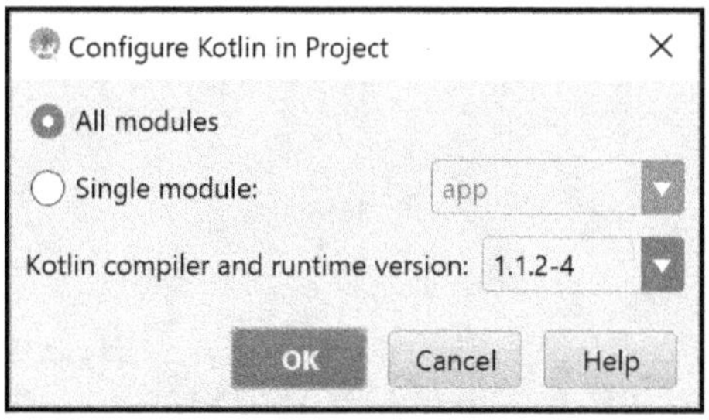

The preceding configuration scenario also applies to all existing Android projects that were initially created in Java. Starting from Android Studio 3.0, we can also check the **Include Kotlin support** checkbox while creating a new project:

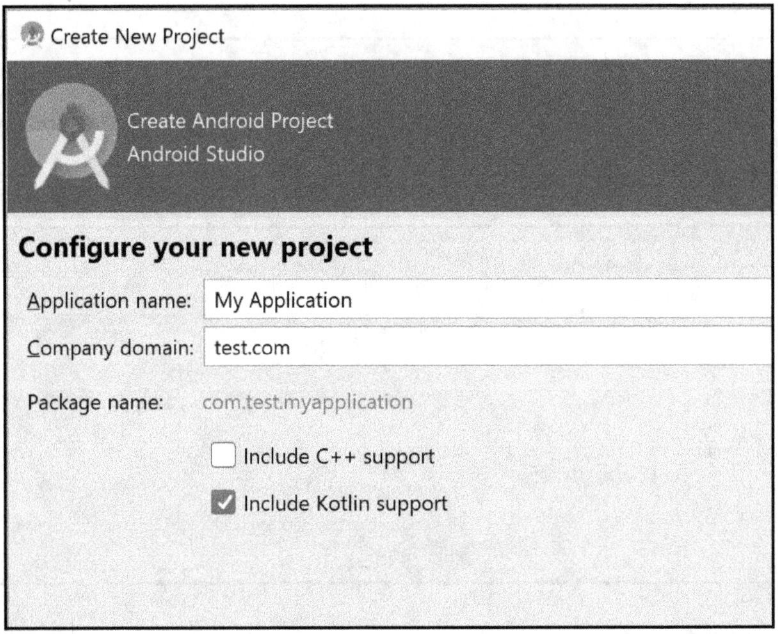

In both scenarios, the `Configure Kotlin in project` command updates the root `build.gradle` file and the `build.gradle` files corresponding to the module(s) by adding Kotlin dependencies. It also adds the Kotlin plugin to the Android module. At the time of writing this book release version of Android Studio 3 is not yet available, but we can review the build script from the pre-release version:

```
//build.gradle file in project root folder
buildscript {
    ext.kotlin_version = '1.1'

    repositories {
        google()
        jcenter()
    }
    dependencies {
       classpath 'com.android.tools.build:gradle:3.0.0-alpha9'
       classpath "org.jetbrains.kotlin:kotlin-gradle-
             plugin:$kotlin_version"
    }
}
```

```
...
//build.gradle file in the selected modules
apply plugin: 'com.android.application'
apply plugin: 'kotlin-android'
apply plugin: 'kotlin-android-extensions'
...
dependencies {
    ...
    implementation 'com.android.support.constraint:constraint-
          layout:1.0.2'
}
...
```

Prior to the Android plugin for Gradle 3.x (delivered with Android Studio 3.0), *compile* dependency configuration was used instead of *implementation*.

To update the Kotlin version (let us say in the future), we need to change the value of the `kotlin_version` variable in the `build.gradle` file (project root folder). Changes in Gradle files mean that the project must be synchronized, so Gradle can update its configuration and download all the required dependencies:

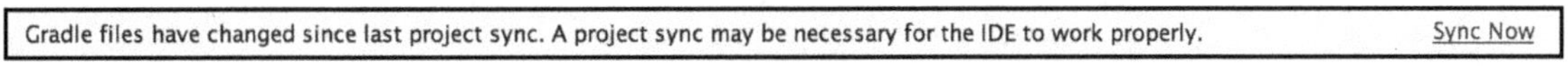

Gradle files have changed since last project sync. A project sync may be necessary for the IDE to work properly.

Using Kotlin in a new Android project

For new Kotlin projects created in Android Studio 3.x, the main activity will be already defined in Kotlin, so that we can start writing Kotlin code right away:

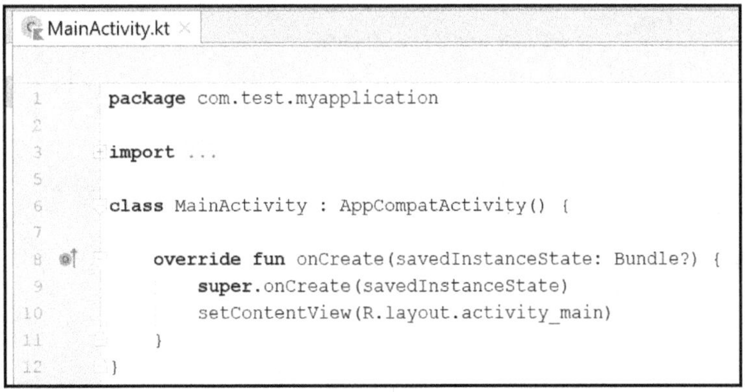

MainActivity.kt
package com.test.myapplication
import ...
class MainActivity : AppCompatActivity() {
override fun onCreate(savedInstanceState: Bundle?) {
super.onCreate(savedInstanceState)
setContentView(R.layout.activity_main)
}
}

Adding a new Kotlin file is similar to adding a Java file. Simply right-click on a package and select **new** | **Kotlin File/Class**:

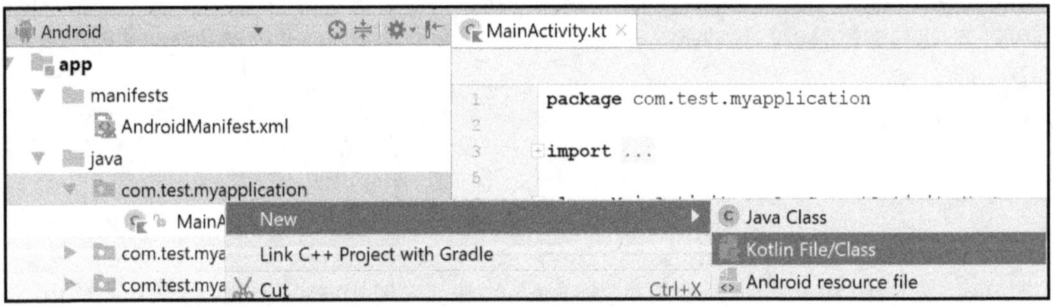

The reason why the IDE says **Kotlin File/Class** and not simply *Kotlin class,* which is analogous to *Java class,* is that we can have more members defined inside a single file. We will discuss this in more detail in `Chapter 2`, *Laying a Foundation.*

Notice that Kotlin source files can be located inside the `java` source folder. We can create a new source folder for Kotlin, but it is not required:

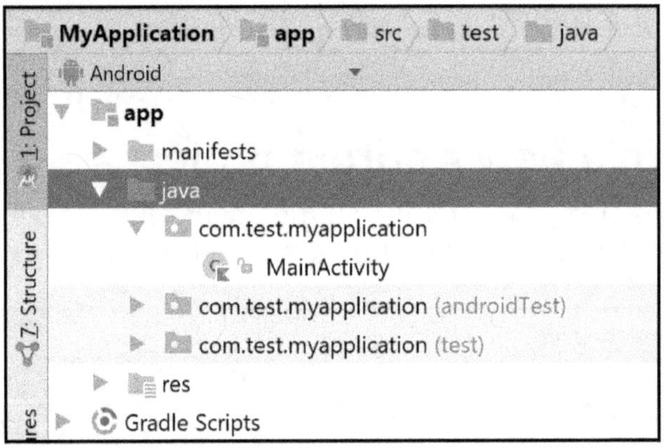

Running and debugging a project is exactly the same as in Java and does not require any additional steps besides configuring Kotlin in the project:

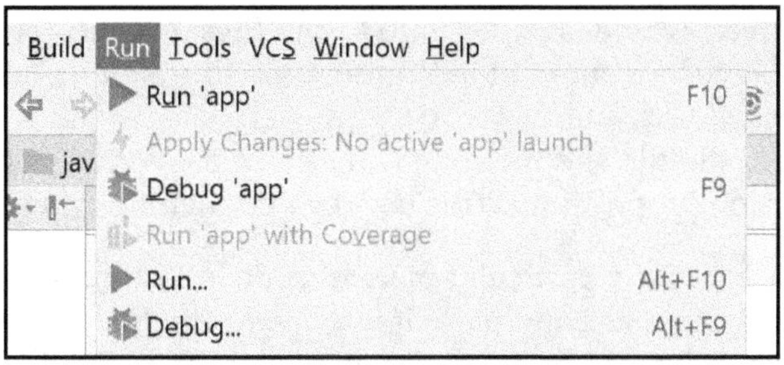

Starting from Android Studio 3.0, various Android templates will also allow us to select a language. This is the new **Configure Activity** wizard:

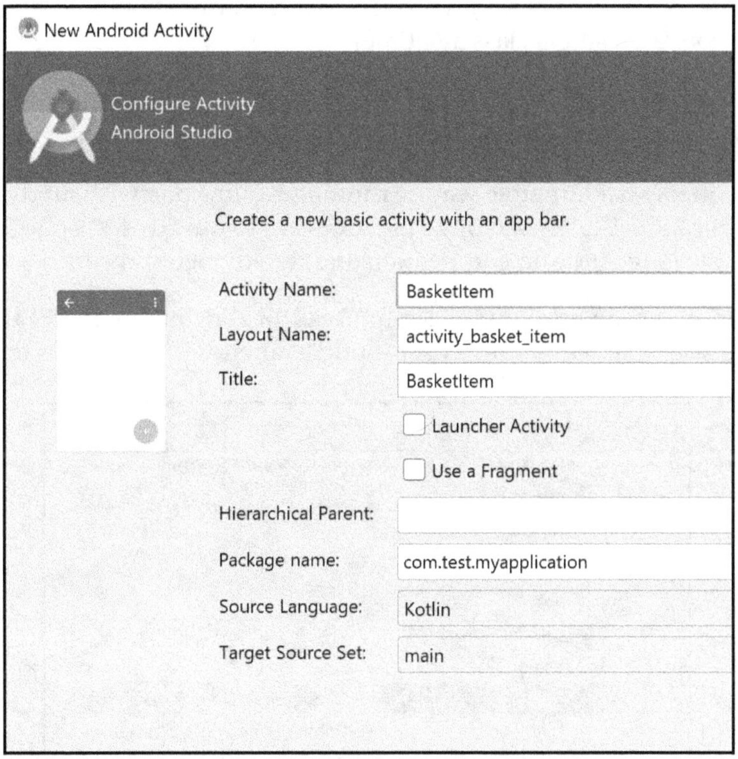

Java to Kotlin converter (J2K)

Migration of existing Java projects is also quite easy, because we can use Java and Kotlin side by side in the same project. There are also ways to convert existing Java code into Kotlin code by using the **Java to Kotlin converter** (J2K).

The first way is to convert whole Java files into Kotlin files using the *convert Java File to Kotlin* command (the keyboard shortcut in Windows is *Alt* + *Shift* + *Ctrl* + *K* and in macOS is *option* + *shift* + *command* + *K*), and this works very well. The second way is to paste Java code into an existing Kotlin file and the code will also be converted (a dialog window will appear with a conversion proposition). This may be very helpful when learning Kotlin.

If we don't know how to write a particular piece of code in Kotlin, we can write it in Java, then simply copy to the clipboard and paste it into the Kotlin file. Converted code will not be the most idiomatic version of Kotlin, but it will work. The IDE will display various intentions to convert the code even more and improve its quality. Before conversion, we need to make sure that the Java code is valid, because conversion tools are very sensitive and the process will fail even if a single semicolon is missing. The J2K converter combined with Java interoperability allows Kotlin be introduced gradually into the existing project (for example, to convert a single class at a time).

Alternative ways to run Kotlin code

Android Studio offers an alternative way of running Kotlin code without the need to run the Android application. This is useful when you want to quickly test some Kotlin code separately from the long Android compilation and deployment process.

The way to run Kotlin code is to use the Kotlin **Read Eval Print Loop** (**REPL**). REPL is a simple language shell that reads single user input, evaluates it, and prints the result:

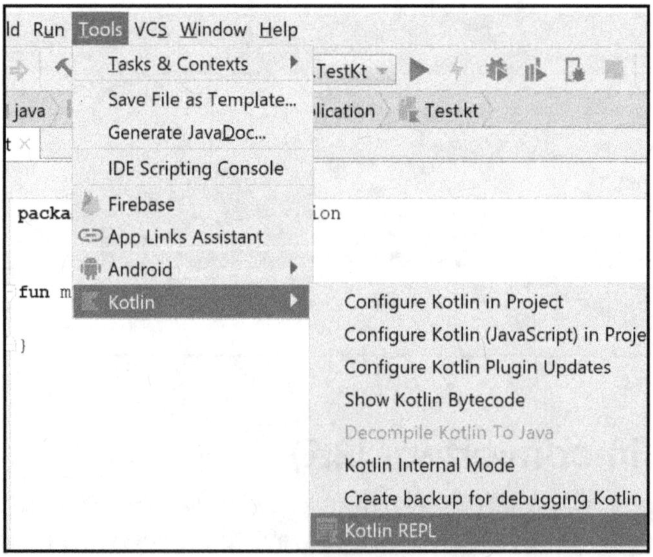

REPL looks like the command-line, but it will provide us with all the required code hints and will give us access to various structures defined inside the project (classes, interfaces, top-level functions, and so on):

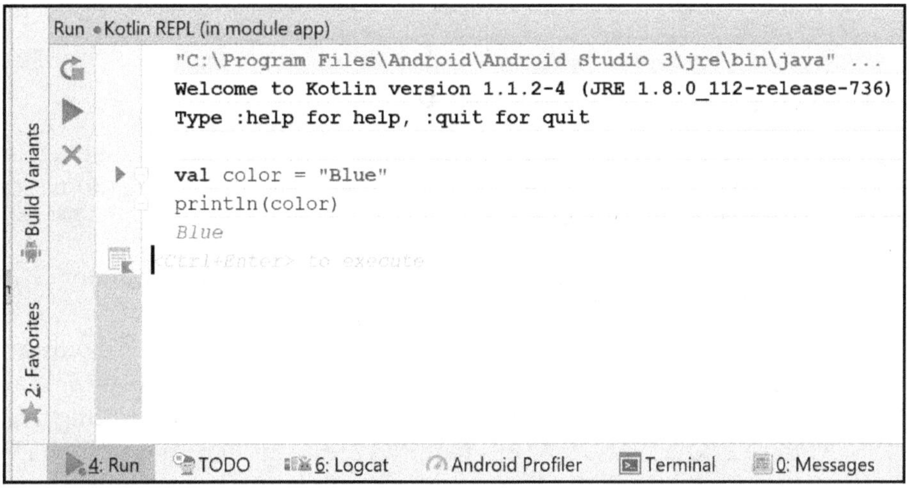

The biggest advantage of REPL is its speed. We can test Kotlin code really quickly.

Kotlin under the hood

We will focus mainly on Android, but keep in mind that Kotlin can be compiled to multiple platforms. Kotlin code can be compiled to *Java bytecode* and then to *Dalvik bytecode*. Here is the simplified version of the Kotlin build process for the Android platform:

- A file with a `.java` extension contains Java code
- A file with a `.kt` extension contains Kotlin code
- A file with a `.class` extension contains Java bytecode
- A file with a `.dex` extension contains Dalvik bytecode
- A file with a `.apk` extension contains the `AndroidManifest` file, resources, and `.dex` file

For pure Kotlin projects, only the Kotlin compiler will be used, but Kotlin also supports cross-language projects, where we can use Kotlin together with Java in the same Android project. In such cases, both compilers are used to compile the Android application and the result will be merged at the class level.

The Kotlin standard library

The **Kotlin standard library** (**stdlib**) is a very small library that is distributed together with Kotlin. It is required to run applications written in Kotlin and it is added automatically to our application during the build process.

> In Kotlin 1.1, `kotlin-runtime` was required to run applications written in Kotlin. In fact, in Kotlin 1.1 there were two artifacts (`kotlin-runtime` and `kotlin-stdlib`) that shared a lot of Kotlin packages. To reduce the amount of confusion, both the artifacts will be merged into a single artifact (`kotlin-stdlib`) in the upcoming 1.2 version of Kotlin. Starting from Kotlin 1.2, `kotlin-stdlib` is required to run applications written in Kotlin.

The Kotlin standard library provides essential elements required for everyday work with Kotlin. These include:

- Data types such as arrays, collections, lists, ranges, and so on
- Extensions
- Higher-order functions
- Various utilities for working with strings and char sequences
- Extensions for JDK classes, making it convenient to work with files, IO, and threading

More reasons to use Kotlin

Kotlin has strong commercial support from JetBrains, a company that delivers very popular IDEs for many popular programming languages (Android Studio is based on JetBrains IntelliJ IDEA). JetBrains wanted to improve the quality of their code and team performance, so they needed a language that would solve all the Java issues and provide seamless interoperability with Java. None of the other JVM languages meet those requirements, so JetBrains finally decided to create their own language and started the Kotlin project. Nowadays, Kotlin is used in their flagship products. Some use Kotlin together with Java while others are pure Kotlin products.

Kotlin is quite a mature language. In fact, its development started many years before Google announced official Android support (the first commit dates back to 2010-11-08):

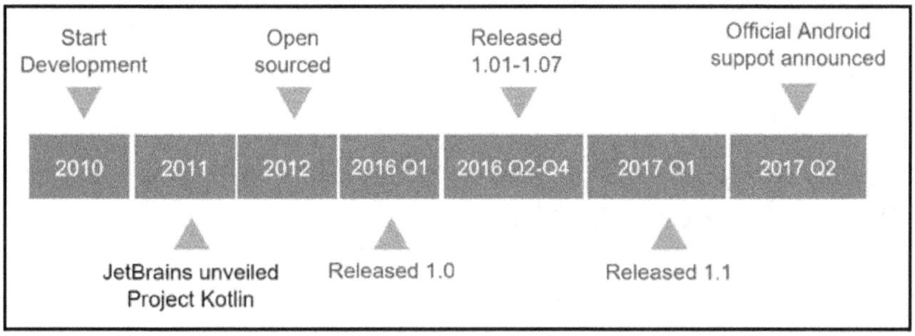

The initial name of the language was **Jet**. At some point, the JetBrains team decided to rename it to Kotlin. The name comes from Kotlin Island near St. Petersburg and is analogous to Java, which was named after an Indonesian island.

After the version 1.0 release in 2016, more and more companies started to support the Kotlin project. Gradle added support for Kotlin into building scripts; Square, the biggest creator of Android libraries posted that they strongly support Kotlin; and finally, Google announced official Kotlin support for the Android platform. This means that every tool that will be released by the Android team will be compatible not only with Java but also with Kotlin. Google and JetBrains have begun a partnership to create a nonprofit foundation for Kotlin, responsible for future language maintenance and development. All of this will greatly increase the number of companies that use Kotlin in their projects.

Kotlin is also similar to Apple's Swift programming language. In fact, such is the resemblance that some articles focus on differences, not similarities. Learning Kotlin will be very helpful for developers eager to develop applications for Android and iOS. There are also plans to port Kotlin to iOS (Kotlin/Native), so maybe we don't have to learn Swift after all. Full stack development is also possible in Kotlin, so we can develop server-side applications and frontend clients that share the same data model as mobile clients.

Summary

We've discussed how the Kotlin language fits into Android development and how we can incorporate Kotlin into new and existing projects. We have seen useful examples where Kotlin simplified the code and made it much safer. There are still many interesting things to discover.

In the next chapter, we will learn about Kotlin building blocks and lay a foundation to develop Android applications using Kotlin.

2

Laying a Foundation

This chapter is largely devoted to the fundamental building blocks that are core elements of the Kotlin programming language. Each one may seem insignificant by itself, but combined together, they create really powerful language constructs. We will discuss the Kotlin type system that introduces strict null safety and smart casts. Also, we will see a few new operators in the JVM world, and many improvements compared to Java. We will also present new ways to handle application flows and deal with equality in a unified way.

In this chapter, we will cover the following topics:

- Variables, values, and constants
- Type inference
- Strict null safety
- Smart casts
- Kotlin data types
- Control structures
- Exceptions handling

Variables

In Kotlin, we have two types of variables: `var` and `val`. The first one, `var`, is a mutable reference (read-write) that can be updated after initialization. The `var` keyword is used to define a variable in Kotlin. It is equivalent to a normal (non-final) Java variable. If our variable needs to change at some point, we should declare it using the `var` keyword. Let's look at an example of a variable declaration:

```
fun main(args: Array<String>) {
    var fruit: String =  "orange" //1
    fruit  = "banana" //2
}
```

1. Create a `fruit` variable and initialize it with the vale of the `orange` variable.
2. Reinitialize the `fruit` variable with the value of the `banana` variable.

The second type of variable is a read-only reference. This type of variable cannot be reassigned after initialization.

> The `val` keyword can contain a custom getter, so technically it can return different objects on each access. In other words, we can't guarantee that the reference to the underlying object is immutable:
>
> ```
> val random: Int
> get() = Random().nextInt()
> ```
>
> Custom getters will be discussed in more detail in `Chapter 4`, *Classes and Objects*.

The `val` keyword is the equivalent of a Java variable with the `final` modifier. Using immutable variables is useful, because it makes sure that the variable will never be updated by mistake. The concept of *immutability* is also helpful for working with multiple threads without worrying about proper data synchronization. To declare immutable variables, we will use the `val` keyword:

```
fun main(args: Array<String>) {
    val fruit: String= "orange"//1
    fruit = "banana" //2  Error
}
```

1. Create the `fruit` variable and initialize it with the value of the `orange` string.
2. The compiler will throw an error, because the `fruit` variable was already initialized.

Kotlin also allows us to define variables and functions at the level of the file. We will discuss this further in `Chapter 3`, *Playing with Functions*.

Notice that the type of the variable reference (`var`, `val`) relates to the reference itself, not the properties of the referenced object. This means that when using a read-only reference (`val`), we will not be able to change the reference that is pointing to a particular object instance (we will not be able to reassign variable values), but we will still be able to modify properties of referenced objects. Let's see it in action using an array:

```
val list = mutableListOf("a","b","c") //1
list = mutableListOf("d", "e") //2 Error
list.remove("a") //3
```

1. Initialize a mutable list.
2. The compiler will throw an error, because a value reference cannot be changed (reassigned).
3. The compiler will allow us to modify the content of the list.

The `val` keyword cannot guarantee that the underlying object is immutable.

If we really want to make sure that the object will not be modified, we must use an immutable reference and an immutable object. Fortunately, Kotlin's standard library contains an immutable equivalent of any collection interface (`List` versus `MutableList`, `Map` versus `MutableMap`, and so on) and the same is true for helper functions that are used to create instances of a particular collection:

Variable/value definition	**Reference can change**	**Object state can change**
`val = listOf(1,2,3)`	No	No
`val = mutableListOf(1,2,3)`	No	Yes
`var = listOf(1,2,3)`	Yes	No
`var = mutableListOf(1,2,3)`	Yes	Yes

Type inference

As we saw in previous examples, unlike Java, the Kotlin type is defined after the variable name:

```
var title: String
```

At first glance, this may look strange to Java developers, but this construct is a building block of a very important feature of Kotlin called **type inference**. Type inference means that the compiler can infer type from context (the value of an expression assigned to a variable). When variable declaration and initialization is performed together (single line), we can omit the type declaration. Let's look at the following variable definition:

```
var title: String = "Kotlin"
```

The type of the `title` variable is `String`, but do we really need an implicit type declaration to determine variable type? On the right side of the expression, we have a string, `Kotlin` and we are assigning it to a variable, `title`, defined on the left-hand side of the expression.

We specified a variable type as `String`, but it was obvious, because this is the same type as the type of assigned expression (`Kotlin`). Fortunately, this fact is also obvious for the Kotlin compiler, so we can omit type when declaring a variable, because the compiler will try to determine the best type for the variable from the current context:

```
var title = "Kotlin"
```

Keep in mind that type declaration is omitted, but the type of variable is still implicitly set to `String`, because Kotlin is a strongly typed language. That's why both of the preceding declarations are the same, and Kotlin compiler will still be able to properly validate all future usages of the variable. Here is an example:

```
var title = "Kotlin"
title = 12 // 1, Error
```

1. The inferred type was `String` and we are trying to assign `Int`.

If we want to assign `Int` (value `12`) to the title variable then we need to specify title type to one that is a `String` and `Int` common type. The closest one, up in the type hierarchy, is `Any`:

```
var title: Any = "Kotlin"
title = 12
```

The `Any` type is an equivalent of the Java object type. It is the root of the Kotlin type hierarchy. All classes in Kotlin explicitly inherit from type `Any`, even primitive types such as `String` or `Int`.

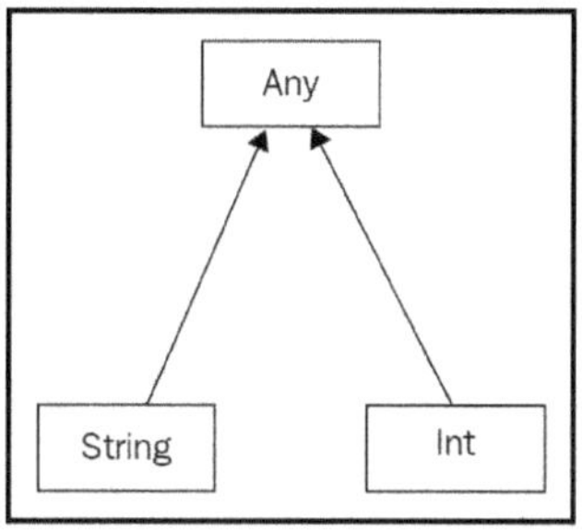

Any defines three methods: `equals`, `toString`, and `hashCode`. The Kotlin standard library contains a few extensions for this type. We will discuss extensions in `Chapter 7`, *Extension Functions and Properties*.

As we can see, *type inference* is not limited to primitive values. Let's look at inferring types directly from functions:

```
var total = sum(10, 20)
```

In the preceding example, the inferred type will be the same as the type returned by the function. We may guess that it will be `Int`, but it may also be a `Double`, `Float`, or some other type. If it's not obvious from the context what type will be inferred, we can use place caret on the variable name and run the Android Studio expression type command (for Windows, it is *Shift* + *Ctrl* + *P*, and for macOS, it is arrow key + *control* + *P*). This will display the variable type in the tooltip, as follows:

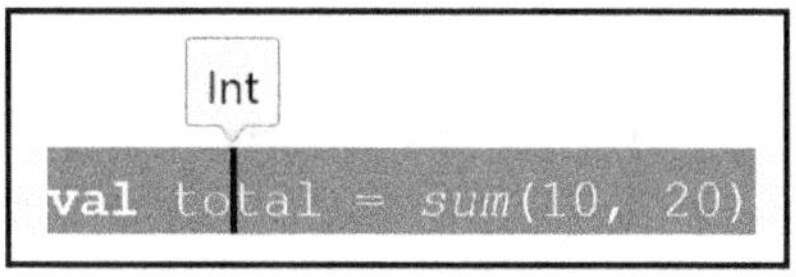

Type inference works also for generic types:

```
var persons = listOf(personInstance1, personInstance2)
// Inferred type: List<Person> ()
```

Assuming that we pass only instances of the `Person` class, the inferred type will be `List<Person>`. The `listOf` method is a helper function defined in the Kotlin standard library that allow us to create collections. We will discuss this subject in `Chapter 7`, *Extension Functions and Properties*. Let's look at more advanced examples that uses the Kotlin standard library type called `Pair`, which contains a pair composed of two values:

```
var pair = "Everest" to 8848 // Inferred type: Pair<String, Int>
```

In the preceding example, a `pair` instance is created using the *infix function*, which will be discussed in `Chapter 4`, *Classes and Objects*, but for now all we need to know is that those two declarations return the same type of the `Pair` object:

```
var pair = "Everest" to 8848
// Create pair using to infix method
var pair2 = Pair("Everest", 8848)
// Create Pair using constructor
```

Type inference works also for more complex scenarios such as inferring type from an inferred type. Let's use the Kotlin standard library's `mapOf` function and infix the `to` method of the `Pair` class to define `map`. The first item in the pair will be used to infer the `map` key type; the second will be used to infer the value type:

```
var map = mapOf("Mount Everest" to 8848, "K2" to 4017)
// Inferred type: Map<String, Int>
```

Generic type of `Map<String, Int>` is inferred from type of `Pair<String, Int>`, which is inferred from type of parameters passed to the `Pair` constructor. We may wonder what happens if inferred type of pairs used to create `map` differs? The first pair is `Pair<String, Int>` and second is `Pair<String, String>`:

```
var map = mapOf("Mount Everest" to 8848, "K2" to "4017")
// Inferred type: Map<String, Any>
```

In the preceding scenario, the Kotlin compiler will try to infer a common type for all pairs. The first parameter in both pairs is `String` (`Mount Everest`, `K2`), so naturally `String` will be inferred here. The second parameter of each pair differs (`Int` for the first pair, `String` for the second pair), so Kotlin needs to find the closest common type. The `Any` type is chosen, because this is the closest common type in the upstream type hierarchy:

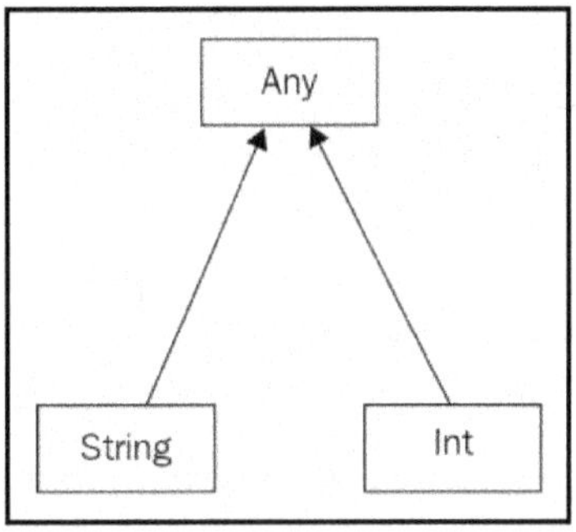

As we can see, type inference does a great job in most cases, but we can still choose to explicitly define a data type if we want, for example, if we want different variable types:

```
var age: Int = 18
```

When dealing with integers, the `Int` type is always the default choice, but we can still explicitly define different types, for example, `Short`, to save some precious Android memory:

```
var age: Short = 18
```

On the other hand, if we need to store larger values, we can define the type of the `age` variable as `Long`. We can use explicit type declaration as previously, or use a *literal constant*:

```
var age: Long = 18 // Explicitly define variable type
var age = 18L
// Use literal constant to specify value type
```

Those two declarations are equal, and both of them will create a variable of type `Long`.

For now, we know that there are more cases in code where the type declaration can be omitted to make code syntax more concise. There are, however, some situations where the Kotlin compiler will not be able to infer type due to a lack of information in context. For example, a simple declaration without assignment will make type inference impossible:

```
val title // Error
```

In the preceding example, the variable will be initialized later, so there is no way to determine its type. That's why type must be explicitly specified. The general rule is that if the type of expression is known for the compiler, then type can be inferred. Otherwise, it must be explicitly specified. Kotlin plugin in Android Studio does a great job because it knows exactly where type cannot be inferred and then it is highlighted as an error. This allows us to display proper error messages instantly in the IDE when writing the code, without the need to complete the application.

Strict null safety

According to **Agile Software Assessment** (`http://p3.snf.ch/Project-144126`) research, a missing null check is the most frequent pattern of bugs in Java systems. The biggest source of errors in Java is `NullPointerExceptions`. It's so big that speaking at a conference in 2009, Sir Tony Hoare apologized for inventing the null reference, calling it a *billion-dollar mistake* (`https://en.wikipedia.org/wiki/Tony_Hoare`).

To avoid `NullPointerException`, we need to write defensive code that checks if an object is null before using it. Many modern programming languages, including Kotlin, made steps to convert runtime errors into compile time errors to improve programming language safety. One of the ways to do it in Kotlin is by adding *nullability safeness mechanisms* to language type systems. This is possible because the Kotlin type system distinguishes between references that can hold null (nullable references) and those that cannot (non-nullable references). This single feature of Kotlin allows us to detect many errors related to `NullPointerException` at very early stages of development. The compiler, together with the IDE, will prevent many `NullPointerException`. In many cases compilation will fail instead of the application failing at runtime.

Strict null safety is part of the Kotlin type system. By default, regular types cannot be null (can't store null references), unless they are explicitly allowed. To store null references, we must mark the variable as nullable (allow it to store null references) by adding a question mark suffix to the variable type declaration. Here is an example:

```
val age: Int = null //1, Error
val name: String? = null //2
```

1. The compiler will throw an error, because this type does not allow null.
2. The compiler will allow null assignment, because type is marked as nullable using the question mark suffix.

We are not allowed to call a method on a potentially nullable object, unless a nullity check is performed before a call:

```
val name: String? = null
// ...
name.toUpperCase() // error, this reference may be null
```

We will learn how to deal with this problem in the next section. Every non-nullable type in Kotlin has its nullable type equivalent: `Int` has `Int?`, `String` has `String?`, and so on. The same rule applies for all classes in the Android framework (`View` has `View?`), third-party libraries (`OkHttpClient` has `OkHttpClient?`), and all custom classes defined by developers (`MyCustomClass` has `MyCustomClass?`). This means that every non-generic class can be used to define two kinds of type, nullable and non-nullable. A non-nullable type is also a subtype of its nullable equivalent. For example, `Vehicle`, as well as being a subtype of `Vehicle?`, is also a subtype of `Any`:

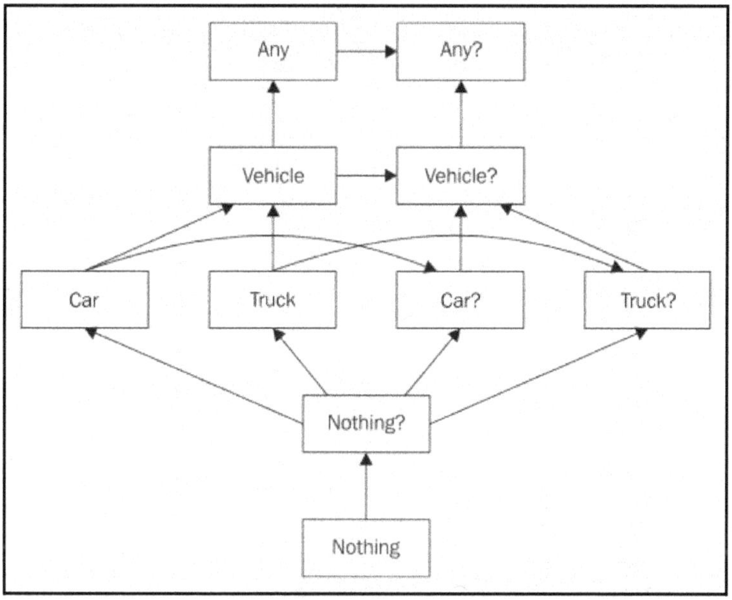

The `Nothing` type is an empty type (uninhabited type), which can't have an instance. We will discuss it in more detail in `Chapter 3`, *Playing with Functions*. This type hierarchy is the reason why we can assign a non-null object (`Vehicle`) in a variable typed as nullable (`Vehicle?`), but we cannot assign a nullable object (`Vehicle?`) in a non-null variable (`Vehicle`):

```
var nullableVehicle: Vehicle?
var vehicle: Vehicle

nullableVehicle = vehicle // 1
vehicle = nullableVehicle // 2, Error
```

1. Assignment possible.
2. Error because `nullableVehicle` may be a null.

We will discuss ways of dealing with nullable types in the following sections. Now let's get back to type definitions. When defining *generic types*, there are multiple possibilities for defining nullability, so let's examine various collection types by comparing different declarations for a generic `ArrayList` containing items of type `Int`. Here is a table that presents the key differences:

Type declaration	List itself can be null	Element can be null
`ArrayList<Int>`	No	No
`ArrayList<Int>?`	Yes	No
`ArrayList<Int?>`	No	Yes
`ArrayList<Int?>?`	Yes	Yes

It's important to understand different ways to specify null type declarations, because the Kotlin compiler enforces it to avoid `NullPointerExceptions`. This means that the compiler enforces a nullity check before accessing any reference that potentially can be null. Now let's examine a common Android/Java error in the `Activity` class's `onCreate` method:

```
//Java
@Override
public void onCreate(Bundle savedInstanceState) {
    super.onCreate(savedInstanceState);
    savedInstanceState.getBoolean("locked");
}
```

In Java, this code will compile fine and accessing null objects will result in an application crash at runtime throwing `NullPointerException`. Now let's examine the Kotlin version of the same method:

```
override fun onCreate(savedInstanceState: Bundle?) { //1
     super.onCreate(savedInstanceState)
     savedInstanceState.getBoolean("key") //2 Error
}
```

1. `savedInstanceState` defined as nullable `Bundle?`.
2. The compiler will throw an error.

The `savedInstanceState` type is a platform type that can be interpreted by Kotlin as nullable or non-nullable. We will discuss platform types in the following sections, but for now we will define `savedInstanceState` as a nullable type. We are doing so because we know that `null` will be passed when an Activity is created for the first time. An instance of `Bundle` will only be passed when an Activity is recreated using a saved instance state.

> We will discuss functions in `Chapter 3`, *Playing with Functions*, but for now, we can already see that the syntax for declaring functions in Kotlin is quite similar to Java.

The most obvious way to fix the preceding error in Kotlin is to check for nullity exactly the same way as in Java:

```
override fun onCreate(savedInstanceState: Bundle?) {
    super.onCreate(savedInstanceState)
}

override fun onCreate(savedInstanceState: Bundle?) {
    super.onCreate(savedInstanceState)

    val locked: Boolean
    if(savedInstanceState != null)
        locked = savedInstanceState.getBoolean("locked")
    else
        locked = false
}
```

The preceding construct presents some boilerplate code, because null-checking is a pretty common operation in Java development (especially in the Android framework, where most elements are nullable). Fortunately, Kotlin allows a few simpler solutions to deal with nullable variables. The first one is the *safe call* operator.

Safe call

The safe call operator is simply a question mark followed by a dot. It's important to understand that the safe cast operator will always return a value. If the left-hand side of the operator is null, then it will return null, otherwise it will return the result of the right-hand side expression:

```
override fun onCreate(savedInstanceState: Bundle?) {
     super.onCreate(savedInstanceState)
     val locked: Boolean? = savedInstanceState?.getBoolean("locked")
}
```

If savedInstanceState is null, then null will be returned, otherwise the result of evaluating a savedInstanceState?.getBoolean("locked") expression will be returned. Keep in mind that a nullable reference call always returns nullable, so the result of the whole expression is a nullable Boolean?. If we want to make sure we will get non-nullable Boolean, we can combine the safe call operator with the *elvis* operator discussed in the next section.

Multiple calls to the *save call* operator can be chained together to avoid a nested if expression or complex conditions like this:

```
//Java idiomatic - multiple checks
val quiz: Quiz = Quiz()
//...
val correct: Boolean?

if(quiz.currentQuestion != null) {
    if(quiz.currentQuestion.answer != null ) {
        //do something
    }
}
//Kotlin idiomatic - multiple calls of save call operator
val quiz: Quiz = Quiz()

//...

val correct = quiz.currentQuestion?.answer?.correct
// Inferred type Boolean?
```

The preceding chain works like this: -correct will be accessed only if the answer value is not null and answer is accessed only if the currentQuestion value is not null. As a result, the expression will return the value returned by correct property or null if any object in the safe call chain is null.

Elvis operator

The elvis operator is represented by a question mark followed by a colon (?:) and has a syntax such as the following:

```
first operand ?: second operand
```

The elvis operator works as follows: if first operand is not null, then this operand will be returned, otherwise second operand will be returned. The elvis operator allows us to write very concise code.

We can apply the elvis operator to our example to retrieve the variable `locked`, which will always be non-nullable:

```
override fun onCreate(savedInstanceState: Bundle?) {
super.onCreate(savedInstanceState)
val locked: Boolean = savedInstanceState?.getBoolean("locked") ?: false
}
```

In the preceding example, the elvis operator will return a value of the `savedInstanceState?.getBoolean("locked")` expression if `savedInstanceState` is not null, otherwise it will return `false`. This way we can make sure that the `locked` variable will always have a non-nullable value. Thanks to the elvis operator, we can define a default value. Also, note that the right-hand side expression is evaluated only if the left-hand side is null. It is then providing a default value that will be used when the expression is nullable. Getting back to our quiz example from the previous section, we can easily modify the code to always return a non-nullable value:

```
val correct = quiz.currentQuestion?.answer?.correct ?: false
```

As the result, the expression will return the value returned by the `correct` property or `false` if any object in the *safe call* chain is null. This means that the value will always be returned, so non-nullable Boolean type is inferred.

The operator name comes from the famous American singer-songwriter Elvis Presley, because his hairstyle is similar to a question mark:

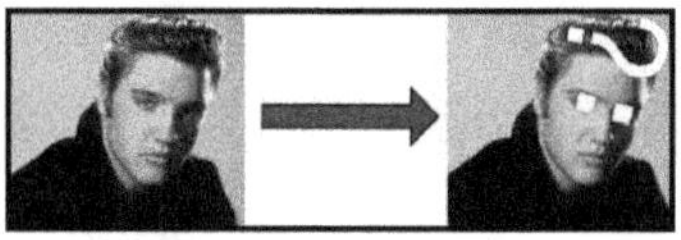

Source: `http://dobsondev.com/2014/06/06/the-elvis-operator/`

Not-null assertion

Another tool to deal with nullity is the *not-null assertion* operator. It is represented by a double exclamation mark (`!!`). This operator explicitly casts nullable variables to non-nullable variables. Here is a usage example:

```
var y: String? = "foo"
var size: Int = y!!.length
```

Normally, we would not be able to assign a value from a nullable property `length` to a non-nullable variable `size`. However, as developers, we can assure the compiler that this nullable variable will have a value here. If we are right, our application will work correctly, but if we are wrong, and the variable has a null value, the application will throw `NullPointerException`. Let's examine our activity method `onCreate()`:

```
override fun onCreate(savedInstanceState: Bundle?) {
    super.onCreate(savedInstanceState)
    val locked: Boolean = savedInstanceState!!.getBoolean("locked")
}
```

The preceding code will compile, but will this code work correctly? As we said before, when restoring an activity instance, `savedInstanceState` will be passed to the `onCreate` method, so this code will work without exceptions. However, when creating an activity instance, the `savedInstanceState` will be null (there is no previous instance to restore), so `NullPointerException` will be thrown at runtime. This behavior is similar to Java, but the main difference is that in Java accessing potentially nullable objects without a nullity check is the default behavior, while in Kotlin we have to force it; otherwise, we will get a compilation error.

There are only few correct applications of this operator, so when you use it or see it in code, think about it as a potential danger or warning. It is suggested that not-null assertion should be used rarely, and in most cases should be replaced with safe call or smart cast.

> The article for combating non-null assertions presents a few useful examples where the not-null assertion operator is replaced with other, safe Kotlin constructs: `http://bit.ly/2xg5JXt`.

In this case, there is no point in using the not-null assertion operator because we can solve our problem in a safer way using the `let` function.

The let function

Another tool to deal with nullable variables is the `let` function. This is actually not an operator, nor a language special construct. It is a function defined in the Kotlin standard library. Let's see the syntax of `let` combined with the *safe call* operator:

```
override fun onCreate(savedInstanceState: Bundle?) {
    super.onCreate(savedInstanceState)

    savedInstanceState?.let {
        println(it.getBoolean("isLocked")) // 1
```

```
    }
}
```

1. `savedInstanceState` inside the `let` function can be accessed using the `it` variable.

As mentioned before, the right-hand expression of the safe call operator will be only evaluated if the left-hand side is not null. In this case, the right-hand side is a `let` function that takes another function (lambda) as a parameter. Code defined in the block after `let` will be executed if `savedInstanceState` is not null. We will learn more about it and how to define such functions in `Chapter 7`, *Extension Functions and Properties*.

Nullability and Java

We know that Kotlin requires us to explicitly define references that can hold null values. Java on the other hand is much more lenient about nullability, so we may wonder how Kotlin handles types coming from Java (basically the whole Android SDK and libraries written in Java). Whenever possible, the Kotlin compiler will determine type nullability from the code and represent types as actual nullable or non-nullable types using nullability annotations.

> The Kotlin compiler supports several flavors of nullability annotations, including:
>
> - Android (`com.android.annotations` and `android.support.annotations`)
> - JetBrains (`@Nullable` and `@NotNull` from the `org.jetbrains.annotations` package)
> - JSR-305 (`Javax.annotation`)
>
> We can find the full list in the Kotlin compiler source code (`https://github.com/JetBrains/kotlin/blob/master/core/descriptor.loader.Java/src/org/jetbrains/kotlin/load/Java/JvmAnnotationNames.kt`).

We have seen this previously in Activity's `onCreate` method, where the `savedInstanceState` type was explicitly set to the nullable type `Bundle?`:

```
override fun onCreate(savedInstanceState: Bundle?) {
    ...
}
```

There are, however, many situations where it is not possible to determine variable nullability. All variables coming from Java can be null, except ones annotated as non-nullable. We could treat all of them as nullable and check before each access, but this would be impractical. As a solution to this problem, Kotlin introduced the concept of *platform types*. These are types that comes from Java types with relaxed null checks, meaning that each platform type may be null or not.

Although we cannot declare platform types by ourselves, this special syntax exists because the compiler and Android Studio need to display them sometimes. We can spot platform types in exception messages or the method parameters list. Platform type syntax is just a single exclamation mark suffix in a variable type declaration:

```
View! // View defined as platform type
```

We could treat each platform type as nullable, but type nullability usually depends on context, so sometimes we can treat them as non-nullable variables. This pseudo code shows the possible meaning of platform type:

```
T! = T or T?
```

It's our responsibility as developers to decide how to treat such types, as nullable or non-nullable. Let's consider the usage of the `findViewById` method:

```
val textView = findViewById(R.id.textView)
```

What will the `findViewById` method actually return? What is the inferred type of the `textView` variable? Nullable type (`TestView`) or not nullable (`TextView?`)? By default, the Kotlin compiler knows nothing about the nullability of the value returned by the `findViewById` method. This is why the inferred type for `TextView` has the platform type `View!`.

This is the kind of developer responsibility that we are talking about. We, as developers, must decide, because only we know if the layout will have `textView` defined in all configurations (portrait, landscape, and so on) or only in some of them. If we define a proper view inside the current layout, the `findViewById` method will return a reference to this view, and otherwise it will return null:

```
val textView = findViewById(R.id.textView) as TextView // 1
val textView = findViewById(R.id.textView) as TextView? // 2
```

1. Assuming that `textView` is present in every layout for each configuration, `textView` can be defined as non-nullable.

2. Assuming that `textView` is not present in all layout configurations (for example, it is present only in landscape), `textView` must be defined as nullable, otherwise the application will throw a `NullPointerException` when trying to assign null to a non-nullable variable (when the layout without `textView` is loaded).

Casts

The casting concept is supported by many programming languages. Basically, casting is a way to convert an object of one particular type into another type. In Java, we need to cast an object explicitly before accessing its member, or cast it and store it in the variable of the casted type. Kotlin simplifies concept of casting and moves it to the next level by introducing *smart casts*.

In Kotlin, we can perform a few types of cast:

- Cast objects to different types explicitly (*safe cast* operator)
- Cast objects to different types, or nullable types to non-nullable types, implicitly (*smart cast* mechanism)

Safe/unsafe cast operator

In strongly typed languages, such as Java or Kotlin, we need to convert values from one type to another explicitly using the cast operator. A typical casting operation is taking an object of one particular type and turning it into another object type that is its supertype (upcasting), subtype (downcasting), or interface. Let's start with a small reminder of casting that can be performed in Java:

```
Fragment fragment = new ProductFragment();
ProductFragment productFragment = (ProductFragment) fragment;
```

In the preceding example, there is an instance of `ProductFragment` that is assigned to a variable storing the `Fragment` data type. To be able to store this data in the `productFragment` variable that can store only the `ProductFragment` data type, so we need to perform an explicit cast. Unlike Java, Kotlin has a special `as` keyword representing the *unsafe cast* operator to handle casting:

```
val fragment: Fragment = ProductFragment()
val productFragment: ProductFragment =  fragment as ProductFragment
```

The `ProductFragment` variable is a subtype of `Fragment`, the preceding example will work fine. The problem is that casting to an incompatible type will throw the exception `ClassCastException`. That's why the `as` operator is called an unsafe cast operator:

```
val fragment : String = "ProductFragment"
val productFragment : ProductFragment =  fragment as
    ProductFragment
// Exception: ClassCastException
```

To fix this problem, we can use the *safe cast* operator `as?`. It is sometimes called the **nullable cast** operator. This operator tries to cast a value to the specified type, and returns `null` if the value cannot be cast. Here is an example:

```
val fragment: String = "ProductFragment"
val productFragment: ProductFragment? =  fragment as?
    ProductFragment
```

Notice that usage of the *safe cast* operator requires us to define the `name` variable as nullable (`ProductFragment?` instead of `ProductFragment`). As an alternative, we can use the *unsafe cast* operator and nullable type `ProductFragment?`, so we can see exactly the type that we are casting to:

```
val fragment: String = "ProductFragment"
val productFragment: ProductFragment? =  fragment as
    ProductFragment?
```

If we would like to have a `productFragment` variable that is non-nullable, then we would have to assign a default value using the elvis operator:

```
val fragment: String = "ProductFragment"
val productFragment: ProductFragment? = fragment as?
    ProductFragment ?: ProductFragment()
```

Now, the `fragment as? ProductFragment` expression will be evaluated without a single error. If this expression returns a non-nullable value (the cast can be performed), then this value will be assigned to the `productFragment` variable, otherwise a default value (the new instance of `ProductFragment`) will be assigned to the `productFragment` variable. Here is a comparison between these two operators:

- Unsafe cast `(as)`: Throws `ClassCastException` when casting is impossible
- Safe cast `(as?)`: Returns null when casting is impossible

Now, when we understand the difference between the *safe cast* and *unsafe cast* operators, we can safely retrieve a fragment from the fragment manager:

```
var productFragment: ProductFragment? = supportFragmentManager
.findFragmentById(R.id.fragment_product) as? ProductFragment
```

The *safe cast* and *unsafe cast* operators are used for casting complex objects. When working with primitive types, we can simply use one of the Kotlin standard library conversion methods. Most of the objects from the Kotlin standard library have standard methods used to simplify common casting to other types. The convention is that this kind of function has a prefix `to`, and the name of the class that we want to cast to. In the line in this example, the `Int` type is cast to the `String` type using the `toString` method:

```
val name: String
    val age: Int = 12
    name = age.toString(); // Converts Int to String
```

We will discuss *primitive types* and their conversions in the primitive data types section.

Smart casts

Smart casting converts a variable of one type to another type, but as opposed to safe casting, it is done implicitly (we don't need to use the `as` or `as?` cast operator). Smart casts work only when the Kotlin compiler is absolutely sure that the variable will not be changed after checking. This makes them perfectly safe for multithreaded applications. Generally, smart casts are available for all immutable references (`val`) and for local mutable references (`var`). We have two kinds of *smart cast*:

- Type *smart casts* cast an object of one type to an object of another type
- Nullity *smart casts* cast nullable references to non-nullable

Type smart casts

Let's represent the `Animal` and `Fish` classes from the previous section:

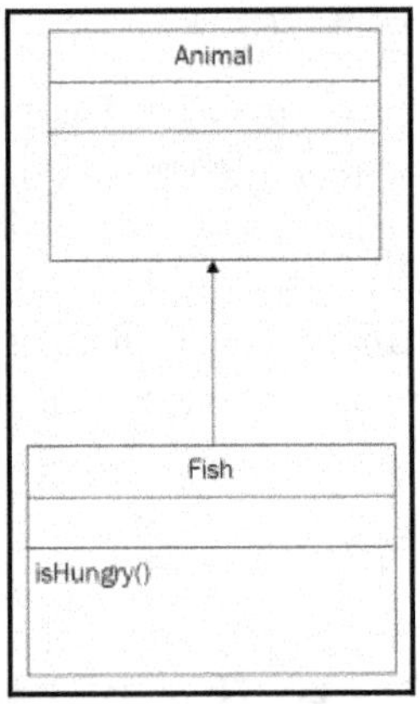

Let's assume we want to call the `isHungry` method and we want to check if the `animal` is an instance of `Fish`. In Java, we would have to do something like this:

```
//Java
if (animal instanceof Fish){
    Fish fish = (Fish) animal;
    fish.isHungry();
    //or
    ((Fish) animal).isHungry();
}
```

The problem with this code is its redundancy. We have to check if the `animal` instance is `Fish` and then we have to explicitly cast `animal` to `Fish` after this check. Wouldn't it be nice if the compiler could handle this for us? It turns out that the Kotlin compiler is really smart when it comes to casts, so it will handle all those redundant casts for us, using the *smart casts* mechanism. Here is an example of smart casting:

```
if(animal is Fish) {
    animal.isHungry()
}
```

Smart casting in Android Studio
Android Studio will display proper errors if smart casting is not possible, so we will know exactly whether we can use it. Android Studio marks variables with a green background when we access a member that required a cast.

```
if(animal is Fish){
    animal.isHungry()
}
```

In Kotlin, we don't have to explicitly cast an `animal` instance to `Fish`, because after the type check, the Kotlin compiler will be able to handle casts implicitly. Now inside the `if` block, the variable `animal` is cast to `Fish`. The result is then exactly the same as in the previous Java example (the Java instance of the operator is called in Kotlin). This is why we can safely call the `isHungry` method without any explicit casting. Notice that in this case, the scope of this *smart cast* is limited by the `if` block:

```
if(animal is Fish) {
    animal.isHungry() //1
}

animal.isHungry() //2, Error
```

1. In this context, the `animal` instance is `Fish`, so we can call the `isHungry` method.
2. In this context, the `animal` instance is still `Animal`, so we can't call the `isHungry` method.

There are, however, other cases where the smart cast scope is larger than a single block, as in the following example:

```
val fish:Fish? = // ...
if (animal !is Fish) //1
    return

animal.isHungry() //1
```

1. From this point, `animal` will be implicitly converted to a non-nullable `Fish`.

In the preceding example, the whole method would return from the function if `animal` is not `Fish`, so the compiler knows that `animal` must be `Fish` across the rest of the code block. Kotlin and Java conditional expressions are evaluated lazily.

This means that in the expression `condition1() && condition2()`, the method `condition2` will be called only when `condition1` returns `true`. This is why we can use a *smart cast* type on the right-hand side of the conditional expression:

```
if (animal is Fish && animal.isHungry()) {
    println("Fish is hungry")
}
```

Notice that if the `animal` was not `Fish`, the second part of the conditional expression would not be evaluated at all. When it is evaluated, Kotlin knows that `animal` is `Fish` (smart cast).

Non-nullable smart cast

Smart casts also handle other cases, including nullity checks. Let's assume that we have a `view` variable that is marked as nullable, because we don't know whether or not `findViewById` will return a view or `null`:

```
val view: View? = findViewById(R.layout.activity_shop)
```

We could use the safe call operator to access `view` methods and properties, but in some cases we may want to perform more operations on the same object. In these situations, smart casting may be a better solution:

```
val view: View?

if ( view != null ){
    view.isShown()
    // view is casted to non-nullable inside if code block
}

view.isShown() // error, outside if the block view is nullable
```

When performing null checks like this, the compiler automatically casts a nullable view (`View?`) to non-nullable (`View`). This is why we can call the `isShown` method inside the `if` block, without using a safe call operator. Outside the `if` block, the view is still nullable.

Each *smart cast* works only with read-only variables, because a read-write variable may change between the time the check was performed and the time the variable is accessed.

Smart casts also work with a function's `return` statements. If we perform nullity checks inside the function with a `return` statement, then the variable will also be cast to non-nullable:

```
fun setView(view: View?){
    if (view == null)
    return
    //view is casted to non-nullable
    view.isShown()
}
```

In this case, Kotlin is absolutely sure that the variable value will not be null, because the function would call `return` otherwise. Functions will be discussed in more detail in `Chapter 3`, *Playing with Functions*. We can make the preceding syntax even simpler by using the Elvis operator and performing a nullity check in a single line:

```
fun verifyView(view: View?){
    view ?: return

    //view is casted to non-nullable
    view.isShown()
    //..
}
```

Instead of just returning from the function, we may want to be more explicit about the existing problem and throw an exception. Then we can use the Elvis operator together with the error throw:

```
fun setView(view: View?){
    view ?: throw RuntimeException("View is empty")
    //view is casted to non-nullable
    view.isShown()
}
```

As we can see, *smart casts* are a very powerful mechanism that allows us to decrease the number of nullity checks. This is why they are heavily exploited by Kotlin. Remember the general rule--*smart casts* work only if Kotlin is absolutely sure that the variable cannot be changed after the cast, even by another thread.

Primitive data types

In Kotlin, everything is an object (reference type, not primitive type). We don't find primitive types, like the ones we can use in Java. This reduces code complexity. We can call methods and properties on any variable. For example, this is how we can convert the `Int` variable to a `Char`:

```
var code: Int = 75
code.toChar()
```

Usually (whenever it is possible), under the hood types such as `Int`, `Long`, or `Char` are optimized (stored as primitive types) but we can still call methods on them as on any other objects.

By default, the Java platform stores numbers as JVM primitive types, but when a nullable number reference (for example, `Int?`), is needed or generics are involved, Java uses *boxed representation*. **Boxing** means wrapping a primitive type into a corresponding boxed primitive type. This means that the instance behaves as an object. Examples of Java boxed representations of primitive types are `int` versus `Integer` or a `long` versus Long Since Kotlin is compiled to JVM bytecode, the same is true here:

```
var weight: Int = 12 // 1
var weight: Int? = null // 2
```

1. The value is stored as a primitive type.
2. The value is stored as a boxed integer (composite type).

This means that each time we create a number (`Byte`, `Short`, `Int`, `Long`, `Double`, and `Float`), or with `Char`, and `Boolean`, it will be stored as a primitive type unless we declare it as a nullable type (`Byte?`, `Char?`, `Array?`, and so on); otherwise, it will be stored as a boxed representation:

```
var a: Int = 1 // 1
var b: Int? = null // 2
b = 12 // 3
```

1. `a` is non-nullable, so it is stored as a primitive type.
2. `b` is null so it is stored as a boxed representation.
3. `b` is still stored as a boxed representation although it has a value.

Generic types cannot be parameterized using primitive types, so boxing will be performed. It's important to remember that using boxed representation (composite type) instead of primary representation can have performance penalties, because it will always create memory overhead compared to primitive type representation. This may be noticeable for lists and arrays containing a huge number of elements, so using primary representation may be crucial for application performance. On the other hand, we should not worry about the type of representation when it comes to a single variable or even multiple variable declarations, even in the Android world where memory is limited.

Now let's discuss the most important Kotlin primitive data types: numbers, characters, Booleans, and arrays.

Numbers

Basic Kotlin data types used for numbers are equivalents of Java numeric primitives:

Type	Bit width
Double	64
Float	32
Long	64
Int	32
Short	16
Byte	8

Kotlin, however, handles numbers a little bit differently than Java. The first difference is that there are no implicit conversions for numbers--smaller types are not implicitly converted to bigger types:

```
var weight : Int = 12
var truckWeight: Long = weight // Error1
```

This means that we cannot assign a value of type `Int` to the `Long` variable without an explicit conversion. As we said, in Kotlin everything is an object, so we can call the method and explicitly convert the `Int` type to `Long` to fix the problem:

```
var weight:I nt = 12
var truckWeight: Long = weight.toLong()
```

At first, this may seem like boilerplate code, but in practice this will allow us to avoid many errors related to number conversion and save a lot of debugging time. This is actually a rare example where Kotlin syntax has more code than Java. The Kotlin standard library supports the following conversion methods for numbers:

- `toByte():Byte`
- `toShort():Short`
- `toInt():Int`
- `toLong():Long`
- `toFloat():Float`
- `toDouble():Double`
- `toChar():Char`

We can, however, explicitly specify a number literal to change the inferred variable type:

```
val a: Int = 1
val b = a + 1 // Inferred type is Int
val b = a + 1L // Inferred type is Long
```

The second difference between Kotlin and Java with numbers is that number literals are slightly different in some cases. There are the following kinds of literal constants for integral values:

```
27 // Decimals by default
27L // Longs are tagged by a upper case L suffix
0x1B // Hexadecimals are tagged by 0x prefix
0b11011 // Binaries are tagged by 0b prefix
```

Octal literals are not supported. Kotlin also supports a conventional notation for floating-point numbers:

```
27.5 // Inferred type is Double
27.5F // Inferred type is Float. Float are tagged by f or F
```

Char

Characters in Kotlin are stored in type `Char`. In many ways, characters are similar to strings, so we will concentrate on the similarities and differences. To define `Char`, we must use single quote, as opposed to a `String` where we are using double quotes:

```
val char = 'a'     // 1
val string = "a"   // 2
```

1. Defines a variable of type `Char`.
2. Defines a variable of type `String`.

In both characters and strings, special characters can be escaped using a backslash. The following escape sequences are supported:

- `\t`: Tabulator
- `\b`: Backspace
- `\n`: New line
- `\r`: Carriage-return
- `\'`: Quote
- `\"`: Double quote
- `\\`: Slash
- `\$`: Dollar character
- `\u`: Unicode escape sequence

Let's define a `Char` containing the Yin Yang Unicode character (`U+262F`):

```
var yinYang = '\u262F'
```

Arrays

In Kotlin, arrays are represented by the `Array` class. To create an array in Kotlin, we can use a number of Kotlin standard library functions. The simplest one is `arrayOf()`:

```
val array = arrayOf(1,2,3)    // inferred type Array<Int>
```

By default, this function will create an array of boxed `Int`. If we want to have an array containing `Short` or `Long`, then we have to specify the array type explicitly:

```
val array2: Array<Short> = arrayOf(1,2,3)
val array3: Array<Long> = arrayOf(1,2,3)
```

As previously mentioned, using boxed representations may decrease application performance. That's why Kotlin has a few specialized classes representing arrays of primitive types to reduce boxing memory overhead: `ShortArray`, `IntArray`, `LongArray`, and so on. These classes have no inheritance relation to the `Array` class, although they have the same set of methods and properties. To create instances of this class, we have to use the corresponding factory function:

```
val array =  shortArrayOf(1, 2, 3)
val array =  intArrayOf(1, 2, 3)
val array =  longArrayOf(1, 2, 3)
```

It's important to notice and keep in mind this subtle difference, because those methods look similar, but create different type representations:

```
val array = arrayOf(1,2,3) // 1
val array = longArrayOf(1, 2, 3) // 2
```

1. The generic array of boxed `Long` elements (inferred type: `Array<Long>`).
2. The array containing primitive `Long` elements (inferred type: `LongArray`).

Knowing the exact size of an array will often improve performance, so Kotlin has another library function, `arrayOfNulls`, that creates an array of a given size filled with null elements:

```
val array = arrayOfNulls(3) // Prints: [null, null, null]
println(array) // Prints: [null, null, null]
```

We can also fill a predefined size array using a factory function that takes the array size as the first parameter and a lambda that can return the initial value of each array element given its index as the second parameter:

```
val array = Array (5) { it * 2 }
println(array) // Prints: [0, 2, 4, 8, 10]
```

We will discuss lambdas (anonymous functions) in more detail in `Chapter 5`, *Functions as First Class Citizen*. Accessing array elements in Kotlin is done the same way as in Java:

```
val array = arrayOf(1,2,3)
println(array[1]) //Prints: 2
```

Element are also indexed the same way as in Java, meaning the first element has index 0, the second has index 1, and so on. Not everything works the same and there are some differences: the main one is that arrays in Kotlin, unlike in Java, are invariant. We will discuss *variance* in `Chapter 6`, *Generics Are Your Friends.*

The Boolean type

Boolean is a logic type that has two possible values: `true` and `false`. We can also use the nullable `Boolean` type:

```
val isGrowing: Boolean = true
val isGrowing: Boolean? = null
```

The Boolean type also supports standard built-in operations that are generally available in most modern programming languages:

- `||`: Logical OR. Returns `true` when any of two predicates return `true`.
- `&&`: Logical AND. Returns `true` when both predicates return `true`.
- `!`: Negation operator. Returns `true` for `false`, and `false` for `true`.

Keep in mind that we can only use a not-null Boolean for any type of condition.

Like in Java, in `||` and `&&` predicates are evaluated lazily, and only when needed (*lazy conjunction*).

Composite data types

Let's discuss more complex types built into Kotlin. Some data types have major improvements compared to Java, while others are totally new.

Strings

Strings in Kotlin behave in a similar way as in Java, but they have a few nice improvements.

To start to access characters at a specified index, we can use the *indexing* operator and access characters the same way we access array elements:

```
val str = "abcd"
println (str[1]) // Prints: b
```

We also have access to various extensions defined in the Kotlin standard library, which make working with strings easier:

```
val str = "abcd"
println(str.reversed()) // Prints: dcba
println(str.takeLast(2)) // Prints: cd
println("john@test.com".substringBefore("@")) // Prints: john
println("john@test.com".startsWith("@")) // Prints: false
```

This is exactly the same `String` class as in Java, so these methods are not part of `String` class. They were defined as extensions. We will learn more about extensions in `Chapter 7`, *Extension Functions and Properties*.

> Check the `String` class documentation for a full list of the methods (`https://kotlinlang.org/api/latest/jvm/stdlib/kotlin/-string/`).

String templates

Building strings is an easy process, but in Java it usually requires long concatenation expressions. Let's jump straight to an example. Here is a string built from multiple elements implemented in Java:

```
//Java
String name = "Eva";
int age = 27;
String message = "My name is" + name + "and I am" + age + "years old";
```

In Kotlin, we can greatly simplify the process of string creation by using *string templates.* Instead of using concatenation, we can simply place a variable inside a string, using a dollar character to create a placeholder. During interpolation, string placeholders will be replaced with the actual value. Here is an example:

```
val name = "Eva"
val age = 27
val message = "My name is $name and I am $age years old"
println(message)
//Prints: My name is Eva  and I am 27 years old
```

This is as efficient as concatenation, because under the hood the compiled code creates a `StringBuilder` and put all the parts together. String templates are not limited to single variables. They can also contain whole expressions between the `${`, and `}` characters. It can be a function call that returns the value or property access, as shown in the following snippet:

```
val name = "Eva"
val message = "My name has ${name.length} characters"
println(message) //Prints: My name has 3 characters
```

This syntax allows us to create much cleaner code without the need to break the string each time a value from a variable or expression is required to construct strings.

Ranges

A range is a way to define a sequence of values. It is denoted by the first and last value in the sequence. We can use ranges to store weights, temperatures, time, and age. A range is defined using double dot notation (under the hood, a range uses the `rangeTo` operator):

```
val intRange = 1..4 // 1
val charRange= 'b'..'g' // 2
```

1. Inferred type is `IntRange` (equivalent of `i >= 1 && i <= 4`).
2. Inferred type is `CharRange` (equivalent of letters from `'b'` to `'g'`).

Notice that we are using single quotes to define the character range.

The `Int`, `Long`, and `Char` type ranges can be used to iterate over next values in the `for... each` loop:

```
for (i in 1..5) print(i) // Prints: 1234
for (i in 'b'..'g') print(i) // Prints: bcdefg
```

Ranges can be used to check a value is bigger than a start value and smaller than an end value:

```
val weight = 52
val healthy = 50..75

if (weight in healthy)
    println("$weight is in $healthy range")
    //Prints: 52 is in 50..75 range
```

It can be also used this way for other types of range, such as `CharRange`:

```
val c = 'k'       // Inferred type is Char
val alphabet = 'a'..'z'

if(c in alphabet)
    println("$c is character") //Prints: k is a character
```

In Kotlin, ranges are closed (end inclusive). This means that the range ending value is included in the range:

```
for (i in 1..1) print(i) // Prints: 123
```

Note that ranges in Kotlin are incremental by default (a step is equal to `1` by default):

```
for (i in 5..1) print(i) // Prints nothing
```

To iterate in reverse order, we must use a `downTo` function, which sets a step to `-1`, as in this example:

```
for (i in 5 downTo 1) print(i) // Prints: 54321
```

We can also set different steps:

```
for (i in 3..6 step 2) print(i) // Prints: 35
```

Notice that in the `3..6` range, the last element was not printed. This is because the *stepping index* moves two steps in each of the loop iterations. So in the first iteration, it has a value of `3`, in the second iteration a value of `5`, and finally in a third iteration the value would be `7`, so it is ignored, because it is outside the range.

A step defined by the `step` function must be positive. If we want to define a negative step, then we should use the `downTo` function together with the `step` function:

```
for (i in 9 downTo 1 step 3) print(i) // Prints: 963
```

Collections

A very important aspect of programming is working with collections. Kotlin offers multiple kinds of collections and many improvements compared to Java. We will discuss this subject in `Chapter 7`, *Extension Functions and Properties*.

Statements versus expressions

Kotlin utilizes expressions more widely than Java, so it is important to know the difference between a *statement* and an *expression*. A program is basically a sequence of statements and expressions. An expression produces a value, which can be used as part of another expression, variable assignment, or function parameter. An expression is a sequence of one or more *operands* (data that is manipulated) and zero or more *operators* (a token that represents a specific operation) that can be evaluated to a single value:

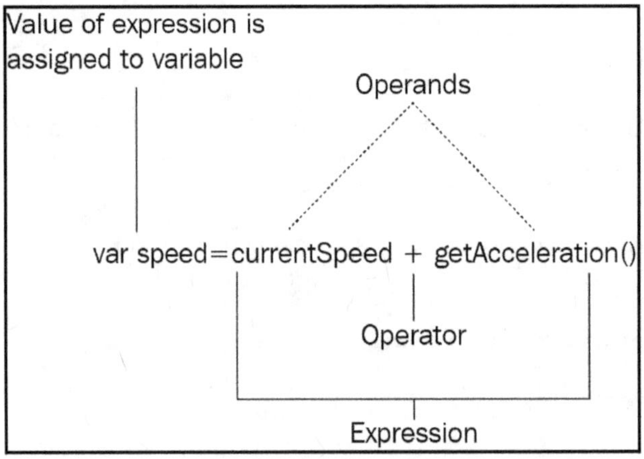

Let's review some examples of expressions from Kotlin:

Expression (produces a value)	Assigned value	Expression of type
`a = true`	`true`	Boolean
`a = "foo" + "bar"`	`"foobar"`	String
`a = min(2, 3)`	`2`	Integer
`a = computePosition().getX()`	Value returned by the `getX` method	Integer

Statements, on the other hand, perform an action and cannot be assigned to a variable, because they simply don't have a value. Statements can contain language keywords that are used to define classes (`class`), interfaces (`interface`), variables (`val`, `var`), functions (`fun`), loop logic (`break`, `continue`) and so on. Expressions can also be treated as a statement when the value returned by the expression is ignored (do not assign a value to the variable, do not return it from a function, do not use it as part of other expressions, and so on).

Kotlin is an expression-oriented language. This means that many constructs that are statements in Java are treated as expressions in Kotlin. The first major difference is the fact that Java and Kotlin have different ways of treating *control structures*. In Java they are treated as statements, while in Kotlin all control structures are treated as expressions, except for loops. This means that in Kotlin we can write very concise syntax using control structures. We will see examples in upcoming sections.

Control flow

Kotlin has many control flow elements known from Java, but they offer a little bit more flexibility and in some cases their usage is simplified. Kotlin introduces a new control flow construct known as `when` as a replacement for Java's `switch... case`.

The if statement

At its core, Kotlin's `if` clause works the same way as in Java:

```
val x = 5

if(x > 10){
    println("greater")
} else {
    println("smaller")
}
```

The version with the block body is also correct if the block contains single statements or expressions:

```
val x = 5

if(x > 10)
    println("greater")
else
    println("smaller")
```

Java, however, treats `if` as a *statement* while Kotlin treats `if` as an *expression*. This is the main difference, and this fact allows us to use more concise syntax. We can, for example, pass the result of an `if` expression directly as a function argument:

```
println(if(x > 10) "greater" else "smaller")
```

We can compress our code into single line, because the result of the `if` expression (of type `String`) is evaluated and then passed to the `println` method. When the condition `x > 10` is `true`, then the first branch (greater) will be returned by this expression; otherwise, the second branch (smaller) will be returned by this expression. Let's examine another example:

```
val hour = 10
val greeting: String
if (hour < 18) {
    greeting = "Good day"
} else {
    greeting = "Good evening"
}
```

In the preceding example, we are using `if` as a statement. But as we know, `if` in Kotlin is an expression and the result of the expression can be assigned to a variable. This way we can assign the result of the `if` expression to a greeting variable directly:

```
val greeting = if (hour < 18) "Good day" else "Good evening"
```

But sometimes there is a need to place some other code inside the branch of the `if` statement. We can still use `if` as an expression. Then, the last line of the matching `if` branch will be returned as a result:

```
val hour = 10
val greeting = if (hour < 18) {
    //some code
    "Good day"
} else {
    //some code
    "Good evening"
}

println(greeting) // Prints: "Good day"
```

If we are using `if` as an expression rather than a statement, the expression is required to have an `else` branch. The Kotlin version is even better than Java. Since the `greeting` variable is defined as non-nullable, the compiler will validate the whole `if` expression and it will check that all cases are covered with branch conditions. Since `if` is an expression, we can use it inside a *string template*:

```
val age = 18
val message = "You are ${ if (age < 18) "young" else "of age" } person"
println(message) // Prints: You are of age person
```

Treating `if` as an *expression* gives us a wide range of possibilities previously unavailable in the Java world.

The when expression

The `when` expression in Kotlin is a multiway branch statement. The `when` expression is designed as a more powerful replacement for the Java `switch... case` statement. The `when` statement often provides a better alternative than a large series of `if... else if` statements, as it provides more concise syntax. Let's look at an example:

```
when (x) {
    1 -> print("x == 1")
    2 -> print("x == 2")
    else -> println("x is neither 1 nor 2")
}
```

The `when` expression matches its argument against all branches one after another until the condition of some branch is satisfied. This behavior is similar to Java's `switch... case`, but we do not have to write a redundant `break` statement after every branch.

Similar to the `if` clause, we can use `when` either as a *statement* ignoring the returned value or as an *expression* and assign its value to a variable. If `when` is used as an *expression*, the value of the last line of the satisfied branch becomes the value of the overall expression. If it is used as a statement, the value is simply ignored. As usual, the `else` branch is evaluated if none of the previous branches satisfy the condition:

```
val vehicle = "Bike"

val message= when (vehicle) {
    "Car" -> {
        // Some code
        "Four wheels"
    }
    "Bike" -> {
        // Some code
        "Two wheels"
    }
    else -> {
        //some code
        "Unknown number of wheels"
    }
}

println(message) //Prints: Two wheels
```

Each time a branch has more than one instruction, we must place it inside the code block, defined by two braces `{... }`. If `when` is treated as an expression (the result of evaluating `when` is assigned to a variable), the last line of each block is treated as the return value. We have seen the same behavior with an `if` expression, so by now you have probably figured out that this is common behavior across many Kotlin constructs, including lambdas, which will be discussed further later in the book.

If `when` is used as an expression, the `else` branch is mandatory, unless the compiler can prove that all possible cases are covered with branch conditions. We can also handle many matching arguments in a single branch using commas to separate them:

```
val vehicle = "Car"

when (vehicle) {
    "Car", "Bike" -> print("Vehicle")
    else -> print("Unidentified funny object")
}
```

Another nice feature of `when` is the ability to check variable type. We can easily validate that a value `is` or `!is` of a particular type. Smart casts become handy again, because we can access the methods and properties of a matching type in a branch block without any extra checks:

```
val name = when (person) {
    is String -> person.toUpperCase()
    is User -> person.name
    //Code is smart casted to String, so we can
    //call String class methods
    //...
}
```

In a similar way, we can check which range or collection contains a particular value. This time, we'll use the `is` and `!is` keywords:

```
val riskAssessment = 47

val risk = when (riskAssessment) {
    in 1..20 -> "negligible risk"
    !in 21..40 -> "minor risk"
    !in 41..60 -> "major risk"
    else -> "undefined risk"
}

println(risk) // Prints: major risk
```

Actually, we can put any kind of expression on the right-hand side of the `when` branch. It can be a method call or any other expression. Consider the following example where the second `when` expression is used for the `else` statement:

```
val riskAssessment = 80
val handleStrategy = "Warn"

val risk = when (riskAssessment) {
    in 1..20 -> print("negligible risk")
    !in 21..40 -> print("minor risk")
    !in 41..60 -> print("major risk")
    else -> when (handleStrategy){
        "Warn" -> "Risk assessment warning"
        "Ignore" -> "Risk ignored"
        else -> "Unknown risk!"
    }
}

println(risk) // Prints: Risk assessment warning
```

As we can see, `when` is a very powerful construct, allowing more control than Java's `switch`, but it is even more powerful because it is not limited only to checking values for equality. In a way, it can even be used as a replacement for an `if... else if` chain. If no argument is supplied to the `when` expression, the branch conditions behave as Boolean expressions, and a branch is executed when its condition is `true`:

```
private fun getPasswordErrorId(password: String) = when {
    password.isEmpty() -> R.string.error_field_required
    passwordInvalid(password) -> R.string.error_invalid_password
    else -> null
}
```

All the presented examples require an `else` branch. Each time when all the possible cases are covered, we can omit an `else` branch (exhaustive `when`). Let's look at the simplest example with Boolean:

```
val large:Boolean = true
when(large){
    true -> println("Big")
    false -> println("Big")
}
```

The compiler can verify that all possible values are handled, so there is no need to specify an `else` branch. The same logic applies to enums and sealed classes, which will be discussed in `Chapter 4`, *Classes and Objects*.

Checks are performed by the Kotlin compiler, so we have certainty that any case will not be missed. This reduces the possibility of a common Java bug where the developer forgets to handle all the cases inside the `switch` statement (although polymorphism is usually a better solution).

Loops

A loop is a control structure that repeats the same set of instructions until a termination condition is met. In Kotlin, loops can iterate through anything that provides an iterator. An iterator is an interface that has two methods: `hasNext` and `next`. It knows how to iterate over a collection, range, string, or any entity that can be represented as a sequence of elements.

> To iterate through something, we have to supply an `iterator()` method. As `String` doesn't have one, in Kotlin it is defined as an extension function. Extensions will be covered in `Chapter 7`, *Extension Functions and Properties*.

Kotlin provides three kinds of loops `for`, `while`, and `do... while`. All of them work the same as in other programming languages, so we will discuss them briefly.

The for loop

The classic Java `for` loop, where we need to define the iterator explicitly, is not present in Kotlin. Here is an example of this kind of loop in Java:

```
//Java
String str = "Foo Bar";
for(int i=0; i<str.length(); i++)
System.out.println(str.charAt(i));
```

To iterate through a collection of items from start to finish, we can simply use the `for` loop instead:

```
var array = arrayOf(1, 2, 3)

for (item in array) {
    print(item)
}
```

It can also be defined without a block body:

```
for (item in array)
    print(item)
```

If a `collection` is a generic collection, then `item` will be smart cast to a type corresponding to a generic collection type. In other words, if a collection contains elements of type `Int`, the item will be smart cast to `Int`:

```
var array = arrayOf(1, 2, 3)

for (item in array)
    print(item) // item is Int
```

We can also iterate through the collection using its index:

```
for (i in array.indices)
    print(array[i])
```

The `array.indices` param returns `IntRange` with all indexes. It is the equivalent of (`1.. array.length - 1`). There is also an alternative `withIndex` library method that returns a list of the `IndexedValue` property, which contains an index and a value. This can be deconstructed into these elements this way:

```
for ((index, value) in array.withIndex()) {
    println("Element at $index is $value")
}
```

The construct `(index, value)` is known as a destructive declaration, and we will discuss it in `Chapter 4`, *Classes and Objects*.

The while loop

The `while` loop repeats a block, while its conditional expression returns `true`:

```
while (condition) {
    //code
}
```

There is also a `do... while` loop that repeats blocks as long as a *conditional expression* is returning `true`:

```
do {
    //code
} while (condition)
```

Kotlin, as opposed to Java, can use variables declared inside the `do... while` loop as a condition:

```
do {
    var found = false
    //..
} while (found)
```

The main difference between the `while` and `do... while` loops is when a conditional expression is evaluated. A `while` loop checks the condition before code execution and if it is not true, the code won't be executed. On the other hand, a `do... while` loop first executes the body of the loop, and then evaluates the conditional expression, so the body will always execute at least once. If this expression is `true`, the loop will repeat. Otherwise, the loop terminates.

Other iterations

There other ways to iterate over collections using built-in standard library functions, such as `forEach`. We will cover them in `Chapter 7`, *Extension Functions and Properties*.

Break and continue

All loops in Kotlin support classic `break` and `continue` statements. The `continue` statement proceeds to the next iteration of that loop, while `break` stops the execution of the most inner enclosing loop:

```
val range = 1..6

for(i in range) {
    print("$i ")
}

// prints: 1 2 3 4 5 6
```

Now let's add a `condition` and `break` the iteration when this condition is `true`:

```
val range = 1..6

for(i in range) {
    print("$i ")

    if (i == 3)
        break
}

// prints: 1 2 3
```

The `break` and `continue` statements are especially useful when dealing with nested loops. They may simplify our control flow and significantly decrease the amount of work performed to save priceless Android resources. Let's perform a nested iteration and break the outer loop:

```
val intRange = 1..6
val charRange = 'A'..'B'

for(value in intRange) {
    if(value == 3)
        break

    println("Outer loop: $value ")

    for (char in charRange) {
        println("\tInner loop: $char ")
    }
}

// prints
Outer loop: 1
    Inner loop: A
    Inner loop: B
Outer loop: 2
    Inner loop: A
    Inner loop: B
```

We used a `break` statement to terminate the outer loop at the beginning of the third iteration, so the nested loop was also terminated. Notice the usage of the `\t` escaped sequence, which adds indents on the console. We can also utilize the `continue` statement to skip the current iteration of the loop:

```
val intRange = 1..5

for(value in intRange) {
    if(value == 3)
        continue

    println("Outer loop: $value ")

    for (char in charRange) {
        println("\tInner loop: $char ")
    }
}

// prints
Outer loop: 1
    Inner loop: A
    Inner loop: B
Outer loop: 2
    Inner loop: A
    Inner loop: B
Outer loop: 4
    Inner loop: A
    Inner loop: B
Outer loop: 5
    Inner loop: A
    Inner loop: B
```

We skip the iteration of the outer loop when the current value equals `3`.

Both `continue` and `break` statements perform corresponding operations on the enclosing loop. There are, however, times when we want to terminate or skip the iteration of one loop from within another; for example, to terminate an outer loop iteration from within an inner loop:

```
for(value in intRange) {
    for (char in charRange) {
        // How can we break outer loop here?
    }
}
```

Fortunately, both `continue` and `break` statements have two forms--labeled and unlabeled. We already saw unlabeled; now we will need labeled to solve our problem. Here is an example of how a labeled break might be used:

```
val charRange = 'A'..'B'
val intRange = 1..6

outer@ for(value in intRange) {
    println("Outer loop: $value ")

    for (char in charRange) {
        if(char == 'B')
            break@outer

        println("\tInner loop: $char ")
    }
}

// prints
Outer loop: 1
    Inner loop: A
```

The `@outer` is the label name. By convention, the label name always starts with `@` followed by the label name. The label is placed before the loop. Labeling the loop allows us to use a qualified break (`break@outer`), which is a way to stop execution of a loop that is referenced by this label. The preceding qualified break (a break with a label) jumps to the execution point right after the loop marked with that label.

Placing the `return` statement will break all the loops and return from enclosing an anonymous or named function:

```
fun doSth() {
    val charRange = 'A'..'B'
    val intRange = 1..6

    for(value in intRange) {
        println("Outer loop: $value ")

        for (char in charRange) {
            println("\tInner loop: $char ")
            return
        }
    }
}

//usage
println("Before method call")
```

```
doSth()
println("After method call")

// prints
Outer loop: 1
    Inner loop: A
```

After the method call:

```
Outer loop: 1
    Inner loop: A
```

Exceptions

Most Java programming guidelines, including the book *Effective Java,* promote the concept of validity checks. This means that we should always verify arguments or the state of the object and throw an exception if a validity check fails. Java exception systems have two kinds of exceptions: checked exceptions and unchecked exceptions.

An unchecked exception means that the developer is not forced to catch exceptions by using a `try... catch` block. By default, exceptions go all the way up the call stack, so we make decisions where to catch them. If we forget to catch them, they will go all the way up the call stack and stop thread execution with a proper message (thus they remind us):

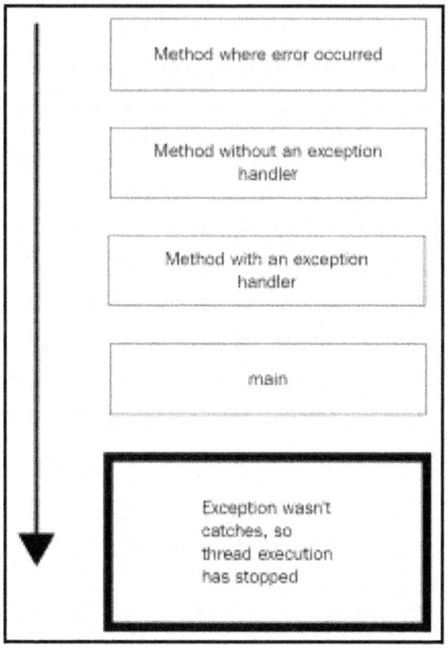

Java has a really strong exception system, which in many cases forces developers to explicitly mark each function that may throw an exception and explicitly catch each exception by surrounding them with `try... catch` blocks (checked exceptions). This works great for very small projects, but in real large-scale applications, this very often leads to the following verbose code:

```
// Java
try {
    doSomething()
} catch (IOException e) {
    // Must be safe
}
```

Instead of passing the exception up in the call stack, it is ignored by providing an empty catch block, so it won't be handled properly and it will vanish. This kind of code may mask critical exceptions, give a false sense of security, and lead to unexpected problems and difficult to find bugs.

Before we discuss how exception handling is done in Kotlin, let's compare both types of exception:

Code	**Checked exceptions**	**Unchecked exceptions**
Function declaration	We have to specify what exceptions can be thrown by functions.	The function declaration does not contain information about all thrown exceptions.
Exception handling	The function that throws an exception must to be surrounded by a `try... catch` block.	We can catch the exception and do something if we want, but we aren't forced to do this. The exception goes up in the call stack.

The biggest difference between the Kotlin and Java exception systems is that in Kotlin all exceptions are unchecked. This means we never have to surround a method with a `try... catch` block, even if this is a Java method that may throw a cached exception. We can still do it, but we are not forced to:

```
fun foo() {
    throw IOException()
}

fun bar() {
    foo () //no need to surround method with try-catch block
}
```

This approach removes code verbosity and improves safety because we don't need to introduce empty `catch` blocks.

The try... catch block

The Kotlin `try... catch` block is the equivalent of the Java `try... catch` block. Let's look at a quick example:

```
fun sendFormData(user: User?, data: Data?) { // 1
    user ?: throw NullPointerException("User cannot be null")
    // 2
    data ?: throw NullPointerException("Data cannot be null")
    //do something
}

fun onSendDataClicked() {
    try { // 3
        sendFormData(user, data)
    } catch (e: AssertionError) { // 4
        // handle error
    }  finally { // 5
        // optional finally block
    }
}
```

1. Exceptions are not specified on function signature like in Java.
2. We check the validity of the data and throw `NullPointerException` (notice that no new keyword is required when creating an object instance).
3. The `try... catch` block is similar construct to Java.
4. Handle only this specific exception (the `AssertionError` exception).
5. The `finally` block is always executed.

There may be zero or more `catch` blocks and the `finally` block may be omitted. However, at least one `catch` or `finally` block should be present.

In Kotlin exception handling, `try` is an expression, so it can return a value and we can assign its value to a variable. The actual assigned value is the last expression of the executed block. Let's check if a particular Android application is installed on the device:

```
val result = try { // 1
    context.packageManager.getPackageInfo("com.text.app", 0)  //2
    true
} catch (ex: PackageManager.NameNotFoundException) { // 3
    false
}
```

1. The `try... catch` block is returning value that was returned by a single expression function.
2. If an application is installed, the `getPackageInfo` method will return a value (this value is ignored) and the next line containing the `true` expression will be executed. This is the last operation performed by a `try` block, so its value will be assigned to a variable (`true`).

If an app is not installed, `getPackageInfo` will throw `PackageManager.NameNotFoundException` and the `catch` block will be executed. The last line of the `catch` block contains a `false` expression, so its value will be assigned to a variable.

Compile-time constants

Since the `val` variable is read-only, in most cases we could treat it as a constant. We need to be aware that its initialization may be delayed, so this means that there are scenarios where the `val` variable may not be initialized at compile time, for example, when assigning the result of the method call to a value:

```
val fruit:String  = getName()
```

This value will be assigned at runtime. There are, however, situations where we need to know the value at compile time. The exact value is required when we want to pass parameters to annotations. Annotations are processed by an annotation processor that runs long before the application is started:

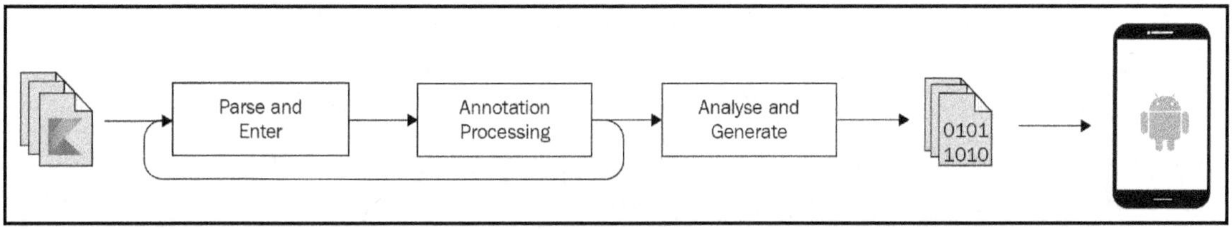

To make absolutely sure that the value is known at compile time (and thus can be processed by an annotation processor), we need to mark it with a `const` modifier. Let's define a custom annotation, `MyLogger`, with a single parameter defining maximum log entries and annotate a `Test` class with it:

```
const val MAX_LOG_ENTRIES = 100
    @MyLogger(MAX_LOG_ENTRIES )
    // value available at compile time
    class Test {}
```

There are couple of limitations regarding usage of `const` that we must be aware of. The first limitation is that it must be initialized with values of primitive types or the `String` type. The second limitation is that it must be declared at the top level or as a member of an object. We will discuss objects in `Chapter 4`, *Classes and Objects*. The third limitation is that it cannot have a custom getter.

Delegates

Kotlin provides first-class support for delegation. It is a very useful improvement on Java. In fact, there are many applications for delegates in Android development, so we have decided to spare a whole chapter on this subject (`Chapter 8`, *Delegates*).

Summary

In this chapter, we have discussed the differences between variables, values, and consts, and discussed basic Kotlin data types, including ranges. We also looked into a Kotlin type system that enforces strict null safety and ways to deal with nullable references using various operators and smart casts. We now know that we can write more concise code by taking advantage of using type inference and various control structures that in Kotlin are treated as expressions. Finally, we discussed ways of exception handling.

In the next chapter, we will learn about functions and present different ways of defining them. We will cover concepts such as single-expression functions, default arguments and named argument syntax, and discuss various modifiers.

3
Playing with Functions

In previous chapters, we've seen Kotlin variables, type systems, and control structures. But to create applications, we need building blocks that allow us to make structures. In Java, the class is the building block of the code. Kotlin, on the other hand, supports functional programming; therefore, it is possible to create whole programs or libraries without any classes. The function is the most basic building block in Kotlin. This chapter introduces functions in Kotlin, together with different function features and types.

In this chapter, we will cover the following topics:

- Basic function usage in Kotlin
- The `Unit` return type
- The vararg parameter
- Single-expression functions
- Tail-recursive functions
- Default argument values
- Named argument syntax
- Top-level functions
- Local functions
- The `Nothing` return type

Basic function declaration and usage

The most common first program that programmers write to test a programming language is the `Hello, World!` program. It is a full program that just displays `Hello, World!` as text on the console. We are also going to start with this program, because in Kotlin it is based on a function and only on a function (no class is needed). So the Kotlin `Hello, World!` program looks as follows:

```
// SomeFile.kt
fun main(args: Array<String>) {          // 1
    println("Hello, World!")             // 2, Prints: Hello, World!
}
```

1. A function defines a single parameter, `args`, which contains an array of all arguments used to run the program (from the command line). It is defined as non-nullable, because an empty array is passed to a method when the program is started without any arguments.
2. The `println` function is a Kotlin function defined in the Kotlin standard library that is equivalent to the Java function `System.out.println`.

This program tells us a lot about Kotlin. It shows what the function looks like and that we can define a function without any classes. First, let's analyze the structure of the function. It starts with the `fun` keyword, and then comes the name of the function, parameters in the bracket, and the function body. Here is another example of a simple function, but this one is returning a value:

```
fun double(i: Int): Int {
    return 2 * i
}
```

Good to know frame

There is much confusion around the difference between methods and functions. Common definitions are as follows:

- A function is a piece of code that is called by name. A method is a function associated with an instance of a class (object). Sometimes it is called member function.
- So in simpler words, functions inside classes are called **methods**. In Java, there are officially only methods, but academics often argue that static Java methods are in fact functions. In Kotlin, we can define functions that are not associated with any object.

The syntax to call a function is the same in Kotlin as in Java, and most modern programming languages:

```
val a = double(5)
```

We call the `double` function and assign a value returned by it to a variable. Let's discuss the details of the parameters and return types of Kotlin functions.

Parameters

Parameters in Kotlin functions are declared using Pascal notation, and the type of each parameter must be explicitly specified. All parameters are defined as read-only variables. There is no way to make parameters mutable, because such behavior is error-prone and in Java it was often abused by programmers. If there is a need for that, then we can explicitly shadow parameters by declaring local variables with the same name:

```
fun findDuplicates(list: List<Int>): Set<Int> {
    var list = list.sorted()
    //...
}
```

This is possible, but it is treated as bad practice, so a warning will be displayed. A better approach is to name parameters by the data they provide and variables by the purpose they serve. These names should then be different in most cases.

Parameters versus arguments

In the programming community, arguments and parameters are often though to be the same thing. These words cannot be used interchangeably because they have different meanings. An argument is an actual value that is passed to a function when the function is called. A parameter refers to the variables declared inside a function declaration. Consider the following example:

```
fun printSum(a1: Int, a2: Int) { // 1.
print(a1 + a2)
}
add(3, 5) // 2.

1 - a1 and a2 are parameters
2 - 3 and 5 are arguments
```

As with Java, functions in Kotlin can contain multiple parameters:

```
fun printSum(a: Int, b: Int) {
    val sum = a + b
    print(sum)
}
```

Arguments provided to functions can be subtypes of the type specified in the parameter declaration. As we know, in Kotlin the supertype of all the non-nullable types is `Any`, so we need to use it if we want to accept all types:

```
fun presentGently(v: Any) {
    println("Hello. I would like to present you: $v")
}

presentGently("Duck")
// Hello. I would like to present you: Duck
presentGently(42)
// Hello. I would like to present you: 42
```

To allow null in arguments, the type needs to be specified as nullable. Note that `Any?` is the supertype of all nullable and non-nullable types, so we can pass objects of any type as arguments:

```
fun presentGently(v: Any?) {
    println("Hello. I would like to present you: $v")
}

presentGently(null)
// Prints: Hello. I would like to present you: null
presentGently(1)
// Prints: Hello. I would like to present you: 1
presentGently("Str")
// Prints: Hello. I would like to present you: Str
```

Returning functions

So far, most of the functions were defined like procedures (functions that do not return any values). But in fact, there are no procedures in Kotlin and all functions return some value. When it is not specified, the default return value is the `Unit` instance. We can set it explicitly for demonstration purposes:

```
fun printSum(a: Int, b: Int): Unit { // 1
    val sum = a + b
    print(sum)
}
```

1. Unlike in Java, we are defining the return type after the function name and parameters.

The `Unit` object is the equivalent of Java's `void`, but it can be treated as any other object. So we can store it in variable:

```
val p = printSum(1, 2)
println(p is Unit) // Prints: true
```

Of course, Kotlin coding conventions claim that when a function returns `Unit`, then the type definition should be omitted. This way, code is more readable and simpler to understand:

```
fun printSum(a: Int, b: Int) {
    val sum = a + b
    print(sum)
}
```

Good to know frame

`Unit` is a singleton, which means that there is only one instance of it. So all three conditions are `true`:

```
println(p is Unit) // Print: true
println(p == Unit) // Print: true
println(p === Unit) // Print: true
```

The singleton pattern is highly supported in Kotlin and it will be more thoroughly covered in `Chapter 4`, *Classes and Objects*.

To return output from functions with the `Unit` return type, we can simply use a return statement without any value:

```
fun printSum(a: Int, b: Int) {  // 1
    if(a < 0 || b < 0) {
        return                  // 2
    }
    val sum = a + b
    print(sum)
    // 3
}
```

1. There is no return type specified, so the return type is implicitly set to `Unit`.
2. We can just use return without any value.
3. When a function returns `Unit`, then the return call is optional. We don't have to use it.

We could also use return type, `Unit`, but it should not be used because that would be misleading and less readable.

When we specify a return type other than `Unit`, then we always need to return the value explicitly:

```
fun sumPositive(a: Int, b: Int): Int {
    if(a > 0 && b > 0) {
        return a + b
    }
    // Error, 1
}
```

1. The function will not compile it, because no return value was specified, as the `if` condition is not fulfilled.

The problem can be fixed by adding a second `return` statement:

```
fun sumPositive(a: Int, b: Int): Int {
    if(a >= 0 && b >= 0) {
        return a + b
    }
    return 0
}
```

Vararg parameter

Sometimes, the number of parameters is not known in advance. In such cases, we can add a `vararg` modifier to a parameter. It allows the function to accept any number of arguments. Here is an example, where the function is printing the sum of multiple integers:

```
fun printSum(vararg numbers: Int) {
    val sum = numbers.sum()
    print(sum)
}

printSum(1,2,3,4,5) // Prints: 15
printSum()          // Prints: 0
```

Arguments will be accessible inside the method as an array that holds all the provided values. The type of the array will correspond to a `vararg` parameter type. Normally we would expect it to be a generic array holding a specified type (`Array<T>`), but as we know, Kotlin has an optimized type for arrays of `Int` called `IntArray`, so this type will be used. Here, for example, is the type of the `vararg` parameter with the type `String`:

```
fun printAll(vararg texts: String) {
//Inferred type of texts is Array<String>
    val allTexts = texts.joinToString(",")
    println("Texts are $allTexts")
}

printAll("A", "B", "C") // Prints: Texts are A,B,C
```

Note that we are still able to specify more parameters before or after the `vararg` parameter, as long as it is clear which argument is directed to which parameter:

```
fun printAll(prefix: String, postfix: String, vararg texts: String)
{
    val allTexts = texts.joinToString(", ")
    println("$prefix$allTexts$postfix")
}

printAll("All texts: ", "!") // Prints: All texts: !
printAll("All texts: ","!" , "Hello", "World")
// Prints: All texts: Hello, World!
```

Additionally, arguments provided to `vararg` parameters can be subtypes of the specified type:

```
fun printAll(vararg texts: Any) {
    val allTexts = texts.joinToString(",") // 1
    println(allTexts)
}

// Usage
printAll("A", 1, 'c') // Prints: A,1,c
```

1. The `joinToString` function can be invoked on lists. It joins elements into a single string. On the first argument, there is a separator specified.

One limitation with `vararg` usage is that there is only one `vararg` parameter allowed per function declaration.

When we call `vararg` parameters, we can pass argument values one by one, but we can also pass an array of values. This can be done using the `spread` operator (`*` prefixing the array), as in the following example:

```
val texts = arrayOf("B", "C", "D")
printAll(*texts) // Prints: Texts are: B,C,D
printAll("A", *texts, "E") // Prints: Texts are: A,B,C,D,E
```

Single-expression functions

In typical programming, many functions contain only one expression. Here is an example of this kind of function:

```
fun square(x: Int): Int {
    return x * x
}
```

Another one, which can be often found in Android projects, is a pattern used in `Activity`, to define methods that just get text from some view or provide some other data from the view to allow a presenter to get it:

```
fun getEmail(): String {
    return emailView.text.toString()
}
```

Both functions are defined to return the results of a single expression. In the first example, it is the result of an `x * x` multiplication, and in the second one it is the result of the expression `emailView.text.toString()`. These kinds of function are used all over Android projects. Here are some common use cases:

- Extracting some small operations (like in the preceding `square` function)
- Using polymorphism to provide values specific to a class
- Functions that only create some object
- Functions that pass data between architecture layers (like in the preceding example, where `Activity` is passing data from the view to the presenter)
- Functional programming-style functions that are based on recurrence

Such functions are often used, so Kotlin has a notation for this kind. When a function returns a single expression, then curly braces and the body of the function can be omitted. We specify the expression directly using the equality character. Functions defined this way are called **single-expression** functions. Let's update our `square` function, and define it as a single-expression function:

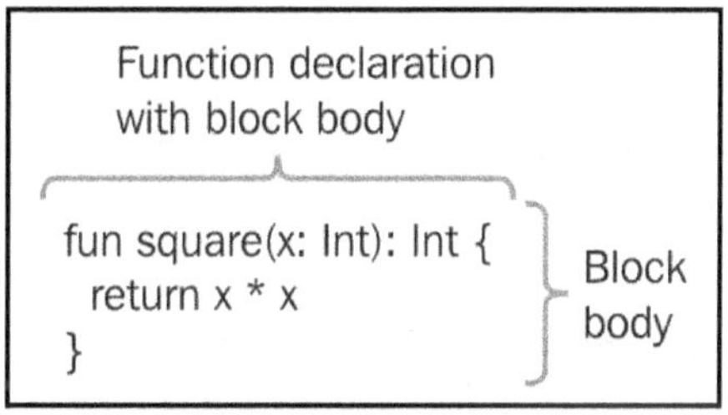

As we can see, single-expression functions have an expression body instead of a block body. This notation is shorter, but the whole body needs to be just a single expression.

In single-expression functions, declaring the return type is optional, because it can be inferred by the compiler from the type of expression. This is why we can simplify the `square` function, and define it this way:

```
fun square(x: Int) = x * x
```

There are many places inside Android applications where we can utilize single-expression functions. Let's consider the `RecyclerView` adapter that provides the layout ID and creates `ViewHolder`:

```
class AddressAdapter : ItemAdapter<AddressAdapter.ViewHolder>() {
    override fun getLayoutId() = R.layout.choose_address_view
    override fun onCreateViewHolder(itemView: View) = ViewHolder(itemView)

    // Rest of methods
}
```

In the following example, we achieve high readability thanks to a single-expression function. Single expression functions are also very popular in the functional world. An example will be described later, in the section about tail-recursive functions. Single expression function notation also pairs well with the `when` structure. Here is an example of their connection, used to get specific data from an object according to a key (a use case from a big Kotlin project):

```
fun valueFromBooking(key: String, booking: Booking?) = when(key) {
    // 1
    "patient.nin" -> booking?.patient?.nin
    "patient.email" -> booking?.patient?.email
    "patient.phone" -> booking?.patient?.phone
    "comment" -> booking?.comment
    else -> null
}
```

1. We don't need a type, because it is inferred from the `when` expression.

Another common Android example is that we can combine `when` expressions with the Activity method `onOptionsItemSelected` which handles top bar menu clicks:

```
override fun onOptionsItemSelected(item: MenuItem): Boolean = when
{
    item.itemId == android.R.id.home -> {
        onBackPressed()
        true
    }
    else -> super.onOptionsItemSelected(item)
}
```

Another example where the syntax of the single-expression function is useful is when we chain multiple operations on a single object:

```
fun textFormatted(text: String, name: String) = text
                  .trim()
                  .capitalize()
                  .replace("{name}", name)

val formatted = textFormatted("hello, {name}", "Marcin")
println(formatted) // Hello, Marcin
```

As we can see, single expression functions can make our code more concise and improve readability. Single-expression functions are commonly used in Kotlin Android projects and they are really popular for functional programming.

Imperative versus declarative programming

Imperative programming: This programming paradigm describes the exact sequence of steps required to perform an operation. It is most intuitive for most programmers.

Declarative programming: This programming paradigm describes a desired result, but not necessarily steps to achieve it (implementation of behavior). This means that programming is done with expressions or declarations instead of statements. Both *functional* and *logic* programming are characterized as declarative programming styles. Declarative programming is often shorter and more readable than imperative.

Tail-recursive functions

Recursive functions are functions that call themselves. Let's see an example of a recursive function, `getState`:

```
fun getState(state: State, n: Int): State =
    if (n <= 0) state // 1
    else getState(nextState(state), n - 1)
```

They are an important part of the functional programming style, but the problem is that each recursive function call needs to keep the return address of the previous function on the stack. When an application recurses too deeply (there are too many functions on the stack), `StackOverflowError` is thrown. This limitation presents a very serious problem for recurrence usage.

A classic solution for this problem was to use iteration instead of recurrence, but this approach is less expressive:

```
fun getState(state: State, n: Int): State {
    var state = state
    for (i in 1..n) {
        state = state.nextState()
    }
    return state
}
```

A proper solution for this problem is usage of the *tail-recursive* function supported by modern languages such as Kotlin. A tail-recursive function is a special kind of recursive function, where the function calls itself as the last operation it performs (in other words, recursion takes place in the last operation of a function). This allows us to optimize recursive calls by compiler and perform recursive operations in a more efficient way, without worrying about a potential `StackOverflowError`. To make a function tail-recursive, we need to mark it with a `tailrec` modifier:

```
tailrec fun getState(state: State, n: Int): State =
    if (n <= 0) state
    else getState(state.nextState(), n - 1)
```

To check out how it works, let's compile this code and decompile it to Java. Here is what can be found then (code after simplification):

```
public static final State getState(@NotNull State state, int n)
{
    while(true) {
        if(n <= 0) {
            return state;
        }
        state = state.nextState();
        n = n - 1;
    }
}
```

Implementation is based on iteration, so there is no way that stack overflow error might happen. To make the `tailrec` modifier work, there are some requirements to be met:

- The function must call itself only as the last operation it performs
- It cannot be used within `try/catch/finally` blocks
- At the time of writing, it was allowed only in Kotlin compiled to JVM

Different ways of calling a function

Sometimes we need to call a function and provide only selected arguments. In Java, we could create multiple overloads of the same method, but this solution has some limitations. The first problem is that the number of possible permutations of a given method is growing very quickly (2^n), making them very difficult to maintain. The second problem is that overloads must be distinguishable from each other, so the compiler may know which overload to call. So when a method defines a few parameters with the same type, we can't define all possible overloads. That's why in Java we often need to pass multiple null values to a method:

```
// Java
printValue("abc", null, null, "!");
```

Multiple null parameters provide boilerplate. Such a situation greatly decreases method readability. In Kotlin, there is no such problem, because Kotlin has a feature called *default arguments* and *named argument syntax*.

Default argument values

Default arguments are mostly known from C++, which is one of the oldest languages supporting them. A default argument provides a value for a parameter in case it is not provided during a method call. Each function parameter can have a default value. It might be any value that matches a specified type, including null. This way we can simply define functions that can be called in multiple ways. This is an example of a function with default values:

```
fun printValue(value: String, inBracket: Boolean = true,
               prefix: String = "", suffix: String = "") {
    print(prefix)
    if (inBracket) {
        print("(${value})")
    } else {
        print(value)
```

```
        }
        println(suffix)
    }
```

We can use this function the same way as a normal function (a function without default argument values) by providing values for each parameter (all arguments):

```
printValue("str", true, "","")  // Prints: (str)
```

Thanks to the default argument values, we can call a function by providing arguments only for parameters without default values:

```
printValue("str")  // Prints: (str)
```

We can also provide all parameters without default values, and only some that have a default value:

```
printValue("str", false)  // Prints: str
```

Named arguments syntax

Sometimes we want only to pass a value for the last argument. Let's suppose that we want to define a value for a suffix, but not for a prefix and `inBracket` (which is defined before the suffix). Normally, we would have to provide values for all previous parameters including the default parameter values:

```
printValue("str", true, true, "!") // Prints: (str)
```

By using named argument syntax, we can pass specific arguments using the argument name:

```
printValue("str", suffix = "!") // Prints: (str)!
```

This allows very flexible syntax, where we can supply only chosen arguments when calling a function (that is, the first one and the second from the end). It is often used to specify what this argument is because such a call is more readable:

```
printValue("str", inBracket = true) // Prints: (str)
printValue("str", prefix = "Value is ") // Prints: Value is str
printValue("str", prefix = "Value is ", suffix = "!! ")
// Prints:  Value is str!!
```

We can set any parameters we want using named parameter syntax in any order, as long as all parameters without default values are provided. The order of the arguments is relevant:

```
printValue("str", inBracket= true, prefix = "Value is ")
```

```
// Prints: Value is (str)
printValue("str", prefix = "Value is ", inBracket= true)
// Prints: Value is (str)
```

The order of arguments is different, but both preceding calls are equivalent.

We can also use *named argument syntax* together with a *classic call*. The only restriction is if we start using named syntax, we cannot use a classic call for the next arguments we are serving:

```
printValue ("str", true, "")
printValue ("str", true, prefix = "")
printValue ("str", inBracket = true, prefix = "")
printValue ("str", inBracket = true, "") // Error
printValue ("str", inBracket = true, prefix = "", "") // Error
```

This feature allows us to call methods in a very flexible way, without the need to define multiple method overloads.

The named argument syntax imposes some extra responsibility for Kotlin programmers. We need to keep in mind that when we change a parameter name, we may cause errors in the project, because the parameter name may be used in other classes. Android Studio will take care of it if we rename the parameter using built-in refactoring tools, but this will work only inside our project. The Kotlin library creators should be very careful while using named argument syntax. A change in the parameter name will break the API. Note that the named argument syntax cannot be used when calling Java functions, because Java bytecode does not always preserve names of function parameters.

Top-level functions

Another thing we can observe in a simple `Hello, World!` program is that the `main` function is not located inside any class. In `Chapter 2`, *Laying a Foundation*, we already mentioned that Kotlin can define various entities at the top level. A function that is defined at the top level is called a **top-level function**. Here is an example of one of them:

```
// Test.kt
package com.example

fun printTwo() {
    print(2)
}
```

Top-level functions can be used all around the code (assuming that they are public, which is the default visibility modifier). We can call them in the same way as functions from the local context. To access a top-level function, we need to explicitly import it into a file by using the `import` statement. Functions are available in the code hint list in Android Studio, so imports are automatically added when a function is selected (used). As an example, let's see a top-level function defined in `Test.kt` and use it inside the `Main.kt` file:

```
// Test.kt
package com.example

fun printTwo() {
    print(2)
}

// Main.kt
import com.example.printTwo

fun main(args: Array<String>) {
    printTwo()
}
```

Top-level functions are often useful, but it is important to use them wisely. Keep in mind that defining public top-level functions will increase the number of functions available in the code *hint list* (by *hint list* I mean a list of methods suggested by the IDE as hints, when we are writing code). This is because public top-level functions are suggested by the IDE in every context (because they can be used everywhere). If the name of the top-level function does not clearly state that this is a top-level function, then it may be confused with a method from the local context and used accidentally. Here are some good examples of top-level functions:

- `factorial`
- `maxOf` and `minOf`
- `listOf`
- `println`

Here are some examples of functions that may be poor candidates for top-level functions:

- `sendUserData`
- `showPossiblePlayers`

This rule is applicable only in Kotlin object-oriented programming projects. In function-oriented programming projects, these are valid top-level names, but then we suppose that nearly all functions are defined in the top level and not as methods.

Often, we define functions we want to use only in specific modules or specific classes. To limit function visibility (the place where it can be used), we can use visibility modifiers. We will discuss visibility modifiers in `Chapter 4`, *Classes and Objects*.

Top-level functions under the hood

With Android projects, Kotlin is compiled to Java bytecode that runs on Dalvik Virtual Machine (before Android 5.0) or Android Runtime (Android 5.0 and newer). Both virtual machines can execute only the code that is defined inside a class. To solve this problem, the Kotlin compiler generates classes for top-level functions. The class name is constructed from the file name and the `Kt` suffix. Inside such a class, all functions and properties are static. For example, let's suppose that we define a function within the `Printer.kt` file:

```
// Printer.kt
fun printTwo() {
    print(2)
}
```

Kotlin code is compiled into Java bytecode. The generated bytecode will be analogical to the code generated from the following Java class:

```
//Java
public final class PrinterKt { // 1
    public static void printTwo() { // 2
        System.out.print(2); // 3
    }
}
```

1. `PrinterKt` is the name made from the name of the file and the `Kt` suffix.

2. All top-level functions and properties are compiled to static methods and variables.
3. `print` is a Kotlin function, but since it is an inline function, its call is replaced by its body during compilation time and its body includes only `System.out.println call.`

Inline functions will be described in `Chapter 5`, *Functions as First-Class Citizens*.

Kotlin classes at the Java bytecode level will contain more data (for example, the names of parameters). We can also access Kotlin top-level functions from Java files by prefixing a function call with the class name:

```
//Java file, call inside some method
PrinterKt.printTwo()
```

This way, Kotlin top-level function calls from Java are fully supported. As we can see, Kotlin is really interoperable with Java. To make Kotlin top-level function usage more comfortable in Java, we can add an annotation that will change the name of a JVM generated class. This comes in handy when making use of top-level Kotlin properties and functions from Java classes. This annotation looks as follows:

```
@file:JvmName("Printer")
```

We need to add the `JvmName` annotation at the top of the file (before the package name). When this is applied, the name of the generated class will be changed to `Printer`. This allows us to call the `printTwo` function in Java using `Printer` as the class name:

```
//Java
Printer.printTwo()
```

Sometimes we are defining top-level functions, and we want to define them in separate files, but we also want them in the same class after compilation to JVM. This is possible if we use the following annotation at the top of the file:

```
@file:JvmMultifileClass
```

For example, let's assume that we are making a library with mathematical helpers that we want to use from Java. We can define the following files:

```
// Max.kt
@file:JvmName("Math")
@file:JvmMultifileClass
package com.example.math

fun max(n1: Int, n2: Int): Int = if(n1 > n2) n1 else n2
```

```
// Min.kt
@file:JvmName("Math")
@file:JvmMultifileClass
package com.example.math

fun min(n1: Int, n2: Int): Int = if(n1 < n2) n1 else n2
```

And we can use them from Java classes this way:

```
Math.min(1, 2)
Math.max(1, 2)
```

Thanks to this, we can keep files short and simple, while keeping them all easy to use from Java.

The `JvmName` annotation to change generated class names is especially useful when we create libraries in Kotlin that are also directed to be used in Java classes. It can be useful in the case of name conflicts too. Such a situation can occur when we create both an `X.kt` file with some top-level functions or properties and an `XKt` class in the same package. But this is rare and should never take place since there is a convention that no classes should have the `Kt` suffix.

Local functions

Kotlin allows defining functions in many contexts. We can define functions at the top level, as members (inside `class`, `interface`, and so on), and inside other functions (local function). Consider the following example of the definition of a local function:

```
fun printTwoThreeTimes() {
    fun printThree() { // 1
        print(3)
    }
    printThree() // 2
    printThree() // 2
}
```

1. `printThree` is a local function, because it is located inside another function.
2. Local functions are not accessible from outside the function they were declared in.

Elements accessible inside local functions don't have to be passed from enclosing functions as arguments because they are accessible directly. For example:

```
fun loadUsers(ids: List<Int>) {
    var downloaded: List<User> = emptyList()

    fun printLog(comment: String) {
        Log.i("loadUsers (with ids $ids): $comment\nDownloaded:
                                          $downloaded") // 1
    }
    for(id in ids) {
        printLog("Start downloading for id $id")
        downloaded += loadUser(id)
        printLog("Finished downloading for id $id")
    }
}
```

1. The local function can access the comment parameter and local variables (`downloaded` and `ids`), defined inside an enclosing function.

If we would like to define `printLog` as a top-level function, then we would have to pass as arguments both `ids` and `downloaded`:

```
fun loadUsers(ids: List<Int>) {
    var downloaded: List<User> = emptyList()

    for(id in ids) {
        printLog("Start downloading for id $id", downloaded, ids)
        downloaded += loadUser(id)
        printLog("Finished downloading for
                 id $id", downloaded, ids))
    }
}

fun printLog(state: String, downloaded: List<User>, ids: List<Int>)
{
    Log.i("loadUsers (with ids $ids):
    $state\nDownloaded: downloaded")
}
```

This implementation is not only longer, but also harder to maintain. Changes in `printLog` might demand different parameters, and a change in parameters demands changes in arguments in this function call. Also, if we change the `loadUsers` parameter type that is used in `printLog`, then we will need to also change the parameter of `printLog`. There would be no such problems if `printLog` was a local function. This explains when local functions should be used: when we are extracting functionality that is used only by a single function, and that functionality is using the elements (variables, values, and parameters) of this function. Also, local functions are allowed to modify local variables, as in this example:

```
fun makeStudentList(): List<Student> {
    var students: List<Student> = emptyList()
    fun addStudent(name: String, state: Student.State =
                    Student.State.New) {
        students += Student(name, state, courses = emptyList())
    }
    // ...
    addStudent("Adam Smith")
    addStudent("Donald Duck")
    // ...
    return students
}
```

This way, we can extract and reuse functionality that could not be extracted in Java. It is good to remember about local functions, because they sometimes allow code extraction that is hard to implement in other ways.

Nothing return type

Sometimes we need to define a function that is always throwing exceptions (never terminating normally). Two real-life use cases are:

- Functions that simplify error throwing. This is especially useful in libraries where the error system is important and there is a need to provide more data about error occurrences. (As an example, look at the `throwError` function presented in this section.)
- Functions used for throwing errors in unit tests. This is useful when we need to test error handling in our code.

For these kinds of situation, there is a special class called `Nothing`. The `Nothing` class is an empty type (uninhabited type), meaning it has no instances. A function that has `Nothing` return type won't return anything and it will never reach the `return` statement. It can only throw an exception. This is why when we see that a function is returning `Nothing`, then it is designed to throw exceptions. This way we can distinguish functions that do not return a value (such as Java's `void`, and Kotlin's `Unit`) from functions that never terminate (return `Nothing`). Let us have a look at an example of functions that might be used to simplify error throwing in unit tests:

```
fun fail(): Nothing = throw Error()
```

Here is a function that construct complex error messages using elements available in the context where it is defined (in the class or function):

```
fun processElement(element: Element) {
    fun throwError(message: String): Nothing
    = throw ProcessingError("Error in element $element: $message")

    // ...
    if (element.kind != ElementKind.METHOD)
        throwError("Not a method")
    // ...
}
```

This kind of function can be used, just like a `throw` statement, as an alternative that is does not influence the function return type:

```
fun getFirstCharOrFail(str: String): Char
    = if(str.isNotEmpty()) str[0] else fail()

val name: String = getName() ?: fail()

val enclosingElement = element.enclosingElement ?: throwError ("Lack of
enclosing element")
```

How is this possible? This is a special trait of the `Nothing` class, which is acting as if it is a subtype of all the possible types, both nullable and not-nullable. This is why `Nothing` is referred to as an **empty type**, which means that no value can have this type at runtime, and it's also a subtype of every other class.

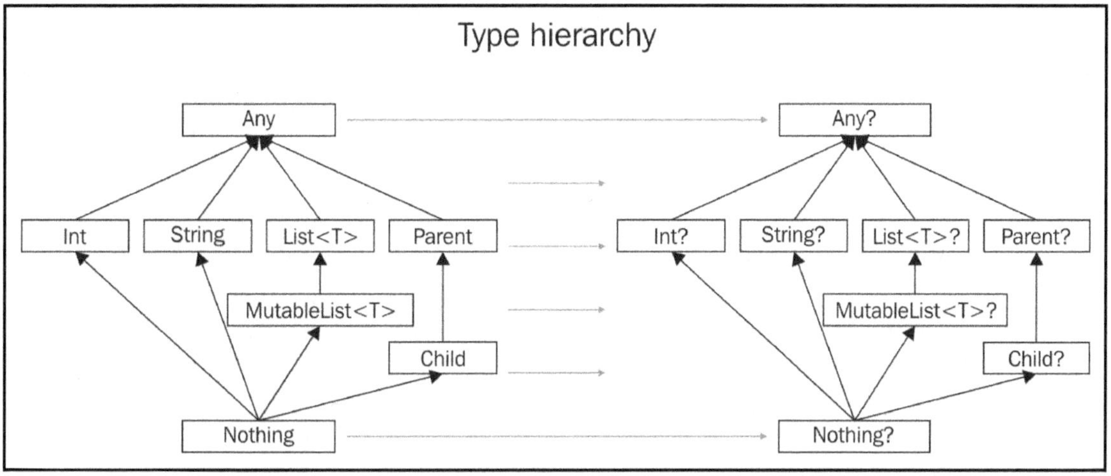

The concept of uninhabited type is new in the world of Java, and this is why it might be confusing. The idea is actually pretty simple. The `Nothing` instance never exists, while there is only an error that might be returned from functions that specify it as a return type. And there is no need for `Nothing` to be added to something to influence its type.

Summary

In this chapter, we've seen how to define and use functions. We learned how functions can be defined at the top-level or inside other functions. There was also a discussion on different features connected to functions: vararg parameters, default names, and named argument syntax. Finally, we saw some Kotlin special return types: `Unit`, which is the equivalent of Java's `void`, and `Nothing`, which is a type that cannot be defined and means that nothing can be returned (only exceptions).

In the next chapter, we are going to see how classes are defined in Kotlin. Classes are also specially supported by the Kotlin language, and there are lots of improvements introduced over Java definitions.

4
Classes and Objects

The Kotlin language provides full support for OOP. We will review powerful structures that allow us to simplify data model definition and operate on it in an easy and flexible way. We'll learn how Kotlin simplifies and improves implementations of many concepts known from Java. We will take a look at different types of class, property, initializer block, and constructor. We will learn about **operator overloading** and interface default implementations.

In this chapter, we will cover the following topics:

- Class declaration
- Properties
- Property access syntax
- Constructors and initializers blocks
- Constructors
- Inheritance
- Interfaces
- Data classes
- Destructive declarations
- Operator overloading
- Object declaration
- Object expression
- Companion objects
- Enum classes
- Sealed classes
- Nested classes

Classes

Classes are a fundamental building block of OOP. In fact, Kotlin classes are very similar to Java classes. Kotlin, however, allows more functionality together with simpler and much more concise syntax.

Class declaration

Classes in Kotlin are defined using the `class` keyword. The following is the simplest class declaration--an empty class named `Person`:

```
class Person
```

The definition of `Person` does not contain any body. Still, it can be instantiated using a default constructor:

```
val person = Person()
```

Even such a simple task as class instantiation is simplified in Kotlin. Unlike Java, Kotlin does not require the `new` keyword to create a class instance. Due to strong Kotlin interoperability with Java, we can instantiate classes defined in Java and Kotlin exactly the same way (without the `new` keyword). The syntax used to instantiate a class depends on the actual language used to create class instance (Kotlin or Java), not the language the class was declared in:

```
// Instantiate Kotlin class inside Java file
Person person = new Person()
// Instantiate class inside Kotlin file
var person = Person()
```

It is a rule of thumb to use the `new` keyword inside a Java file and never use the `new` keyword inside a Kotlin file.

Properties

A property is just a combination of a *backing field* and its accessors. It could be a *backing field* with both a getter and a setter or a backing field with only one of them. Properties can be defined at the top level (directly inside the file) or as a member (for example, inside the class or interface).

In general, it is advisable to define properties (private fields with getters/setters) instead of accessing public fields directly (according to *Effective Java, by Joshua Bloch,* item 14: in public classes, use accessor methods, not public fields).

Java getter and setter conventions for private fields

Getter: A parameterless method with a name that corresponds to the property name and a `get` prefix (for a `Boolean` property there might be an `is` prefix instead).

Setter: Single-argument methods with names starting with `set`: for example, `setResult(String resultCode).`

Kotlin guards this principle by language design, because this approach provides various encapsulation benefits:

- The ability to change the internal implementation without changing an external API
- It enforces invariants (it calls methods that validate an object's state)
- The ability to perform additional actions when accessing a member (for example, a log operation)

To define a top-level property, we simply define it in the Kotlin file:

```
//Test.kt
val name:String
```

Let's imagine that we need a class to store basic data regarding a person. This data may be downloaded from an external API (backend) or retrieved from a local database. Our class will have to define two (member) properties, `name` and `age`. Let's look at the Java implementation first:

```
public class Person {

    private int age;
    private String name;

    public Person(String name, int age) {
        this.name = name;
        this.age = age;
    }

    public int getAge() {
        return age;
```

```
        }

        public void setAge(int age) {
            this.age = age;
        }

        public String getName() {
            return name;
        }

        public void setName(String name) {
            this.name = name;
        }
    }
```

This class contains only two properties. Since we can make the Java IDE generate accessor code for us, at least we don't have to write the code by ourselves. However, the problem with this approach is that we cannot get along without these automatically generated chunks, and that makes the code very verbose. We (developers) spend most of our time just reading code, not writing it, so reading redundant code wastes a lot of valuable time. Also, a simple task such as refactoring the property name becomes a little bit trickier, because the IDE might not update constructor parameter names.

Fortunately, boilerplate code can be decreased significantly by using Kotlin. Kotlin solves this problem by introducing the concept of *properties*, which is built into the language. Let's look at a Kotlin equivalent of the preceding Java class:

```
class Person {
    var name: String
    var age: Int

    constructor(name: String, age: Int) {
        this.name = name
        this.age = age
    }
}
```

This is an exact equivalent of the preceding Java class:

- The `constructor` method is equivalent to the Java constructor that is called when an object instance is created
- Getters and setters are generated by the Kotlin compiler

We can still define custom implementations of getters and setters. We will discuss this in more detail in the *Custom getters/setters* section.

All the constructors that we have already defined are called *secondary constructors*. Kotlin also provides alternative, very concise syntax for defining constructors. We can define a constructor (with all parameters) as part of the class header. This kind of constructor is called a *primary constructor*. Let's move a property declaration from the secondary constructor into the primary constructor to make our code a little bit shorter:

```
class Person constructor(name: String, age: Int) {
    var name: String
    var age: Int

    init {
        this.name = name
        this.age = age
        println("Person instance created")
    }
}
```

In Kotlin, the primary constructor, as opposed to the secondary constructor, can't contain any code, so all initialization code must be placed inside the initializer block (`init`). An initializer block will be executed during class creation, so we can assign constructor parameters to fields inside it.

To simplify code, we can remove the initializer block and access constructor parameters directly in property initializers. This allows us to assign constructor parameters to a field:

```
class Person constructor(name: String, age: Int) {
    var name: String = name
    var age: Int = age
}
```

We managed to make the code shorter, but it still contains a lot of boilerplate, because type declarations and property names are duplicated (the constructor parameter, field assignment, and field itself). When properties do not have any custom getters or setters, we can define them directly inside primary constructor by adding a `val` or `var` modifier:

```
class Person constructor (var name: String, var age: Int)
```

Finally, if the primary constructor does not have any annotations (such as `@Inject`) or visibility modifiers (such as `public` or `private`), then the `constructor` keyword can be omitted:

```
class Person (var name: String, var age: Int)
```

When the constructor takes a few parameters, it is good practice to define each parameter in a new line to improve code readability and decrease the chance of potential merge conflicts (when merging branches from a source code repository):

```
class Person(
    var name: String,
    var age: Int
)
```

Summing up, the preceding example is equivalent to the Java class presented at the beginning of this section--both properties are defined directly in the class's primary constructor and the Kotlin compiler does all the work for us--it generates the appropriate fields and accessors (getters/setters).

Note that this notation contains only the most important information about this data model class--its name, parameter names, types, and mutability (`val`/`var`) information. The implementation has nearly zero boilerplate. This makes the class very easy to read, understand, and maintain.

Read-write versus read-only

All the properties in the previous examples were defined as read-write (a setter and a getter are generated). To define read-only properties, we need to use the `val` keyword, so only a getter will be generated. Let's look at a simple example:

```
class Person(
    var name: String,
    // Read-write property (generated getter and setter)
    val age: Int      // Read-only property (generated getter)
)
//usage
val person = Person("Eva", 25)

val name = person.name
person.name = "Kate"

val age = person.age
person.age = 28 //error: read-only property
```

Kotlin does not support write-only properties (properties of which only setter is generated).

Keyword	Read	Write
`var`	Yes	Yes
`val`	Yes	No
(unsupported)	No	Yes

Property access syntax between Kotlin and Java

Another big improvement introduced by Kotlin is the way to access properties. In Java, we access a property using the corresponding method (`setSpeed`/`getSpeed`). Kotlin promotes *property access syntax*, which is a more expressive way of accessing properties. Let's compare both approaches, assuming we have a simple `Car` class that has a single `speed` property:

```
class Car (var speed: Double)

//Java access properties using method access syntax
Car car = new Car(7.4)
car.setSpeed(9.2)
Double speed = car.getSpeed();

//Kotlin access properties using property access syntax
val car: Car = Car(7.4)
car.speed = 9.2
val speed = car.speed
```

As we can see, in Kotlin there is no need to add `get` or `set` prefixes and parentheses to access or modify an object property. Using property access syntax permits the direct use of the increment (++) and decrement (--) operators together with property access:

```
val car = Car(7.0)
println(car.speed)  //prints 7.0
car.speed++
println(car.speed)  //prints 8.0
car.speed--
car.speed--
println(car.speed) //prints: 6.0
```

Increment and decrement operators

There are two kinds of increment (++) and decrements (--) operator: pre-increment/pre-decrement, where the operator is defined before the expression, and post-increment/post-decrement, where the operator is defined after the expression:

```
++speed //pre increment
--speed //pre decrement

speed++ //post increment
speed-- //post decrement
```

In the preceding example, using post- instead of pre-increment/decrement would change nothing because those operations are executed in sequence. But this makes a huge difference when the increment/decrement operator is combined with a function call.

In the pre-increment operator, `speed` is retrieved, incremented, and passed to a function as an argument:

```
var speed = 1.0
println(++speed) // Prints: 2.0
println(speed)   // Prints: 2.0
```

In post-increment operator, `speed` is retrieved, passed to a function as an argument, and then it is incremented, so the old value is passed to a function:

```
var speed = 1.0
println(speed++) // Prints: 1.0
println(speed) // Prints: 2.0
```

This works in an analogical way for pre-decrement and post-decrement operators.

Property access syntax is not limited to classes defined in Kotlin. Each method that follows the Java conventions for getters and setters is represented as a property in Kotlin.

This means that we can define a class in Java and access its properties in Kotlin using *property access* syntax. Let's define a Java `Fish` class with two properties, `size` and `isHungry`, and let's instantiate this class in Kotlin and access the properties:

```
//Java class declaration
public class Fish {
    private int size;
    private boolean hungry;
```

```
    public Fish(int size, boolean isHungry) {
        this.size = size;
        this.hungry = isHungry;
    }

    public int getSize() {
        return size;
    }

    public void setSize(int size) {
        this.size = size;
    }

    public boolean isHungry() {
        return hungry;
    }

    public void setHungry(boolean hungry) {
        this.hungry = hungry;
    }
}

//Kotlin class usage
val fish = Fish(12, true)
fish.size = 7
println(fish.size) // Prints: 7
fish.isHungry = true
println(fish.isHungry) // Prints: true
```

This works both ways, so we can define the `Fish` class in Kotlin using very concise syntax and access it in the usual Java way, because the Kotlin compiler will generate all the required getters and setters:

```
//Kotlin class declaration
class Fish(var size: Int, var hungry: Boolean)

//class usage in Java
Fish fish = new Fish(12, true);
fish.setSize(7);
System.out.println(fish.getSize());
fish.setHungry(false);
System.out.println(fish.getHungry());
```

As we can see, the syntax used to access the class property depends on the actual language that the class uses, not the language that the class was declared in. This allows for more idiomatic usage of many classes defined in the Android framework. Let's see some examples:

Java method access syntax	Kotlin property access syntax
`activity.getFragmentManager()`	`activity.fragmentManager`
`view.setVisibility(Visibility.GONE)`	`view.visibility = Visibility.GONE`
`context.getResources().getDisplayMetrics().density`	`context.resources.displayMetrics.density`

Property access syntax results in more concise code that decreases the original Java complexity. Notice that it is still possible to use method access syntax with Kotlin, although property access syntax is often the better alternative.

There are some methods in the Android framework that use the `is` prefix for their name; in these cases, Boolean properties also have the `is` prefix:

```
class MainActivity : AppCompatActivity() {

    override fun onDestroy() { // 1
        super.onDestroy()

        isFinishing() // method access syntax
        isFinishing // property access syntax
        finishing // error
    }
}
```

1. Kotlin marks overridden members using the `override` modifier, not `@Override` annotation like Java.

Although using `finishing` would be the most natural and consistent approach, it's impossible to use it by default due to potential conflicts.

Another case where we can't use property access syntax is when the property defines a setter without a getter, because Kotlin does not support write-only properties, as in this example:

```
fragment.setHasOptionsMenu(true)
fragment.hasOptionsMenu = true // Error!
```

Custom getters/setters

Sometimes, we want to have more control over the use of properties. We may want to perform other auxiliary operations when using a property, for example, verify a value before it's assigned to a field, log the whole operation, or invalidate an instance state. We can do this by specifying custom setters and/or getters. Let's add the `ecoRating` property to our `Fruit` class. In most cases, we would add this property to the class declaration header like this:

```
class Fruit(var weight: Double,
            val fresh: Boolean,
            val ecoRating: Int)
```

If we want to define custom getters and setters, we need to define a property in the class body instead of the class declaration header. Let's move the `ecoRating` property into the class body:

```
class Fruit(var weight: Double, val fresh: Boolean, ecoRating: Int)
{
    var ecoRating: Int = ecoRating
}
```

When the property is defined inside the body of a class, we have to initialize it with a value (even nullable properties need to be initialized with a null value). We can provide the default value instead of filling a property with the constructor argument:

```
class Fruit(var weight: Double, val fresh: Boolean) {
    var ecoRating: Int = 3
}
```

We can also compute default values based on some other properties:

```
class Apple(var weight: Double, val fresh: Boolean) {
    var ecoRating: Int = when(weight) {
        in 0.5..2.0 -> 5
        in 0.4..0.5 -> 4
        in 0.3..0.4 -> 3
        in 0.2..0.3 -> 2
        else -> 1
    }
}
```

Different values will be set for different weight constructor arguments.

When a property is defined in a class body, the type declaration can be omitted, because it can be inferred from the context:

```
class Fruit(var weight: Double) {
    var ecoRating = 3
}
```

Let's define a custom getter and setter with the default behavior that will be the equivalent of the preceding property:

```
class Fruit(var weight: Double) {
    var ecoRating: Int = 3
    get() {
        println("getter value retrieved")
        return field
    }
    set(value) {
        field = if (value < 0) 0 else value
        println("setter new value assigned $field")
    }
}

// Usage
val fruit = Fruit(12.0)
val ecoRating = fruit.ecoRating
// Prints: getter value retrieved
fruit.ecoRating = 3;
// Prints: setter new value assigned 3
fruit.ecoRating = -5;
// Prints: setter new value assigned 0
```

Inside the `get` and `set` block, we can have access a special variable called `field`, which refers to the corresponding backing field of the property. Notice that the Kotlin property declaration is closely positioned to a custom getter/setter. This is in contrast to Java and solves the issue in which the field declaration is usually at the top of the file containing the class and the corresponding getter/setter is at the bottom of this file, so we can't really see them on a single screen, and thus code is more difficult to read. Apart from the location, Kotlin property behavior is quite similar to Java. Each time we retrieve a value from the `ecoRating` property, a `get` block will be executed, and each time we assign a new value to the `ecoRating` property, a `set` block will be executed.

This is a read-write property (`var`), so it may contain both the corresponding getters and setters. If we explicitly define only one of them, the default implementation will be used for the other.

To compute a value each time a property value is retrieved, we need to explicitly define a getter:

```
class Fruit(var weight: Double) {
    val heavy               // 1
    get() = weight > 20
}

//usage
var fruit = Fruit(7.0)
println(fruit.heavy) //prints: false
fruit.weight = 30.5
println(fruit.heavy) //prints: true
```

1. Since Kotlin 1.1, the type can be omitted (it is to be inferred).

The getter versus property default value

In the preceding example, we used a getter, so the property value is calculated each time the value is retrieved. By omitting the getter, we can create a default value for the property. This value will be computed only once during class creation and it will never change (changing the `weight` property will have no effect on the `isHeavy` property value):

```
class Fruit(var weight: Double) {
    val isHeavy = weight > 20
}
var fruit = Fruit(7.0)
println(fruit.isHeavy) // Prints: false
fruit.weight = 30.5
println(fruit.isHeavy) // Prints: false
```

This type of property does have a backing field, because its value is always computed during object creation. We can also create read-write properties without a backing field:

```
class Car {
    var usable: Boolean = true
    var inGoodState: Boolean = true

   var crashed: Boolean
   get() = !usable && !inGoodState
   set(value) {
       usable = false
       inGoodState = false
   }
}
```

This type of property does not have a backing field, because its value is always computed using another property.

Late-initialized properties

Sometimes, we know that a property won't be null, but it won't be initialized with the value at declaration time. Let's look at a common Android example--retrieving a reference to a layout element:

```
class MainActivity : AppCompatActivity() {

   private var button: Button? = null

   override fun onCreate(savedInstanceState: Bundle?) {
       super.onCreate(savedInstanceState)
       button = findViewById(R.id.button) as Button
   }
}
```

The `button` variable can't be initialized at declaration time because the `MainActivity` layout is not yet initialized. We can retrieve the reference to the button defined in the layout inside the `onCreate` method, but to do this we need to declare a variable as nullable (`Button?`).

Such an approach seems quite impractical because after the `onCreate` method is called, a `button` instance is available all the time. However, the client still needs to use the safe call operator or other nullity checks to access it.

To avoid nullity checks when accessing a property, we need a way to inform the Kotlin compiler that this variable will be filled before it is used, but its initialization will be delayed. To do this, we can use the `lateinit` modifier:

```
class MainActivity : AppCompatActivity() {

    private lateinit var button: Button

    override fun onCreate(savedInstanceState: Bundle?) {
        button = findViewById(R.id.button) as Button
        button.text = "Click Me"
    }
}
```

Now, with the property marked as `lateinit`, we can access our application instance without performing nullity checks.

The `lateinit` modifier tells the compiler that this property is non-nullable, but its initialization is delayed. Naturally, when we try to access the property before it is initialized, the application will throw `UninitializedPropertyAccessException`. This is fine because we assume that this scenario should not happen.

Scenarios where a variable initialization is not possible at declaration time are quite common, and they are not always related to views. Properties can be initialized through Dependency Injection or via the `setup` method of a unit test. In such scenarios, we cannot supply a non-nullable value in the constructor, but we still want to avoid nullity checks.

The lateinit property and frameworks

The `lateinit` property is also helpful when a property is injected by the Dependency Injection framework. The popular Android Dependency Injection framework, **Dagger** uses the `@Inject` annotation to mark properties that need to be injected:

```
@Inject lateinit var locationManager: LocationManager
```

We know that the property will never be null (because it will be injected), but the Kotlin compiler does not understand this annotation.

Similar scenarios happen with the popular framework **Mockito**:

```
@Mock lateinit var mockEventBus: EventBus
```

The variable will be mocked, but it will happen sometime later, after test class creation.

Annotating properties

Kotlin generates multiple JVM bytecode elements from a single property (`private` field, getter, and setter). Sometimes, the framework annotation processor or the reflection-based library requires a particular element to be defined as a public field. A good example of this behavior is the JUnit test framework. It requires rules to be provided through a test class field or a getter method. We may encounter this problem when defining `ActivityTestRule` or Mockito's (mocking framework for unit tests) `Rule` annotation:

```
@Rule
val activityRule = ActivityTestRule(MainActivity::class.Java)
```

The preceding code annotates the Kotlin property that JUnit won't recognize, so `ActivityTestRule` can't be properly initialized. The JUnit annotation processor expects the `Rule` annotation on the field or getter. There are a few ways to solve this problem. We can expose the Kotlin property as a Java field by annotating it with the `@JvmField` annotation:

```
@JvmField @Rule
val activityRule = ActivityTestRule(MainActivity::class.Java)
```

The field will have the same visibility as the underlying property. There are a few limitations regarding `@JvmField` annotation usage. We can annotate a property with `@JvmField` if it has a backing field; it is not private; does not have open, override, or const modifiers; and is not a delegated property.

We can also annotate a getter by adding an annotation directly to it:

```
val activityRule
@Rule get() = ActivityTestRule(MainActivity::class.java)
```

If we don't want to define getter, we can still add an annotation to the getter using the use-site target (`get`). By doing so, we simply specify which element generated by the Kotlin compiler will be annotated:

```
@get:Rule
val activityRule = ActivityTestRule(MainActivity::class.Java)
```

Inline properties

We can optimize property calls by using the `inline` modifier. During compilation, each property call will be optimized. Instead of really calling a property, the call will be replaced with the property body:

```
inline val now: Long
    get() {
        println("Time retrieved")
        return System.currentTimeMillis()
    }
```

With inline properties, we are using the `inline` modifier. The preceding code will be compiled to the following:

```
println("Time retrieved")
System.currentTimeMillis()
```

Inlining improves performance because there is no need to create additional objects. No getter will be invoked because the body replaces the property usage. Inlining has only one limitation--it can be applied to properties that do not have a backing field.

Constructors

Kotlin allows us to define classes without any constructors. We can also define a primary constructor and one or more secondary constructors:

```
class Fruit(val weight: Int) {
    constructor(weight: Int, fresh: Boolean) : this(weight) { }
}

//class instantiation
val fruit1 = Fruit(10)
val fruit2 = Fruit(10, true)
```

Declaring properties is not allowed for secondary constructors. If we need a property that is initialized by secondary constructors, we must declare it in the class body, and we can initialize it in the secondary constructor body. Let's define the `fresh` property:

```
class Test(val weight: Int) {
    var fresh: Boolean? = null
    //define fresh property in class body

    constructor(weight: Int, fresh: Boolean) : this(weight) {
        this.fresh = fresh
        //assign constructor parameter to fresh property
    }
}
```

Notice that we defined our `fresh` property as nullable because when an instance of the object is created using a primary constructor, the `fresh` property will be `null`:

```
val fruit = Fruit(10)
println(fruit.weight) // prints: 10
println(fruit.fresh) // prints: null
```

We can also assign the default value to the `fresh` property to make it non-nullable:

```
class Fruit(val weight: Int) {
    var fresh: Boolean = true

    constructor(weight: Int, fresh: Boolean) : this(weight) {
        this.fresh = fresh
```

```
        }
    }

    val fruit = Fruit(10)
    println(fruit.weight) // prints: 10
    println(fruit.fresh) // prints: true
```

When a primary constructor is defined, every secondary constructor must call the primary constructor implicitly or explicitly. An implicit call means that we call the primary constructor directly. An explicit call means that we call another secondary constructor that calls the primary constructor. To call another constructor, we use the `this` keyword:

```
class Fruit(val weight: Int) {

    constructor(weight: Int, fresh: Boolean) : this(weight) // 1

    constructor(weight: Int, fresh: Boolean, color: String) :
            this(weight, fresh) // 2
}
```

1. The call to the primary constructor.
2. The call to the secondary constructor.

If the class has no primary constructor and the superclass has a non-empty constructor, then each secondary constructor has to initialize the base class using the `super` keyword or call another constructor that does that:

```
class ProductView : View {
   constructor(ctx: Context) : super(ctx)
   constructor(ctx: Context, attrs : AttributeSet) :
            super(ctx, attrs)
}
```

A view example can be greatly simplified by using the `@JvmOverloads` annotation that will be described in the `@JvmOverloads` section.

By default, this generated constructor will be public. If we want to prevent the generation of such an implicit `public` constructor, we have to declare an empty primary constructor with a `private` or `protected` visibility modifier:

```
class Fruit private constructor()
```

To change the constructor visibility, we need to explicitly use the `constructor` keyword in the class definition header. The `constructor` keyword is also required when we want to annotate a constructor. A common example is to annotate a class constructor using Dagger's `@Inject` annotation:

```
class Fruit @Inject constructor()
```

Both the visibility modifier and annotation can be applied at the same time:

```
class Fruit @Inject private constructor {
    var weight: Int? = null
}
```

Properties versus constructor parameters

The important thing to notice is the fact that if we remove the `var/val` keyword from the constructor property declaration, we'll end up with a constructor parameter declaration. This means that the property will be changed to a constructor parameter, so no accessors will be generated and we will not be able to access the property on the class instance:

```
class Fruit(var weight:Double, fresh:Boolean)

val fruit = Fruit(12.0, true)
println(fruit.weight)
println(fruit.fresh) // error
```

In the preceding example, we have an error because `fresh` is missing a `val` or `var` keyword, so it is a constructor parameter, not a class property such as `weight`. The following table summarizes the compiler accessor generation:

Class declaration	**Getter generated**	**Setter generated**	**Type**
`class Fruit (name:String)`	No	No	Constructor parameter
`class Fruit (val name:String)`	Yes	No	Property
`class Fruit (var name:String)`	Yes	Yes	Property

Sometimes, we may wonder when we should use a property and when we should use a method. A good guideline to follow is to use a property instead of a method in the following circumstances:

- It does not throw an exception
- It is cheap to calculate (or cached on the first run)
- It returns the same result over multiple invocations

Constructors with default arguments

Since the early days of Java, there has been a serious flaw with object creation. It is difficult to create an object instance when an object requires multiple parameters and some of those parameters are optional. There are a few ways to solve this problem, such as the Telescoping constructor pattern, the JavaBeans pattern, and even the Builder pattern. Each of them has their pros and cons.

Patterns

The patterns solve the issue of object creation. Each of them is explained as follows:

- **Telescoping constructor pattern**: A class with a list of constructors where each constructor adds a new parameter. Nowadays it's considered an anti-pattern, but Android still uses it in a few places; for example, the `android.view.View` class:

```
val view1 = View(context)
val view1 = View(context, attributeSet)
val view1 = View(context, attributeSet, defStyleAttr)
```

- **JavaBeans pattern**: A parameterless constructor plus one or more setters methods to configure objects. The main problem with this pattern is that we can't say whether or not all the required methods have been called on an object, so it may be only partially constructed:

```
val animal = Animal()
fruit.setWeight(10)
fruit.setSpeed(7.4)
fruit.setColor("Gray")
```

- **Builder pattern**: This uses another object, a builder, that receives initialization arguments step by step and then returns the resulting constructed object at once when the `build` method is called. Examples are `android.app.Notification.Builder`, and `android.app.AlertDialog.Builder`:

```
Retrofit retrofit = new Retrofit.Builder()
                        .baseUrl("https://api.github.com/")
                        .build();
```

For a long time, the builder pattern was most widely used, but a combination of *default arguments* and *named argument syntax* is an even more concise option. Let's define a default value:

```
class Fruit(weight: Int = 0, fresh: Boolean = true, color:
            String = "Green")
```

By defining default parameter values, we can create objects in multiple ways, without needing to pass all arguments:

```
val fruit = Fruit(7.4, false)
println(fruit.fresh) // prints: false

val fruit2 = Fruit(7.4)
println(fruit.fresh) // prints: true
```

Using argument syntax with default parameters gives us much more flexibility in object creation. We can pass the required parameters only in any order that we want without defining multiple methods and constructors, as in the following example:

```
val fruit1 = Fruit (weight = 7.4, fresh = true, color = "Yellow")

val fruit2 = Fruit (color = "Yellow")
```

Inheritance

As we already know, a supertype of all Kotlin types is `Any`. It is the equivalent of the Java `Object` type. Each Kotlin class explicitly or implicitly extends the `Any` class. If we do not specify the parent class, `Any` will be implicitly set as the parent of the class:

```
class Plant // Implicitly extends Any
class Plant : Any // Explicitly extends Any
```

Kotlin, like Java, promotes single inheritance, so a class can have only one parent class, but it can implement multiple interfaces.

In contrast to Java, every class and every method in Kotlin is final by default. This conforms to the *Item 17* in *Effective Java*, the *Design and document for inheritance or else prohibit it* rule. This is used to prevent unexpected behavior from a subclass changing. Modification of a base class can cause incorrect behavior of subclasses because the changed code of the base class no longer matches the assumptions in its subclasses.

This means that a class cannot be extended and a method cannot be overridden until it's explicitly declared as open using the `open` keyword. This is the exact opposite of the Java `final` keyword.

Let's say we want to declare a base class called `Plant` and subclass called `Tree`:

```
class Plant
class Tree : Plant() // Error
```

The preceding code will not compile because the class `Plant` is final by default. Let's make it `open`:

```
open class Plant
class Tree : Plant()
```

Notice that we define inheritance in Kotlin simply by using the colon character (:). There are no `extends` or `implements` keywords, in contrast Java.

Now let's add some methods and properties to our `Plant` class, and try to override it in the `Tree` class:

```
open class Plant {
    var height: Int = 0
    fun grow(height: Int) {}
}

class Tree : Plant() {
    override fun grow(height: Int) { // Error
        this.height += height
    }
}
```

This code will also not compile. We have said already that all methods are closed by default, so each method we want to override must be explicitly marked as `open`. Let's fix the code by marking the `grow` method as `open`:

```
open class Plant {
    var height: Int = 0
    open fun grow(height: Int) {}
}

class Tree : Plant() {
    override fun grow(height: Int) {
        this.height += height
    }
}
```

In a similar way, we could open and override the `height` property:

```
open class Plant {
    open var height: Int = 0
    open fun grow(height: Int) {}
}

class Tree : Plant() {
    override var height: Int = super.height
        get() = super.height
        set(value) { field = value}

    override fun grow(height: Int) {
        this.height += height
    }
}
```

TIP

To quickly override any member, go to a class where a member is declared, add the `open` modifier, and then go to a class where we want to override member, run the `override` members action (the shortcut for Windows is *Ctrl* + *O*, and for macOS it is *Command* + *O*), and select all the members you want to override. This way, all the required code will be generated by Android Studio.

Let's assume that all trees grow in the same way (the same computation of the growing algorithm is applicable for all trees). We want to allow the creation of new subclasses of the `Tree` class to have more control over trees, but at the same time we want to preserve our growing algorithm--not allowing any subclasses of the `Tree` class to override this behavior. To achieve this, we need to explicitly mark the `grow` method in the `Tree` class as `final`:

```
open class Plant {
    var height: Int = 0

    open fun grow(height: Int) {}
}

class Tree : Plant() {
    final override fun grow(height: Int) {
        this.height += height
    }
}

class Oak : Tree() {
    // 1
}
```

1. It's not possible to override grow method here because it's `final`.

Let's sum up all this `open` and `final` behavior. To make a method overridable in a subclass, we needed to explicitly mark it as `open` in the superclass. To make sure that overridden method will not be overridden again by any subclass, we need to mark it as `final`.

In the preceding example, the `grow` method in the `Plant` class does not really provide any functionality (it has an empty body). This is a sign that maybe we don't want to instantiate the `Plant` class at all, but treat it as a base class and only instantiate various classes, such as `Tree`, which extends the `Plant` class. We should mark the `Plant` class as `abstract` to prohibit its instantiation:

```
abstract class Plant {
    var height: Int = 0

    abstract fun grow(height: Int)
}

class Tree : Plant() {
    override fun grow(height: Int) {
        this.height += height
    }
}
```

```
val plant = Plant()
// error: abstract class can't be instantiated
val tree = Tree()
```

Marking the class as `abstract` will also make the method class open by default, so we don't have to explicitly mark each member as `open`. Notice that when we are defining the `grow` method as abstract, we have to remove its body, because the `abstract` method can't have a body.

The JvmOverloads annotation

Some classes in the Android platform use Telescoping constructors, which is considered an anti-pattern. A good example of such a class is the `android.view.View` class. There may be a case when only a single constructor is used (inflating the custom view from Kotlin code), but it is much safer to override all three constructors when the subclassing `android.view.View`, because the class will work correctly in all scenarios. Normally, our `CustomView` class would look like this:

```
class CustomView : View {

    constructor(context: Context?) : this(context, null)

    constructor(context: Context?, attrs: AttributeSet?) :
                this(context, attrs, 0)

    constructor(context: Context?, attrs: AttributeSet?, defStyleAttr:
Int) : super(context, attrs, defStyleAttr) {
        //...
    }
}
```

This case introduces a lot of boilerplate code just for constructors that delegate calls to other constructors. Kotlin's solution to this problem is to use the `@JvmOverload` annotation:

```
class KotlinView @JvmOverloads constructor(
    context: Context,
    attrs: AttributeSet? = null,
    defStyleAttr: Int = 0
) : View(context, attrs, defStyleAttr)
```

Annotating a constructor with the `@JvmOverload` annotation informs the compiler to generate in additional JVM bytecode constructor overload for every parameter with a default value. In this case, all the required constructors will be generated:

```
public SampleView(Context context) {
    super(context);
}

public SampleView(Context context, @Nullable AttributeSet attrs) {
    super(context, attrs);
}

public SampleView(Context context, @Nullable AttributeSet attrs, int
defStyleAttr) {
    super(context, attrs, defStyleAttr);
}
```

Interfaces

Kotlin interfaces are similar to Java 8 interfaces and different to interfaces in previous version Java. An interface is defined using the `interface` keyword. Let's define an `EmailProvider` interface:

```
    interface EmailProvider {
        fun validateEmail()
    }
```

To implement the preceding interface in Kotlin, use the same syntax as for extending classes--a single colon character (`:`). There is no `implements` keyword, in contrast to Java:

```
    class User:EmailProvider {
        override fun validateEmail() {
            //email validation
        }
    }
```

The question of how to extend a class may arise and implement an interface at the same time. Simply place the class name after the colon, and use a comma to add one or more interfaces. It's not required to place the superclass in the first position, although it's considered good practice:

```
    open class Person {

        interface EmailProvider {
            fun validateEmail()
```

```
    }

    class User: Person(), EmailProvider {
    override fun validateEmail(){
        //email validation
    }
}
```

As with Java, the Kotlin class can only extend one class, but it can implement one or more interfaces. We can also declare properties in the interfaces:

```
interface EmailProvider {
    val email: String
    fun validateEmail()
}
```

All methods and properties have to be overridden in a class implementing an interface:

```
class User() : EmailProvider {

    override val email: String = "UserEmailProvider"

    override fun validateEmail() {
        //email validation
    }
}
```

Also, properties defined in a primary constructor can be used to override parameters from an interface:

```
class User(override val email: String) : EmailProvider {
    override fun validateEmail() {
        //email validation
    }
}
```

All methods and properties defined in an interface that does not have a default implementation are treated by default as abstract, so we don't have to explicitly define them as abstract. All abstract methods and properties must be implemented (overridden) by a concrete (non-abstract) class that implements an interface.

There is, however, another way to define methods and properties in the interface. Kotlin, similar to Java 8, introduces major improvements to interfaces. An interface not only defines behavior, but also implements it. This means that the default method of property implementation can be provided by an interface. The only limitation is that an interface cannot reference any backing fields or store a state (because there is no good place to store it). This is a difference between an interface and an abstract class. Interfaces are stateless (they can't have a state), while abstract classes are stateful (they can have a state). Let's see an example:

```
interface EmailProvider {

    fun validateEmail(): Boolean

    val email: String

    val nickname: String
    get() = email.substringBefore("@")
}
class User(override val email: String) : EmailProvider {
    override fun validateEmail() {
        //email validation
    }
}
```

The `EmailProvider` interface provides the default implementation for the `nickname` property, so we don't have to define it in the `User` class, and we can still use the property as any other property defined in the class:

```
val user = User (" johnny.bravo@test.com")
print(user.nickname) //prints: johnny
```

The same applies to methods. Simply define a method with the body in the interface, so the `User` class will take all the default implementation from the interface and will only have to override only the `email` member--the member in the inference without a default implementation:

```
interface EmailProvider {

    val email: String

    val nickname: String
    get() = email.substringBefore("@")

    fun validateEmail() = nickname.isNotEmpty()
}
```

```
class User(override val email: String) : EmailProvider

//usage
val user = User("joey@test.com")
print(user.validateEmail()) // Prints: true
print(user.nickname) // Prints: joey
```

There is one interesting case related to default implementations. A class can't inherit from multiple classes, but it can implement multiple interfaces. We can have two interfaces containing methods with the same signature and default implementations:

```
interface A {
    fun foo() {
        println("A")
    }
}

interface B {
    fun foo() {
        println("B")
    }
}
```

In such cases, conflicts must be resolved explicitly by overriding the `foo` method in a class implementing the interfaces:

```
class Item : A, B {
    override fun foo() {
        println("Item")
    }
}

//usage
val item = Item()
item.foo() //prints: Item
```

We can still call both default interface implementations by qualifying `super` using angle brackets and specifying the parent interface type name:

```
class Item : A, B {
    override fun foo() {
        val a = super<A>.foo()
        val b = super<B>.foo()
        print("Item $a $b")
    }
}

//usage
```

```
val item = Item()
item.foo()

//Prints: A
          B
          ItemsAB
```

Data classes

Often, we create a class whose only purpose is to store data, such as, data retrieved from a server or a local database. These classes are the building blocks of application data models:

```
class Product(var name: String?, var price: Double?) {

   override fun hashCode(): Int {
       var result = if (name != null) name!!.hashCode() else 0
       result = 31 * result + if (price != null) price!!.hashCode()
       else 0
       return result
   }

   override fun equals(other: Any?): Boolean = when {
       this === other -> true
       other == null || other !is Product -> false
       if (name != null) name != other.name else other.name !=
                         null -> false
       price != null -> price == other.price
       else -> other.price == null
   }

   override fun toString(): String {
       return "Product(name=$name, price=$price)"
   }
}
```

In Java, we need to generate a lot of redundant getters and setters together with the `hashCode` and `equals` methods. Android Studio can generate most of the code for us, but maintaining this code is still an issue. In Kotlin, we can define a special kind of class called the data class by adding the `data` keyword to a class declaration header:

```
class Product(var name: String, var price: Double)
// normal class

data class Product(var name: String, var price: Double)
// data class
```

A data class adds additional capabilities to a class in the form of methods generated by the Kotlin compiler. Those methods are `equals`, `hashCode`, `toString`, `copy`, and multiple `componentN` methods. The limitation is that data classes can't be marked as `abstract`, `inner`, and `sealed`. Let's discuss methods added by a data modifier in more detail.

The equals and hashCode methods

When dealing with data classes, there is often a need to compare two instances for structural equality (they contain the same data, but are not necessarily the same instance). We many simply want to check whether one instance of the `User` class equals another `User` instance or if two product instances represent the same product. A common pattern used to check whether objects are equal is to use an `equals` method that uses the `hashCode` method internally:

```
product.equals(product2)
```

The general contract for overridden implementations of `hashCode` is that two equal objects (according to the `equals` implementation) need to have the same hash code. The reason behind this is that `hashCode` is often compared before `equals`, because of its performance--it's much cheaper to compare hash code than every field in the object.

If `hashCode` is the same then the `equals` method checks whether the two objects are the same instance, or the same type, and then verifies equality by comparing all significant fields. If at least one of the fields of the first object is not equal to a corresponding field of a second object then the objects are not considered equal. Another way to describe this is: two objects are equal when they have the same `hashCode` and all significant (compared) fields have the same value. Let's check an example of the Java `Product` class, which contains two fields, `name` and `price`:

```
public class Product {

    private String name;
    private Double price;

    public Product(String name, Double price) {
        this.name = name;
        this.price = price;
    }

    @Override
    public int hashCode() {
        int result = name != null ? name.hashCode() : 0;
     result = 31 * result + (price != null ?
```

```
                                  price.hashCode() : 0);
            return result;
        }

        @Override
        public boolean equals(Object o) {
            if (this == o) {
                return true;
            }
            if (o == null || getClass() != o.getClass()) {
                return false;
            }

            Product product = (Product) o;

            if (name != null ? !name.equals(product.name) :
            product.name != null) {
                return false;
            }
            return price != null ? price.equals(product.price) :
            product.price == null;
        }

        public String getName() {
            return name;
        }

        public void setName(String name) {
            this.name = name;
        }

        public Double getPrice() {
            return price;
        }

        public void setPrice(Double price) {
            this.price = price;
        }
    }
```

This approach is widely used in Java and other OOP languages. In the early days, programmers had to write this code manually for every class that needed to be compared and maintained the code, making sure that it was correct and it compared every significant value.

Nowadays, modern IDEs such as Android Studio can generate this code and update the appropriate methods. We don't have to write the code, but we still have to maintain it by making sure that all the required fields are compared by the `equals` method. Sometimes, we don't know whether it is a standard code generated by the IDE or it is a tweaked version. For each Kotlin data class, those methods are automatically generated by a compiler, so this problem does not exist. Here is a definition of `Product` in Kotlin, that contains all methods defined in the previous Java classes:

```
data class Product(var name: String, var price: Double)
```

The preceding class contains all methods defined in previous Java classes, but there is no massive boilerplate code to maintain.

In `Chapter 2`, *Laying a Foundation*, we mentioned that, in Kotlin, using the structural equality operator (==) will always call the `equals` method under the hood, so it means that we can easily and safely compare instances of our `Product` data class:

```
data class Product(var name:String, var price:Double)

val productA = Product("Spoon", 30.2)
val productB = Product("Spoon", 30.2)
val productC = Product("Fork", 17.4)

print(productA == productA) // prints: true
print(productA == productB) // prints: true
print(productB == productA) // prints: true
print(productA == productC) // prints: false
print(productB == productC) // prints: false
```

By default, the `hashCode` and `equals` methods are generated based on every property declared in the primary constructor. In most scenarios this is enough, but if we need more control we are still allowed to override these methods by ourselves in the data class. In this case, the default implementation won't be generated by the compiler.

The toString method

Generated methods contain the names and values of all properties declared in the primary constructor:

```
data class Product(var name:String, var price:Double)
val productA = Product("Spoon", 30.2)
println(productA) // prints: Product(name=Spoon, price=30.2)
```

We can actually log meaningful data to a console or log file, instead of the class name and memory address as in Java (`Person@a4d2e77`). This makes the debugging process much simpler, because we have a proper, human-readable format.

The copy method

By default, the Kotlin compiler will also generate an appropriate `copy` method that will allow us to easily create a copy of an object:

```
data class Product(var name: String, var price: Double)
val productA = Product("Spoon", 30.2)
print(productA) // prints: Product(name=Spoon, price=30.2)
val productB = productA.copy()
print(productB) // prints: Product(name=Spoon, price=30.2)
```

Java does not have named argument syntax, so when calling the `copy` method in Java, we need to pass all arguments (the order of the arguments corresponds to the order of properties defined in the primary constructor). In Kotlin, this approach decreases the need for `copy` constructors or `copy` factories:

- The `copy` constructor takes a single argument whose type is the class containing the constructor, and it returns the `newInstance` of this class:

  ```
  val productB = Product(productA)
  ```

- The `copy` factory is a static factory that takes a single argument whose type is the class containing the factory, and returns a new instance of this class:

  ```
  val productB = ProductFactory.newInstance(productA)
  ```

The `copy` method takes arguments that correspond to all the properties declared in the primary constructor. When combined with the default arguments syntax, we can provide all or only some of the properties to create a modified instance copy:

```
data class Product(var name:String, var price:Double)

val productA = Product("Spoon", 30.2)
print(productA) // prints: Product(name=Spoon, price=30.2)

val productB = productA.copy(price = 24.0)
print(productB) // prints: Product(name=Spoon, price=24.0)

val productC = productA.copy(price = 24.0, name = "Knife")
print(productB) // prints: Product(name=Knife, price=24.0)
```

This is a very flexible way of creating a copy of the object in such as way that we can easily say if, and how, the copy should differ from the original instances. On the other hand, the programming approach promotes the concept of immutability, which can be easily implemented with an argumentless call of the `copy` method:

```
//Mutable object - modify object state
data class Product(var name:String, var price:Double)

var productA = Product("Spoon", 30.2)
productA.name = "Knife"

//immutable object - create new object instance
data class Product(val name:String, val price:Double)

var productA = Product("Spoon", 30.2)
productA = productA.copy(name = "Knife")
```

Instead of defining mutable properties (`var`) and modifying the object state, we can define immutable properties (`val`), make an object immutable, and operate on it by getting its copy with the changed values. This approach reduces the need for data synchronization in multithreading applications and the number of potential errors related with it because immutable objects can be freely shared across threads.

Destructing declarations

Sometimes it makes sense to restructure objects into multiple variables. This syntax is called a **destructuring declaration**:

```
data class Person(val firstName: String, val lastName: String,
                  val height: Int)

val person = Person("Igor", "Wojda", 180)
var (firstName, lastName, height) = person
println(firstName) // prints: "Igor"
println(lastName) // prints: "Wojda"
println(height) // prints: 180
```

A destructuring declaration allows us to create multiple variables at once. The preceding code will create values of the `firstName`, `lastName`, and `height` variables. Under the hood, the compiler will generate code like this:

```
val person = Person("Igor", "Wojda", 180)
var firstName = person.component1()
var lastName = person.component2()
var height = person.component3()
```

For every property declared in the primary constructor of the data class, the Kotlin compiler generates a single `componentN` method. The suffix of the `component` function corresponds to the order of properties declared in the primary constructor, so `firstName` corresponds to `component1`, `lastName` corresponds to `component2`, and `height` corresponds to `component3`. In fact, we could invoke those methods directly on the `Person` class to retrieve a property value, but there is no point in doing so, because their names are meaningless and the code would be very difficult to read and maintain. We should leave those methods for the compiler to destructure the object and use property access syntax such as `person.firstName`.

We can also omit one or more properties using an underscore:

```
val person = Person("Igor", "Wojda", 180)
var (firstName, _, height) = person
println(firstName) // prints: "Igor"
println(height) // prints: 180
```

In this case, we want only to create two variables, `firstName` and `height`; `lastName` is ignored. The code generated by the compiler will look as follows:

```
val person = Person("Igor", "Wojda", 180)
var firstName= person.component1()
var height = person.component3()
```

We can also destructure simple types such as string:

```
val file = "MainActivity.kt"
val (name, extension) = file.split(".", limit = 2)
```

Destructive declarations can also be used with a `for` loop:

```
val authors = listOf(
   Person("Igor", "Wojda", 180),
   Person("Marcin", "Moskała", 180)
)

println("Authors:")
for ((name, surname) in authors) {
    println("$name $surname")
}
```

Operator overloading

Kotlin has a predefined set of operators with fixed symbolic representation (such as +, and *) and fixed precedence. Most of the operators are translated directly into method calls; some are translated into more complex expressions. The following table contains a list of all the operators available in Kotlin:

Operator token	Corresponding method/expression
`a + b`	`a.plus(b)`
`a - b`	`a.minus(b)`
`a * b`	`a.times(b)`
`a / b`	`a.div(b)`
`a % b`	`a.rem(b)`
`a..b`	`a.rangeTo(b)`
`a += b`	`a.plusAssign(b)`
`a -= b`	`a.minusAssign(b)`
`a *= b`	`a.timesAssign(b)`
`a /= b`	`a.divAssign(b)`
`a %= b`	`a.remAssign(b)`
`a++`	`a.inc()`
`a--`	`a.dec()`
`a in b`	`b.contains(a)`
`a !in b`	`!b.contains(a)`
`a[i]`	`a.get(i)`
`a[i, j]`	`a.get(i, j)`
`a[i_1, ..., i_n]`	`a.get(i_1, ..., i_n)`
`a[i] = b`	`a.set(i, b)`
`a[i, j] = b`	`a.set(i, j, b)`
`a[i_1, ..., i_n] = b`	`a.set(i_1, ..., i_n, b)`
`a()`	`a.invoke()`

`a(i)`	`a.invoke(i)`
`a(i, j)`	`a.invoke(i, j)`
`a(i_1, ..., i_n)`	`a.invoke(i_1, ..., i_n)`
`a == b`	`a?.equals(b) ?: (b === null)`
`a != b`	`!(a?.equals(b) ?: (b === null))`
`a > b`	`a.compareTo(b) > 0`
`a < b`	`a.compareTo(b) < 0`
`a >= b`	`a.compareTo(b) >= 0`
`a <= b`	`a.compareTo(b) <= 0`

The Kotlin compiler translates tokens that represent specific operations (left column) to corresponding methods or expressions that will be invoked (right column).

We can provide custom implementations for each operator by using them in `operator` method corresponding with an `operator` token. Let's define a simple `Point` class containing `x` and `y` properties together and `plus` and `times`:

```
data class Point(var x: Double, var y: Double) {
   operator fun plus(point: Point) = Point(x + point.x, y+ point.y)

   operator fun times(other: Int) = Point(x * other, y * other)
}

//usage
var p1 = Point(2.9, 5.0)
var p2 = Point(2.0, 7.5)

println(p1 + p2)      // prints: Point(x=4.9, y=12.5)
println(p1 * 3)       // prints: Point(x=8.7, y=21.0)
```

By defining the `plus` and `times` operators, we can perform addition and multiplication operations on any `Point` instance. Each time the + or * operations are called, Kotlin calls the corresponding operator method, `plus` or `times`. Under the hood, the compiler will generate method calls:

```
p1.plus(p2)
p1.times(3)
```

In our example, we are passing the other `Point` instance to the `plus` operator method, but this type is not mandatory. Operator methods do not actually override any methods from the super class, so they have no fixed declaration with fixed parameters and fixed types. We don't have to inherit from a particular Kotlin type to be able to overload operators. All we need to have is a method with a proper signature marked as `operator`. The Kotlin compiler will do the rest by running the method that corresponds to the operator. In fact, we can define multiple operators with the same name and different parameter types:

```
data class Point(var x: Double, var y: Double) {
   operator fun plus(point: Point) = Point(x + point.x, y +point.y)

   operator fun plus(vector:Double) = Point(x + vector, y + vector)
}

var p1 = Point(2.9, 5.0)
var p2 = Point(2.0, 7.5)

println(p1 + p2) // prints: Point(x=4.9, y=12.5)
println(p1 + 3.1) // prints: Point(x=6.0, y=10.1)
```

Both operators are working fine because the Kotlin compiler can select the proper overload for the operator. Many basic operators have a corresponding compound assign operator (`plus` has `plusAssign`, times has `timesAssign`, and so on), so when we define an operator such as the + operator, Kotlin supports the + operation and += operation as well:

```
var p1 = Point(2.9, 7.0)
var p2 = Point(2.0, 7.5)

p1 += p2
println(p1) // prints: Point(x=4.9, y=14.5)
```

Notice the important difference that in some scenarios may be performance critical. A compound assign operator (for example, the += operator) has the `Unit` return type, so it just modifies the state of the existing object, while the basic operator (for example, the + operator) always returns a new instance of an object:

```
var p1 = Wallet(39.0, 14.5)
p1 += p2          // update state of p1
val p3 = p1 + p2  //creates new object p3
```

If we define both the `plus` and `plusAssign` operators with the same parameter types, when we try to use the `plusAssign` (compound) operator, the compiler will throw an error because it does not know which method should be invoked:

```
data class Point(var x: Double, var y: Double) {
    init {
```

```
            println("Point created $x.$y")
        }
        operator fun plus(point: Point) = Point(x + point.x, y + point.y)

        operator fun plusAssign(point:Point) {
            x += point.x
            y += point.y
        }
    }

    // usage
    var p1 = Point(2.9, 7.0)
    var p2 = Point(2.0, 7.5)
    val p3 = p1 + p2
    p1 += p2 // Error: Assignment operations ambiguity
```

Operator overloading also works for classes defined in Java. All we need is a method with the proper signature and a name that corresponds to the operator method's name. The Kotlin compiler will translate the operator's usage to this method. The `operator` modifier is not present in Java, so it's not required in the Java class:

```
// Java
public class Point {
    private final int x;
    private final int y;
    public Point(int x, int y) {
        this.x = x;
        this.y = y;
    }
    public int getX() {
        return x;
    }
    public int getY() {
        return y;
    }
    public Point plus(Point point) {
        return new Point(point.getX() + x, point.getY() + y);
    }
}
//Main.kt
val p1 = Point(1, 2)
val p2 = Point(3, 4)
val p3 = p1 + p2;
println("$x:{p3.x}, y:${p3.y}") //prints: x:4, y:6
```

Object declaration

There are a few ways to declare singletons in Java. Here is the most common way to define a class that has a private constructor and retrieves instances via a static factory method:

```
public class Singleton {

    private Singleton() {
    }

    private static Singleton instance;

    public static Singleton getInstance() {
        if (instance == null) {
            instance = new Singleton();
        }

        return instance;
    }
}
```

The preceding code works fine for a single thread, but it's not thread-safe, so in some cases two instances of `Singleton` can be created. There are a few ways to fix it. We can use the `synchronized` block, presented as follows:

```
//synchronized
public class Singleton {

    private static Singleton instance = null;

    private Singleton(){
    }

    private synchronized static void createInstance() {
        if (instance == null) {
            instance = new Singleton();
        }
    }

    public static Singleton getInstance() {
        if (instance == null) createInstance();
        return instance;
    }
}
```

This solution, however, is very verbose. In Kotlin, there is a special language construct for creating singletons called **object declaration**, so we can achieve the same result in a much simpler way. Defining objects is similar to defining classes; the only difference is that we use the `object` keyword instead of the `class` keyword:

```
object Singleton
```

We can add methods and properties to an object declaration exactly the same way as a class:

```
object SQLiteSingleton {
    fun getAllUsers(): List<User> {
        //...
    }
}
```

This method is accessed the same way as any Java static method:

```
SQLiteSingleton.getAllUsers()
```

Object declarations are initialized lazily and they can be nested inside other object declarations or non-inner classes. Also, they cannot be assigned to a variable.

Object expression

An object expression is equivalent to Java's anonymous class. It is used to instantiate objects that might inherit from some class or that implements an interface. A classic use case is when we need to define objects that are implement an interface. This is how in Java we could implement the `ServiceConnection` interface and assign it to a variable in Java:

```
ServiceConnection serviceConnection = new ServiceConnection() {
    @Override
    public void onServiceDisconnected(ComponentName name) {
        ...
    }

    @Override
    public void onServiceConnected(ComponentName name,
        IBinder service)
    {
        ...
    }
}
```

The closest Kotlin equivalent of the preceding implementation is the following:

```
val serviceConnection = object: ServiceConnection {

 override fun onServiceDisconnected(name: ComponentName?) { }

 override fun onServiceConnected(name: ComponentName?,
     service: IBinder?) { }
}
```

The preceding example uses an object expression, which creates instance of an anonymous class that implements `ServiceConnection` interface. An object expression can also extend classes. Here is how we can create an instance of the `BroadcastReceiver`:

```
val broadcastReceiver = object : BroadcastReceiver() {
   override fun onReceive(context: Context, intent: Intent) {
       println("Got a broadcast ${intent.action}")
   }
}

val intentFilter = IntentFilter("SomeAction");
registerReceiver(broadcastReceiver, intentFilter)
```

While object expressions allow us to create objects of an anonymous type that can implement an interface and extend a class, we can use them to easily solve interesting problems related to the Adapter pattern.

> The Adapter design pattern allows otherwise incompatible classes to work together by converting the interface of one class into an interface expected by the clients.

Let's say that we have a `Player` interface and function that requires `Player` as a parameter:

```
interface Player {
    fun play()
}

fun playWith(player: Player) {
    print("I play with")
    player.play()
}
```

Also, we have `VideoPlayer` class from a public library that has the `play` method defined, but it is not implementing our `Player` interface:

```
open class VideoPlayer {
    fun play() {
        println("Play video")
    }
}
```

The `VideoPlayer` class meets all the interface requirements, but it cannot be passed as `Player` because it is not implementing the interface. To use it as a `player`, we need to make an Adapter. In this example, we will implement it as an object of an anonymous type that implements the `Player` interface:

```
val player = object: VideoPlayer(), Player { }
playWith(player)
```

We were able to solve our problem without defining the `VideoPlayer` subclass. We can also define custom methods and properties in the object expression:

```
val data = object {
    var size = 1
    fun update() {
        //...
    }
}

data.size = 2
data .update()
```

This is a very easy way to define custom anonymous objects that are not present in Java. To define similar types in Java, we need to define the custom interface. We can now add a behavior to our `VideoPlayer` class to fully implement the `Player` interface:

```
open class VideoPlayer {
    fun play() {
        println("Play video")
    }
}

interface Player{
    fun play()
    fun stop()
}

//usage
val player = object: VideoPlayer(), Player {
```

```
    var duration:Double = 0.0

    fun stop() {
        println("Stop  video")
    }
}

player.play() // println("Play video")
player.stop() // println("Stop  video")
player.duration = 12.5
```

In the preceding code, we can call on anonymous object (`player`) methods defined in the `VideoPlayer` class and the expression object.

Companion objects

Kotlin, as opposed to Java, lacks the ability to define static members, but instead it allows us to define objects that are associated with a class. In other words, an object is initialized only once; therefore, only one instance of an object exists, sharing its state across all instances of a particular class. When a singleton object is associated with a class of the same name, it is called the companion object of the class, and the class is called the companion class of the object:

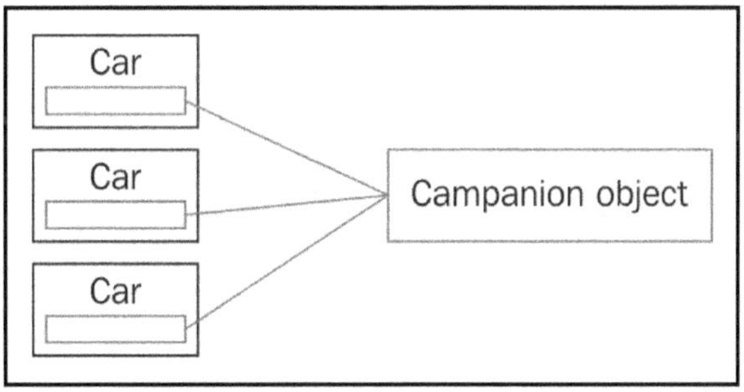

The preceding diagram presents three instances of the `Car` class sharing a single instance of an object.

Members, such as methods and properties, defined inside a companion object may be accessed similarly to the way we access static fields and methods in Java. The main purpose of a companion object is to have code that is related to a class, but not necessary to any particular instance of this class. It is a good way to define members that would be defined as static in Java, for example, `factory`, which creates a class instance method converting units, activity request codes, shared preference keys, and so on. To define the simplest companion object, we need to define a single block of code:

```
class ProductDetailsActivity {

    companion object {
    }
}
```

Now let's define a `start` method that will allow us to start an activity easily:

```
//ProductDetailsActivity.kt
class ProductDetailsActivity : AppCompatActivity() {
    override fun onCreate(savedInstanceState: Bundle?) {
        super.onCreate(savedInstanceState)
        val product = intent.getParcelableExtra<Product>
            (KEY_PRODUCT) // 3
        //...
    }

    companion object {

        const val KEY_PRODUCT = "product" // 1

        fun start(context: Context, product: Product) { // 2
            val intent = Intent(context,
                ProductDetailsActivity::class.java)
            intent.putExtra(KEY_PRODUCT, product) // 3
            context.startActivity(intent)
        }
    }
}

// Start activity
ViewProductActivity.start(context, productId) // 2
```

1. Only a single instance of `key` exists.
2. The `start` method can be invoked without creating an object instance, just like Java static methods.
3. Retreive the value after the instance is created.

Notice that we are able to call `start` prior to the creation of activity instance. Let's use the companion object to track how many instances of the `Car` class were created. To achieve this we need to define a `count` property with a `private` setter. It could also be defined as a top-level property, but it is better to place it inside a companion object because we don't want to allow counter modification outside of this class:

```
class Car {
    init {
        count++;
    }

    companion object {
        var count:Int = 0
        private set
    }
}
```

The class can access all the methods and properties defined in the companion object, but the companion object can't access any of the class's content. The companion object is assigned to a specific class, but not to a particular instance:

```
println(Car.count) // Prints 0
Car()
Car()
println(Car.count) // Prints: 2
```

To access an instance of the companion object directly, we can use the class name.

We can also access the companion object by using more verbose syntax, `Car.Companion.count`, but in most cases there is no point in doing so, unless we want to access `companion` from Java code.

Companion object instantiation

A companion object is a singleton created by a companion class and kept in its static property. The instantiation of a `companion` object is lazy. This means that `companion` object will be instantiated when it is needed for the first time--when its members are accessed, or an instance of a class containing the `companion` object is created. To mark when the `Car` class instance and its corresponding `companion` object are created, we need to add two initializer blocks--one for the `Car` class, another for the companion object.

The initializer block inside the `companion` object works exactly the same way as in the class--it's executed when an instance is created:

```
class Car {
    init {
        count++;
        println("Car created")
    }

    companion object {
        var count: Int = 0
        init {
            println("Car companion object created")
        }
    }
}
```

While the class initialization block is equivalent to the Java constructor body, the compilation object initialization block is equivalent to the Java static initialization block in Kotlin. For now, the `count` property can be updated by any client, because it's accessible from outside of the `Car` class. We will fix this issue later in this chapter in the *Visibility modifiers* section. Now let's access the `Car` companion object class member:

```
Car.count  // Prints: Car companion object created
Car() // Prints: Car created
```

By accessing the `count` property defined in the companion object, we trigger its creation, but notice that an instance of `Car` class has not been created. Later, when we create a `Car` class instance, the `companion` object has already created. Now, let's instantiate the `Car` class before been accessing the `companion` object:

```
Car()
//Prints: Car companion object created
//Prints: Car created

Car()  //Prints: Car created
Car.count
```

The companion object is created together with first instance of the `Car` class, so when we create some other instances of the `user` class, the `companion` object for the class already exists, so it's not created.

Keep in mind that the preceding instantiation describes two separate examples. Both could not be true in a single program, because only a single instance of class `companion` object can exist, and it is created the first time it is needed.

The `companion` objects can also contain functions, implement interfaces, and even extend classes. We can define a companion object that will include a static constriction method with the additional option to override the implementation for testing purposes:

```
abstract class Provider<T> { // 1

    abstract fun creator(): T // 2

    private var instance: T? = null // 3
    var override: T? = null // 4

    fun get(): T = override ?: instance ?: creator().also { instance = it
} //5
}
```

1. `Provider` is a generic class.
2. The abstract function is used to the create an instance.
3. The field is used to keep the created instance.
4. The field is used in tests to provide an alternative implementation of the instance.
5. The function that returns an override instance if it was set, an instance if it was created, or creating instance using the `create` method and filling `instance` field with it.

With this implementation, we can define the interface with a default static constructor:

```
interface MarvelRepository {

    fun getAllCharacters(searchQuery: String?):
Single<List<MarvelCharacter>>

    companion object : Provider<MarvelRepository>() {
        override fun creator() = MarvelRepositoryImpl()
    }
}
```

To get the instance, we need to use the following code:

```
MarvelRepository.get()
```

If we need to specify a different instance for testing purposes (for example, in Espresso tests) then we can always specify them using an object expression:

```
MarvelRepository.override = object : MarvelRepository {
    override fun getAllCharacters(searchQuery: String?):
    Single<List<MarvelCharacter>> {
        //...
    }
}
```

Companion objects are really popular in the Kotlin Android world. They are mostly used to define all the elements that were static in Java (constant fields, static creators, and so on), but they also provide additional capabilities.

Enum classes

An enumerated type (`enum`) is a data type consisting of a set of named values. To define an enum type, we need to add the `enum` keyword to the class declaration header:

```
enum class Color {
    RED,
    ORANGE,
    BLUE,
    GRAY,
    VIOLET
}

val favouriteColor = Color.BLUE
```

To parse a string into enum, use the `valueOf` method (like in Java):

```
val selectedColor = Color.valueOf("BLUE")
println(selectedColor == Color.BLUE) // prints: true
```

Or you can use the Kotlin helper method:

```
val selectedColor = enumValueOf<Color>("BLUE")
println(selectedColor == Color.BLUE) // prints: true
```

To display all values in the `Color` enum, use the `values` function (like in Java):

```
for (color in Color.values()) {
    println("name: ${it.name}, ordinal: ${it.ordinal}")
}
```

Or you can use the Kotlin `enumerateValues` helper method:

```
for (color in enumValues<Color>()) {
    println("name: ${it.name}, ordinal: ${it.ordinal}")
}

// Prints:
name: RED, ordinal: 0
name: ORANGE, ordinal: 1
name: BLUE, ordinal: 2
name: GRAY, ordinal: 3
name: VIOLET, ordinal: 4
```

The `enum` type can also have its constructor, and there can be custom data associated with each `enum` constant. Let's add properties with values of `red`, `green`, and `blue` color components:

```
enum class Color(val r: Int, val g: Int, val b: Int) {
    RED(255, 0, 0),
    ORANGE(255, 165, 0),
    BLUE(0, 0, 255),
    GRAY(49, 79, 79),
    VIOLET(238, 130, 238)
}

val color = Color.BLUE
val rValue =color.r
val gValue = color.g
val bValue = color.b
```

With these values, we can define a function that will calculate an RGB value for each color.

Notice that the last constant (`VIOLET`) is followed by a semicolon. This is a rare situation where a semicolon is actually required in Kotlin code. It separates the constant definitions from the member definitions:

```
enum class Color(val r: Int, val g: Int, val b: Int) {
    BLUE(0, 0, 255),
    ORANGE(255, 165, 0),
    GRAY(49, 79, 79),
    RED(255, 0, 0),
    VIOLET(238, 130, 238);

    fun rgb() = r shl 16 + g shl 8 + b
}

fun printHex(num: Int) {
```

```
        println(num.toString(16))
    }

    printHex(Color.BLUE.rgb()) // Prints: ff
    printHex(Color.ORANGE.rgb()) // Prints: ffa500
    printHex(Color.GRAY.rgb()) // Prints: 314f4f
```

The `rgb()` method accesses the `r`, `g`, and `b` variable data for a particular enum and calculates the value for each `enum` element separately. We can also add a validation for the enum constructor arguments using the `init` block and the Kotlin standard library's `require` function:

```
    enum class Color(val r: Int, val g: Int, val b: Int) {
        BLUE(0, 0, 255),
        ORANGE(255, 165, 0),
        GRAY(49, 79, 79),
        RED(255, 0, 0),
        VIOLET(238, 130, 238);

        init {
            require(r in 0..255)
            require(g in 0..255)
            require(b in 0..255)
        }

        fun rgb() = r shl 16 + g shl 8 + b
    }
```

Defining an incorrect enum will result in an exception:

```
    GRAY(33, 33, 333) // IllegalArgumentException: Failed requirement.
```

There are cases where we want to associate fundamentally different behavior with each constant. To do this, we can define an abstract method or property and override it in each enum block. Let's define the `Temperature` enum and `temperature` property:

```
    enum class Temperature { COLD, NEUTRAL, WARM }

    enum class Color(val r: Int, val g: Int, val b: Int) {
        RED(255, 0, 0) {
            override val temperature = Temperature.WARM
        },
        ORANGE(255, 165, 0) {
            override val temperature = Temperature.WARM
        },
        BLUE(0, 0, 255) {
            override val temperature = Temperature.COLD
```

```
    },
    GRAY(49, 79, 79) {
        override val temperature = Temperature.NEUTRAL
    },
    VIOLET(238, 130, 238 {
        override val temperature = Temperature.COLD
    };
     init {
        require(r in 0..256)
        require(g in 0..256)
        require(b in 0..256)
    }

    fun rgb() = (r * 256 + g) * 256 + b

    abstract val temperature: Temperature
}

println(Color.BLUE.temperature) //prints: COLD
println(Color.ORANGE.temperature) //prints: WARM
println(Color.GRAY.temperature) //prints: NEUTRAL
```

Now, each color contains not only RGB information, but also an additional enum describing its temperature. We have added a property, but in an analogical way we could add custom methods to each enum element.

Infix calls for named methods

Infix calls are features of Kotlin that allow us to create more fluid and readable code. They allow us to write code that is closer to natural human language. We have already seen the infix methods in `Chapter 2`, *Laying a Foundation,* which allowed us to easily create an instance of a `Pair` class. Here is a quick reminder:

```
var pair = "Everest" to 8848
```

The `Pair` class represents a generic pair of two values. There is no meaning attached to values in this class, so it can be used for any purpose. `Pair` is a data class, so it contains all data class methods (`equals`, `hashCode`, `component1`, and so on). Here is a definition of the `Pair` class from the Kotlin standard library:

```
public data class Pair<out A, out B>( // 1
   public val first: A,
   public val second: B
) : Serializable {
```

```
    public override fun toString(): String = "($first, $second)"
    // 2
}
```

1. The meaning of this `out` modifier when used behind a generic type will be described in `Chapter 6`, *Generic Are Your Friends*.
2. Pairs have a custom `toString` method. This is implemented to make printed syntax more readable because first and second names are not meaningful in most usage contexts.

Before we dive deeper and learn how to define our own infix method, let's translate the presented code into a more familiar form. Each infix method can be used like any other method:

```
val mountain = "Everest";
var pair = mountain.to(8848)
```

In essence, the infix notation is simply the ability to call a method without using the dot operator and call operator (parentheses). The infix notation only looks different, but it's still a regular method call underneath. In the preceding examples, we simply called the `to` method on the `String` class instance. The `to` function is an extension function, and it will be explained in `Chapter 7`, *Extension Functions and Properties*, but we can imagine it is a method of the `String` class, in this case, which is just returning an instance of `Pair` containing itself and the passed argument. We can operate on the returned `Pair` like on any data class object:

```
val mountain = "Everest";
var pair = mountain.to(8848)
println(pair.first) //prints: Everest
println(pair.second) //prints: 8848
```

In Kotlin, this method is allowed to be an infix only when it has a single parameter. Also, an infix notation does not happen automatically--we need to explicitly mark the method as infix. Let's define our `Point` class with the `infix` method:

```
data class Point(val x: Int, val y: Int) {
    infix fun moveRight(shift: Int) = Point(x + shift, y)
}
```

Here's an usage example:

```
val pointA = Point(1,4)
val pointB = pointA moveRight 2
println(pointB) //prints: Point(x=3, y=4)
```

Notice that we are creating a new `Point` instance, but we could also modify an existing one (if the type was mutable). This decision is for the developer to make, but infix methods are more often used with immutable types.

We can use `infix` methods combined with enums to achieve very fluent syntax. Let's implement a natural syntax that will allow us to define cards from a classic playing card deck. It includes 13 ranks of each of the four suits: clubs, diamonds, hearts, and spades:

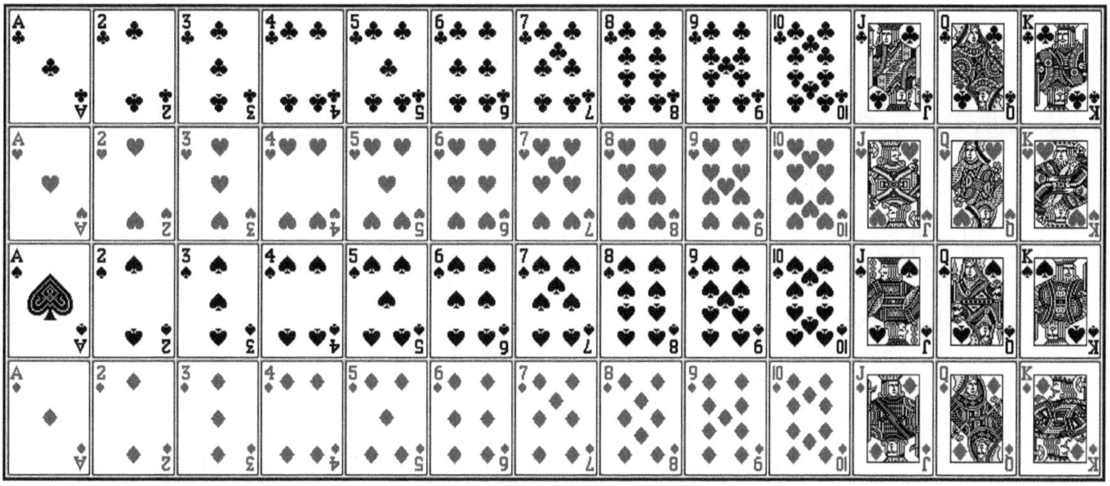

Source for the preceding image: `https://mathematica.stackexchange.com/questions/16108/standard-deck-of-52-playing-cards-in-curated-data`

The goal is to define the syntax that will allow us to define a card from its suit and rank it this way:

```
val card = KING of HEARTS
```

First of all, we need two enums to represent all the ranks and suits:

```
enum class Suit {
    HEARTS,
    SPADES,
    CLUBS,
    DIAMONDS
}

enum class Rank {
    TWO, THREE, FOUR, FIVE,
```

```
        SIX, SEVEN, EIGHT, NINE,
        TEN, JACK, QUEEN, KING, ACE;
    }
```

Then we need a class that will represent a card composed of a particular rank and a particular suite:

```
data class Card(val rank: Rank, val suit: Suit)
```

Now we can instantiate a `Card` class like this:

```
val card = Card(Rank.KING, Suit.HEARTS)
```

To simplify the syntax, we introduce a new `infix` method into the `Rank` enum:

```
enum class Rank {
    TWO, THREE, FOUR, FIVE,
    SIX, SEVEN, EIGHT, NINE,
    TEN, JACK, QUEEN, KING, ACE;

    infix fun of(suit: Suit) = Card(this, suit)
}
```

This will allow us to create a `Card` call like this:

```
val card = Rank.KING.of(Suit.HEARTS)
```

Because the method is marked as infix, we can remove the dot call operator and parentheses:

```
val card = Rank.KING of Suit.HEARTS
```

Using static imports will allow us to shorten the syntax even more and achieve our final result:

```
import Rank.KING
import Suit.HEARTS

val card = KING of HEARTS
```

Besides being super simple, this code is also 100% type safe. We can only define cards using the predefined enums of `Rank` and `Suit`, so we are unable to define a fictional card by mistake.

Visibility modifiers

Kotlin supports four types of visibility modifier (access modifiers)--`private`, `protected`, `public`, and `internal`. Kotlin does not support `private` Java modifiers. The main difference between a Kotlin and Java modifier is that the default visibility modifier in Kotlin is `public`, and it's not required to specify it explicitly, so it can be omitted for a particular declaration. All of the modifiers can be applied to various elements divided into two main groups based on their declaration site: top-level elements and nested members.

> TIP
>
> A quick reminder from `Chapter 3`, *Playing with Functions*: top level elements are elements declared directly inside the Kotlin file, as opposed to elements nested inside a class, object, interface, or function. In Java, we can only declare classes and interfaces at the top level, while Kotlin also allows functions, objects, properties, and extensions there.

First, we have top-level element visibility modifiers:

- `public` (default): Element is visible everywhere.
- `private`: Element is visible inside the file containing the declaration.
- `protected`: Not available at the top level.
- `internal`: Element is visible everywhere in the same module. It is public for elements in the same module.

> **What is a module in Java and Kotlin?**
>
> A module is just a set of Kotlin files compiled together, for example, IntelliJ IDEA module and Gradle project. The modular structure of applications allows better distributed responsibilities and speeds up build time, because only the changed modules are recompiled.

Let's look at an example:

```
//top.kt
public val version: String = "3.5.0" // 1

internal class UnitConveter // 3

private fun printSomething() {
    println("Something")
}

fun main(args: Array<String>) {
    println(version) // 1, Prints: "3.5.0"
```

```
    UnitConveter() // 2, Accessible
    printSomething() // 3, Prints: Something
}

// branch.kt
fun main(args: Array<String>) {
    println(version) // 1, Accessible
    UnitConveter() // 2, Accessible
    printSomething() // 3, Error
}

// main.kt in another module
fun main(args: Array<String>) {
    println(version) // 1, Accessible
    UnitConveter() // 2, Error
    printSomething() // 3, Accessible
}
```

1. The `version` property is public, so it is accessible in all files.
2. `UnitConveter` is accessible in the `branch.kt` file, while it is in the same module, but not in `main.kt` because it is located in another module.
3. The `printSomething` function is only accessible in the file where it is defined.

Note that the package in Kotlin does not give any extra visibility privileges.

The second group consists of members--elements declared inside a top level element. These will be mainly methods, properties, constructors, sometimes objects, companion objects, getters and setters, and occasionally nested classes and nested interfaces. Here are the obligatory rules:

- `public` (default): Clients who see the declaring class see its public members.
- `private`: The element is only visible inside the class or interface containing the member.
- `protected`: The element is visible inside the class containing the declaration and subclasses. It is not applicable inside an object because an object cannot be opened.
- `internal`: Any client inside this module who sees the declaring class sees its internal members.

Let's define a top level element. In this example, we will define class, but the same logic is applied to any top level element that has nested members:

```
class Person {
    public val name: String = "Igor"
```

```
    protected var age:Int = 23
    internal fun learn() {}
    private fun speak() {}
}
```

When we create an instance of the Person class, we can only access the name property marked with the public modifier and the learn method marked with internal modifier:

```
// main.kt inside the same package as Person definition
val person = Person()
println(person.name)    // 1
person.speak()          // 2, Error
person.age              // 3, Error
person.learn()          // 4
```

1. Client who can access the Person instance can also access the name property.
2. The speak method is accessible only inside the Person class.
3. The age property is accessible inside the Person class and its subclasses.
4. Client inside the module that can access the Person class instance can also access its public members.

Inheritance accessibility is similar to external access accessibility, but the main difference is that the member marked with the protected modifier is also visible inside the subclasses:

```
open class Person {
    public val name: String = "Igor"
    private fun speak() {}
    protected var age: Int = 23
    internal fun learn() {}
}

class Student() : Person() {
    fun doSth() {
        println(name)
        learn()
        print(age)
        // speak()   // 1
    }
}
```

1. In the Student subclass, we can access members marked with the public, protected modifier, and internal, but not members marked with the private modifier.

The internal modifier and Java bytecode

It is pretty obvious how the `public`, `private`, and `protected` modifiers are compiled to Java, because they have direct analogs. But there is a problem with the `internal` modifier because it has no direct analog in Java, so there is also no support in Java bytecode. This is why the `internal` modifier is actually compiled to the `public` modifier, and to communicate that it shouldn't be used in Java, its name is mashed (changed so that it is not usable anymore). For example, here we have the `Foo` class:

```
open class Foo {
    internal fun boo() { }
}
```

It could be possible to use it in Java like this:

```
public class Java {
    void a() {
        new Foo().boo$production_sources_for_module_SmallTest();
    }
}
```

It is pretty controversial that internal visibility is guarded by Kotlin and it can be bypassed using a Java adapter, but there is no other way to implement it.

Besides defining visibility modifiers in a class, we are also able to override them while overriding a member. This gives us the ability to weaken access restrictions in the inheritance hierarchy:

```
open class Person {
    protected open fun speak() {}
}

class Student() : Person() {
    public override fun speak() {
    }
}

val person = Person()
//person.speak() // 1

val student = Student()
student.speak() // 2
```

1. Error, the `speak` method is not accessible because it's `protected`.
2. The visibility of the `speak` method was changed to `public` so we can access it.

Defining modifiers for members and their visibility scope is quite straightforward, so let's see how to define class and constructor visibility. As we know, the primary constructor definition is in the class header, so two visibility modifiers are required in a single line:

```
internal class Fruit private constructor {
   var weight: Double? = null

   companion object {
       fun create() = Fruit()
   }
}
```

Assuming the preceding class is defined at the top level, it will be visible inside the module, but it can be only instantiated from within the file containing the class declaration:

```
var fruit: Fruit? = null     // Accessible
fruit = Fruit()              // Error
fruit = Fruit.create()       // Accessible
```

Getter and setters by default have the same visibility modifier as the property, but we can modify it. Kotlin allows us to place a visibility modifier before the `get/set` keyword:

```
class Car {
    init {
        count++;
        println("Car created")
    }

    companion object {
        init {
            println("Car companion object created")
        }
        var count: Int = 0
            private set
    }
}
```

In the preceding example, we have changed the getter's visibility. Notice that this approach allows us to change the visibility modifier without changing its default implementation (generated by the compiler). Now, our instance counter is safe, because it's read-only external clients, but we can still modify the property value from inside the `Car` class.

Sealed classes

A sealed class is a class with a limited number of subclasses (sealed subtyping hierarchy). Prior to Kotlin 1.1, these subclasses had to be defined inside a sealed class body. Kotlin 1.1 weakened this restriction and allowed us to define sealed class subclasses in the same file as a sealed class declaration. All the classes are declared close to each other, so we can easily see all possible subclasses by simply looking at one file:

```
//vehicle.kt

sealed class Vehicle()
class Car : Vehicle()
class Truck : Vehicle()
class Bus : Vehicle()
```

To mark a class as `sealed`, simply add a `sealed` modifier to the class declaration header. The preceding declaration means that the `Vehicle` class can be only extended by three classes, `Car`, `Truck`, and `Bus` because they are declared inside the same file. We could add a fourth class in our `vehicle.kt` file, but it would not be possible to define such a class in another file.

The `sealed` subtyping restriction only applies to direct inheritors of the `Vehicle` class. This means that `Vehicle` can only be extended by classes defined in the same file (`Car`, `Truck`, or `Bus`), but assuming that the `Car`, `Truck`, or `Bus`, classes are open, they could be extended by a class declared inside any file:

```
//vehicle.kt
sealed class Vehicle()
open class Bus : Vehicle()

//data.kt
class SchoolBus:Bus()
```

To prevent this behavior, we would need to also mark the `Car`, `Truck`, and `Bus` classes as `sealed`:

```
//vehicle.kt
sealed class Vehicle()
sealed class Bus : Vehicle()

//data.kt
class SchoolBus:Bus() //Error cannot access Bus
```

The sealed classes work really well with the `when` expression. There is no need for an `else` clause, because a compiler can verify that each subclass of a sealed class has a corresponding clause inside the `when` block:

```
when (vehicle) {
    is Car -> println("Can transport 4 people")
    is Truck -> println("Can transport furnitures ")
    is Bus -> println("Can transport 50 people ")
}
```

We can safely add a new subclass to the `Vehicle` class, because if somewhere in the application the corresponding clause of the `when` expression is missing, the application will not compile. This fixes problems with the Java `switch` statement, where programmers often forget to add proper capsules, which leads to program crashes at runtime or undetected bugs.

Sealed classes are abstract by default, so an `abstract` modifier is redundant. Sealed classes can never be `open` or `final`. We can also substitute a subclass with objects in case we need to make sure that only a single instance exists:

```
sealed class Employee()

class Programmer : Employee()
class Manager : Employee()
object CEO : Employee()
```

The preceding declaration not only protects the inheritance hierarchy, but also limits `CEO` to a single instance. There are a few interesting applications of sealed classes that go beyond the scope of this book, but it's good to be aware of them:

- Defining data types such as a linked list or a binary tree (`https://en.wikipedia.org/wiki/Algebraic_data_type`)
- Protecting inheritance hierarchy when building an application module or library by prohibiting clients from extending our class and still keeping the ability to extend it ourselves
- State machines where some states contain data that makes no sense in other states (`https://en.wikipedia.org/wiki/Finite-state_machine`)
- A list of possible token types for lexical analysis

Nested classes

A nested class is a class defined inside another class. Nesting small classes within top-level classes places the code closer to where it is used, and allows a better way of grouping classes. Typical examples are `Tree`/`Leaf` listeners or presenter states. Kotlin in a similar way to Java, allows us to define a nested class, and there are two main ways to do this. We can define a class as a member inside a class:

```
class Outer {
    private val bar: Int = 1

    class Nested {
        fun foo() = 2
    }
}

val demo = Outer.Nested().foo() // == 2
```

The preceding example allows us to create an instance of the `Nested` class without creating instances of the `Outer` class. In this case, a class cannot refer directly to instance variables or methods defined in its enclosing class (it can use them only through an object reference). This is equivalent to a Java static nested class and, in general, static members.

To be able to access the members of an outer class, we must create a second kind of class by marking a nested class as `inner`:

```
class Outer {
    private val bar: Int = 1

    inner class Inner {
        fun foo() = bar
    }
}

val outer = Outer()
val demo = outer.Inner().foo() // == 1
```

Now, to instantiate the `inner` class we must first instantiate the `Outer` class. In this case, the `Inner` class can access all the methods and properties defined in the outer class and share state with outer class. Only a single instance of the `Inner` class can exist per instance of the `Outer` class. Let's sum up the differences:

Behavior	**Class (member)**	**Inner class (member)**
Behaves as a Java static member	Yes	No
Instances of this class can exist without an instance of the enclosing class	Yes	No
Has a reference to the outer class	No	Yes
Shares state with the outer class (can access outer class members)	No	Yes
Number of instances	Unlimited	One per outer class instance

When deciding whether we should define `inner` class or a top-level class we should think about potential class usage. If the class is only useful for a single class instance, we should declare it as `inner`. If an `inner` class at some point may be useful in another context than serving its outer class, then we should declare it as a top-level class.

Import aliases

An alias is a way to introduce new names for types. If the type name is already used in the file, is inappropriate, or is too long, you can introduce a different name and use it instead of the original type name. An alias does not introduce a new type, and it is available only before compile time (when writing code). The compiler replaces a class alias with an actual class, so it does not exist at runtime.

Sometimes, we need to use a few classes with the same name in a single file. For example, the `InterstitialAd` type is defined both in the Facebook and Google advertising libraries. Let's suppose that we want to use them both in a single file. This situation is common in projects where we need to implement both ad providers to allow a profit comparison between them. The problem is that using both data types in a single file would mean that we need to access one or both of them with a fully qualified class name (namespace and class name):

```
import com.facebook.ads.InterstitialAd

val fbAd = InterstitialAd(context, "...")
val googleAd = com.google.android.gms.ads.InterstitialAd(context)
```

Qualified versus unqualified class name

An unqualified class name is simply the name of the class, for example, `Box`. A qualified class name is a namespace combined with a class name, for example, `com.test.Box`.

In these situations, people often say that the best fix is to rename one of the classes, but sometimes this may not be possible (such as when the class is defined in an external library) or desirable (such as when class name is consistent with the backend database). In this situation, where both the classes are located in an external library, the solution to the class naming conflict is to use an `import` alias. We can use it to rename Google's `InterstitialAd` to `GoogleAd`, and Facebook's `InterstitialAd` to `FbAd`:

```
import com.facebook.ads.InterstitialAd as FbAd
import com.google.android.gms.ads.InterstitialAd as GoogleAd
```

And now we can use these aliases around the file as if they were actual types:

```
val fbAd = FbAd(context, "...")
val googleAd = GoogleAd(context)
```

Using the `import` alias, we can explicitly redefine the names of a class that are imported into a file. In this situation, we didn't have to use two aliases, but this serves to improve readability--it's better to have `FbAd` and `GoogleAd` than `InterstitialAd` and `GoogleAd`. We don't have to use fully qualified class names any more, because we simply said to the compiler, each time when you encounter the `GoogleAd` alias, translate it to `com.google.android.gms.ads.InterstitialAd` during compilation and each time you encounter the `FbAd` alias, translate it to `com.facebook.ads.InterstitialAd`. Import alias work inside a files only where the alias is defined.

Summary

In this chapter, we have discussed constructors, which are the buildings blocks of OOP. We've learned how to define interfaces and various classes and the differences between `inner`, `sealed`, `enum`, and data classes. We've learned that all elements are `public` by default and all classes/interfaces are `final` by default, so we need to explicitly open them to allow inheritance and member overriding.

We've discussed how to define proper data models using very concise data classes combined with even more powerful properties. We know how to properly operate on data using various methods generated by the compiler and how to overload operators.

We learned how to create singletons by using object declarations and how to define objects of an anonymous type that may extend a class and/or implement an interface using object expressions. We've also presented the usage of the `lateinit` modifier, which allows us to define non-nullable data types with delayed initialization.

In the next chapter, we will cover the more functional side of Kotlin by looking into concepts related to **functional programming** (**FP**). We will discuss functional types, lambdas, and higher-order functions.

5
Functions as First-Class Citizens

In the previous chapter, we saw how Kotlin features relate to OOP. This chapter will introduce advanced functional programming features that were previously not present in standard Android development. Some of them were introduced in Java 8 (in Android through the Retrolambda plugin), but Kotlin introduces many more functional programming features.

This chapter is about high-level functions and functions as first-class citizens. Most of the concepts are going to be familiar to readers who have used functional languages in the past.

In this chapter, we will cover the following topics:

- Function types
- Anonymous functions
- Lambda expressions
- The implicit name of a single parameter in a lambda expression
- Higher-order functions
- The last lambda in an argument convention
- The Java **Single Abstract Method** (**SAM**) lambda interface
- Using Java methods with Java SAM on parameter
- Named parameters in function types
- Type aliases
- Inline functions
- Function references

Function types

Kotlin supports functional programming, and functions are first-class citizens in Kotlin. A first-class citizen in a given programming language is a term that describes an entity that supports all the operations generally available to other entities. These operations typically include being passed as an argument, returned from a function, and assigned to a variable. The sentence *a function is a first-class citizen in Kotlin* should then be understood as: *it is possible in Kotlin to pass functions as an argument, return them from functions, and assign them to variables*. While Kotlin is a statically typed language, there needs to be a function type defined to allow these operations. In Kotlin, the notation used to define a function type is the following:

```
(types of parameters)->return type
```

Here are some examples:

- `(Int)->Int`: A function that takes `Int` as an argument and returns `Int`
- `()->Int`: A function that takes no arguments and returns `Int`
- `(Int)->Unit`: A function that takes `Int` and does not return anything (only `Unit`, which does not need to be returned)

Here are some examples of properties that can hold functions:

```
lateinit var a: (Int) -> Int
lateinit var b: ()->Int
lateinit var c: (String)->Unit
```

The term *function type* is most often defined as the type of a variable or parameter to which a function can be assigned, or the argument or result type of a higher-order function taking or returning a function. In Kotlin, the function type can be treated like an interface.

We will see later in this chapter that Kotlin functions can take other functions in arguments, or even return them:

```
fun addCache(function: (Int) -> Int): (Int) -> Int {
    // code
}

val fibonacciNumber: (Int)->Int = // function implementation
val fibonacciNumberWithCache = addCache(fibonacciNumber)
```

If a function can take or return a function, then the function type also needs to be able to define functions that take a function as an argument or return a function. This is done by simply placing a function type notation as a parameter or a return type. Here are some examples:

- `(String)->(Int)->Int`: A function that takes `String` and returns a function that takes an `Int` type and returns `Int`.
- `(()->Int)->String`: A function that takes another function as an argument and returns `String` type. A function in an argument takes no arguments and returns `Int`.

Each property with a function type can be called like a function:

```
val i = a(10)
val j = b()
c("Some String")
```

Functions can not only be stored in variables, they can also be used as a generic. For example, we can keep functions in a list:

```
var todoList: List<() -> Unit> = // ...
for (task in todoList) task()
```

The preceding list can store functions with the `() -> Unit` signature.

What is function type under the hood?

Under the hood, function types are just a syntactic sugar for generic interfaces. Let's look at some examples:

- The `()->Unit` signature is an interface for `Function0<Unit>`. The expression is `Function0`, because it has zero parameters, and `Unit` because it is the return type.
- The `(Int)->Unit` signature is interface for `Function1<Int, Unit>`. The expression is `Function1` because it has one parameter.
- The `()->(Int, Int)->String` signature is an interface for `Function0<Function2<Int, Int, String>>`.

All of these interfaces have only one method, `invoke`, which is an operator. It allows an object to be used like a function:

```
val a: (Int) -> Unit = //...
a(10)         // 1
a.invoke(10) // 1
```

1. These two statements have the same meaning.

Function interfaces are not present in a standard library. They are synthetic compiler-generated types (they are generated during compilation). Because of this, there is no artificial limit to the number of function type arguments, and the standard library size does not increase.

Anonymous functions

One way of defining a function as an object is by using **anonymous functions**. They work the same way as normal functions, but they have no name between the `fun` keyword and the parameter declaration, so by default they are treated as objects. Here are a few examples:

```
val a: (Int) -> Int = fun(i: Int) = i * 2 // 1
val b: ()->Int = fun(): Int { return 4 }
val c: (String)->Unit = fun(s: String){ println(s) }
```

1. This is an anonymous single-expression function. Note that, as in a normal single expression function, the return type does not need to be specified when it is inferred from the expression return type.

Consider the following usage:

```
// Usage
println(a(10))      // Prints: 20
println(b())        // Prints: 4
c("Kotlin rules")   // Prints: Kotlin rules
```

In the previous examples, function types were defined explicitly, but while Kotlin has a good type inference system, the function type can also be inferred from types defined by an anonymous default function:

```
var a = fun(i: Int) = i * 2
var b = fun(): Int { return 4 }
var c = fun(s: String){ println(s) }
```

It also works in the opposite way. When we define the type of a property, we don't need to set parameter types in anonymous functions explicitly, because they are inferred:

```
var a: (Int)->Int = fun(i) = i * 2
var c: (String)->Unit = fun(s){ println(s) }
```

If we check out the methods of function types, then we will see that there is only the `invoke` method inside. The `invoke` method is an operator function, and it can be used in the same way as function invocation. This is why the same result can be achieved by using the `invoke` call inside brackets:

```
println(a.invoke(4))          // Prints: 8
println(b.invoke())           // Prints: 4
c.invoke("Hello, World!")     // Prints: Hello, World!
```

This knowledge can be helpful, for example, when we are keeping function in a nullable variable. We can, for example, use the `invoke` method by using the safe call:

```
var a: ((Int) -> Int)? = null // 1
if (false) a = fun(i: Int) = i * 2
print(a?.invoke(4)) // Prints: null
```

1. Variable `a` is nullable; we are using `invoke` with a safe call.

Let's look at an Android example. We often want to define a single error handler that will include multiple logging methods and pass it to different objects as an argument. Here is how we can implement this using anonymous functions:

```
val TAG = "MainActivity"
val errorHandler = fun (error: Throwable) {
    if(BuildConfig.DEBUG) {
        Log.e(TAG, error.message, error)
    }
    toast(error.message)
    // Other methods, like: Crashlytics.logException(error)
}

// Usage in project
val adController = AdController(errorHandler)
val presenter = MainPresenter(errorHandler)

// Usage
val error = Error("ExampleError")
errorHandler(error) // Logs: MainActivity: ExampleError
```

Anonymous functions are simple and useful. They are a simple way of defining functions that can be used and passed as objects. But there is a simpler way of achieving similar behavior,with lambda expressions.

Lambda expressions

The simplest way to define anonymous functions in Kotlin is by using a feature called lambda expressions. They are similar to Java 8 lambda expressions, but the biggest difference is that Kotlin lambdas are actually closures, so they allow us to change variables from the creation context. This is not allowed in Java 8 lambdas. We will discuss this difference later in this section. Let's start with some simple examples. Lambda expressions in Kotlin have the following notation:

```
{ arguments -> function body }
```

Instead of `return`, the result of the last expression is returned. Here are some simple lambda expression examples:

- `{ 1 }`: A lambda expression that takes no arguments and returns 1. Its type is `()->Int`.
- `{ s: String -> println(s) }`: A lambda expression that takes one argument of type `String`, and prints it. It returns `Unit`. Its type is `(String)->Unit`.
- `{ a: Int, b: Int -> a + b }`: A lambda expression that takes two `Int` arguments and returns the sum of them. Its type is `(Int, Int)->Int`.

The functions we defined in the previous chapter can be defined using lambda expressions:

```
var a: (Int) -> Int = { i: Int -> i * 2 }
var b: ()->Int = { 4 }
var c: (String)->Unit = { s: String -> println(s) }
```

While the returned value is taken from the last statement in lambda expressions, `return` is not allowed unless it has a `return` statement qualified by a label:

```
var a: (Int) -> Int = { i: Int -> return i * 2 }
// Error: Return is not allowed there
var l: (Int) -> Int = l@ { i: Int -> return@l i * 2 }
```

Lambda expressions can be multiline:

```
val printAndReturn = { i: Int, j: Int ->
    println("I calculate $i + $j")
```

```
        i + j // 1
    }
```

1. This is the last statement, so the result of this expression will be a returned value.

Multiple statements can also be defined in a single line when they are separated by semicolons:

```
val printAndReturn = {i: Int, j: Int -> println("I calculate $i + $j");
                      i + j }
```

A lambda expression does not need to only operate on values provided by arguments. Lambda expressions in Kotlin can use all properties and functions from the context where they are created:

```
val text = "Text"
var a: () -> Unit = { println(text) }
a() // Prints: Text
a() // Prints: Text
```

This is the biggest difference between Kotlin and Java 8 lambda usage. Both Java anonymous objects and Java 8 lambda expressions allow us to use fields from the context, but Java does not allow us to assign different values to these variables (Java variables used in lambda must be final):

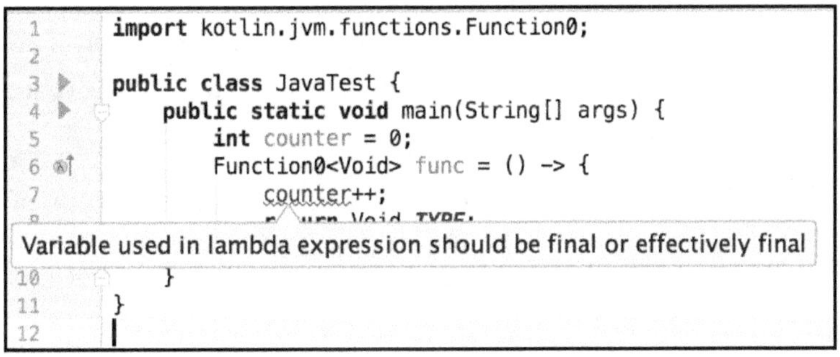

import kotlin.jvm.functions.Function0;
public class JavaTest {
public static void main(String[] args) {
int counter = 0;
Function0<Void> func = () -> {
counter++;
Variable used in lambda expression should be final or effectively final
}
}

Kotlin has gone a step further by allowing lambda expressions and anonymous functions to modify these variables. Lambda expressions that enclose local variables and allow us to change them inside the function body are called **closures**. Kotlin fully supports closure definition. To avoid confusion between lambdas and closures, in this book we will always call both of them lambdas. Let's look at an example:

```
var i = 1
val a: () -> Int = { ++i }
println (i)      // Prints: 1
println (a())    // Prints: 2
```

```
println (i)      // Prints: 2
println (a())    // Prints: 3
println (i)      // Prints: 3
```

Lambda expressions can use and modify variables from the local context. Here is an example of `counter`, where the value is kept in a local variable:

```
fun setUpCounter() {
    var value: Int = 0
    val showValue = { counterView.text = "$value" }
    counterIncView.setOnClickListener { value++; showValue() }
    // 1
    counterDecView.setOnClickListener { value--; showValue() }
    // 1
}
```

1. Here is how the View `onClickListener` can be set in Kotlin using a lambda expression. This will be described in the *Java SAM support in Kotlin* section.

Thanks to this feature, it is simpler to use lambda expressions. Note that, in the preceding example, the `showValue` type was not specified. This is because, in Kotlin lambdas, typing arguments is optional when the compiler can infer them from the context:

```
val a: (Int) -> Int = { i -> i * 2 }  // 1
val c: (String)->Unit = { s -> println(s) } // 2
```

1. The inferred type of `i` is `Int`, because the function type defines an `Int` parameter.
2. The inferred type of `s` is `String`, because the function type defines a `String` parameter.

As we can see in the following example, we don't need to specify the type of parameter because it is inferred from the type of the property. Type inference also works in another way. We can define the type of a lambda expression's parameter to infer the property type:

```
val b = { 4 }                          // 1
val c = { s: String -> println(s) }   // 2
val a = { i: Int -> i * 2 }           // 3
```

1. The inferred type is `()->Int`, because `4` is `Int` and there is no parameter type.
2. The inferred type is `(String)->Unit`, because the parameter is typed as `String`, and the return type of the `println` method is `Unit`.
3. The inferred type is `(Int)->Int`, because `i` is typed as `Int`, and the return type of the times operation from `Int` is also `Int`.

This inference simplifies lambda expression definition. Often, when we are defining lambda expressions as function parameters, we don't need to specify parameter types each time. But there is also another benefit--while the parameter type can be inferred, a simpler notation for single-parameter lambda expressions can be used. Let's discuss this in the next section.

The implicit name of a single parameter

We can omit lambda parameter definitions and access parameters using the `it` keyword when two conditions are met:

- There is only one parameter
- Parameter type can be inferred from the context

As an example, let's define the properties `a` and `c` again, but this time using the implicit name of a single parameter:

```
val a: (Int) -> Int = { it * 2 }            // 1
val c: (String)->Unit = { println(it) }  // 2
```

1. The same as `{ i -> i * 2 }`.
2. The same as `{ s -> println(s) }`.

This notation is really popular in Kotlin, mostly because it is shorter and it allows us to avoid parameter type specification. It also improves the readability of processing defined in LINQ style. This style needs components that have not yet been introduced, but just to demonstrate the idea, let's look at an example:

```
strings.filter { it.length = 5 }.map { it.toUpperCase() }
```

Supposing that `strings` is `List<String>`, this expression filters strings with a length equal to `5` and converts them to uppercase.

Note that in the body of lambda expressions, we can use methods of the `String` class. This is because function type (such as `(String)->Boolean` for the `filter`) is inferred from the method definition, which infers `String` from the iterable type (`List<String>`). Also, the type of the returned list (`List<String>`) depends on what is returned by the lambda (`String`).

LINQ style is popular in functional languages because it makes the syntax of collections or string processing really simple and concise. It will be discussed in much more detail in `Chapter 7`, *Extension Functions and Properties*.

Higher-order functions

A higher-order function is a function that takes at least one function as an argument, or returns a function as its result. It is fully supported in Kotlin, as functions are first-class citizens. Let's look at it in an example. Let's suppose that we need two functions: a function that will add all `BigDecimal` numbers from a list, and a function that will get the product (the result of multiplication between all the elements in this list) of all these numbers:

```
fun sum(numbers: List<BigDecimal>): BigDecimal {
    var sum = BigDecimal.ZERO
    for (num in numbers) {
        sum += num
    }
    return sum
}

fun prod(numbers: List<BigDecimal>): BigDecimal {
    var prod = BigDecimal.ONE
    for (num in numbers) {
        prod *= num
    }
    return prod
}

// Usage
val numbers = listOf(
    BigDecimal.TEN,
    BigDecimal.ONE,
    BigDecimal.valueOf(2)
)
print(numbers)          //[10, 1, 2]
println(prod(numbers))  // 20
println(sum(numbers))   // 13
```

These are readable functions, but these functions are also nearly the same. The only difference is name, accumulator (`BigDecimal.ZERO` or `BigDecimal.ONE`), and operation. If we use the **DRY (Don't Repeat Yourself)** rule, then we shouldn't leave two pieces of similar code in the project. While it is easy to define a function that will have similar behavior and just differ in the objects used, it is harder to define a function that will differ in the operation performed (here, functions differ by the operation used to accumulate). The solution comes with the function type, because we can pass the operation as an argument. In this example, it is possible to extract the common method this way:

```
fun sum(numbers: List<BigDecimal>) =
    fold(numbers, BigDecimal.ZERO) { acc, num -> acc + num }
```

```
fun prod(numbers: List<BigDecimal>) =
   fold(numbers, BigDecimal.ONE) { acc, num -> acc * num }

private fun fold(
    numbers: List<BigDecimal>,
    start: BigDecimal,
    accumulator: (BigDecimal, BigDecimal) -> BigDecimal
): BigDecimal {
    var acc = start
    for (num in numbers) {
        acc = accumulator(acc, num)
    }
    return acc
}

// Usage

fun BD(i: Long) = BigDecimal.valueOf(i)
val numbers = listOf(BD(1), BD(2), BD(3), BD(4))
println(sum(numbers))   // Prints: 10
println(prod(numbers))  // Prints: 24
```

The `fold` function iterates through numbers and updates `acc` using each element. Note that the function parameter is defined like any other type, and it can be used like any other function. For example, we can have the `vararg` function type parameter:

```
fun longOperation(vararg observers: ()->Unit) {
    //...
    for(o in observers) o()
}
```

In `longOperation`, `for` is used to iterate over all the observers and invokes them one after another. This function allows multiple functions to be provided as arguments. Here's an example:

```
longOperation({ notifyMainView() }, { notifyFooterView() })
```

Functions in Kotlin can also return functions. For example, we can define a function that will create custom error handlers with the same error logging but different tags:

```
fun makeErrorHandler(tag: String) = fun (error: Throwable) {
    if(BuildConfig.DEBUG) Log.e(tag, error.message, error)
    toast(error.message)
    // Other methods, like: Crashlytics.logException(error)
}

// Usage in project
val adController = AdController(makeErrorHandler("Ad in MainActivity"))
```

```
    val presenter = MainPresenter(makeErrorHandler("MainPresenter"))

    // Usage
    val exampleHandler = makeErrorHandler("Example Handler")
    exampleHandler(Error("Some Error")) // Logs: Example Handler: Some
Error
```

The three most common cases when functions in arguments are used are:

- Providing operations to functions
- The Observer (Listener) pattern
- A callback after a threaded operation

Let's look at them in detail.

Providing operations to functions

As we saw in the previous section, sometimes we want to extract common functionality from functions, but they differ in an operation they use. In such situations, we can still extract this functionality, but we need to provide an argument with the operation that distinguishes them. This way, any common pattern can be extracted and reused. For example, we often only need elements of the list that match some predicate, such as when we only want to show elements that are active. Classically, this would be implemented like this:

```
var visibleTasks = emptyList<Task>()
for (task in tasks) {
    if (task.active)
    visibleTasks += task
}
```

While it is a common operation, we can extract the functionality of only filtering some elements according to the predicate to separate the function and use it more easily:

```
fun <T> filter(list: List<T>, predicate: (T)->Boolean) {
    var visibleTasks = emptyList<T>()
    for (elem in list) {
        if (predicate(elem))
            visibleTasks += elem
    }
}

var visibleTasks = filter(tasks, { it.active })
```

This method of using higher-order functions is very important and it will be described a number of times throughout the book, but this is not the only way that higher-order functions are used.

Observer (Listener) pattern

We use the Observer (Listener) pattern when we want to perform operations when an event occurs. In Android development, observers are often set to view elements. Common examples are on-click listeners, on-touch listeners, or text watchers. In Kotlin, we can set listeners with no boilerplate. For example, setting listener on button click looks as follows:

```
button.setOnClickListener({ someOperation() })
```

Note that the `setOnClickListener` is a Java method from the Android library. Later, we will see in detail why we can use it with lambda expressions. The creation of listeners is very simple. Here is an example:

```
var listeners: List<()->Unit> = emptyList() // 1
fun addListener(listener: ()->Unit) {
    listeners += listener // 2
}

fun invokeListeners() {
    for( listener in listeners) listener() // 3
}
```

1. Here, we create an empty list to hold all listeners.
2. We can simply add a listener to the listeners list.
3. We can iterate through the listeners and invoke them one after another.

It is hard to imagine a simpler implementation of this pattern. There is another common use case where parameters with function types are commonly used; a callback after a threaded operation.

A callback after a threaded operation

If we need to do a long operation, and we don't want to make the user wait for it, then we have to start it in another thread. To be able to use a callback after a long operation called in a separate thread, we need to pass it as an argument. Here's an example function:

```
fun longOperationAsync(longOperation: ()->Unit, callback: ()->Unit) {
      Thread({ // 1
```

```
        longOperation() // 2
        callback() // 3
    }).start() // 4
}

// Usage
longOperationAsync(
        longOperation = { Thread.sleep(1000L) },
        callback = { print("After second") }
        // 5, Prints: After second
)
println("Now") // 6, Prints: Now
```

1. Here, we create `Thread`. We also pass a lambda expression that we would like to execute on the constructor argument.
2. Here, we are executing a long operation.
3. Here, we start the callback operation provided in the argument.
4. `start` is a method that starts the defined thread.
5. This is printed after a one-second delay.
6. This is printed immediately.

Actually, there are some popular alternatives to using callbacks, such as RxJava. Still, classic callbacks are in common use, and in Kotlin they can be implemented with no boilerplate.

These are the most common use cases where higher-order functions are used. All of them allow us to extract common behavior and decrease boilerplate. Kotlin allows a few more improvements regarding higher-order functions.

Combination of named arguments and lambda expressions

Using default named arguments and lambda expressions can be really useful in Android. Let's look at some practical Android examples. Let's suppose we have a function that downloads elements and shows them to the user. We will add a few parameters:

- `onStart`: This will be called before the network operation
- `onFinish`: This will be called after the network operation

```
fun getAndFillList(onStart: () -> Unit = {},
    onFinish: () -> Unit = {}){
        // code
    }
```

Then, we can show and hide the loading spinner in `onStart` and `onFinish`:

```
getAndFillList(
    onStart = { view.loadingProgress = true } ,
    onFinish = { view.loadingProgress = false }
)
```

If we start it from `swipeRefresh`, then we just need to hide it when it finishes:

```
getAndFillList(onFinish = { view.swipeRefresh.isRefreshing =
   false })
```

If we want to make a quiet refresh, then we just call this:

```
getAndFillList()
```

Named argument syntax and lambda expressions are a perfect match for multi-purpose functions. This connects both the ability to choose the arguments we want to implement and the operations that should be implemented. If a function contains more than one function type parameter, then in most cases it should be used by named argument syntax. This is because lambda expressions are rarely self-explanatory when more than one are used as arguments.

The last lambda in an argument convention

In Kotlin, higher-order functions are really important, and so it is also important to make their usage as easy as possible. This is why Kotlin introduced a special convention that makes higher-order functions simpler and clearer. It works this way: if the last parameter is a function, then we can define a lambda expression outside of the brackets. Let's see how it looks if we use it with the `longOperationAsync` function, which is defined as follows:

```
fun longOperationAsync(a: Int, callback: ()->Unit) {
    // ...
}
```

The function type is in the last position in the arguments. This is why we can execute it this way:

```
longOperationAsync(10) {
    hideProgress()
}
```

Thanks to the last lambda in an argument convention, we can locate the lambda after the brackets. It looks as if it is outside the arguments.

As an example, let's see how the invocation of code in another thread can be done in Kotlin. The standard way of starting a new thread in Kotlin is by using the `thread` function from the Kotlin standard library. Its definition is as follows:

```
public fun thread(
    start: Boolean = true,
    isDaemon: Boolean = false,
    contextClassLoader: ClassLoader? = null,
    name: String? = null,
    priority: Int = -1,
    block: () -> Unit): Thread {
        // implementation
    }
```

As we can see, the `block` parameter, which takes operations that should be invoked asynchronously, is in the last position. All other parameters have a default argument defined. That is why we can use the `thread` function in this way:

```
thread { /* code */ }
```

The `thread` definition has lots of other arguments, and we can set them either by using named argument syntax or just by providing them one after another:

```
thread (name = "SomeThread") { /*...*/ }
thread (false, false) { /*...*/ }
```

The last lambda in an argument convention is syntactic sugar, but it makes it much easier to use higher-order functions. These are the two most common cases where this convention really makes a difference:

- Named code surrounding
- Processing data structures using LINQ style

Let's look at them closely.

Named code surrounding

Sometimes, we need to mark part of the code to be executed in a different way. The `thread` function is this kind of situation. We need some code to be executed asynchronously, so we surround it with brackets, starting from the `thread` function:

```
thread {
    operation1()
    operation2()
}
```

From the outside, it looks as if it is a part of code that is surrounded by a block named `thread`. Let's look at another example. Let's suppose that we want to log the execution time of a certain code block. As a helper, we will define the `addLogs` function, which will print logs together with the execution time. We will define it in the following way:

```
fun addLogs(tag: String, f: () -> Unit) {
    println("$tag started")
    val startTime = System.currentTimeMillis()
    f()
    val endTime = System.currentTimeMillis()
    println("$tag finished. It took " + (endTime - startTime))
}
```

The following is the usage of the function:

```
addLogs("Some operations") {
    // Operations we are measuring
}
```

Here's an example of its execution:

```
addLogs("Sleeper") {
    Thread.sleep(1000)
}
```

On executing the preceding code, the following output is presented:

```
Sleeper started
Sleeper finished. It took 1001
```

The exact number of printed milliseconds may differ a little bit.

This pattern is really useful in Kotlin projects because some patterns are connected to blocks of code. For example, it is common to check whether the version of the API is after Android 5.x Lollipop before the execution of features that need at least this version to work. To check this, we used the following condition:

```
if (Build.VERSION.SDK_INT >= Build.VERSION_CODES.LOLLIPOP) {
    // Operations
}
```

But in Kotlin, we can just extract the function in the following way:

```
fun ifSupportsLolipop(f:()->Unit) {
    if (Build.VERSION.SDK_INT >= Build.VERSION_CODES.LOLLIPOP)
    {
        f()
    }
}

//Usage
ifSupportsLollipop {
    // Operation
}
```

This is not only easy, but also it also reduces redundancy in the code. This is often referred to as very good practice. Also note that this convention allows us to define control structures that work in a similar way to standard ones. We can, for example, define a simple control structure that runs as long as the statement in the body does not return an error. Here is the definition and usage:

```
fun repeatUntilError(code: ()->Unit): Throwable {
    while (true) {
        try {
            code()
        } catch (t: Throwable) {
            return t
        }
    }
}

// Usage
val tooMuchAttemptsError = repeatUntilError {
    attemptLogin()
}
```

An additional advantage is that our custom data structure can return a value. The impressive part is that is doesn't need any extra language support, and we can define nearly any control structure we want.

Processing data structures using LINQ style

We've already mentioned that Kotlin allows LINQ-style processing. The last lambda in an argument convention is another component that aids its readability. For example, look at the following code:

```
strings.filter { it.length == 5 }.map { it.toUpperCase() }
```

It is more readable than notation that does not use the last lambda in an argument convention:

```
strings.({ s -> s.length == 5 }).map({ s -> s.toUpperCase() })
```

Again, this processing will be discussed in detail later, in `Chapter 7`, *Extension Functions and Properties*, but for now, we have learned about two features that improve its readability (the last lambda in an argument convention and the implicit name of a single parameter).

The last lambda in an argument convention is one of the Kotlin features that was introduced to improve the use of lambda expressions. There are more such improvements, and how they work together is important to make the use of higher-order functions simple, readable, and efficient.

Java SAM support in Kotlin

It is really easy to use higher-order functions in Kotlin. The problem is that we often need to interoperate with Java, which natively doesn't support it. It achieves substitution by using interfaces with only one method. This kind of interface is called a **Single Abstract Method** (**SAM**) or functional interface. The best example, of situation in which we need to set up a function this way is when we use `setOnClickListener` on a `View` element. In Java (until 8), there was no simpler way than by using an anonymous inner class:

```
//Java
button.setOnClickListener(new OnClickListener() {
    @Override public void onClick(View v) {
        // Operation
    }
});
```

In the preceding example, the `OnClickListener` method is the SAM, because it contains only a single method, `onClick`. While SAMs are very often used as a replacement for function definitions, Kotlin also generates a constructor for them that contains the function type as a parameter. It is called a SAM constructor. A SAM constructor allows us to create an instance of a Java SAM interface just by calling its name and passing a *function literal*. Here's an example:

```
button.setOnClickListener(OnClickListener {
    /* ... */
})
```

A *function literal* is an expression that defines an unnamed function. In Kotlin, there are two kinds of *function literal*:

1. Anonymous functions
2. Lambda expressions

Both Kotlin *function literals* have already been described:

```
val a = fun() {} // Anonymous function
val b = {} // Lambda expression
```

Even better, for each Java method that takes a SAM, the Kotlin compiler generates a version that instead takes a function as an argument. This is why we can set `OnClickListener` as follows:

```
button.setOnClickListener {
    // Operations
}
```

Remember that the Kotlin compiler generates SAM constructors and function methods only for Java SAMs. It does not generate SAM constructors for Kotlin interfaces with a single method. This is because the Kotlin community is pushing to use function types and not SAMs in Kotlin code. When a function is written in Kotlin and includes a SAM, then we cannot use it as in Java methods, with SAM on a parameter:

```
interface OnClick {
    fun call()
}

fun setOnClick(onClick: OnClick) {
    //...
}
```

```
setOnClick {  } // 1. Error
```

1. This does not work because the `setOnClick` function is written in Kotlin.

In Kotlin, interfaces shouldn't be used this way. The preferred way is to use function types instead of SAMs:

```
fun setOnClick(onClick: ()->Unit) {
    //...
}

setOnClick {  } // Works
```

The Kotlin compiler generates a SAM constructor for every SAM interface defined in Java. This interface only includes the function type that can substitute a SAM. Look at the following interface:

```
// Java, inside View class
public interface OnClickListener {
    void onClick(View v);
}
```

We can use it in Kotlin this way:

```
val onClick = View.OnClickListener { toast("Clicked") }
```

Or we can provide it as a function argument:

```
fun addOnClickListener(d: View.OnClickListener) {}
addOnClickListener( View.OnClickListener { v -> println(v) })
```

Here are more examples of the Java SAM lambda interface and methods from Android:

```
view.setOnLongClickListener { /* ... */; true }
view.onFocusChange { view, b -> /* ... */ }

val callback = Runnable { /* ... */ }
view.postDelayed(callback, 1000)
view.removeCallbacks(callback)
```

And here's some examples from RxJava:

```
observable.doOnNext { /* ... */ }
observable.doOnEach { /* ... */ }
```

Now, let's look at how a Kotlin alternative to SAM definition can be implemented.

Named Kotlin function types

Kotlin does not support SAM conversions of types defined in Kotlin, because the preferred way is to use function types instead. But SAM has some advantages over classic function types: named function types and named parameters. It is good to have the function type named when its definition is long or it is passed multiple times as an argument. It is also good to have named parameters when it is not clear what each parameter means just by its type.

In the upcoming sections, we are going to see that it is possible to name both the parameters and the whole definition of a function type. This can be done with type aliases and named parameters in the function type. This way, it is possible to have all the advantages of SAM while sticking with function types.

Named parameters in function types

Until now, we've only seen definitions of function types where only the types were specified, but not parameter names. Parameter names have been specified in *function literals*:

```
fun setOnItemClickListener(listener: (Int, View, View)->Unit) {
    // code
}
setOnItemClickListener { position, view, parent -> /* ... */ }
```

The problem comes when the parameters are not self-explanatory, and the developer does not know what the parameters mean. With SAMs there were suggestions, while in the function type defined in the previous example, they are not really helpful:

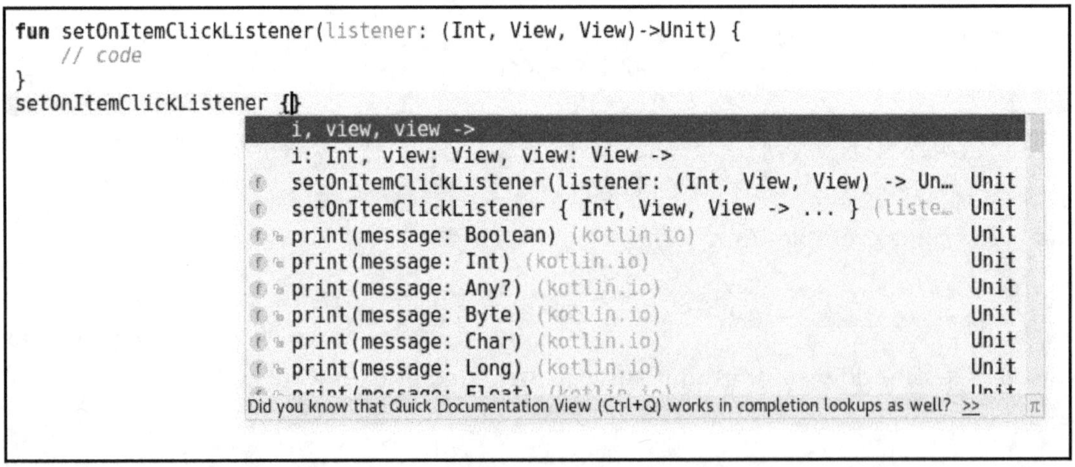
fun setOnItemClickListener(listener: (Int, View, View)->Unit) {
// code
}
setOnItemClickListener {}
i, view, view ->
i: Int, view: View, view: View ->
setOnItemClickListener(listener: (Int, View, View) -> Un... Unit
setOnItemClickListener { Int, View, View -> ... } (liste... Unit
print(message: Boolean) (kotlin.io) Unit
print(message: Int) (kotlin.io) Unit
print(message: Any?) (kotlin.io) Unit
print(message: Byte) (kotlin.io) Unit
print(message: Char) (kotlin.io) Unit
print(message: Long) (kotlin.io) Unit
Did you know that Quick Documentation View (Ctrl+Q) works in completion lookups as well? >>

The solution is to define function types with named parameters. Here is what this looks like:

```
(position: Int, view: View, parent: View)->Unit
```

The benefit of this notation is that the IDE suggests these names as the names of the parameters in the *function literal*. Because of this, the programmer can avoid any confusion:

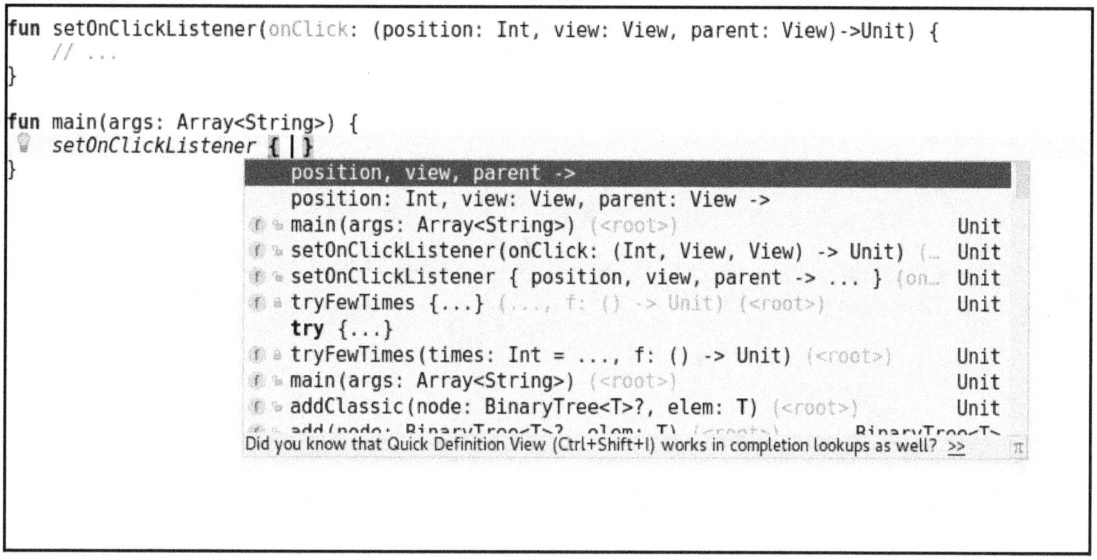
fun setOnClickListener(onClick: (position: Int, view: View, parent: View)->Unit) {
// ...
}
fun main(args: Array<String>) {
setOnClickListener { | }
}
position, view, parent ->
position: Int, view: View, parent: View ->
main(args: Array<String>) (<root>) Unit
setOnClickListener(onClick: (Int, View, View) -> Unit) Unit
setOnClickListener { position, view, parent -> ... } Unit
tryFewTimes {...} (..., f: () -> Unit) (<root>) Unit
try {...}
tryFewTimes(times: Int = ..., f: () -> Unit) (<root>) Unit
main(args: Array<String>) (<root>) Unit
addClassic(node: BinaryTree<T>?, elem: T) (<root>) Unit
Did you know that Quick Definition View (Ctrl+Shift+I) works in completion lookups as well? >>

The problem occurs when the same function type is used multiple times, then it is not easy to define those parameters for each definition. In that situation, a different Kotlin feature is used--one we describe in the next section, *type alias*.

Type alias

Since version 1.1, Kotlin has had a feature called **type alias**, which allows us to provide alternative names for existing types. Here is an example of a type alias definition where we have made a list of `Users`:

```
data class User(val name: String, val surname: String)
typealias Users = List<User>
```

This way, we can add more meaningful names to existing data types:

```
typealias Weight = Double
typealias Length = Int
```

Type aliases must be declared at the top level. A visibility modifier can be applied to a type alias to adjust its scope, but they are public by default. This means that the type aliases defined previously can be used without any limitations:

```
val users: Users = listOf(
    User("Marcin", "Moskala"),
    User("Igor", "Wojda")
)

fun calculatePrice(length: Length) {
    // ...
}
calculatePrice(10)

val weight: Weight = 52.0
val length: Length = 34
```

Keep in mind that aliases are used to improve code readability, and the original types can still be used interchangably:

```
typealias Length = Int
var intLength: Int = 17
val length: Length = intLength
intLength = length
```

Another application of `typealias` is to shorten long generic types and give them more meaningful names. This improves code readability and consistency when the same type is used in multiple places in the code:

```
typealias Dictionary<V> = Map<String, V>
typealias Array2D<T> = Array<Array<T>>
```

Type aliases are often used to name function types:

```
typealias Action<T> = (T) -> Unit
typealias CustomHandler = (Int, String, Any) -> Unit
```

We can use them together with function type parameter names:

```
    typealias OnElementClicked = (position: Int, view: View, parent:
View)->Unit
```

And then we get parameter suggestions:

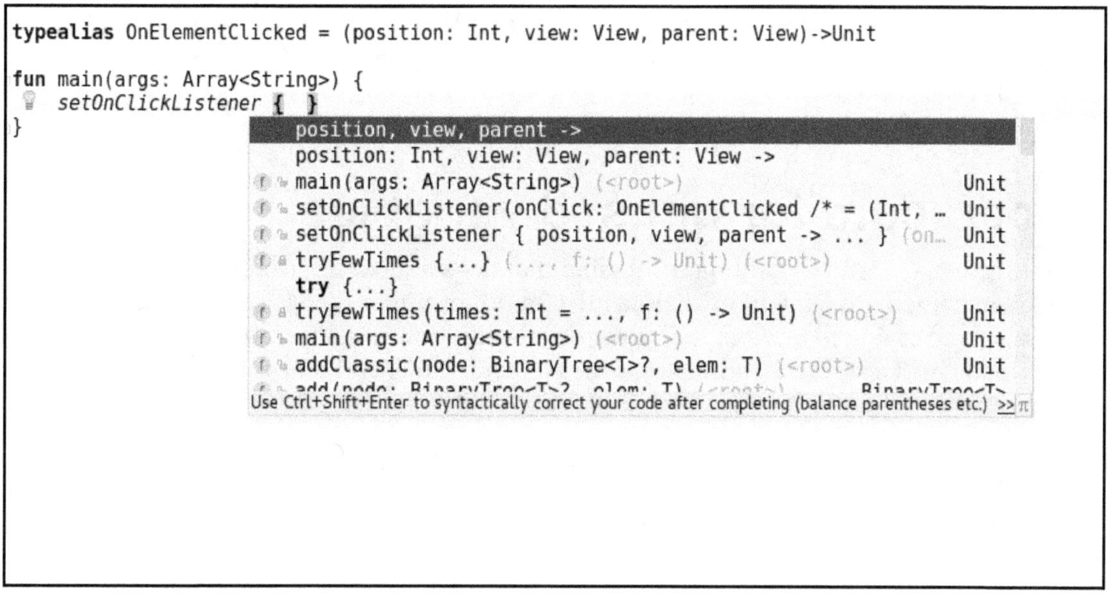
typealias OnElementClicked = (position: Int, view: View, parent: View)->Unit
fun main(args: Array<String>) {
setOnClickListener { }
}
position, view, parent ->
position: Int, view: View, parent: View ->
main(args: Array<String>) (<root>) Unit
setOnClickListener(onClick: OnElementClicked /* = (Int, ... Unit
setOnClickListener { position, view, parent -> ... } (on... Unit
tryFewTimes {...} (..., f: () -> Unit) (<root>) Unit
try {...}
tryFewTimes(times: Int = ..., f: () -> Unit) (<root>) Unit
main(args: Array<String>) (<root>) Unit
addClassic(node: BinaryTree<T>?, elem: T) (<root>) Unit
Use Ctrl+Shift+Enter to syntactically correct your code after completing (balance parentheses etc.) >>

Let's look at an example of how function types named by type alias can be implemented by class. Parameter names from function types are also suggested as method parameter names in this example:

```
    typealias OnElementClicked = (position: Int, view: View, parent:
View)->Unit

    class MainActivity: Activity(), OnElementClicked {

        override fun invoke(position: Int, view: View, parent: View) {
            // code
        }
    }
```

These are the main reasons why we are using named function types:

- Names are often shorter and easier than whole function type definitions
- When we are passing functions, after changing their definitions, we don't have to change them everywhere if we are using type aliases
- It is easier to have defined parameter names when we use type aliases

These two features (named parameters in function types and type aliases) combined are the reasons why there is no need to define SAMs in Kotlin--all the advantages of SAMs over function types (a name and named parameters) can be achieved with named parameters in function type definitions and type aliases. This is another example of how Kotlin supports functional programming.

Underscore for unused variables

In some cases, we define a lambda expression that does not use all its parameters. When we leave them named, they might be distracting to a programmer who is reading the lambda expression and trying to understand its purpose. Let's look at the function that filters every second element. The second parameter is the element value, and it is unused in this example:

```
list.filterIndexed { index, value -> index % 2 == 0 }
```

To prevent a misunderstanding, there are some conventions used, such as ignoring the parameter names:

```
list.filterIndexed { index, ignored -> index % 2 == 0 }
```

Because these conventions were unclear and problematic, Kotlin introduced underscore notation, which is used as a replacement for the names of parameters that are not used:

```
list.filterIndexed { index, _ -> index % 2 == 0 }
```

This notation is suggested, and there is a warning displayed when a lambda expression parameter is unused:

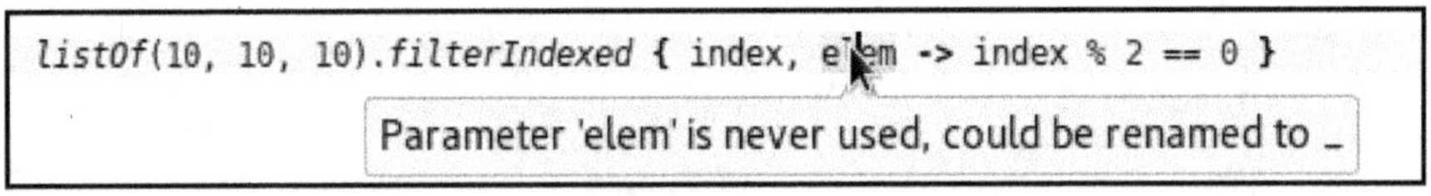
listOf(10, 10, 10).filterIndexed { index, elem -> index % 2 == 0 }
Parameter 'elem' is never used, could be renamed to _

Destructuring in lambda expressions

In `Chapter 4`, *Classes and Objects,* we saw how objects can be destructured into multiple properties using destructuring declarations:

```
data class User(val name: String, val surname: String, val phone: String)

val (name, surname, phone) = user
```

Since version 1.1, Kotlin can use destructuring declarations syntax for lambda parameters. To use them, you should use parentheses that include all the parameters that we want to destructure into:

```
val showUser: (User) -> Unit = { (name, surname, phone) ->
    println("$name $surname have phone number: $phone")
}

val user = User("Marcin", "Moskala", "+48 123 456 789")
showUser(user)
// Marcin Moskala have phone number: +48 123 456 789
```

Kotlin's destructing declaration is position-based, as opposed to the property name-based destructuring declaration that can be found, for example, in TypeScript. In position-based destructuring declarations, the order of properties decides which property is assigned to which variable. In property name-based destructuring, it is determined by the names of variables:

```
//TypeScript
const obj = { first: 'Jane', last: 'Doe' };
const { last, first } = obj;
console.log(first); // Prints: Jane
console.log(last); // Prints: Doe
```

Both solutions have their pros and cons. Position-based destructing declarations are secure for renaming a property, but they are not safe for property reordering. Name-based destructuring declarations are safe for property reordering but are vulnerable for property renaming.

Destructuring declarations can be used multiple times in a single lambda expression, and they can be used together with normal parameters:

```
val f1: (Pair<Int, String>)->Unit = { (first, second) ->
    /* code */ } // 1
val f2: (Int, Pair<Int, String>)->Unit = { index, (f, s)->
    /* code */ } // 2
val f3: (Pair<Int, String>, User) ->Unit = { (f, s), (name,
    surname, tel) ->/* code */ } // 3
```

1. The deconstruction of `Pair`.
2. The deconstruction of `Pair` and other element.
3. Multiple deconstructions in a single lambda expression.

Note that we can destructure a class into less than all its components:

```
val f: (User)->Unit = { (name, surname) -> /* code */ }
```

Underscore notation is allowed in destructuring declarations. It is most often used to get to further components:

```
val f: (User)->Unit = { (name, _, phone) -> /* code */ }
val third: (List<Int>)->Int = { (_, _, third) -> third }
```

It is possible to specify the type of the destructured parameter:

```
val f = { (name, surname): User -> /* code */ } //1
```

1. The type is inferred from the lambda expression.

Also, parameters can be defined by a destructuring declaration:

```
val f = { (name: String, surname: String): User ->
   /* code */}// 1
val f: (User)->Unit = { (name, surname) ->
  /* code */ } // 2
```

1. The type is inferred from the lambda expression.
2. The type cannot be inferred because there is not enough information about types inside the lambda expression.

This all makes destructuring in lambdas a really useful feature. Let's look at some of the most common use cases in Android where deconstruction in lambdas is used. It is used to process the elements of `Map` because they are of type `Map.Entry`, which can be destructured to the `key` and `value` parameters:

```
val map = mapOf(1 to 2, 2 to "A")
val text = map.map { (key, value) -> "$key: $value" }
println(text) // Prints: [1: 2, 2: A]
```

Similarly, lists of pairs can be destructed:

```
val listOfPairs = listOf(1 to 2, 2 to "A")
val text = listOfPairs.map { (first, second) ->
    "$first and $second" }
println(text) // Prints: [1 and 2, 2 and A]
```

Destructuring declarations are also used when we want to simplify data object processing:

```
fun setOnUserClickedListener(listener: (User)->Unit) {
    listView.setOnItemClickListener { _, _, position, _ ->
        listener(users[position])
    }
}

setOnUserClickedListener { (name, surname) ->
    toast("Clicked to $name $surname")
}
```

This is especially useful in libraries that are used to asynchronously process elements (such as RxJava). Their functions are designed to process single elements, and if we want multiple elements to be processed, then we need to pack them in `Pair`, `Triple`, or some other data class and use a destructuring declaration on each step:

```
getQuestionAndAnswer()
    .flatMap { (question, answer) ->
      view.showCorrectAnswerAnimationObservable(question, answer)
    }
    .subscribe( { (question, answer) -> /* code */ } )
```

Inline functions

Higher-order functions are very helpful and they can really improve the reusability of code. However, one of the biggest concerns about using them is efficiency. Lambda expressions are compiled to classes (often anonymous classes), and object creation in Java is a heavy operation. We can still use higher-order functions in an effective way, while keeping all the benefits, by making functions inline.

The concept of inline functions is pretty old, and it is mostly related to C++ or C. When a function is marked as inline, during code compilation the compiler will replace all the function calls with the actual body of the function. Also, lambda expressions provided as arguments are replaced with their actual body. They will not be treated as functions, but as actual code. This makes bytecode longer, but runtime execution is much more efficient. Later, we will see that nearly all higher-order functions from the standard library are marked as inline. Let's look at the example. Suppose we marked the `printExecutionTime` function with the `inline` modifier:

```
inline fun printExecutionTime(f: () -> Unit) {
    val startTime = System.currentTimeMillis()
    f()
    val endTime = System.currentTimeMillis()
    println("It took " + (endTime - startTime))
}

fun measureOperation() {
    printExecutionTime {
        longOperation()
    }
}
```

When we compile and decompile the `measureOperation`, we are going to find out that the function call is replaced with its actual body, and the parameter function call is replaced by the lambda expression's body:

```
fun measureOperation() {
    val startTime = System.currentTimeMillis() // 1
    longOperation() // 2
    val endTime = System.currentTimeMillis()
    println("It took " + (endTime - startTime))
}
```

1. Code from `printExecutionTime` was added to `measureOperation` function body.
2. Code located inside the lambda was located on its call. If the function used it multiple times, then the code would replace each call.

> The body of `printExecutionTime` can still be found in the code. It was skipped to make the example more readable. It is kept in the code because it might be used after compilation, for example, if this code is added to a project as a library. What is more, this function will still work as inline when used by Kotlin.

While there is no need to create classes for lambda expressions, inline functions can speed up the execution of functions with function parameters. This difference is so important that it is recommended to use the inline modifier for all short functions with at least one function parameter. Unfortunately, using the inline modifier also has its bad sides. The first we've already mentioned: the bytecode produced is longer. This is because function calls are replaced by function bodies and because lambda calls inside this body are replaced with the body of the *function literal*. Also, inline functions cannot be recursive and they cannot use functions or classes that have a more restrictive visibility modifier than this lambda expression. For example, public inline functions cannot use private functions. The reason is that this could lead to the injection of code into functions that cannot use them. This would lead to a compilation error. To prevent this, Kotlin does not permit the use of elements with less restrictive modifiers than the lambda expression in which they are placed. Here's an example:

```
internal fun someFun() {}
inline fun inlineFun() {
    someFun() // ERROR
}
```

In fact, it is possible in Kotlin to use elements with more restrictive visibility in `inline` functions if we suppress this warning, but this is bad practice and it should never be used this way:

```
// Tester1.kt
fun main(args: Array<String>) { a() }

// Tester2.kt
inline fun a() { b() }
private fun b() { print("B") }
```

How is this possible? For the internal modifier it is simpler, because the internal modifier is public under the hood. For private functions, there is an additional `access$b` function created, which has `public` visibility and only invokes the `b` function:

```
public static final void access$b() { b(); }
```

This behavior is presented here just to explain why less restrictive modifiers can sometimes be used inside `inline` functions (these situations can be found in the Kotlin standard library in Kotlin 1.1). In the projects, we should design elements in such a way that there is no need to use such suppression.

Another problem is less intuitive. While no lambda has been created, we cannot pass parameters that are of the function type to another function. Here is an example:

```
fun boo(f: ()->Int) {
    //...
}

inline fun foo(f: () -> Int) {
    boo (f) // ERROR, 1
}
```

When a function is `inline`, then its function arguments cannot be passed to a function that is not inline.

This doesn't work because no `f` parameter has been created. It has just been defined to be replaced by the *function literal* body. This is why it cannot be passed to another function as an argument.

The simplest way to deal with it is by making the `boo` function inline as well. Then it will be OK. In most cases, we cannot make too many functions inline. Here are a few reasons why:

- The `inline` functions should be used for smaller functions. If we make `inline` function that use other `inline` functions, then it can lead to a large structure being generated after compilation. This is a problem both because of compilation time and because of the resulting code's size.
- While `inline` functions cannot use an element with visibility modifiers more strict than the one they have, it would be a problem if we would like to use them in libraries where as many functions as possible should be private to protect the API.

The simplest way to deal with this problem is by making function parameters that we want to pass to another function `noinline`.

The noinline modifier

The `noinline` modifier is for function type parameters. It makes a specific argument be treated as a normal function type parameter (its calls are not replaced with the *function literal* body). Let's look at a `noinline` example:

```
fun boo(f: ()->Unit) {
    //...
}
```

```
inline fun foo(before: ()->Unit, noinline f: () -> Unit) { // 1
    before() // 2
    boo (f) // 3
}
```

1. The `noinline` annotation modifier is before parameter `f`.
2. The `before` function will be replaced by the body of the lambda expression used as an argument.
3. `f` is `noinline` so it can be passed to the `boo` function.

Two main reasons to use the `noinline` modifier are as follows:

- When we need to pass a specific lambda to another function
- When we are calling the lambda intensively and we don't want to bloat the code too much

Note that when we make all function parameters the `noinline`, there will be almost no performance improvement from making the functions inline. While it is unlikely that using `inline` will be beneficial, the compiler will show a warning. This is why, in most cases, `noinline` is only used when there are multiple function parameters and we only apply it to some of them.

Non-local returns

Functions with function parameters might act similarly to native structures (such as loops). We've already seen the `ifSupportsLolipop` function and the `repeatUntilError` function. An even more common example is the `forEach` modifier. It is an alternative to the `for` control structure, and it calls a parameter function with each element one after another. This is how it could be implemented (there is a `forEach` modifier in the Kotlin standard library, but we will look at it later because it includes elements that have not yet been presented):

```
fun forEach(list: List<Int>, body: (Int) -> Unit) {
    for (i in list) body(i)
}

// Usage
val list = listOf(1, 2, 3, 4, 5)
forEach(list) { print(it) } // Prints: 12345
```

The big problem is that inside a `forEach` function defined this way, we cannot return from an outer function. For example, this is how we could implement the `maxBounded` function using a `for` loop:

```
fun maxBounded(list: List<Int>, upperBound: Int, lowerBound: Int):
Int {
    var currentMax = lowerBound
    for(i in list) {
        when {
            i > upperBound -> return upperBound
            i > currentMax -> currentMax = i
        }
    }
    return currentMax
}
```

If we want to treat `forEach` as an alternative to a `for` loop, then a similar possibility should be allowed there. The problem is that the same code, but with `forEach` used instead of a `for` loop, would not compile:

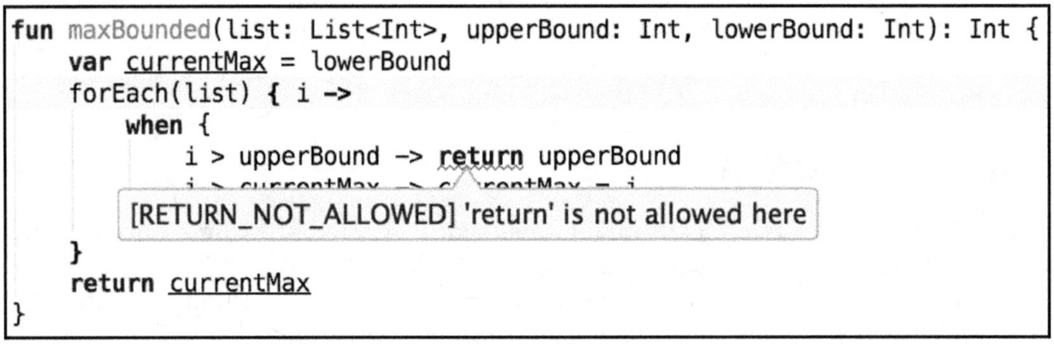
fun maxBounded(list: List<Int>, upperBound: Int, lowerBound: Int): Int {
var currentMax = lowerBound
forEach(list) { i ->
when {
i > upperBound -> return upperBound
[RETURN_NOT_ALLOWED] 'return' is not allowed here
}
return currentMax
}

The reason is related to how the code is compiled. We have already discussed that lambda expressions are compiled to a class of anonymous objects with a method that includes the defined code, and over there we cannot return from the `maxBounded` function because we are in a different context.

We encounter a situation where the `forEach` function is marked as `inline`. As we have already mentioned, the body of this function replaces its calls during compilation, and all of the functions from the parameters are replaced with their body. So, there is no problem with using the `return` modifier there. Then, if we make `forEach` inline, we can use `return` inside the lambda expression:

```
inline fun forEach(list: List<Int>, body: (Int)->Unit) {
    for(i in list) body(i)
}

fun maxBounded(list: List<Int>, upperBound: Int,
    lowerBound: Int): Int {
    var currentMax = lowerBound
    forEach(list) { i ->
        when {
            i > upperBound -> return upperBound
            i > currentMax -> currentMax = i
        }
    }
    return currentMax
}
```

This is how the `maxBounded` function has compiled in Kotlin, and the code looks like this (after some cleanup and simplification) when it is decompiled to Java:

```
public static final int maxBounded(@NotNull List list,
int upperBound, int lowerBound) {
    int currentMax = lowerBound;
    Iterator iter = list.iterator();
    while(iter.hasNext()) {
        int i = ((Number)iter.next()).intValue();
        if(i > upperBound) {
            return upperBound; // 1
        }

        if(i > currentMax) {
            currentMax = i;
        }
    }

    return currentMax;
}
```

In the preceding code, `return` is important--it was defined in the lambda expression, and it is returned from the `maxBounded` function.

The `return` modifier used inside the lambda expression of the `inline` function is called a non-local return.

Labeled returns in lambda expressions

Let's look at a case in which we need to return from a lambda expression and not from a function. We can do this using labels. Here is an example of a return from a lambda expression using labels:

```
inline fun <T> forEach(list: List<T>, body: (T) -> Unit) { // 1
    for (i in list) body(i)
}

fun printMessageButNotError(messages: List<String>) {
    forEach(messages) messageProcessor@ { // 2
        if (it == "ERROR") return@messageProcessor // 3
        print(it)
    }
}

// Usage
val list = listOf("A", "ERROR", "B", "ERROR", "C")
processMessageButNotError(list) // Prints: ABC
```

1. This is a generic implementation of the `forEach` function, where a list with any type can be processed.
2. We define a label for the lambda expression inside a `forEach` argument.
3. We return from a lambda expression specified by a label.

Another Kotlin feature is that lambda expressions that are defined as function arguments have a default label whose name is the same as the function in which they are defined. This label is called an **implicit label**. When we want to return from a lambda expression defined in a `forEach` function, we can do so just by using `return@forEach`. Let's look at an example:

```
inline fun <T> forEach(list: List<T>, body: (T) -> Unit) { // 1
    for (i in list) body(i)
}

fun processMessageButNotError(messages: List<String>) {
    forEach(messages) {
```

```
        if (it == "ERROR") return@forEach // 1
        process(it)
    }
}

// Usage
val list = listOf("A", "ERROR", "B", "ERROR", "C")
processMessageButNotError(list) // Prints: ABC
```

1. The implicit label name is taken from the function name.

Note that while the `forEach` function is inline, we can also use a non-local return to return from the `processMessageButNotError` function:

```
inline fun <T> forEach(list: List<T>, body: (T) -> Unit) {
    for (i in list) body(i)
}

fun processMessageButNotError(messages: List<String>) {
    forEach(messages) {
        if (it == "ERROR") return
        process(it)
    }
}

// Usage
val list = listOf("A", "ERROR", "B", "ERROR", "C")
processMessageButNotError(list) // Prints: A
```

Let's move on to a more complex example of using non-local return labels. Let's suppose that we have two `forEach` loops, one inside another. When we use an implicit label, it will return from the deeper loop. In our example, we can use it to skip the processing of the specific message:

```
inline fun <T> forEach(list: List<T>, body: (T) -> Unit) { // 1
    for (i in list) body(i)
}

fun processMessageButNotError(conversations: List<List<String>>) {
    forEach(conversations) { messages ->
        forEach(messages) {
            if (it == "ERROR") return@forEach // 1.
            process(it)
        }
    }
}
```

```
// Usage
val conversations = listOf(
    listOf("A", "ERROR", "B"),
    listOf("ERROR", "C"),
    listOf("D")
)
processMessageButNotError(conversations) // ABCD
```

1. This will return from the lambda defined in the `forEach` function that also takes messages as an argument.

We cannot return from another lambda expression in the same context using an implicit label, because it is shadowed by a deeper implicit label.

In these situations, we need to use a non-local implicit label return. It is only permissible with inline function parameters. In our example, while `forEach` is inline, we can return from a *function literal* this way:

```
inline fun <T> forEach(list: List<T>, body: (T) -> Unit) { // 1
    for (i in list) body(i)
}

fun processMessageButNotError(conversations: List<List<String>>) {
    forEach(conversations) conv@ { messages ->
        forEach(messages) {
            if (it == "ERROR") return@conv // 1.
            print(it)
        }
    }
}

// Usage
val conversations = listOf(
    listOf("A", "ERROR", "B"),
    listOf("ERROR", "C"),
    listOf("D")
)
processMessageButNotError(conversations) // AD
```

1. This will return from the lambda defined in `forEach` called on conversations.

We can also just use a non-local return (a return without any labels) to finish the processing:

```
inline fun <T> forEach(list: List<T>, body: (T) -> Unit) { // 1
    for (i in list) body(i)
}

fun processMessageButNotError(conversations: List<List<String>>) {
    forEach(conversations) { messages ->
        forEach(messages) {
            if (it == "ERROR") return // 1.
            process(it)
        }
    }
}
```

1. This will return from the `processMessageButNotError` function and finish the processing.

Crossinline modifier

Sometimes we need to use function type parameters from inline functions not directly in the function body, but in another execution context, such as a local object or a nested function. But standard function type parameters of inline functions are not allowed to be used this way because they allow non-local returns, which should not be allowed if this function could be used inside another execution context. To inform the compiler that non-local returns are not allowed, this parameter must be annotated as `crossinline`. Then it will act like a substitution that we are expecting in an `inline` function, even when it is used inside another lambda expression:

```
fun boo(f: () -> Unit) {
    //...
}

inline fun foo(crossinline f: () -> Unit) {
    boo { println("A"); f() }
}

fun main(args: Array<String>) {
    foo { println("B") }
}
```

This will be compiled as follows:

```
fun main(args: Array<String>) {
    boo { println("A"); println("B") }
}
```

While no property has been created with the function, it is not possible to pass the crossinline parameter to another function as an argument:

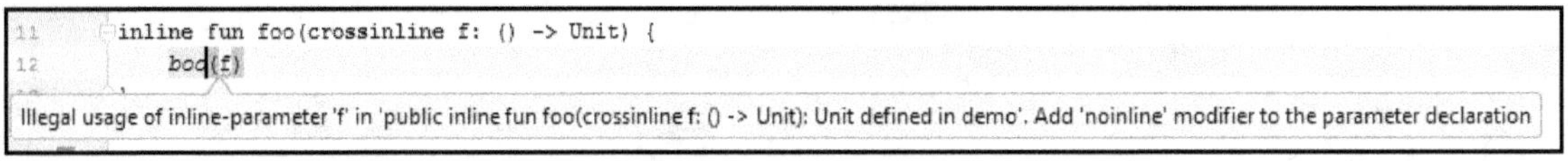

inline fun foo(crossinline f: () -> Unit) {
boo(f)
Illegal usage of inline-parameter 'f' in 'public inline fun foo(crossinline f: () -> Unit): Unit defined in demo'. Add 'noinline' modifier to the parameter declaration

Let's look at a practical example. In Android, we don't need `Context` to execute an operation on the main thread of the application because we can get a main loop using the `getMainLooper` static function from the `Looper` class. Therefore, we can write a top-level function that will allow a simple thread change into the main thread. To optimize it, we are first check whether the current thread is not the main thread. When it is, the action is just invoked. When it is not, we create a handler that operates on the main thread and a `post` operation to invoke it from there. To make the execution of this function faster, we are going to make the `runOnUiThread` function inline, but then to allow the action invocation from another thread, we need to make it `crossinline`. Here is an implementation of this described function:

```
inline fun runOnUiThread(crossinline action: () -> Unit) {
    val mainLooper = Looper.getMainLooper()
    if (Looper.myLooper() == mainLooper) {
        action()
    } else {
        Handler(mainLooper).post { action() } // 1
    }
}
```

1. We can run `action` inside a lambda expression thanks to the `crossinline` modifier.

The `crossinline` annotation is useful because it allows to use function types in the context of lambda expressions or local functions while maintaining the advantages of making the function `inline` (there's no need for lambda creation in this context).

Inline properties

Since Kotlin 1.1, the `inline` modifier can be used on properties that do not have a backing field. It can be either applied to separate accessors, which will result in their body replacing usage, or it can be used for a whole property, which will have the same result as making both accessors inline. Let's make an inline property that will be used to check and change an element's visibility. Here is an implementation where both accessors are inline:

```
var viewIsVisible: Boolean
inline get() = findViewById(R.id.view).visibility == View.VISIBLE
inline set(value) {
  findViewById(R.id.view).visibility = if (value) View.VISIBLE
  else View.GONE
}
```

We can achieve the same result if we annotate the whole property as inline:

```
inline var viewIsVisible: Boolean
get() = findViewById(R.id.view).visibility == View.VISIBLE
  set(value) {
    indViewById(R.id.view).visibility = if (value) View.VISIBLE
      else View.GONE
    }

// Usage
if (!viewIsVisible)
viewIsVisible = true
```

The preceding code can be compiled as follows:

```
if (!(findViewById(R.id.view).getVisibility() == View.VISIBLE))
{
  findViewById(R.id.view).setVisibility(true?View.VISIBLE:View.GONE);
}
```

This way, we have omitted the setter and getter function calls, and we should expect a performance improvement at the cost of increased compiled code size. Still, for most properties it should be profitable to use the `inline` modifier.

Function references

Sometimes, functions that we want to pass as an argument are already defined as a separate function. Then we can just define the lambda with its call:

```
fun isOdd(i: Int) = i % 2 == 1

list.filter { isOdd(it) }
```

But Kotlin also allows us to pass a function as a value. To be able to use a top-level function as a value, we need to use a function reference, which is used as a double colon and the function name (`::functionName`). Here is an example of how it can be used to provide a predicate to `filter`:

```
list.filter(::isOdd)
```

Here is an example:

```
fun greet(){
    print("Hello! ")
}

fun salute(){
    print("Have a nice day ")
}

val todoList: List<() -> Unit> = listOf(::greet, ::salute)

for (task in todoList) {
    task()
}

// Prints: Hello! Have a nice day
```

A function reference is example of reflection, and this is why the object returned by this operation also contains information about the referred function:

```
fun isOdd(i: Int) = i % 2 == 1

val annotations = ::isOdd.annotations
val parameters = ::isOdd.parameters
println(annotations.size) // Prints: 0
println(parameters.size) // Prints: 1
```

But this object also implements the function type, and it can be used this way:

```
val predicate: (Int)->Boolean = ::isOdd
```

It is also possible to reference to methods. To do this, we need to write the type name, two colons, and the method name (`Type::functionName`). Here is an example:

```
val isStringEmpty: (String)->Boolean = String::isEmpty

// Usage
val nonEmpty = listOf("A", "", "B", "")
.filter(String::isNotEmpty)
print(nonEmpty) // Prints: ["A", "B"]
```

As in the preceding example, when we are referencing a non-static method, there needs to be an instance of the class provided as an argument. The `isEmpty` function is a `String` method that takes no arguments. The reference to `isEmpty` has a `String` parameter that will be used as an object on which the function is invoked. The reference to the object is always located as the first parameter. Here is another example, where the method has the `food` already defined:

```
class User {

    fun wantToEat(food: Food): Boolean {
        // ...
    }
}

val func: (User, Food) -> Boolean = User::wantToEat
```

It is a different situation when we are referencing a Java static method, because it does not need an instance of the class on which it is defined. This is similar to methods of *objects* or *companion objects*, where the object is known in advance and does not need to be provided. In these situations, there is a function created with the same parameters as the referenced function and the same return type:

```
object MathHelpers {
    fun isEven(i: Int) = i % 2 == 0
}

class Math {
    companion object {
        fun isOdd(i: Int) = i % 2 == 1
    }
}

// Usage
val evenPredicate: (Int)->Boolean = MathHelpers::isEven
val oddPredicate: (Int)->Boolean = Math.Companion::isOdd
```

```
val numbers = 1..10
val even = numbers.filter(evenPredicate)
val odd = numbers.filter(oddPredicate)
println(even) // Prints: [2, 4, 6, 8, 10]
println(odd) // Prints: [1, 3, 5, 7, 9]
```

In function reference usage, there are common use cases where we want to use function references to provide method from a class we have a reference to. A common example is when we want to extract some operations as methods of the same class, or when we want to reference functions from reference member function of a class we have reference to. A simple example is when we define what should be done after a network operation. This is defined in a `Presenter` (such as `MainPresenter`), but it references all the View operations that are defined by the `view` property (which is, for example, of type `MainView`):

```
getUsers().smartSubscribe (
    onStart = { view.showProgress() }, // 1
    onNext = { user -> onUsersLoaded(user) }, // 2
    onError = { view.displayError(it) }, // 1
    onFinish = { view.hideProgress() } // 1
)
```

1. `showProgress`, `displayError`, and `hideProgress` are defined in `MainView`.
2. `onUsersLoaded` is a method defined in `MainPresenter`.

To help in this kind of situation, in Version 1.1 Kotlin introduced a feature called **bound references**, which provide references that are bound to a specific object. Thanks to that, this object does not need to be provided by an argument. Using this notation, we can replace the previous definition like this:

```
getUsers().smartSubscribe (
    onStart = view::showProgress,
    onNext = this::onUsersLoaded,
    onError = view::displayError,
    onFinish = view::hideProgress
)
```

Another function that we might want to reference is a constructor. An example use case is when we need to map from a **data transfer object** (**DTO**) to a class that is part of a model:

```
fun toUsers(usersDto: List<UserDto>) = usersDto.map { User(it) }
```

Here, `User` needs to have a constructor that defines how it is constructed from `UserDto`.

A DTO is an object that carries data between processes. It is used because classes used during communications between a system (in an API) are different than actual classes used inside the system (a model).

In Kotlin, constructors are used and treated similarly to functions. We can also reference them with a double colon and a class name:

```
val mapper: (UserDto)->User = ::User
```

This way, we can replace the lambda with a constructor call that has a constructor reference:

```
fun toUsers(usersDto: List<UserDto>) = usersDto.map(::User)
```

Using function references instead of lambda expressions gives us shorter and often more readable notation. It is also especially useful when we are passing multiple functions as parameters, or functions that are long and need to be extracted. In other cases, there is the useful bound reference, which provides a reference that is bound to a specific object.

Summary

In this chapter, we've discussed using functions as first-class citizens. We've seen how function types are used. We have seen how to define *function literals* (anonymous functions and lambda expressions), and that any function can be used as an object thanks to function references. We've also discussed higher-order functions and the different Kotlin features that support them: the implicit name of a single parameter, the last lambda in an argument convention, Java SAM support, using an underscore for unused variables, and destructuring declarations in lambda expressions. These features provide great support for higher-order functions, and they make functions even more than first-class citizens.

In the next chapter, we are going to see how generics work in Kotlin. This will allow us to define much more powerful classes and functions. We will also see how well they can be used when connected to higher-order functions.

6
Generics Are Your Friends

In the previous chapter, we discussed concepts related to functional programming and functions as first-class citizens in Kotlin.

In this chapter, we will discuss the concepts of generic types and generic functions, known as generics. We will learn why they exist and how to use them and also how to define generic classes, interfaces, and functions. We will discuss how to deal with generics at runtime, take a look at subtyping relations, and deal with generic nullability.

In this chapter, we will cover the following topics:

- Generic classes
- Generic interfaces
- Generic functions
- Generic constraints
- Generic nullability
- Variance
- Use-site target versus declaration-site target
- Declaration-site target
- Type erasure
- Reified and erased type parameters
- Star-projection syntax
- Variance

Generics

Generics is a programming style where classes, functions, data structures, or algorithms are written in such a way that the exact type can be specified later. In general, generics provide type safety together with the ability to reuse a particular code structure for various data types.

Generics are present in both Java and Kotlin. They work in a similar way, but Kotlin offers a few improvements over the Java generic type system, such as use-site variance, start-projection syntax, and reified type parameters. We will discuss them in this chapter.

The need for generics

Programmers often need a way to specify that a collection only contains elements of a particular type, such as `Int`, `Student`, or `Car`. Without generics, we would need to separate classes for each data type (`IntList`, `StudentList`, `CarList`, and so on). Those classes would have a very similar internal implementation, which would only differ in the stored data type. This means that we would need to write the same code (such as adding or removing an item from a collection) multiple times and maintain each class separately. This is a lot of work, so before generics were implemented, programmers usually operated on a universal list. This forced them to cast elements each time they were accessed:

```
// Java
ArrayList list = new ArrayList();
list.add(1);
list.add(2);
int first = (int) list.get(0);
int second = (int) list.get(1);
```

Casting adds boilerplate, and there is no type validation when an element is added to a collection. Generics are the solution for this problem, because a generic class defines and uses a placeholder instead of a real type. This placeholder is called a **type parameter**. Let's define our first generic class:

```
class SimpleList<T> // T is type parameter
```

The type parameter means that our class will use a certain type, but this type will be specified during class creation. This way, our `SimpleList` class can be instantiated for a variety of types. We can parametrize a generic class with various data types using *type arguments*. This allows us to create multiple data types from a single class:

```
 // Usage
var intList: SimpleList<Int>
```

```
var studentList: SimpleList<Student>
var carList:SimpleList<Car>
```

The `SimpleList` class is parametrized with *type arguments* (`Int`, `Student`, and `Car`) that define what kind of data can be stored in the given list.

Type parameters versus type arguments

Functions have parameters (variables declared inside a function declaration) and arguments (the actual value that is passed to a function). Similar terminology applies to generics. A *type parameter* is a blueprint or placeholder for a type declared in a generic, and a *type argument* is an actual type used to parametrize a generic.

We can use a *type parameter* in a method signature. This way, we can make sure that we will be able to add items of a certain type to our list and retrieve items of a certain type:

```
class SimpleList<T> {

    fun add(item:T) { // 1
        // code
    }
    fun get(intex: Int): T { // 2
        // code
    }
}
```

1. The generic type parameter `T` is used as the type for the item.
2. The type parameter is used as the return type.

The type of item that can be added to a list or retrieved from a list depends on the *type argument*. Let's see an example:

```
class Student(val name: String)
val studentList = SimpleList<Student>()
studentList.add(Student("Ted"))
println(studentList.getItemAt(0).name)
```

We can only add and get items of type `Student` from the list. The compiler will automatically perform all necessary type checks. It is guaranteed that the collection will only contain objects of a particular type. Passing an object of an incompatible type to the `add` method will result in a compile-time error:

```
var studentList: SimpleList<Student>
studentList.add(Student("Ted"))
studentList.add(true) // error
```

We cannot add a Boolean, because the expected type is `Student`.

> The Kotlin standard library defines various generic collections in the `kotlin.collections` package, such as `List`, `Set`, and `Map`. We will discuss them in `Chapter 7`, *Extension Functions and Properties*.

In Kotlin, generics are often used in combination with higher-order functions (discussed in `Chapter 5`, *Functions as First Class Citizens*) and extension functions (which we will discuss in `Chapter 7`, *Extension Functions and Properties*). Examples of such connections are the `map`, `filter`, and `takeUntil` functions. We can perform common operations that will differ in the details. For example, we can find matching elements in the collection using the `filter` function and specifying how matching elements will be detected:

```
val fruits = listOf("Babana", "Orange", "Apple", "Blueberry")
val bFruits = fruits.filter { it.startsWith("B") } //1
println(bFruits) // Prints: [Babana, Blueberry]
```

1. We can call the `startsWith` method because the collection can contain only `Strings`, so the lambda parameter (`it`) has the same type.

Generic constraints

By default, we can parametrize a generic class with any type of *type argument*. However, we can limit the possible types that can be used as *type arguments*. To limit the possible values of a *type argument*, we need to define a *type parameter bound*. The most common type of *constraint* is an *upper bound*. By default, all type parameters have `Any?` as an implicit *upper bound*. This is why both the following declarations are equivalent:

```
class SimpleList<T>
class SimpleList<T: Any?>
```

The preceding bounds mean that we can use any type we want as a *type argument* for our `SimpleList` class (including nullable types). This is possible because all nullable and non-nullable types are subtypes of `Any?`:

```
class SimpleList<T>
class Student
//usage

var intList = SimpleList<Int>()
var studentList = SimpleList<Student>()
var carList = SimpleList<Boolean>()
```

In some situations, we want to limit the data types that can be used as *type arguments*. To make it happen, we need to explicitly define a *type parameter* upper bound. Let's assume that we only want to be able to use numeric types as *type arguments* for our `SimpleList` class:

```
class SimpleList<T: Number>
//usage

var numberList = SimpleList<Number>()
var intList = SimpleList<Int>()
var doubleList = SimpleList<Double>()
var stringList = SimpleList<String>() //error
```

The `Number` class is an abstract class, that is, a superclass of Kotlin numeric types (`Byte`, `Short`, `Int`, `Long`, `Float`, and `Double`). We can use the `Number` class and all its subclasses (`Int`, `Double`, and so on) as a *type argument*, but we can't use the `String` class, because it's not a subclass of `Number`. Any attempt to add an incompatible type will be rejected by the IDE and compiler. Type parameters also incorporate Kotlin type system nullability.

Nullability

When we define a class with an unbounded type parameter, we can use both non-nullable and nullable types as *type arguments*. Occasionally, we need to make sure that a particular generic type will not be parametrized with nullable *type arguments*. To block the ability to use nullable types as *type arguments*, we need to explicitly define a non-nullable type parameter upper bound:

```
class Action (val name:String)
class ActionGroup<T : Action>

// non-nullable type parameter upper bound

var actionGroupA: ActionGroup<Action>
var actionGroupB: ActionGroup<Action?> // Error
```

Now we can't pass a nullable *type argument* (`Action?`) to the `ActionGroup` class.

Let's consider another example. Imagine that we want to retrieve the last `Action` in `ActionGroup`. A simple definition of the `last` method would look like this:

```
class ActionGroup<T : Action>(private val list: List<T>) {
    fun last(): T = list.last()
}
```

Let's analyze what will happen when we pass an empty list to the constructor:

```
val actionGroup = ActionGroup<Action>(listOf())

//...
val action = actionGroup.last
//error: NoSuchElementException: List is empty

println(action.name)
```

Our application crashes, because the `last` method throws an error when there is no element with such an index on the list. Instead of an exception, we might prefer a null value when the list is empty. The Kotlin standard library already has a corresponding method that will return a null value:

```
class ActionGroup<T : Action>(private val list: List<T>) {
    fun lastOrNull(): T = list.lastOrNull() //error
}
```

The code will not compile because there is a possibility that the last method will return null irrespective of *type argument* nullability (there may be no elements in the list to return). To solve this problem, we need to enforce a nullable return type by adding a question mark to the type parameter use-site (`T?`):

```
class ActionGroup<T : Action>(private val list: List<T>) { // 1
    fun lastOrNull(): T? = list.lastOrNull() // 2
}
```

1. The type parameter *declaration-site* (place in the code where the type parameter is declared).
2. The type parameter *use-site* (place in code where type parameter is used).

The `T?` parameter means that the `lastOrNull` method will always be nullable regardless of potential *type argument* nullability. Notice that we restored the type parameter `T` bound as the non-nullable `Action` type, because we want to store non-nullable types and deal with nullability only in certain scenarios (such as a non-existing last element). Let's use our updated `ActionGroup` class:

```
val actionGroup= ActionGroup<Action>(listOf())
```

```
val actionGroup = actionGroup.lastOrNull()
// Inferred type is Action?
println(actionGroup?.name) // Prints: null
```

Notice that the `actionGroup` inferred type is nullable even if we parameterized the generic with a non-nullable *type argument*.

A nullable type at the use-site does not stop us from allowing non-null types in the declaration-site:

```
open class Action
class ActionGroup<T : Action?>(private val list: List<T>) {
    fun lastOrNull(): T? = list.lastOrNull()
}

// Usage
val actionGroup = ActionGroup(listOf(Action(), null))
println(actionGroup.lastOrNull()) // Prints: null
```

Let's sum up the preceding solution. We specified a non-nullable bound for type parameter to disallow parameterizing the `ActionGroup` class with nullable types as *type arguments*. We parameterized the `ActionGroup` class with the non-nullable *type argument* `Action`. Finally, we enforced type parameter nullability at the use-site (`T?`) because the last property can return `null` if there are no elements in the list.

Variance

Subtyping is a popular concept in the OOP paradigm. We define inheritance between two classes by extending the class:

```
open class Animal(val name: String)
class Dog(name: String): Animal(name)
```

The `Dog` class extends the `Animal` class, so the `Dog` type is a subtype of `Animal`. This means that we can use an expression of type `Dog` whenever an expression of type `Animal` is required; for example, we can use it as a function argument or assign a variable of type `Dog` to a variable of type `Animal`:

```
fun present(animal: Animal) {
    println( "This is ${ animal. name } " )
}
present(Dog( "Pluto" )) // Prints: This is Pluto
```

Before we move on, we need to discuss the difference between class and type. Type is a more general term--it can be defined by class or interface, or it can be built into the language (primitive type). In Kotlin, for each class (for example, Dog), we have at least two possible types--non-nullable (Dog) and nullable (Dog?). What's more, for each generic class (for example, class Box<T>) we can define multiple data types (Box<Dog>, Box<Dog?>, Box<Animal>, Box<Box<Dog>>, and so on).

The previous example applies only to simple types. Variance specifies how subtyping between more complex types (for example, Box<Dog> and Box<Animal>) relates to subtyping between their components (for example, Animal and Dog).

In Kotlin, generics are *invariant* by default. This means that there is no subtyping relation between the Box<Dog> and Box<Animal> generic type. The Dog component is subtype of Animal, but Box<Dog> is neither a subtype nor a supertype of Box<Animal>:

```
class Box<T>
open class Animal
class Dog : Animal()

var animalBox = Box<Animal>()
var dogBox = Box<Dog>()

//one of the lines below line must be commented out,
//otherwise Android Studio will show only one error
animalBox = dogBox // 2, error
dogBox = animalBox // 1, error
```

1. Error type mismatch. Required Box<Animal>, found Box<Dog>.
2. Error type mismatch. Required Box<Dog>, found Box<Animal>.

The Box<Dog> type is neither a subtype nor a supertype of Box<Animal>, so we can't use any of the assignments shown in the preceding code.

We can define subtyping relations between Box<Dog> and Box<Animal>. In Kotlin, a subtyping relation of a generic type can be preserved (co-variant), reversed (contra-variant), or ignored (invariant).

When a subtyping relation is co-variant, it means that subtyping is preserved. The generic type will have the same relation as the *type arguments*. If Dog is a subtype of Animal, then Box<Dog> is a subtype of Box<Animal>.

Contra-variant is the exact opposite of co-variant, where subtyping is reversed. The generic type will have a reversed relationship with respect to *type arguments*. If `Dog` is a subtype of `Animal`, then `Box<Animal>` is a subtype of `Box<Dog>`. The following diagram presents all types of variance:

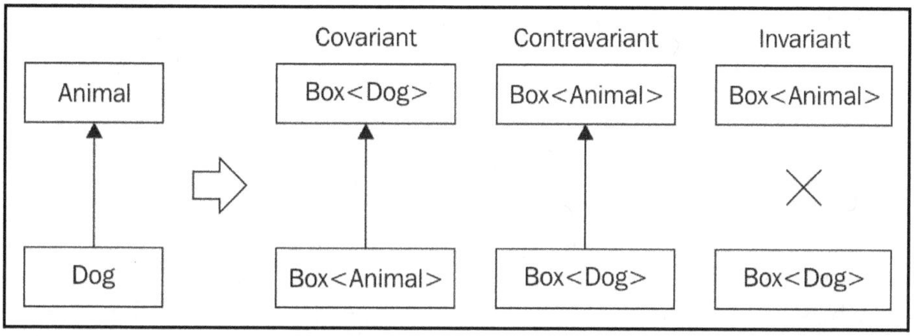

To define co-variant or contra-variant behavior, we need to use *variance modifiers*.

Variance modifiers

Generics in Kotlin are invariant by default. This means that we need to use the type as the type of declared variable or function parameter:

```
public class Box<T> { }
fun sum(list: Box<Number>) { /* ... */ }

// Usage
sum(Box<Any>()) // Error
sum(Box<Number>()) // Ok
sum(Box<Int>()) // Error
```

We can't use a generic type parametrized with `Int`, which is a subtype of `Number`, and `Any`, which is a supertype of `Number`. We can relax this restriction and change the default variance by using variance modifiers. In Java, there is the question mark (`?`) notation (wildcard notation) used to represent an unknown type. Using it, we can define two types of wildcard bounds--upper bound and lower bound. In Kotlin, we can achieve similar behavior using `in` and `out` modifiers.

In Java, the upper bound wildcard allows us to define a function that accepts any argument that is a certain type of its subtype. In the following example, the `sum` function will accept any `List` that was parametrized with the `Number` class or a subtype of the `Number` class (`Box<Integer>`, `Box<Double>`, and so on):

```
//Java
public void sum(Box<? extends Number> list) { /* ... */ }

// Usage
sum(new Box<Any>()) // Error
sum(new Box<Number>()) // Ok
sum(new Box<Int>()) // Ok
```

We can now pass `Box<Number>` to our `sum` function and all the subtypes, for example, `Box<Int>`. This Java behavior corresponds to the Kotlin `out` modifier. It represents covariance, which restricts the type to be a specific type or a subtype of that type. This means that we can safely pass instances of the `Box` class that are parametrized with any direct or indirect subclass of `Number`:

```
class Box<T>
fun sum(list: Box<out Number>) { /* ... */ }

//usage
sum(Box<Any>()) // Error
sum(Box<Number>()) // Ok
sum(Box<Int>()) // Ok
```

In Java, the lower bound wildcard allows us to define a function that accepts any argument that is a certain type or its supertype. In the following example, the `sum` function will accept any `List` that was parametrized with the `Number` class or a supertype of the `Number` class (`Box<Number>` and `Box<Object>`):

```
//Java
public void sum(Box<? super Number> list) { /* ... */ }

//usage
sum(new Box<Any>()) // Ok
sum(new Box<Number>()) // Ok
sum(new Box<Int>()) // Error
```

We can now pass `Box<Any>` to our `sum` function and all the subtypes, for example, `Box<Any>`. This Java behavior corresponds to the Kotlin `in` modifier. It represents contravariance, which restricts the type to be a specific type or a supertype of that type:

```
class Box<T>
fun sum(list: Box<in Number>) { /* ... */ }
```

```
//usage
sum(Box<Any>()) // Ok
sum(Box<Number>()) // Ok
sum(Box<Int>()) // Error
```

It's forbidden to use `in` and `out` modifiers together. We can define variance modifiers in two different ways. Let's look at them in the upcoming section.

Use-site variance versus declaration-site variance

Use-site variance and *declaration-site* variance basically describes the place in the code (site) where the variance modifier is specified. Let's consider a `View` and `Presenter` example:

```
interface BaseView
interface ProductView : BaseView
class Presenter<T>

// Usage
var preseter = Presenter<BaseView>()
var productPresenter = Presenter<ProductView>()
preseter = productPresenter

// Error: Type mismatch
// Required: Presenter<BaseView>
// Found: Presenter<ProductView>
```

The `Presenter` class is invariant on its `parameterT` type. To fix the problem, we can explicitly define the subtyping relationship. We can do it in two ways (use-site and declaration-site). First, let's define the variance at the use-site:

```
var preseter: Presenter<out BaseView> = Presenter<BaseView>() //1
var productPresenter = Presenter<ProductView>()
preseter = productPresenter
```

1. The variance modifier is defined at the type argument use-site.

Now the `preseter` variable can store subtypes of `Presenter<BaseView>`, including `Presenter<ProductView>`. Our solution works, but our implementation can be improved. There are two problems with this approach. Now we need to specify this `out` variance modifier each time we want to use a generic type, for example, use it in multiple variables across different classes:

```
//Variable declared inside class A and class B

var preseter = Presenter<BaseView>()
```

```
var preseter: Presenter<out BaseView> = Presenter<ProductView>()
preseter = productPresenter
```

Both classes A and B contain the preseter variable that has a variance modifier. We lose the ability to use type inference, and this results in the code being more verbose. To improve our code, we can specify a variance modifier at the type parameter declaration-site:

```
interface BaseView
interface ProductView: BaseView
class Presenter<out T> // 1

//usage
//Variable declared inside class A and B

var preseter = Presenter<BaseView>()
var productPresenter = Presenter<ProductView>()
preseter = productPresenter
```

1. The variance modifier is defined at the type parameter declaration-site.

We only need to define the variance modifier once inside Presenter class. In fact, both preceding implementations are equivalent, although *declaration-site* variance is more concise and can be more easily used by external clients of the class.

Collection variance

In Java, arrays are co-variant. By default, we can pass an array of String[] even if an array of Object[] is expected:

```
public class Computer {
    public Computer() {
        String[] stringArray = new String[]{"a", "b", "c"};
        printArray(stringArray); //Pass instance of String[]
    }

    void printArray(Object[] array) {
        //Define parameter of type Object[]
        System.out.print(array);
    }
}
```

This behavior was important in early versions of Java, because it allowed us to use different types of array as arguments:

```
// Java
static void print(Object[] array) {
    for (int i = 0; i <= array.length - 1; i++)
    System.out.print(array[i] + " ");
    System.out.println();
}

// Usage
String[] fruits = new String[] {"Pineapple","Apple", "Orange",
                                "Banana"};
print(fruits); // Prints: Pineapple Apple Orange Banana
Arrays.sort(fruits);
print(fruits); // Prints: Apple Banana Orange Pineapple
```

But this behavior also may lead to potential runtime errors:

```
public class Computer {
    public Computer() {
        Number[] numberArray = new Number[]{1, 2, 3};
        updateArray(numberArray);
    }
    void updateArray(Object[] array) {
        array[0] = "abc";
        // Error, java.lang.ArrayStoreException: java.lang.String
    }
}
```

The `updateArray` function accepts parameters of type `Object[]`, and we are passing `String[]`. We are calling the `add` method with a `String` parameter. We can do so because array items are of type `Object`, so we can use the `String`, which is a new value. Finally, we want to add `String` into the generic array that may only contain items of `String` type. Due to default co-variant behavior, the compiler can't detect this problem, and this will lead to an `ArrayStoreException` exception.

The corresponding code would not compile in Kotlin, because the Kotlin compiler treats this behavior as potentially dangerous. This is the reason why arrays in Kotlin are invariant.

```
public class Array<T> { /*...*/ }
```

Therefore, passing a type other than `Array<Number>` when `Array<Any>` is required will result in a compile-time error:

```
public class Array<T> { /*...*/ }
class Computer {
    init {
        val numberArray = arrayOf<Number>(1, 2, 3)
        updateArray(numberArray)
    }
    internal fun updateArray(array: Array<Any>) {
        array[0] = "abc"
        //error, java.lang.ArrayStoreException: java.lang.String
    }
}
```

Notice that a potential runtime exception may only occur when we can modify the object. Variance is also applied to Kotlin collection interfaces. In the Kotlin standard library, we have two list interfaces that are defined in different ways. The Kotlin `List` interface is defined as co-variant because it is immutable (it does not contain any methods that would allow us to change the inner state), while the Kotlin `MutableList` interface is invariant. Here are the definitions of their type parameters:

```
interface List<out E> : Collection<E> { /*...*/ }
public interface MutableList<E> : List<E>, MutableCollection<E> {
    /*...*/
}
```

Let's see the consequences of such definitions in action. It makes mutable lists safe from the risks of covariance:

```
fun addElement(mutableList: MutableList<Any>) {
    mutableList.add("Cat")
}

// Usage
val mutableIntList = mutableListOf(1, 2, 3, 4)
val mutableAnyList = mutableListOf<Any>(1, 'A')
addElement(mutableIntList) // Error: Type mismatch
addElement(mutableAnyList)
```

The list is safe because it has no methods used to change its inner state, and its covariance behavior allows more general usage of functions:

```
fun printElements(list: List<Any>) {
    for(e in list) print(e)
}
```

```
// Usage
val intList = listOf(1, 2, 3, 4)
val anyList = listOf<Any>(1, 'A')
printElements(intList) // Prints: 1234
printElements(anyList) // Prints: 1A
```

We can pass `List<Any>` or any of its subtypes to the `printElements` function because the `List` interface is co-variant. We can only pass `MutableList<Any>` to the `addElement` function because the `MutableList` interface is invariant.

Using `in` and `out` modifiers, we can manipulate variance behavior. We should also be aware that variance has some limitations. Let's discuss them.

Variance producer/consumer limitation

By applying a variance modifier, we gain co-variant/contra-variant behavior for a certain type parameter of the class/interface (declaration-site variance) or *type argument* (use-site variance). However, there is a limitation that we need to be aware of. To make it safe, the Kotlin compiler limits the positions where type parameters can be used.

With an invariant modifier (default no variance modifier on type parameter) we can use a type parameter on both the `in` (the type of function parameter) and `out` (the function return type) positions:

```
interface Stack<T> {
    fun push(t:T) // Generic type at in position
    fun pop():T // Generic type at out position
    fun swap(t:T):T // Generic type at in and out positions
    val last: T // Generic type at out position
    var special: T // Generic type at out position
}
```

With a variance modifier, we are only limited to a single position. This means that we can use a type parameter only as a type for method parameters (`in`) or the method return value (`out`). Our class can be a producer or consumer, but never both. We can say that the class *takes in parameters* or *gives out parameters.*

Let's look at how this restriction relates to variance modifiers specified at the declaration-site. Here are all the correct and incorrect usages of the type parameters `R` and `T`:

```
class ConsumerProducer<in T, out R> {
    fun consumeItemT(t: T): Unit { } // 1

    fun consumeItemR(r: R): Unit { } // 2, error
```

```
        fun produceItemT(): T { // 3, error
            // Return instance of type T
        }
        fun produceItemR(): R { // 4
            //Return instance of type R
        }
    }
```

1. OK, type parameter `T` is in the `in` position.
2. Error, type parameter `R` is in the `in` position.
3. Error, type parameter `T` is in the `out` position.
4. OK, type parameter `R` is in the `out` position.

As we can see, the compiler will report an error if the configuration is prohibited. Notice that we can add different modifiers for the type parameters `R` and `T`.

Position restriction applies only for methods accessible (visible) outside the class. This means not only all `public` methods (`public` is the default modifier) as used previously, but also methods marked with `protected` or `internal`. When we change method visibility to `private`, then we can use our type parameters (`R` and `T`) on any position, just like invariant type parameters:

```
class ConsumerProducer<in T, out R> {
    private fun consumeItemT(t: T): Unit { }
    private fun consumeItemR(r: R): Unit { }
    private fun produceItemT(): T {
        // Return instance of type T
    }
    private fun produceItemR(): R {
        //Return instance of type R
    }
}
```

Let's look at the following table, which presents all the allowed positions for type parameters used as a type:

Visibility modifier	Invariance	Covariance (out)	Contravariance (in)
`public`, `protected`, `internal`	in/out	out	in
`private`	in/out	in/out	in/out

Invariant constructor

There is one important exception for the `in` and `out` position rules described in the previous section: constructor parameters are always invariant:

```
class Producer<out T>(t: T)
// Usage
val stringProducer = Producer("A")
val anyProducer: Producer<Any> = stringProducer
```

The constructor is public, the type parameter `T` is declared as `out`, but we can still use it as a constructor parameter type at the `in` position. The reason is that a `constructor` method can't be called after an instance is created, so it is always safe to call it.

As we discussed in `Chapter 4`, *Classes and Objects*, we can also define a property directly in the class constructor using a `val` or `var` modifier. When covariance is specified, we can only define a read-only property (`val`) in the constructor that has the co-variant type. It is safe because only the getter will be generated, so the value of this property can't change after class instantiation:

```
class Producer<out T>(val t: T) // Ok, safe
```

With `var`, both the getter and setter are generated by the compiler, so the property value can potentially change at some point. That's why we can't declare a read-write (`var`) property of the co-variant type in the constructor:

```
class Producer<out T>(var t: T) // Error, not safe
```

We have already said that variance restriction only applies for external clients, so we could still define a co-variant read-write property by adding a private visibility modifier:

```
class Producer<out T>(private var t:T)
```

Another popular generic type restriction, known from Java, relates to type erasure.

Type erasure

Type erasure was introduced into JVM to make JVM bytecode backward compatible with versions that predate the introduction of generics. On the Android platform, both Kotlin and Java are compiled to JVM bytecode, so they both are vulnerable to *type erasure*.

Type erasure is the process of removing a *type argument* from a generic type so that the generic type loses some of its type information (*type argument*) at runtime:

```
package test
class Box<T>

val intBox = Box<Int>()
val stringBox = Box<String>()

println(intBox.javaClass) // prints: test.Box
println(stringBox.javaClass) // prints: test.Box
```

The compiler can distinguish between these types and guarantee type safety. However, during compilation, the parameterized types `Box<Int>` and `Box<String>` are translated by the compiler to a `Box` (raw type). The generated Java bytecode does not contain any information related to *type arguments*, so we can't distinguish betweengeneric types at runtime.

Type erasure leads to a few problems. In JVM, we can't declare two overloads of the same method with the same JVM signature:

```
/*
java.lang.ClassFormatError: Duplicate method name&signature...
*/
fun sum(ints: List<Int>) {
    println("Ints")
}

fun sum(strings: List<String>) {
    println("Ints")
}
```

When the *type argument* is removed, those two methods will have exactly the same declaration:

```
/*
java.lang.ClassFormatError: Duplicate method name&signature...
*/
fun sum(ints: List) {
    println("Ints")
}
fun sum(strings: List) {
    println("Ints")
}
```

We can also solve this problem by changing the JVM name of the generated function. We can do it using `JvmName` annotation to change the name of one of the methods when the code is compiled to JVM bytecode:

```
@JvmName("intSum") fun sum(ints: List<Int>) {
    println("Ints")
}
fun sum(strings: List<String>) {
    println("Ints")
}
```

Nothing changed in this function usage from Kotlin, but since we changed the JVM name of the first function, we need to use a new name to use it from Java:

```
// Java
TestKt.intSum(listOfInts);
```

Sometimes we want to preserve the *type argument* at runtime, and this is where `reified` *type parameters* are quite handy.

Reified type parameters

There are some cases where accessing the type parameter at runtime would be useful, but they are not allowed because of type erasure:

```
fun <T> typeCheck(s: Any) {
    if(s is T){
    // Error: cannot check for instance of erased type: T
        println("The same types")
    } else {
        println("Different types")
    }
}
```

To overcome JVM limitation, Kotlin allows us to use a special modifier that can preserve a *type argument* at runtime. We need to mark the type parameter with the `reified` modifier:

```
interface View
class ProfileView: View
class HomeView: View
inline fun <reified T> typeCheck(s: Any) { // 1
    if(s is T){
        println("The same types")
    } else {
    println("Different types")
    }
```

```
}
// Usage
typeCheck<ProfileView>(ProfileView()) // Prints: The same types
typeCheck<HomeView>(ProfileView()) // Prints: Different types
typeCheck<View>(ProfileView()) // Prints: The same types
```

1. Type parameter marked as refined and function marked as `inline`.

Now we can safely access the *type argument* type at runtime. Reified type parameters work only with inline functions, because during compilation (inlining), the Kotlin compiler replaces reified *type argument* class. This way, the *type argument* will not be removed by type erasure.

We can also use reflection on a `reified` type to retrieve more information about the type:

```
inline fun <reified T> isOpen(): Boolean {
    return T::class.isOpen
}
```

Occurrences of a reified type parameter are represented at the JVM bytecode level as an actual type or a wrapper type for primitive types. That's why reified type parameters are not affected by type erasure.

Using reified type parameters allows us to write methods in a whole new way. To start a new `Activity` in Java, we need code like this:

```
//Java
startActivity(Intent(this, ProductActivity::class.java))
```

In Kotlin, we can define the `startActivity` method, which will allow us to navigate to `Activity` in a much simpler way:

```
inline fun <reified T : Activity> startActivity(context: Context) {
    context.startActivity(Intent(context, T::class.java))
}

// Usage
startActivity<UserDetailsActivity>(context)
```

We defined the `startActivity` method and we passed information about the `Activity` we want to start (`ProductActivity`) by using a *type argument*. We also defined an explicit reified type parameter bound to make sure that we can only use `Activity` (and its subclasses) as the *type argument*.

The startActivity method

To make proper use of the `startActivity` method, we need a way to pass parameters to the `Activity` being started (`Bundle`). It is possible to update the preceding implementation to support arguments like this:

```
startActivity<ProductActivity>("id" to 123, "extended" to true)
```

In the preceding example, arguments are filled using a key and value provided by pairs (defined by the inline `to` function). This function implementation is, however, outside of the scope of this book. We can, however, use an existing one. The **Anko** library (`https://github.com/Kotlin/anko`) already implements the `startActivity` method with all the required functionality. We just need to import the `Appcompat-v7-commons` dependency:

```
compile "org.jetbrains.anko:anko-appcompat-v7-commons:$anko_version"
```

Anko defines extensions for the `Context` and `Fragment` classes so we can use this method in any `Activity` or `Fragment` just like any other method defined in the class, without the need to define the method in the class. We will discuss extensions in `Chapter 7`, *Extension Functions and Properties*.

Be aware that reified type parameters have one main limitation: we can't create an instance of a class from a reified type parameter (without using reflection). The reason behind this is that a constructor is always only associated with a concrete instance (it is never inherited), so there is no constructor that could be safely used for all possible type parameters.

Star-projections

Because of type erasure, incomplete type information is available at runtime. For example, type parameters of generic types are not available:

```
val list = listOf(1,2,3)
println(list.javaClass) // Prints: class java.util.Arrays$ArrayList
```

This leads to a few problems. We can't perform any checks to verify what types of element `List` contains:

```
/*
Compile time error: cannot check instance of erased type:
List<String>
*/
if(collection is List<Int>) {
    //...
```

```
}
```

The problem occurs because a check is performed at runtime where information about type parameters is not available. Kotlin, however, as opposed to Java, does not allow us to declare a raw type (a generic type that is not parametrized with a *type argument*):

```
SimpleList<> // Java: ok
SimpleList<> // Kotlin: error
```

Kotlin allows us to use *star-projection* syntax instead, which is basically a way to say that information about the *type argument* is missing or it is not important:

```
if(collection is List<*>) {
    //...
}
```

By using star-projection syntax, we say that `Box` stores arguments of a certain type:

```
class Box<T>

val anyBox = Box<Any>()
val intBox = Box<Int>()
val stringBox = Box<String>()
var unknownBox: Box<*>

unknownBox = anyBox // Ok
unknownBox = intBox // Ok
unknownBox = stringBox // Ok
```

Notice that there is a difference between `Box<*>` and `Box<Any>`. If we want to define a list that contains items of `Any` we would use `Box<Any>`. However, if we want to define a list that contains terms of a certain type, but this type is unknown (it may be `Any`, `Int`, `String`, and so on. But we don't have information about this type), while `Box<Any>` means that list contains items of the `Any` type. We will use `Box<*>`:

```
val anyBox: Box<Any> = Box<Int> // Error: Type mismatch
```

If a generic type is defined with multiple type parameters, we need to use a star (`*`) for each missing the *type argument*:

```
class Container<T, T2>
val container: Container<*, *>
```

Star-projection is also helpful when we want to perform an operation on the type, but information about *type argument* is not important:

```
fun printSize(list: MutableList<*>) {
    println(list.size)
}

//usage
val stringList = mutableListOf("5", "a", "2", "d")
val intList = mutableListOf(3, 7)
printSize(stringList) // prints: 4
printSize(intList) // prints: 2
```

In the preceding example, information about the *type argument* is not required to determine the collection size. Using star-projection syntax reduces the need for variance modifiers as long as we don't use any methods that depend on a *type argument*.

Type parameter naming convention

The official Java type parameter naming convention (`https://docs.oracle.com/javase/tutorial/java/generics/types.html`) defines the following guidelines for parameter naming:

"By convention, type parameter names are single, uppercase letters. This stands in sharp contrast to the variable naming conventions that you already know about, and with good reason. Without this convention, it would be difficult to tell the difference between a type variable and an ordinary class or interface name. The most commonly used type parameter names are:

- *E: Element (used extensively by the Java Collections Framework)*
- *K: Key*
- *N: Number*
- *T: Type*
- *V: Value*
- *S,U,V, and so on: 2nd, 3rd, 4th types"*

Many classes in the Kotlin standard library follow this convention. It works fine for popular kinds of classes such as common classes (`List`, `Mat`, `Set`, and so on) or classes that define a simple type parameter (the `Box<T>` class). However, with custom classes and multiple type parameters, we quickly realize that a single letter does not contain a sufficient amount of information and sometimes it's hard to quickly tell what kind of data the type parameter represents. There are a few solutions for this problem.

We could make sure that generics are properly documented and, yes, this would definitely help, but we still wouldn't be able to determine the meaning of a type parameter just by looking at the code. Documentation is important, but we should treat documentation as an auxiliary source of information and strive for the highest possible code readability.

Over the years, programmers have started to migrate to more meaningful naming conventions. The **Google Java Style Guide** (`https://google.github.io/styleguide/javaguide.html#s5.2.8-type-variable-names`) briefly describes a mix of the official Java type parameter naming convention and custom naming conventions. They promote two distinct styles. The first is to use a single capital letter, optionally followed by a single numeral (as opposed to the `S`, `U`, and `V` names described by Java):

```
class Box<T, T2>
```

The second style is more descriptive because it adds a meaningful prefix to the type parameter:

```
class Box<RequestT>
```

Unfortunately, there is no single standard for type parameter names. The most common solution is the use of a single uppercase letter. Those are simplified examples, but keep in mind that classes usually use generics in multiple places, so proper naming will improve your code readability.

Summary

In this chapter, we have learned why generics exist and we have discussed various ways of defining a generic class and interface, and declaring generic types. We know how to deal with subtyping relations by using use-site and declaration-site variance modifiers. We learned how to deal with type erasure and how to preserve generic types at runtime using reified type parameters.

In the next chapter, we will discuss one of the most exciting Kotlin features, extensions. This feature allows us to add new behavior to an existing class. We will learn how we can implement new methods and properties for any given class, including final classes from the Android framework and third-party libraries.

7
Extension Functions and Properties

In previous chapters, most of the concepts we covered were familiar to Java developers. In this chapter, we are introducing a feature that is not known in Java at all--extensions. It is one of the best Kotlin features, and lots of Kotlin developers mention it as their favorite one. Extensions provide big improvements in Android development.

In this chapter, we will cover the following topics:

- Extension functions
- Extension properties
- Member extension functions
- Generic extension functions
- Collection processing
- Function type with receiver and function literal with receiver
- Kotlin generic extension functions for any object
- Kotlin's domain-specific language

Extension functions

All big Java projects have utility classes, such as `StringUtils`, `ListUtils`, and `AndroidUtils`. They are so popular because util functions capture common patterns and allow them to be tested and used in a simple way. The problem is that Java really poorly supports the creation and usage of such functions because they have to be implemented as static functions of some class. Let's discuss this problem with an example. Every Java Android developer knows well following code which is used to show `Toast`:

```
Toast.makeText(context, text, Toast.LENGTH_SHORT).show();
```

It is commonly used in Android projects to show errors or short messages, and often it is presented at the beginning of most Android tutorials. Code that implements this functionality is verbose because it uses a static function that is used like a builder. Probably every Java Android developer has forgotten at least once to invoke the `show` method on a returned object, which made him check all the surrounding conditions to find out why it is not working. This all makes this simple functionality a perfect candidate to be packed as a `util` function. But it is really rarely used this way. Why? To understand it, let's first look at how it could be implemented in Java:

```
public class AndroidUtils {
    public static void toast(Context context, String text) {
        Toast.makeText(context, text, Toast.LENGTH_SHORT).show();
    }
}

// Usage
AndroidUtils.toast(context, "Some toast");
```

When a programmer wants to use the preceding function, they need to remember that there is such a function, where the class is localized and what its name is. Therefore, its usage is not simpler than it was previously. It is impossible to implement it as a method of `Context` (a superclass of `Activity`) without changing the Android SDK implementation, but in Kotlin, it is possible to create an extension function, which acts similarly to an actual method defined inside a class. Here is how we can implement `toast` as an extension to `Context`:

```
fun Context.toast(text: String) { // 1
    Toast.makeText(this, text, LENGTH_LONG).show() //2
}

// Usage
context.toast("Some toast")
```

1. `Context` is not in the argument list, but before the function name. This is how we define what type we are extending.
2. Inside the function body, we can use the `this` keyword to reference the object on which the extension function is invoked.

The only difference in the general structure between an extension function and a standard function is that there is a receiver type specified before the function name. A less visible change is inside the body--there, we can access the receiver object (the object on which an extension is called) with the `this` keyword, or directly call its functions or properties. With such a definition, the `toast` function acts like a method defined in `Context`:

```
context.toast("Some toast")

Alternatively:
class MainActivity :Activity() {
    override fun onCreate(savedInstanceState: Bundle?){
        super.onCreate(savedInstanceState)
        toast("Some text")
    }
}
```

This makes usage of the `toast` function much easier than the implementation of the whole `toast` displaying code. We also get suggestions from the IDE that we can invoke this function when we are inside `Context` (like inside `Activity`) or on an instance of `Context`:

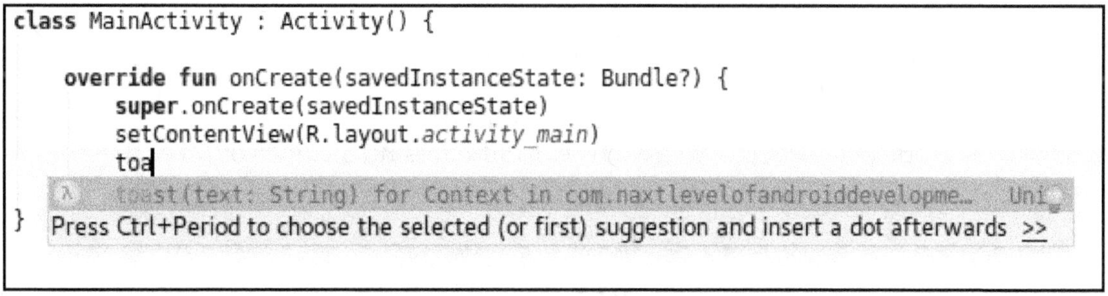
class MainActivity : Activity() {
override fun onCreate(savedInstanceState: Bundle?) {
super.onCreate(savedInstanceState)
setContentView(R.layout.activity_main)
toa
st(text: String) for Context in com.naxtlevelofandroiddevelopme...
}
Press Ctrl+Period to choose the selected (or first) suggestion and insert a dot afterwards >>

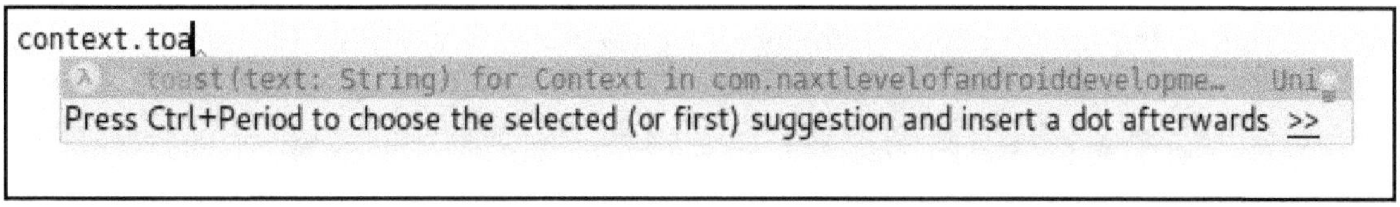
context.toa
st(text: String) for Context in com.naxtlevelofandroiddevelopme...
Press Ctrl+Period to choose the selected (or first) suggestion and insert a dot afterwards >>

In the preceding example, `Context` is a receiver type of the `toast` function, and the `this` instance is a reference to the receiver object. All functions and properties of the receiver object can be accessed explicitly, so we can take the following definition:

```
fun Collection<Int>.dropPercent(percent: Double)
    = this.drop(floor(this.size * percent)
```

We can then replace it with the following:

```
fun Collection<Int>.dropPercent(percent: Double)
    = drop(floor(size * percent))
```

There are multiple use cases in which extension functions are useful. Similar extension functions can be defined for `View`, `List`, `String`, other classes defined in the Android framework or a third-party library, and custom classes defined by the developer. Extension functions can be added to any accessible type, even to the `Any` object. Here is an extension function that can be called on every object:

```
fun Any?.logError(error: Throwable, message: String = "error") {
    Log.e(this?.javaClass?.simpleName ?: "null", message, error)
}
```

Here are some call examples:

```
user.logError(e, "NameError") // Logs: User: NameError ...
"String".logError(e) // String: error ...
logError(e) // 1, MainActivity: error ...
```

1. This supposes that we are invoking this in `MainActivity`.

We can simply add any method to any class we want. This is a great improvement for Android development. With it, we have a way to add missing methods or properties to types.

Extension functions under the hood

While Kotlin extension functions might look magical, they are really simple under the hood. A top-level extension function is compiled to a static function with a receiver object on the first argument. Let's look at the already presented `toast` function:

```
// ContextExt.kt
fun Context.toast(text: String) {
    Toast.makeText(this, text, LENGTH_LONG).show()
}
```

This function, after compilation and decompilation to Java, will look similar to the following function:

```
//Java
public class ContextExtKt {
    public static void toast(Context receiver, String text) {
        Toast.makeText(receiver, text, Toast.LENGTH_SHORT).show();
    }
}
```

Kotlin top-level extension functions are compiled to static functions with a receiver object on the first parameter. This is why we can still use extensions from Java:

```
// Java
ContextExtKt.toast(context, "Some toast")
```

Also, this means that from a JVM bytecode perspective, the method is not really added, but during compilation all extension function usages are compiled to static function calls. While extension functions are just functions, function modifiers can be applied to them in the same way as they can be applied to any other function. For example, an extension function can be marked as `inline`:

```
inline fun Context.isPermissionGranted (permission: String): Boolean =
ContextCompat.checkSelfPermission (this, permission) ==
PackageManager.PERMISSION_GRANTED
```

As with other `inline` functions, the function call will be replaced with an actual body during application compilation. We can do with extension functions practically everything we can do with other functions. They can be single expressions, have default arguments, be used by named parameters, and so on. But there are also other less intuitive consequences of such implementations. In the next sections, we are going to describe them.

No method overriding

When there is a member function and an extension function with the same name and parameters, the member function always wins. Here is an example:

```
class A {
    fun foo() {
        println("foo from A")
    }
}

fun A.foo() {
    println("foo from Extension")
```

```
}

A().foo() // Prints: foo from A
```

This is always true. Even methods from a superclass win with extension functions:

```
open class A {
    fun foo() {
        println("foo from A")
    }
}

class B: A()

fun B.foo() {
    println("foo from Extension")
}

A().foo() // foo from A
```

The point is that the extension function is not allowed to modify the behavior of a real object. We can only add extra functionalities. This keeps us secure, because we know that no one will change the behavior of objects that we are using, which might lead to errors that are hard to track.

Access to receiver elements

An extension function is compiled to a static function with a receiver object on the first parameter, so we have no extra access privilege. The `private` and `protected` elements are not accessible, and elements with Java's `default`, Java's `package`, or Kotlin's `internal` modifiers are accessed in the same way as if we just operate on a standard object.

Thanks to that, these elements are protected as they should be. Remember that extension functions, while being really powerful and useful, are just syntactic sugar, and there is no magic there.

Extensions are resolved statically

Extension functions are just functions with a receiver as the first parameter, so their calls are resolved at compile time by the type on which the function is invoked. For example, when there are extension functions for both superclass and subclass, then the extension functions that will be chosen during invocation depend on the type of property on which we are operating. Here is an example:

```
abstract class A
class B: A()

fun A.foo() { println("foo(A)") }
fun B.foo() { println("foo(B)") }

val b = B()
b.foo() // prints: foo(B)
(b as A).foo() // 1, prints: foo(A)
val a: A = b
a.foo() // 1, prints: foo(A)
```

1. Here we would expect `foo(B)` while the object is, in fact, of type `B`, but while extensions are resolved statically, it is using an extension function for `A` because the variable is of type `A` and there is no information as to what object is there during compilation.

This fact is sometimes problematic because when we define an extension function to the type we are most often cast to, we should not implement extension functions to its subclasses.

This is an important limitation, and should be kept in mind, especially during public library implementation, because this way, some extension functions can block others and cause unexpected behavior.

Companion object extensions

If a class has a companion object defined, then you can also define extension functions (and properties) for this companion object. To distinguish between an extension to a class and an extension to a companion object, `.Companion` needs to be added between the extension type and function name:

```
class A {
    companion object {}
}
fun A.Companion.foo() { print(2) }
```

When it is defined, the `foo` method can be used as if it were defined inside the `A` companion object:

```
A.foo()
```

Note that we are calling this extension using the class type, not the class instance. To allow the creation of an extension function for a companion object, a companion object needs to be explicitly defined inside the class, even an empty one. Without it, it is impossible to define an extension function:

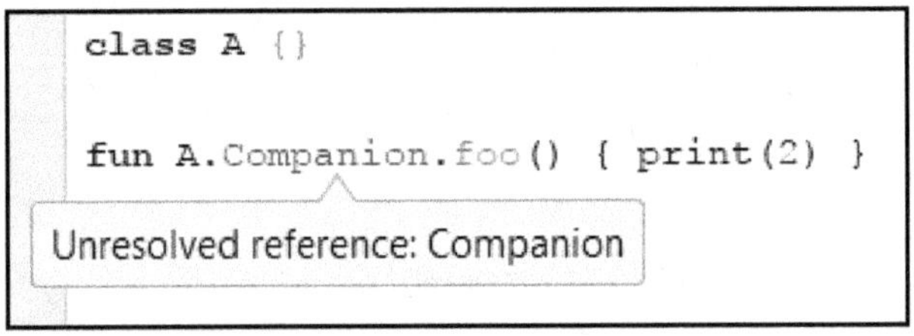
class A {}
fun A.Companion.foo() { print(2) }
Unresolved reference: Companion

Operator overloading using extension functions

Operator overloading is a big Kotlin feature, but we often need to use Java libraries and operators that are not defined there. For example, in RxJava, we use the `CompositeDisposable` function to manage subscriptions. This collection uses the `add` method to add new elements. This is an example subscription added to `CompositeDisposable`:

```
val subscriptions = CompositeDisposable()

subscriptions.add(repository
   .getAllCharacters(qualifiedSearchQuery)
   .subscribeOn(Schedulers.io())
   .observeOn(AndroidSchedulers.mainThread())
   .subscribe(this::charactersLoaded, view::showError))
```

The standard Kotlin way to add a new element to a mutable collection is by using the `plusAssign` operator (+=). It is not only more universal, but also cleaner, because we can omit brackets:

```
val list = mutableListOf(1,2,3)
list.add(1)
list += 1
```

To apply it to our example, we can add the following extension:

```
operator fun CompositeDisposable.plusAssign(disposable: Disposable)
{
    add(disposable)
}
```

And now we can use the `plusAssign` method on `CompositeDisposable`:

```
    subscriptions += repository
       .getAllCharacters(qualifiedSearchQuery)
       .subscribeOn(Schedulers.io())
       .observeOn(AndroidSchedulers.mainThread())
       .subscribe(this::charactersLoaded, view::showError)
```

Where should top-level extension functions be used?

Extension functions are most often used when we feel that a class defined by other programmers is missing a method. For example, if we think that `View` should contain the `show` and the `hide` methods, usage for which would be easier than visibility field setting, then we can just implement it ourselves:

```
    fun View.show() { visibility = View.VISIBLE }
    fun View.hide() { visibility = View.GONE }
```

There is no need to remember the names of classes that hold util functions. In the IDE, we just put a dot after the object, and we can search through all the methods that are provided together with this object extension function from the project and libraries. Invocation looks good, while it looks like an original object member. This is the beauty of extension functions, but it is also a danger. Right now, there are already tons of Kotlin libraries that are just packs of extension functions. When we use lots of extension functions, we can make our Android code unlike normal Android code. This has both pros and cons. Here are the pros:

- Code is short and more readable
- Code presents more logic instead of Android boilerplate
- Extension functions are most often tested, or at least used in multiple places, so it is simpler to find out if they are working correctly
- When we use extension functions, there is a smaller chance that we will make a stupid error that will lead to hours of code debugging

To illustrate the last two points, we will go back to the `toast` function. It is hard to make an error when writing the following:

```
toast("Some text")
```

But it is much easier to make an error in the following:

```
Toast.makeText(this, "Some text",Toast.LENGTH_LONG).show()
```

The biggest problem with strong extension usage in a project is that we are, in fact, making our own API. We are naming and implementing functions and we decide what arguments should be there. When a developer joins the team, they need to learn the entire API we've created. The Android API has lots of shortcomings, but its strength is that it is universal and it is known to all Android developers.

Does this mean we should resign from extensions? Absolutely not! This is a great feature that is helping us to make code short and clean. The point is that we should use them in a smart way:

- Avoid multiple extensions that do the same thing.
- Short and simple functionality often doesn't need to be an extension.
- Keep one coding style around the project. Talk to your team and specify some standards.
- Be careful when you use public libraries with extensions. Keep them as code that you cannot change and match your extensions to them to keep the API clear.

Extension properties

In this section, we will first understand what extension properties are, and then we will move on to learn where these properties can be used. As we already know, properties in Kotlin are defined by their accessors (getter and setter):

```
class User(val name: String, val surname: String) {
    val fullName: String
    get() = "$name $surname"
}
```

We can also define the extension property. The only limitation is that this property can't have a backing field. The reason for this is that extension can't store state, so there is no good place to store this field. Here is an example of an extension property definition for `TextView`:

```
val TextView.trimmedText: String
get() = text.toString().trim()

// Usage
textView.trimmedText
```

As with extension functions, the preceding implementation will be compiled as an accessor function with a receiver on the first parameter. Here is the simplified result in Java:

```
public class AndroidUtilsKt {
    String getTrimmedText(TextView receiver) {
        return receiver.getText().toString().trim();
    }
}
```

If it was a read-write property, then both the setter and getter would be implemented. Remember that only properties that don't need a Java field are allowed to be defined as an extension property. For example, this is illegal:

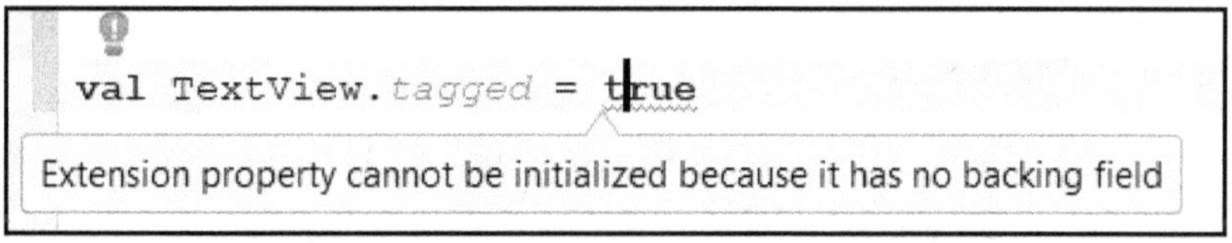
val TextView.tagged = true
Extension property cannot be initialized because it has no backing field

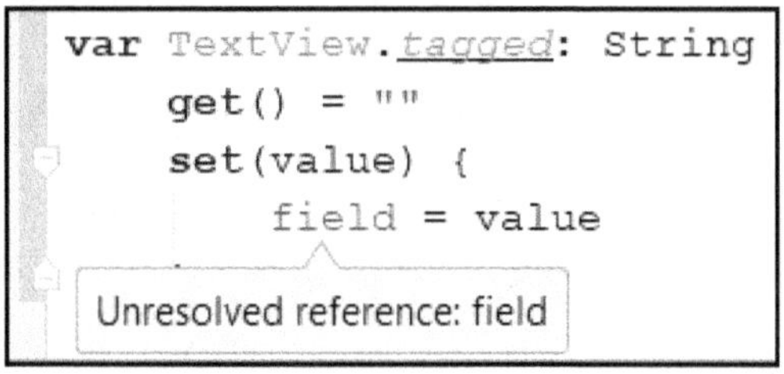
var TextView.tagged: String
get() = ""
set(value) {
field = value
Unresolved reference: field

Where should extension properties be used?

Extension properties can often be used interchangeably with extension functions. They are both most often used as top-level utils. Extension properties are used when we would like an object to have a property that was not developed natively. The decision as to whether we should use an extension function or an extension property is nearly the same as the decision as to whether we should use a function or property without a backing field inside a class. Just to remind you, according to convention, you should choose a property over a function when the underlying algorithm fulfills the following conditions:

- Does not throw errors
- Has **O**(*1*) complexity
- Is cheap to calculate (or cached on the first run)
- Returns the same result over invocations

Let's look at a simple problem. We often need to get some services in Android, but the code used to get them is complicated:

```
PreferenceManager.getDefaultSharedPreferences(this)
getSystemService(Context.LAYOUT_INFLATER_SERVICE) as LayoutInflater
getSystemService(Context.ALARM_SERVICE) as AlarmManager
```

To use a service such as `AlarmManager` or `LayoutInflater`, the programmer has to remember the following for each of them:

- The name of the function that is providing it (such as `getSystemService`) and what class contains it (such as `Context`)
- The name of the field that is specifying this service (such as `Context.ALARM_SERVICE`)
- The name of the class that the service should be cast to (such as `AlarmManager`)

This is complex, and this is the perfect place where we can optimize usage thanks to extension properties. We can define extension properties like this:

```
val Context.preferences: SharedPreferences
    get() = PreferenceManager
        .getDefaultSharedPreferences(this)

val Context.inflater: LayoutInflater
    get() = getSystemService(Context.LAYOUT_INFLATER_SERVICE)
        as LayoutInflater

val Context.alarmManager: AlarmManager
```

```
        get() = getSystemService(Context.ALARM_SERVICE)
            as AlarmManager
```

And from now on, we can use `preferences`, `inflater`, and `alarmManager` as if they are properties of `Context`:

```
context.preferences.contains("Some Key")
context.inflater.inflate(R.layout.activity_main, root)
context.alarmManager.setRepeating(ELAPSED_REALTIME, triggerAt,
   interval, pendingIntent)
```

These are perfect examples of good read-only extension function usage. Let's focus on the `inflater` extension property. It is helping to get elements that are often needed, but hard to get without extensions. It is helpful because the programmer just needs to remember that what they need is an inflater and that they need `Context` to have it, and the programmer does not need to remember the name of method that is providing system services (`getSystemService`), the name of the key used to get the `inflater` property (`ALARM_SERVICE`), where it is located (in `Context`), and what this service should be cast to (`AlarmManager`). In other words, this extension is saving a lot of work and programmer memory. Also, it is correct according to the guidelines, because of property getter execution time is short and its complexity is **O**(*1*), it is not throwing any errors, and it always returns the same `inflater` (in fact, it might be a different instance, but from a programmer's perspective, its usage is always the same, and this is what is important).

We've seen read-only extension properties, but we have not seen read-write extension properties. Here is a good example that is an alternative to the `hide` and `show` functions that we saw in the *Extension functions* section:

```
var View.visible: Boolean
get() = visibility == View.VISIBLE
set(value) {
    visibility = if (value) View.VISIBLE else View.GONE
}
```

We can change the visibility of the `View` element using this property:

```
button.visible = true // the same as show()
button.visible = false // the same as hide()

Also, we can check view element visibility:

if(button.visible) { /* ... */ }
```

Once we define it, we can treat is as if it really were a `View` property. It is also important that what we are setting is consistent with what we are getting. So, supposing that there is no other thread that is changing element visibility, we can set a property value:

```
view.visible = true
```

Then the getter will always provide the same value:

```
println(view.visible) // Prints: true
```

Finally, there is no other logic inside the getter and setter--only a change in specific properties. So, other conventions we've presented before are satisfied too.

Member extension functions and properties

We've seen top-level extension functions and properties, but it is also possible to define them inside a class or object. Extensions defined there are called member extensions, and they are most often used for different kinds of problem than top-level extensions.

Let's start from the simplest use case where member extensions are used. Let's suppose that we need to drop every third element of a list of `String`. Here is the extension function that allows us to drop every ith element:

```
fun List<String>.dropOneEvery(i: Int) =
    filterIndexed { index, _ -> index % i == (i - 1) }
```

The problem with that function is that it should not be extracted as a util extension, because of the following reason:

- It is not prepared for different types of list (such as a list of `User` or `Int`)
- It is a rarely used function, so it probably won't be used anywhere else in the project

This is why we would want to keep it private, and it is a good idea to keep it inside the class where we are using it as a member extension function:

```
class UsersItemAdapter : ItemAdapter() {
    lateinit var usersNames: List<String>

    fun processList() {
    usersNames = getUsersList()
        .map { it.name }
        .dropOneEvery(3)
    }
```

```
    fun List<String>.dropOneEvery(i: Int) =
        filterIndexed { index, _ -> index % i == (i - 1) }

    // ...
}
```

This is the first reason we use member extension functions, to protect the accessibility of functions. In this case, it could be done by defining a function at the top level, in the same file, and with a private modifier. But member extension functions act differently to top-level functions. The function used in the preceding code is public, but it can only be called on `List<String>` and only in `UsersItemAdapter`. So, it can be used only inside the `UsersItemAdapter` class and its subclasses or inside an extension function to `UsersItemAdapter`:

```
fun UsersItemAdapter.updateUserList(newUsers: List<User>) {
    usersNames = newUsers
        .map { it.name }
        .dropOneEvery(3)
}
```

Note that to use a member extension function, we need both the object in which it is implemented and the object on which this extension functions will be called. It is this way because we can use elements of both of these objects. This is important information about member extensions: they can use both elements from receiver type and from member type without a qualifier. Let's see how they might be used. Here is another example, which is similar to the previous one, but it is using the private `category` property:

```
class UsersItemAdapter(
    private val category: Category
) : ItemAdapter() {

   lateinit var usersNames: List<String>

   fun processList() {
        usersNames = getUsersList()
            .fromSameCategory()
            .map { it.name }
   }

   fun List<User>.fromSameCategory() =
       filter { u -> u.category.id == category.id }

   private fun getUsersList() = emptyList<User>()
}
```

Inside the `fromSameCategory` member extension function, we are operating on an extension receiver (`List<User>`), but we are also using the `category` property from `UsersItemAdapter`. We see here that a function defined this way needs to be a method and it can be used similarly to other methods. The advantage over the standard method is that we can call a function on `List`, so we can keep clean stream processing, instead of non-extension method usage:

```
// fromSameCategory defined as standard method
usersNames = fromSameCategory(newUsers)
      .dropLast(3)

// fromSameCategory defined as member extension function
usersNames = newUsers
      .fromSameCategory()
      .dropLast(3)
```

Another common usage is the member extension functions or properties can be used like normal methods, but we are using the fact that inside member functions we can use receiver properties and methods without naming them. This way we can have shorter syntax, and that we are actually calling them on a receiver instead of calling them with the same type as an argument. As an example, we can take the following method:

```
private fun setUpRecyclerView(recyclerView: RecyclerView) {
    recyclerView.layoutManager
        = LinearLayoutManager(recyclerView.context)
    recyclerView.adapter
        = MessagesAdapter(mutableListOf())
}

// Usage
setUpRecyclerView(recyclerView)
```

Then we can replace it with the following member extension function:

```
private fun RecyclerView.setUp() {
    layoutManager = LinearLayoutManager(context)
    adapter = MessagesAdapter(mutableListOf())
}

// Usage
recyclerView.setUp()
```

Using member extension functions, we can achieve both a simpler call and a simpler function body. The biggest problem with this attempt is that it is not clear which functions we are using are members of `RecyclerView`, and which are members of the `Activity` and `RecyclerView` extensions. This problem will be tackled in the next sections.

Types of receivers

When we have a member extension function, then it becomes more complicated to administer the elements we are calling. Inside a member extension, we have implicit access to the following:

- Member functions and properties, both from this class and superclasses
- Receiver type functions and properties, both from the receiver type and its supertypes
- Top-level functions and properties

So inside the `setUp` extension function, we can use both member and receiver methods and properties:

```
class MainActivity: Activity() {

    override fun onCreate(savedInstanceState: Bundle?) {
        super.onCreate(savedInstanceState)
        setContentView(R.layout.main_activity)
        val buttonView = findViewById(R.id.button_view) as Button
        buttonView.setUp()
    }

    private fun Button.setUp() {
        setText("Click me!") // 1, 2
        setOnClickListener { showText("Hello") } // 2
    }

    private fun showText(text: String) {
        toast(text)
    }
}
```

1. `setText` is the `Button` class method.
2. We can use the `Button` class and `MainActivity` class members alternately.

It might be tricky--most people probably wouldn't notice if there was an error and the `setText` call was swapped with the `showText` call.

While we can use inside member extension elements from different receivers, to allow distinction between them, all kinds of receiver were named. First of all, all objects that can be used by the `this` keyword are called **implicit receivers**. They're members which can be accessed without a qualifier. Inside `setUp` functions, there are two implicit receivers:

- **Extension receiver**: An instance of the class that the extension is defined for (`Button`)
- **Dispatch receiver**: An instance of the class in which the extension is declared (`MainActivity`)

Note that while members of both the extension receiver and dispatch receiver are implicit receivers in the same body, it is possible to have a situation where we use members that have the same signature in both of them. For example, if we change the previous class to show text in `textView` instead of showing it in the `toast` function, and change the method name to `setText`, then we are going to have dispatch and extension receiver methods with the same signature (one defined in the `Button` class, the other defined in the `MainActivity` class):

```
class MainActivity: Activity() {
    override fun onCreate(savedInstanceState: Bundle?) {
        super.onCreate(savedInstanceState)
        setContentView(R.layout.main_activity)
        val buttonView = findViewById(R.id.button_view) as Button
        buttonView.setUp()
    }

    private fun Button.setUp() {
        setText("Click me!")
        setOnClickListener { setText("Hello") } // 1
    }
    private fun setText(text: String) {
        textView.setText(text)
    }
}
```

1. `setText` is the method of both the dispatch receiver and the extension receiver. Which one will be called?

As a result, the `setText` function will be invoked from the **extension receiver** and a button click will change the text of the clicked button! This is because the extension receiver always takes precedence over the dispatch receiver. Still, it is possible to use a dispatch receiver in this situation by using qualified `this` syntax (the `this` keyword with a label distinguishing which receiver we want to reference):

```
private fun Button.setUp() {
    setText("Click me!")
    setOnClickListener {
        this@MainActivity.setText("Hello")
    }
}
```

This way, we can solve the problem of distinguishing between the dispatch and extension receivers.

Member extension functions and properties under the hood

Member extension functions and properties are compiled the same way as top-level extension functions and properties, with the only difference being that they are inside a class and they are not static. Here is a simple example of an extension function:

```
class A {
    fun boo() {}

    fun Int.foo() {
        boo()
     }
}
```

This is what it is compiled to (after simplification):

```
public final class A {
    public final void boo() {
        ...
    }

    public final void foo(int $receiver) {
        this.boo();
    }
}
```

Note that while they are just methods with a receiver as the first parameter, we can do with them everything we can with other functions. Access modifiers work the same way, and if we define the member extension function as open, then we can override it in its subclasses.

Generic extension functions

When we are writing utility functions, often we want them to be generic. The most common examples are extensions for collections: `List`, `Map`, and `Set`. Here is an example of an extension property for `List`:

```
val <T> List<T>.lastIndex: Int
    get() = size - 1
```

The preceding example defines an extension property for a generic type. This kind of extension is used for lots of different problems. As an example, starting another `Activity` is a repetitive task that most often needs to be implemented in multiple places in the project. The methods provided by the Android IDE for starting an `Activity` do not make it easy. Here is the code used to start a new Activity called `SettingsActivity`:

```
startActivity(Intent (this, SettingsActivity::class.java))
```

Note that this simple and repetitive task needs a lot of code that is not really clear. But we can define extension functions that will make `Intent` creation and `Activity` without arguments much simpler using a generic inline extension function with the `reified` type:

```
inline fun <reified T : Any> Context.getIntent()
   = Intent(this, T::class.java)

inline fun <reified T : Any> Context.startActivity()
   = startActivity(getIntent<T>())
```

Now we can start `Activity` by simply using the following:

```
startActivity<SettingsActivity>()
```

Or we can create `intent` like this:

```
val intent = getIntent<SettingsActivity>()
```

This way, we can make this common task easier at a low cost. To go further, libraries such as **Anko** (`https://github.com/Kotlin/anko`) provide extension functions that provide a simple way to start an `Activity` with additional parameters or flags, as in this example:

```
startActivity<SettingsActivity>(userKey to user)
```

Internal implementation of the library is outside the scope of this book, but we can use this extension simply by adding an Anko library dependency to our project. The point of this example is that nearly all repetitive code can be replaced with simpler code using extensions. There are also alternative ways to start an `Activity`, such as the `ActivityStarter` library (`https://github.com/MarcinMoskala/ActivityStarter`), which is based on parameter injection and strongly supports Kotlin. It allows classic argument injection:

```
class StudentDataActivity : BaseActivity() {
    lateinit @Arg var student: Student
    @Arg(optional = true) var lesson: Lesson = Lesson.default()
}
```

Or, as an alternative, it allows lazy injection in Kotlin property delegates (which are described in `Chapter 8`, *Delegates*):

```
class StudentDataActivity : BaseActivity() {
    @get:Arg val student: Student by argExtra()
    @get:Arg(optional = true)
    var lesson: Lesson by argExtra(Lesson.default())
}
```

`Activity` with such arguments can be started using generated static functions:

```
StudentDataActivityStarter.start(context, student, lesson)
StudentDataActivityStarter.start(context, student)
```

Let's see another example. In Android, we often need to store objects in JSON format such as, when we need to send them to an API or store them in a file. The most popular library used for serializing and deserializing objects into JSON is Gson. Let's look at the standard way of using the Gson library:

```
val user = User("Marcin", "Moskala")
val json: String = globalGson.toJson(user)
val userFromJson = globalGson.fromJson(json, User::class.java)
```

We can improve it in Kotlin thanks to extension functions with an `inline` modifier. Here is an example of extension functions that use Gson to pack and unpack objects to `String` in JSON format:

```
inline fun Any.toJson() = globalGson.toJson(this)!!

inline fun <reified T : Any> String.fromJson()
  = globalGson.fromJson(this, T::class.java)

// Usage
val user = User("Marcin", "Moskala")
val json: String = user.toJson()
val userFromJson: User = json.fromJson<User>()
```

The `globalGson` instance is a global instance of `Gson`. It is common practice because we often define some serializers and deserializers, and it is a simpler and more effective way to define them and build an instance of `Gson` once.

These examples shows what are possibilities of generic extension functions given to the developer. They are the next level of code extraction:

- They are top-level, but also invoked on an object, so they are simple to manage
- They are generic, so are universal and can be applied to anything
- When inline, they allow us to define `reified` type parameters

This is why generic extension functions are commonly used in Kotlin. Also, the standard library provides lots of generic extensions. In the next section, we will see some collection extension functions. This section is important, not only because it provides knowledge about generic extension function usage, but also because it ultimately describes how list processing in Kotlin works and how it can be used.

Collection processing

Collection processing is one of the most common tasks in programming. This is why one of the first things that developers learn is how to iterate over a collection to operate on elements. Young developers asked to print all users from a list will most probably use a `for` loop:

```
for (user in users) {
    println(user)
}
```

If we asked them to show only the users that are passing in school, then they would most probably add an `if` condition inside this loop:

```
for (user in users) {
    if ( user.passing ) {
        println(user)
    }
}
```

This is still a correct implementation, but the real problem starts when the task becomes more complex. What if they were asked to print the three best students that are passing? It is really complex to implement this in loops, but it is trivial to implement it using Kotlin stream processing. Let's see it in an example. Here is example list of students:

```
data class Student(
    val name: String,
    val grade: Double,
    val passing: Boolean
)

val students = listOf(
    Student("John", 4.2, true),
    Student("Bill", 3.5, true),
    Student("John", 3.2, false),
    Student("Aron", 4.3, true),
    Student("Jimmy", 3.1, true)
)
```

Let's filter out students using an imperative approach from Java (using loops and a sorting method):

```
val filteredList = ArrayList<Student>()
for (student in students) {
    if(student.passing) filteredList += student
}

Collections.sort(filteredList) { p1, p2 ->
    if(p1.grade > p2.grade) -1 else 1
}

for (i in 0..2) {
    val student = filteredList[i]
    println(student)
}

// Prints:
// Student(name=Aron, grade=4.3, passing=true)
```

```
// Student(name=John, grade=4.2, passing=true)
// Student(name=Bill, grade=3.5, passing=true)
```

We can achieve the same result in a much simpler way using Kotlin stream processing:

```
students.filter { it.passing } // 1
   .sortedByDescending { it.grade } // 2
   .take(3) // 3
   .forEach(::println) // 4
```

1. Take only students who passed.
2. Sort students according to their grade (descending, so that students with better grades are in a higher position).
3. Take only the first three of them.
4. Print each of them.

The key is that each stream processing function, such as `sortedByDescending`, `take`, and `forEach` from the preceding example, is extracting a small functionality and the power comes from the composition of them. The result is much simpler and more readable than using the classic loops.

Stream processing is actually a pretty common language feature. It is known in C#, JavaScript, Scala, and many other languages, including Java since version 8. Popular reactive programming libraries, such as RxJava, also heavily utilize this concept to process data. In this section, we are going to go deeper into Kotlin collection processing.

The Kotlin collection type hierarchy

The Kotlin type hierarchy is really well designed. Standard collections are actually collections from a native language (such as Java) that are hidden behind interfaces. They are created by standard top-level functions (`listOf`, `setOf`, `mutableListOf`, and so on), so they can be created and used in common modules (modules compiled to more than one platform). Also, Kotlin interfaces can act like their equivalent interfaces from Java (such as `List`, and `Set`), which makes Kotlin collections efficient and highly compatible with external libraries. At the same time, the Kotlin collection interface hierarchy can be used in common modules. This hierarchy is simple and it is useful to understand it:

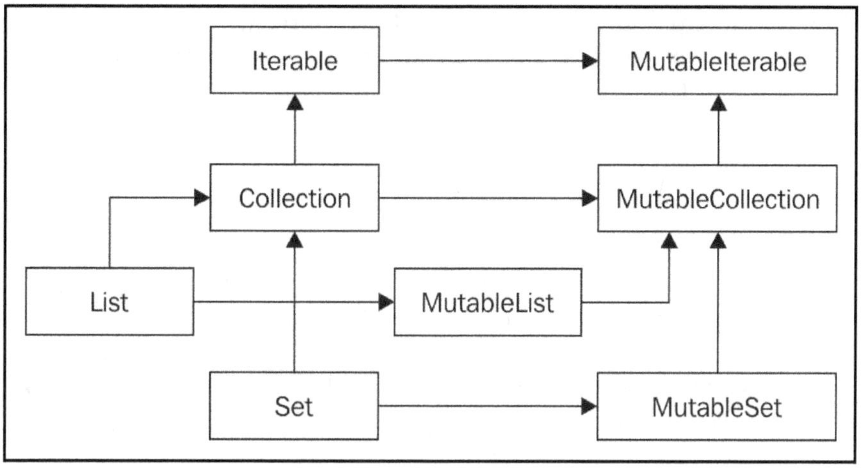

Kotlin collection interfaces hierarchy

The most general interface is `Iterable`. It represents a sequence of elements that can be iterated over. Any object that implements `iterable` can be used in a `for` loop:

```
for (i in iterable) { /* ... */ }
```

Lots of different types implement an iterable interface: all collections, progressions (`1..10`, `'a'..'z'`), and even `String`. They all allow us to iterate over their elements:

```
for (char in "Text") { print("($char)") } // Prints: (T)(e)(x)(t)
```

The `Collection` interface represents a collection of elements and extends `Iterable`. It adds property `size` and the `contains`, `containsAll`, and `isEmpty` methods.

Two main interfaces that inherit from `Collection` are `List` and `Set`. The difference between them is that `Set` is unordered and does not contain repetitive elements (according to the `equals` method). Neither the `List` nor `Set` interface contain any methods that would allow us to mutate the object state. This is why, by default, Kotlin collections are treated as immutable. When we have an instance of `List`, then it is most often `ArrayList` in Android. `ArrayList` is a mutable collection, but while it is hidden behind the `List` interface, it is actually acting as if it was immutable because it is not exposing any methods that would allow us to apply changes (unless it is downcast).

In Java, collections are mutable, but Kotlin collection interfaces only provide immutable behavior by default (not methods that change the state of collections, such as, `add` and `removeAt`):

```
val list = listOf('a', 'b', 'c')
println(list[0]) // Prints: a
println(list.size) // Prints: 3
list.add('d') // Error
list.removeAt(0) // Error
```

All immutable interfaces (such as `Collection`, and `List`) have their mutable equivalents (such as `MutableCollection`, and `MutableList`) that inherit from corresponding immutable interfaces. Mutable means that the actual object can be modified. These are the interfaces that represent mutable collections from the standard library:

- `MutableIterable` allows iteration with changes applied
- `MutableCollection` includes methods for adding and removing elements
- `MutableList` and `MutableSet` are mutable equivalents of `List` and `Set`

Now we can fix our previous example and change the collection using the `add` and `remove` methods:

```
val list = mutableListOf('a', 'b', 'c')
println(list[0]) // Prints: a
println(list.size) // Prints: 3
list.add('d')
println(list) // Prints: [a, b, c, d]
list.removeAt(0)
println(list) // Prints: [b, c, d]
```

Both immutable and mutable interfaces only provide a few methods, but the Kotlin standard library provides many useful extensions for them:

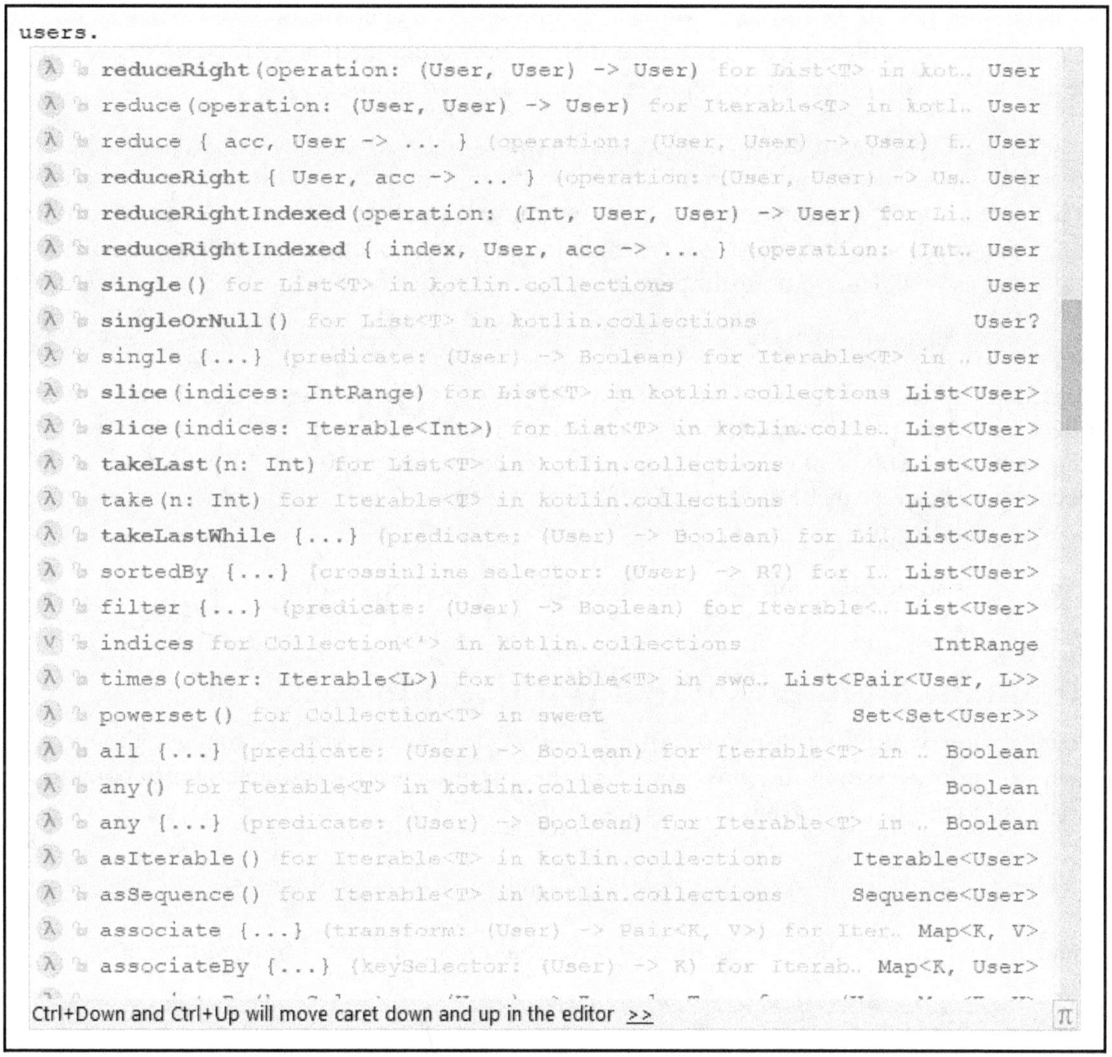

This makes dealing with collections a much easier task than in Java.

Kotlin implements collection processing methods using extensions. This approach has many advantages; for example, if we want to implement a custom collection (such as `List`), we only need to implement an `iterable` interface containing a few methods. We can still use all the extensions that are provided for the `iterable` interface.

Another reason is how flexibly these functions can be used when they are extensions for interfaces. For example, most of these collection processing functions are actually extensions for `Iterable`, which is implemented by many more types than `Collection`, for example, by `String` or `Range`. Therefore, it is possible to use all extension functions for `Iterable` on `IntRange` as well. Here is an example:

```
(1..5).map { it * 2 }.forEach(::print) // Prints: 246810
```

This makes all these extensions really universal. There is also a downside to the fact that collection stream processing methods are implemented as extension functions. While extensions are resolved statically, it is incorrect to override an extension function for a specific type because its behavior will be different when it is behind an interface than when it is accessed directly.

Let's analyze some extension functions used for collection processing.

The map, filter, and flatMap functions

We have already briefly presented `map`, `filter`, and `flatMap`, because they are the most basic stream processing functions. The `map` function returns a list with elements changed according to the function from the argument:

```
val list = listOf(1,2,3).map { it * 2 }
println(list) // Prints: [2, 4, 6]
```

The `filter` function allows only the elements that match the provided predicate:

```
val list = listOf(1,2,3,4,5).map { it > 2 }
println(list) // Prints: [3, 4, 5]
```

The `flatMap` function returns a single list of all elements yielded by the `transform` function, which is invoked on each element of the original collection:

```
val list = listOf(10, 20).flatMap { listOf(it, it+1, it + 2) }
println(list) // Prints: [10, 11, 12, 20, 21, 22]
```

It is most often used to flatten lists of collections:

```
shops.flatMap { it.products }
schools.flatMap { it.students }
```

Let's look at simplified implementations of these extension functions:

```
inline fun <T, R> Iterable<T>.map(transform: (T) -> R): List<R> { //1
    val destination = ArrayList<R>()
    for (item in this) destination.add(transform(item)) // 2
    return destination
}

inline fun <T> Iterable<T>.filter(predicate: (T) -> Boolean): List<T> { //
1
    val destination = ArrayList<T>()
    for (item in this) if(predicate(item)) destination.add(item) // 2
    return destination
}

inline fun <T, R> Iterable<T>.flatMap(transform: (T) -> Collection<R>):
List<R> {
// 1
    val destination = ArrayList<R>()
    for (item in this) destination.addAll(transform(item)) // 2
    return destination
}
```

1. All these functions are inline.
2. All these functions use a `for` loop internally, and return a new list containing proper elements.

Most Kotlin standard library extension functions with a function type are `inline` because it makes lambda expression usage efficient. As a result, whole collection stream processing is actually mostly compiled at runtime into nested loops. As an example, here is this simple processing:

```
students.filter { it.passing }
    .map { "${it.name} ${it.surname}" }
```

After compilation and decompilation to Java, it looks like the following (cleaned up):

```
Collection destination1 = new ArrayList();
Iterator it = students.iterator();
while(it.hasNext()) {
    Student student = (Student) it.next();
    if(student.getPassing()) {
```

```
            destination1.add(student);
        }
    }
    Collection destination2 = new ArrayList(destination1.size());
    it = destination2.iterator();
    while(it.hasNext()) {
        Student student = (Student) it.next();
        String var = student.getName() + " " + student.getSurname();
        destination2.add(var);
    }
```

The forEach and onEach functions

The `forEach` function was discussed in the chapter about functions. It is an alternative to a `for` loop, so it performs an action on each element of the list:

```
listOf("A", "B", "C").forEach { print(it) } // prints: ABC
```

Since Kotlin 1.1, there is a similar function, `onEach`, that also invokes an action on each element. It returns an extension receiver so we can invoke an action on each element in the middle of stream processing. This is commonly used for logging purposes. Here is an example:

```
(1..10).filter { it % 3 == 0 }
    .onEach(::print) // Prints: 369
    .map { it / 3 }
    .forEach(::print) // Prints: 123
```

The withIndex and indexed variants

Sometimes, the element processing method depends on its index in the list. The most universal way to solve this problem is by using the `withIndex` function, which returns a list of values with indexes:

```
listOf(9,8,7,6).withIndex() // 1
    .filter { (i, _) -> i % 2 == 0 } // 2
    .forEach { (i, v) -> print("$v at $i,") }
// Prints: 9 at 0, 7 at 2,
```

1. The `withIndex` function packs each element into `IndexedValue`, which contains both the elements and its index.

2. In a lambda, IndexedValue is deconstructed into index and value, but while the value is unused, an underscore is placed instead. It might be omitted, but this code is more readable. This line only filters elements with an even index.

Also, there are variants for different stream processing methods that provide an index:

```
val list1 = listOf(2, 2, 3, 3)
    .filterIndexed { index, _ -> index % 2 == 0 }
println(list1) // Prints: [2, 3]

val list2 = listOf(10, 10, 10)
    .mapIndexed { index, i -> index * i }
println(list2) // Prints: [0, 10, 20]

val list3 = listOf(1, 4, 9)
    .forEachIndexed { index, i -> print("$index: $i,") }
println(list3) // Prints: 0: 1, 1: 4, 2: 9
```

The sum, count, min, max, and sorted functions

The sum function counts the sum of all elements in a list. It can be invoked on List<Int>, List<Long>, List<Short>, List<Double>, List<Float> , and List<Byte>:

```
val sum = listOf(1,2,3,4).sum()
println(sum) // Prints: 10
```

Often we need to sum some properties of elements, such as summing points of all users. It might be handled by mapping the list of users to the list of points and then counting the sum:

```
class User(val points: Int)
val users = listOf(User(10), User(1_000), User(10_000))

val points = users.map { it.points }. sum()
println(points) // Prints: 11010
```

But we unnecessarily create an intermediate collection by calling the map function, and it would be more efficient to directly sum points. To do this, we can use sumBy with an appropriate selector:

```
val points = users.sumBy { it.points }
println(points) // Prints: 11010
```

`sumBy` is expecting `Int` to be returned from the selector, and it is returning `Int` with the sum of all elements. If values are not `Int` but `Double`, then we can use `sumByDouble`, which returns `Double`:

```
class User(val points: Double)
val users = listOf(User(10.0), User(1_000.0), User(10_000.0))

val points = users.sumByDouble { it.points }
println(points) // Prints: 11010.0
```

A similar functionality is provided by the `count` function, which is used when we need to count elements that match a predicate:

```
val evens = (1..5).count { it % 2 == 1 }
val odds = (1..5).count { it % 2 == 0 }
println(evens) // Prints: 3
println(odds) // Prints: 2
```

Using the `count` function without a predicate returns the size of the collection or iterable:

```
val nums = (1..4).count()
println(nums) // Prints: 4
```

The next important functions are `min` and `max`, which are functions that return the minimal and maximal elements in a list. They can be used on a list of elements that have natural ordering (they implement `Comparable<T>` interface). Here is an example:

```
val list = listOf(4, 2, 5, 1)
println(list.min()) // Prints: 1
println(list.max()) // Prints: 5
println(listOf("kok", "ada", "bal", "mal").min()) // Prints: ada
```

The `sorted` function is similarly used. It returns a sorted list, but it needs to be invoked on collections of elements that implement the `Comparable<T>` interface. Here is an example of how `sorted` can be used to get a list of strings sorted alphanumerically:

```
val strs = listOf("kok", "ada", "bal", "mal").sorted()
println(strs) // Prints: [ada, bal, kok, mal]
```

What if items are not comparable? There are two ways to sort them. The first way is to sort according to a comparable member. We've already seen an example when we were sorting students according to their grades:

```
students.filter { it.passing }
   .sortedByDescending { it.grade }
   .take(3)
   .forEach(::println)
```

In the preceding example, we sort students using the comparable `grade` property. There, `sortedByDescending` is used, which works like `sortedBy`, the only difference being that the order is descending (from biggest to smallest). The selector inside the function can return any value that is comparable to itself. Here is an example, where `String` is used to specify the order:

```
val list = listOf(14, 31, 2)
print(list.sortedBy { "$it" }) // Prints: [14, 2, 31]
```

Similar functions can be used to find the minimal and maximal elements according to the selector:

```
val minByLen = listOf("ppp", "z", "as")
    .minBy { it.length }
println(minByLen) // Prints: "z"

val maxByLen = listOf("ppp", "z", "as")
    .maxBy { it.length }
println(maxByLen) // Prints: "ppp"
```

The second way to specify the sorting order is to define a `Comparator` that will determine how elements should be compared. Function variants that accept comparators should have a `With` suffix. Comparators can be defined by an adapter function that converts a lambda to the SAM type:

```
val comparator = Comparator<String> { e1, e2 ->
    e2.length - e1.length
}
val minByLen = listOf("ppp", "z", "as")
   .sortedWith(comparator)
println(minByLen) // Prints: [ppp, as, z]
```

Kotlin also includes standard library top-level functions (`compareBy`, and `compareByDescending`) used to simplify `Comparator` creation. Here is how we can create a comparator to sort students alphanumerically by `surname` and `name`:

```
data class User(val name: String, val surname: String) {
    override fun toString() = "$name $surname"
}

val users = listOf(
   User("A", "A"),
   User("B", "A"),
   User("B", "B"),
   User("A", "B")
)
```

```
val sortedUsers = users
   .sortedWith(compareBy({ it.surname }, { it.name }))

print(sortedUsers) // [A A, B A, A B, B B]
```

Note that we can use property references instead of lambda expressions:

```
val sortedUsers = users
   .sortedWith(compareBy(User::surname, User::name))
print(sortedUsers) // [A A, B A, A B, B B]
```

Another important function is `groupBy`, which groups elements according to the selector. `groupBy` returns `Map`, which maps from the chosen key to a list of elements that are selected to map to the following key:

```
    val grouped = listOf("ala", "alan", "mulan", "malan")
        .groupBy { it.first() }
    println(grouped) // Prints: {'a': ["ala", "alan"], "m": ["mulan",
"malan"]}
```

Let's look at a more complex example. We need to get a list of the best students from each class. Here is how we can get them from the list of students:

```
    class Student(val name: String, val classCode: String, val meanGrade:
Float)

    val students = listOf(
       Student("Homer", "1", 1.1F),
       Student("Carl", "2", 1.5F),
       Student("Donald", "2", 3.5F),
       Student("Alex", "3", 4.5F),
       Student("Marcin", "3", 5.0F),
       Student("Max", "1", 3.2F)
    )

    val bestInClass = students
       .groupBy { it.classCode }
       .map { (_, students) -> students.maxBy { it.meanGrade }!! }
       .map { it.name }

    print(bestInClass) // Prints: [Max, Donald, Marcin]
```

Other stream processing functions

There are lots of different stream processing functions, and there is no need to describe them all here, while Kotlin contains great documentation on its website. The names of most of the extension functions are self-explanatory and there is no need to really read the documentation to guess what they are doing. In Android Studio, we can check the real implementation by pressing *Ctrl* (the *command* key on Mac) and clicking the function whose implementation we want to read.

The important difference in collection processing comes when you are operating on mutable collections because while they can use additional extensions defined for mutable types (`MutableIterable`, and `MutableCollection`), the important distinction is that functions that change objects are formulated in present imperative form (for example, `sort`), while functions that returns a new collection with changed values are most often formulated in the past form of a verb (for example, `sorted`). Here is an example:

- `sort`: The function that is sorts a mutable object. It returns `Unit`.
- `sorted`: The function that is returns a sorted collection. It does not change the collection on which it is invoked.

```
val list = mutableListOf(3,2,4,1)
val list2 = list.sorted()
println(list) // [3,2,4,1]
println(list2) // [1,2,3,4]
list.sort()
println(list) // [1,2,3,4]
```

Examples of stream collection processing

We've already seen a few stream processing functions, but it needs some skill and creativity to use them for complex use cases. This is why in this section, we are going to discuss some complex stream processing examples.

Let's suppose that we again need to find the best three students who are passing, according to their grade. The key difference is that, in this case, the final order of students must be the same as it was in the beginning. Note that during a sorting by grade operation, this order is lost. But we can preserve it if we keep the value and index together. Thanks to that, we can later sort elements according to this preserved index. Here is how to implement this processing:

```
data class Student(
   val name: String,
   val grade: Double,
```

```
    val passing: Boolean
)

val students = listOf(
    Student("John", 4.2, true),
    Student("Bill", 3.5, true),
    Student("John", 3.2, false),
    Student("Aron", 4.3, true),
    Student("Jimmy", 3.1, true)
)

val bestStudents = students.filter { it.passing } // 1
    .withIndex() // 2
    .sortedBy { it.value.grade } // 3
    .take(3) // 4
    .sortedBy { it.index } // 5
    .map { it.value } // 6

// Print list of names
println(bestStudents.map { it.name }) // [John, Bill, Jimmy]
```

1. Filter to only keep students that are passing.
2. Add indexes to elements to reproduce the element order.
3. Sort students according to their grade.
4. Take only the best 10 students.
5. Reproduce the order by sorting according to indexes.
6. Map values with indexes to just values.

Note that this implementation is concise and each operation performed on the collection is easy to read line by line.

> The big advantage of collection stream processing is that it is easy to manage the complexity of this process. We know that the complexity of most operations, such as `map` or `filter`, is **O**(n) and the complexity of sorting operations is **O**($n*log(n)$). The complexity of stream operations is the maximal complexity of each of the steps, so the complexity of the previous processing is **O**($n*log(n)$) because `sortedBy` is the step with the most complexity.

As the next example, let's suppose that we have a list containing the results of players in different categories:

```
class Result(
   val player: Player,
   val category: Category,
   val result: Double
)
class Player(val name: String)
enum class Category { SWIMMING, RUNNING, CYCLING }
```

And we have some example data:

```
val results = listOf(
   Result("Alex", Category.SWIMMING, 23.4),
   Result("Alex", Category.RUNNING, 43.2),
   Result("Alex", Category.CYCLING, 15.3),
   Result("Max", Category.SWIMMING, 17.3),
   Result("Max", Category.RUNNING, 33.3),
   Result("Bob", Category.SWIMMING, 29.9),
   Result("Bob", Category.CYCLING, 18.0)
)
```

Here is how we can find the best player in each category:

```
val bestInCategory = results.groupBy { it.category } // 1
   .mapValues { it.value.maxBy { it.result }?.player } // 2
print(bestInCategory)
// Prints: {SWIMMING=Bob, RUNNING=Alex, CYCLING=Bob}
```

1. We group results into categories. The return types are `Map<Category>` and `List<Result>`.
2. We are mapping values of the `map` function. Inside, we find the best result in this category and we take the player who is associated with this result. The return of the `mapValues` function is `Map<Category, Player?>`.

The preceding example shows how complex problems related to collections can be easily solved in Kotlin thanks to collection processing functions. After working with Kotlin for a while, most of those functions are well known to programmers, and then collection processing problems are quite easy to solve. Of course, functions as complicated as presented previously are rare, but simple processing with a few step is quite common in everyday programming.

Sequence

`Sequence` is an interface that is also used to refer to a collection of elements. It is an alternative for `Iterable`. For `Sequence`, there are separate implementations of most collection processing functions (`map`, `flatMap`, `filter`, `sorted`, and so on). The key difference is that all these functions are constructed in such a way that they return a sequence that is packaged over the previous sequence. Due to this, the following points become true:

- The size of the sequence does not need to be known in advance
- Sequence processing is more efficient, especially for large collections where we want to perform several transformations (details will be described later)

In Android, sequences are used for processing very big collections or for processing elements whose size is not known in advance (such as reading lines of a potentially long document). There are different ways to create sequences, but the easiest is the `asSequence` function called on `Iterable` or by using the `sequenceOf` top-level function to make a sequence in a similar way to a list.

Sequence size does not need to be known in advance, because values are calculated just when they are needed. Here is an example:

```
    val = generateSequence(1) { it + 1 } // 1. Instance of
GeneratorSequence
        .map { it * 2 } // 2. Instance of TransformingSequence
        .take(10) // 3. Instance of  TakeSequence
        .toList() // 4. Instance of List

    println(numbers) // Prints: [2, 4, 6, 8, 10, 12, 14, 16, 18, 20]
```

1. The `generateSequence` function is a method of sequence generation. This sequence contains the next numbers from 1 to infinity.

2. The `map` function packs a sequence into another that takes the value from the first sequence and then calculates the value after transformation.
3. The `take(10)` function will also pack a sequence into another one that finishes on the 10th element. Without this line execution, processing time would be infinite while we are operating on an infinite sequence.
4. Finally, the `toList` function processes each value and returns the final list.

It is important to stress that elements are processed one after another in the last step (in terminal operation). Let's look at another example, where every operation also prints values for logging purposes. Let's start with the following code:

```
val seq = generateSequence(1) { println("Generated ${it+1}"); it + 1 }
   .filter { println("Processing of filter: $it"); it % 2 == 1 }
   .map { println("Processing map: $it"); it * 2 }
   .take(2)
```

What would be printed in the console? Absolutely nothing. No values were calculated. The reason is that all those intermediate operations are lazy. To retrieve a result, we need to use a terminal operation, such as `toList`. Let's use the following:

```
seq.toList()
```

Then we will see the following in the console:

```
Processing of filter: 1
Processing map: 1
Generated 2
Processing of filter: 2
Generated 3
Processing of filter: 3
Processing map: 3
```

Notice that elements are fully processed one after another. In standard list processing, the order of operation would be totally different:

```
(1..4).onEach { println("Generated $it") }
   .filter { println("Processing filter: $it"); it % 2 == 1 }
   .map { println("Processing map: $it"); it * 2 }
```

The preceding code prints the following:

```
Generated 1
Generated 2
Generated 3
Generated 4
Processing filter: 1
```

```
Processing filter: 2
Processing filter: 3
Processing filter: 4
Processing map: 1
Processing map: 3
```

This explains why sequences are more efficient than classic collection processing--there is no need to create collections in intermediate steps. Values are processed one by one on demand.

Function literals with a receiver

Just as functions have a function type, that allows them to be kept as an object, extension functions have a type that allows them to be kept this way. It is called function type with a receiver. It looks like a simple function type, but the receiver type is located before arguments (like in an extension definition):

```
var power: Int.(Int) -&gt; Int
```

The introduction of a function type with receiver makes full cohesion between functions and types possible, because all functions can now be represented as objects. It can be defined using a lambda expression with a receiver or with an anonymous function with the receiver.

In a lambda expression with a receiver definition, the only difference is that we can refer to a receiver with `this`, and we can explicitly use receiver elements. For lambda expressions, the type must be specified in a parameter, because there is no syntax to specify receiver type. Here is `power` defined as a lambda expression with a receiver:

```
power = { n -> (1..n).fold(1) { acc, _ -> this * acc } }
```

An anonymous function also allows us to define the receiver, and its type is placed before the function name. In such a function, we can use `this` inside the body to refer to the extension receiver object. Note that anonymous extension functions specify the receiver type, so the property type can be inferred. Here is `power` defined as an anonymous extension function:

```
power = fun Int.(n: Int) = (1..n).fold(1) { acc, _ -> this * acc }
```

A function type with a receiver can be used as if it is a method of a receiver type:

```
val result = 10.power(3)
println(result) // Prints: 1000
```

A function type is most often used as a function parameter. Here is an example in which a parameter function is used to configure an element after its creation:

```
fun ViewGroup.addTextView(configure: TextView.()->Unit) {
    val view = TextView(context)
    view.configure()
    addView(view)
}

// Usage
val linearLayout = findViewById(R.id.contentPanel) as LinearLayout

linearLayout.addTextView { // 1
    text = "Marcin" // 2
    textSize = 12F // 2
}
```

1. Here we are using a lambda expression as an argument.
2. Inside the lambda expression, we can directly invoke receiver methods.

Kotlin standard library functions

The Kotlin standard library provide a set of extension functions (`let`, `apply`, `also`, `with`, `run`, and `to`) with generic non-restricted receivers (generic types have no restrictions). They are small and handy extensions, and it is very profitable to understand them, because they are very useful across all Kotlin projects. One of these functions, `let`, was briefly introduced in `Chapter 2`, *Laying a Foundation*, where we saw how it can be used as an alternative to a nullity check:

```
savedInstanceState?.let{ state ->
    println(state.getBoolean("isLocked"))
}
```

All that `let` does is call the specified function and return its result. While in the preceding example it is used together with a safe call operator, it will be called only when the `savedInstanceState` property is not null. The `let` function is actually just a generic extension function with a parameter function:

```
inline fun <T, R> T.let(block: (T) -> R): R = block(this)
```

In standard library, there are more functions similar to `let`. These functions are `apply`, `also`, `with`, and `run`. They are similar, so we are going to describe them together. Here are definitions of the rest of the functions:

```
inline fun <T> T.apply(block: T.() -> Unit): T {
    block();
    return this
}
inline fun <T> T.also(block: (T) -> Unit): T {
    block(this);
    return this
}
inline fun <T, R> T.run(block: T.() -> R): R = block()
inline fun <T, R> with(receiver: T, block: T.() -> R): R = receiver.block()
```

Let's see usage examples:

```
val mutableList = mutableListOf(1)
val mutableList = mutableListOf(1)
val letResult = mutableList.let {
    it.add(2)
    listOf("A", "B", "C")
}
println(letResult) // Prints: [A, B, C]
val applyResult = mutableList.apply {
    add(3)
    listOf("A", "B", "C")
}
println(applyResult) // Prints: [1, 2, 3]
val alsoResult = mutableList.also {
   it.add(4)
   listOf("A", "B", "C")
}
println(alsoResult) // Prints: [1, 2, 3, 4]
val runResult = mutableList.run {
   add(5)
   listOf("A", "B", "C")
}
println(runResult) // Prints: [A, B, C]
val withResult = with(mutableList) {
   add(6)
   listOf("A", "B", "C")
}
println(withResult) // Prints: [A, B, C]
println(mutableList) // Prints: [1, 2, 3, 4, 5, 6]
```

The differences are summarized in the following table:

Returned object/parameter function type	**Function literal with receiver** (receiver object represented as `this`)	**Function literal** (receiver object represented as `it`)
Receiver object	`apply`	`also`
Result of function literal	`run/with`	`let`

While those functions are similar and, in many cases, it is possible to use them interchangeably, there are conventions that define which functions are preferred for certain use cases.

The let function

The `let` function is preferred when we want to use standard functions as if they are extension functions in stream processing:

```
val newNumber = number.plus(2.0)
   .let { pow(it, 2.0) }
   .times(2)
```

Like other extensions, it can be combined with a save call operator:

```
val newNumber = number?.plus(2.0)
   ?.let { pow(it, 2.0) }
```

The `let` function is also preferred which we just want to unpack a nullable read-write property. In this situation, it is not possible to smart cast this property and we need to shadow it, like in this solution:

```
var name: String? = null

fun Context.toastName() {
    val name = name
    if(name != null) {
        toast(name)
    }
}
```

The `name` variable is the shadowing property name, what is necessary if name is a read-write property, because smart casting is only allowed on a mutable or local variable.

We can replace the preceding code with `let` and a safe call operator:

```
name?.let { setNewName(it) }
```

Note that by using Elvis operator, we can easily add a `return` or throw an exception when `name` is `null`:

```
name?.let { setNewName(it) } ?: throw Error("No name setten")
```

Similarly, `let` can be used as a replacement for the following statement:

```
val comment = if(field == null) getComment(field) else "No comment
```

An implementation that uses the `let` function would look like the following:

```
val comment = field?.let { getComment(it) } ?: "No comment"
```

The `let` function used this way is preferred in method chains that transform the receiver:

```
val text = "hello {name}"

fun correctStyle(text: String) = text
   .replace("hello", "hello,")

fun greet(name: String) {
    text.replace("{name}", name)
        .let { correctStyle(it) }
        .capitalize()
        .let { print(it) }
}

// Usage
greet("reader") // Prints: Hello, reader
```

We can also use simpler syntax by passing a function reference as an argument:

```
text.replace("{name}", name)
   .let(::correctStyle)
   .capitalize()
   .let(::print)
```

Using the apply function for initialization

Sometimes we need to create and initialize an object by calling some methods or modifying some properties, such as when we are creating a `Button`:

```
val button = Button(context)
button.text = "Click me"
button.isVisible = true
button.setOnClickListener { /* ... */ }
this.button = button
```

We can reduce code verbosity by using the `apply` extension function. We can call all these methods from the context where `button` is the receiver object:

```
button = Button(context).apply {
    text = "Click me"
    isVisible = true
    setOnClickListener { /* ... */ }
}
```

The also function

The `also` function is similar to `apply`, with the only difference being that the parameter function accepts an argument as an parameter rather than as an receiver. It is preferable when we want to do some operations on an object that are not initializations:

```
abstract class Provider<T> {

   var original: T? = null
   var override: T? = null

   abstract fun create(): T

   fun get(): T = override ?: original ?: create().also { original = it
}
}
```

The `also` function is also preferable when we need to do an operation in the middle of processing, for example, during object construction using the Builder pattern:

```
fun makeHttpClient(vararg interceptors: Interceptor) =
    OkHttpClient.Builder()
        .connectTimeout(60, TimeUnit.SECONDS)
        .readTimeout(60, TimeUnit.SECONDS)
        .also { it.interceptors().addAll(interceptors) }
        .build()
```

Another situation where `also` is preferable is when we are already in an extension function and we don't want to add another extension receiver:

```
class Snail {
    var name: String = ""
    var type: String = ""
    fun greet() {
        println("Hello, I am $name")
    }
}

class Forest {
    var members = listOf<Sneil>()
   fun Sneil.reproduce(): Sneil = Sneil().also {
       it.name = name
       it.type = type
       members += it
   }
}
```

The run and with functions

The `run` and `with` functions are both accepts a lambda literal with a receiver as an argument and return its result. The difference between them is that `run` accepts a receiver, while the `with` function is not an extension function and it takes the object we are operating in as a parameter. Both functions can be used as an alternative to the `apply` function when we are setting up an object:

```
val button = findViewById(R.id.button) as Button

button.apply {
    text = "Click me"
    isVisible = true
    setOnClickListener { /* ... */ }
}
```

```
button.run {
    text = "Click me"
    isVisible = true
    setOnClickListener { /* ... */ }
}

with(button) {
    text = "Click me"
    isVisible = true
    setOnClickListener { /* ... */ }
}
```

The difference between `apply`, `run`, and `with` is that `apply` returns a receiver object, while `run` and `with` returns the result of a function literal. However, when we need any of these, we should choose the function that is returning it. It is debatable which should be used when we do not need a returned value. Most often, it is recommended to use the `run` or `with` function rather than `apply`, because `also` is often used in situations when a returned value is needed.

Regarding the differences between the `run` and `with` functions, the `run` function is used instead of the `with` function when a value is nullable because then we can use a safe call or a not-null assertion:

```
val button = findViewById(R.id.button) as? Button

button?.run {
    text = "Click me"
    isVisible = true
   setOnClickListener { /* ... */ }
}
```

The `with` function is preferable to run, when an expression is short:

```
val button = findViewById(R.id.button) as Button

with(button) {
    text = "Click me"
    isVisible = true
    setOnClickListener { /* ... */ }
}
```

On the other hand, `run` is preferable to `with` when an expression is long:

```
itemAdapter.holder.button.run {
    text = "Click me"
    isVisible = true
    setOnClickListener { /* ... */ }
}
```

The to function

Infix functions were introduced in `Chapter 4`, *Classes and Objects*, but they can be defined not only as member classes, but also as extension functions. This makes it possible to create an infix extension function to any object. One of this kinds of extension functions is `to`, which was briefly described in `Chapter 2`, *Laying a Foundation*. Now we have the knowledge needed to understand its implementation. This is how `to` is defined:

```
infix fun <A, B> A.to(that: B): Pair<A, B> = Pair(this, that)
```

This makes it possible to place `to` between any two objects and make this way `Pair` with them:

```
println( 1 to 2 == Pair(1, 2) ) // Prints: true
```

Note that the fact that we can make `infix` extension functions allows us to define `infix` functions as an extension to any type. Here is an example:

```
infix fun <T> List<T>.intersection(other: List<T>)
    = filter { it in other }

listOf(1, 2, 3) intersection listOf(2, 3, 4) // [2,3]
```

Domain-specific language

Features such as a lambda literal with a receiver and member extension functions make it possible to define type-safe builders, which are used in Groovy. The most well-known Android example is the Gradle configuration `build.gradle`, which is currently written in Groovy. These kinds of builder are a good alternative to XML, HTML, or configuration files. The advantage of using Kotlin is that we can make such configurations fully type-safe and provide a better IDE. Such builders are one example of a Kotlin **domain-specific language** (**DSL**).

The most popular Kotlin DSL pattern in Android is the implementation of optional callback classes. They are used to solve a problem with a lack of functional support to callback interfaces with multiple methods. Classically, the implementation would require using an object-expression, as shown in the following example:

```
searchView.addTextChangedListener(object : TextWatcher {
  override fun beforeTextChanged(s: CharSequence, start: Int, count: Int,
after: Int) {}

  override fun onTextChanged(s: CharSequence, start: Int, before: Int,
count: Int) {
    presenter.onSearchChanged(s.toString())
  }

  override fun afterTextChanged(s: Editable) {}
})
```

The main problems with such implementations are as follows:

- We need to implement all methods present in the interface
- The function structure needs to be implemented for each method
- We need to use object expressions

Let's define the following class, which keeps callbacks as mutable properties:

```
class TextWatcherConfig : TextWatcher {

  private var beforeTextChangedCallback: (BeforeTextChangedFunction)? =
null // 1
  private var onTextChangedCallback: (OnTextChangedFunction)? = null // 1
  private var afterTextChangedCallback: (AfterTextChangedFunction)? = null
// 1

  fun beforeTextChanged(callback: BeforeTextChangedFunction){  // 2
    beforeTextChangedCallback = callback
  }

  fun onTextChanged(callback: OnTextChangedFunction) { // 2
    onTextChangedCallback = callback
  }

  fun afterTextChanged(callback: AfterTextChangedFunction) { // 2
    afterTextChangedCallback = callback
  }

  override fun beforeTextChanged (s: CharSequence?, start: Int, count: Int,
  after: Int) { // 3
```

```
        beforeTextChangedCallback?.invoke(s?.toString(), start, count, after)
    // 4
      }

      override fun onTextChanged(s: CharSequence?, start: Int, before:
      Int, count: Int) { // 3
        onTextChangedCallback?.invoke(s?.toString(), start, before, count) // 4
      }

      override fun afterTextChanged(s: Editable?) { // 3
        afterTextChangedCallback?.invoke(s)
      }
    }

    private typealias BeforeTextChangedFunction =
    (text: String?, start: Int, count: Int, after: Int)->Unit
    private typealias OnTextChangedFunction =
    (text: String?, start: Int, before: Int, count: Int)->Unit

    private typealias AfterTextChangedFunction =
    (s: Editable?)->Unit
```

1. Callbacks that are used when any of the overridden functions are called.
2. Functions are used to set new callbacks. Their names correspond to handler function names, but they include `callback` as a parameter.
3. Each event handler function invokes a callback if it exists.
4. To simplify usage, we also changed types, `CharSequence` in the original methods was changed to `String`.

Now all we need is an extension function that will simplify callback configuration. Its name cannot be the same as any name of `TextView`, but all we need to make a small modification:

```
fun TextView.addOnTextChangedListener(config: TextWatcherConfig.()->Unit) {
    val textWatcher = TextWatcherConfig()
    textWatcher.config()
    addTextChangedListener(textWatcher)
}
```

With such definitions, we can define the callbacks we need like this:

```
searchView.addOnTextChangedListener {
   onTextChanged { text, start, before, count ->
       presenter.onSearchChanged(text)
   }
}
```

We use underscore to hide unused parameters, to improve our implementation:

```
searchView.addOnTextChangedListener {
    onTextChanged { text, _, _, _ ->
        presenter.onSearchChanged(text)
    }
}
```

Now two other callbacks, `beforeTextChanged` and `afterTextChanged`, are ignored, but we can still add other implementations:

```
searchView.addOnTextChangedListener {
    beforeTextChanged { _, _, _, _ ->
        Log.i(TAG, "beforeTextChanged invoked")
    }
    onTextChanged { text, _, _, _ ->
        presenter.onSearchChanged(text)
    }
    afterTextChanged {
        Log.i(TAG, "beforeTextChanged invoked")
    }
}
```

A listener defined this way has the following properties:

- It is shorter than an object expression implementation
- It includes default function implementations
- It allows us to hide unused parameters

While in Android SDK there are multiple listeners with more than one handler, DSL implementation of optional callback classes is really popular in Android projects. Similar implementations can be also found in libraries such as the already-mentioned Anko.

Another example is DSL, which will be used to define the layout structure without using XML layout files. We will define a function to add and configure `LinearLayout` and `TextView`, and use it to define a simple view:

```
fun Context.linearLayout(init: LinearLayout.() -> Unit): LinearLayout {
    val layout = LinearLayout(this)
    layout.layoutParams = LayoutParams(WRAP_CONTENT, WRAP_CONTENT)
    layout.init()
    return layout
}

fun ViewGroup.linearLayout(init: LinearLayout.() -> Unit): LinearLayout
{
```

```
    val layout = LinearLayout(context)
    layout.layoutParams = LayoutParams(WRAP_CONTENT, WRAP_CONTENT)
    layout.init()
    addView(layout)
    return layout
}

fun ViewGroup.textView(init: TextView.() -> Unit): TextView {
    val layout = TextView(context)
    layout.layoutParams = LayoutParams(WRAP_CONTENT, WRAP_CONTENT)
    layout.init()
    addView(layout)
    return layout
}

// Usage
class MainActivity : AppCompatActivity() {

   override fun onCreate(savedInstanceState: Bundle?) {
       super.onCreate(savedInstanceState)
       val view = linearLayout {
           orientation = LinearLayout.VERTICAL
           linearLayout {
               orientation = LinearLayout.HORIZONTAL
               textView { text = "A" }
               textView { text = "B" }
           }
           linearLayout {
               orientation = LinearLayout.HORIZONTAL
               textView { text = "C" }
               textView { text = "D" }
           }
       }
       setContentView(view)
   }
}
```

We can also define our custom DSL from scratch. Let's make a simple DSL that defines a list of articles. We know that each article should be defined in a different category, and that each has its name, URL, and tags. What we would like to achieve is the following definition:

```
category("Kotlin") {
    post {
        name = "Awesome delegates"
        url = "SomeUrl.com"
    }
    post {
        name = "Awesome extensions"
```

```
            url = "SomeUrl.com"
        }
    }
    category("Android") {
        post {
            name = "Awesome app"
            url = "SomeUrl.com"
            tags = listOf("Kotlin", "Google Login")
        }
    }
```

The simplest object here is the `Post` class. It holds a post's properties and allows them to be changed:

```
class Post {
    var name: String = ""
    var url: String = ""
    var tags: List<String> = listOf()
}
```

Next, we need to define a class that will hold the category. It needs to store a list of posts and it also needs to contain its name. There must also be a defined function that will allow simple post addition. This function needs to contain a function parameter in which `Post` is the receiver type. Here is the definition:

```
class PostCategory(val name: String) {
    var posts: List<Post> = listOf()

    fun post(init: Post.()->Unit) {
        val post = Post()
        post.init()
        posts += post
    }
}
```

Also, we need a class that will hold a list of categories and allow simple category definition:

```
class PostList {

    var categories: List<PostCategory> = listOf()

    fun category(name: String, init: PostCategory.()->Unit) {
        val category = PostCategory(name)
        category.init()
        categories += category
    }
}
```

All we need now is the `definePosts` function, the definition of which might be the following:

```
fun definePosts(init: PostList.()->Unit): PostList {
    val postList = PostList()
    postList.init()
    return postList
}
```

And that's all we need. Now we can define the object structure with a simple, type-safe builder:

```
val postList = definePosts {
    category("Kotlin") {
        post {
            name = "Awesome delegates"
            url = "SomeUrl.com"
        }
        post {
            name = "Awesome extensions"
            url = "SomeUrl.com"
        }
    }
    category("Android") {
        post {
            name = "Awesome app"
            url = "SomeUrl.com"
            tags = listOf("Kotlin", "Google Login")
        }
    }
}
```

A DSL is a really powerful concept that is being used is more and more around the Kotlin community. It is already possible, thanks to libraries, to use the Kotlin DSL to fully replace the following:

- Android layout files (Anko)
- Gradle configuration files
- HTML files (`kotlinx.html`)
- JSON files (Kotson)

And lots of other configuration files. Let's look at an example library that defines a Kotlin DSL to provide type-safe builders.

Anko

Anko is a library that provides a DSL to define Android views without any XML layouts. This is pretty similar to examples we've already seen, but Anko made it possible to fully remove XML layout files from a project. Here is an example view written in the Anko DSL:

```
verticalLayout {
    val name = editText()
    button("Say Hello") {
        onClick { toast("Hello, ${name.text}!") }
    }
}
```

And here is the result:

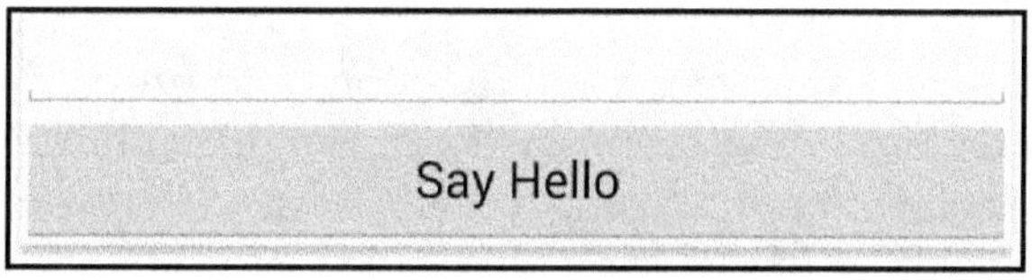

Source: `https://github.com/Kotlin/anko`

It is also possible to define much more complex layouts using the Anko DSL. These views can be placed either on a custom class that serves as a view or even directly inside the `onCreate` method:

```
override fun onCreate(savedInstanceState: Bundle?) {
    super.onCreate(savedInstanceState)

   verticalLayout {
       padding = dip(30)
       editText {
           hint = "Name"
           textSize = 24f
       }
       editText {
            hint = "Password"
            textSize = 24f
       }
       button("Login") {
          textSize = 26f
       }
   }
}
```

To learn more about this example, you can visit the Anko wiki at `https://github.com/Kotlin/anko/wiki/Anko-Layouts`.

It is still debatable if DSL layout definitions are going to replace XML definitions. At the time of writing, it is not very popular to define views this way because of a lack of support from Google, but Google have announced that they are going to support Kotlin, so it is possible that this idea will become more popular and DSL-based layouts will be better supported and maybe even be universal someday.

Summary

In this chapter, we discussed Kotlin extension functions and properties, both defined at the top level and as type member. We've seen how Kotlin standard library extension functions can be used to simplify collection processing and perform various operations. We have also described function types with a receiver together with function literals with a receiver. Also, we've seen a few important generic functions from the standard library that use extensions: `let`, `apply`, `also`, `with`, `run`, and `to`. Finally, we've seen how a DSL can be defined in Kotlin, and where it is useful.

In the next chapter, we will explore another feature that is not present in Java, but that provides a lot of functionality in Kotlin: class and property delegates.

8
Delegates

Kotlin takes design patterns pretty seriously. Previously, we've seen how the usage of the Singleton pattern can be simplified using object declarations, and how usage of the Observator pattern can be trivialized using higher-order functions and functional types. Kotlin also simplifies the usage of most functional patterns, thanks to lambda expressions and functional types. In this chapter, we will see how the use of the Delegation and Decorator patterns can be simplified thanks to class delegation. We will also look at a feature that is pretty new in the programming world--property delegation--and how it is used to make Kotlin properties much more powerful.

In this chapter, we will cover the following topics:

- The Delegation pattern
- Class delegation
- The Decorator pattern
- Property delegation
- Property delegates from the standard library
- The creation of a custom property delegate

Class delegation

Kotlin has a feature called **class delegation**. It is a really inconspicuous feature that has many practical applications. It is worth noticing, that it is strongly connected with two design patterns: the Delegation pattern and the Decorator patterns. We will discuss those patterns in more detail in upcoming sections. Delegation and Decorator pattern have been around for many years, but in Java their implementation required a lot of boilerplate code. Kotlin was one of the first languages to provide native support for those patterns, reducing boilerplate code to a minimum.

The Delegation pattern

In object-oriented programming, the Delegation pattern is a design pattern that is an alternative to inheritance. Delegation means that the object handles a request by delegating it to another object (delegate), instead of extending the class.

To support the polymorphic behavior known from Java, both objects should implement the same interface which holds all the delegated methods and properties. A simple example of the Delegation pattern is the following:

```
interface Player { // 1
    fun playGame()
}

class RpgGamePlayer(val enemy: String) : Player {
    override fun playGame() {
        println("Killing $enemy")
    }
}

class WitcherPlayer(enemy: String) : Player {
    val player = RpgGamePlayer(enemy) // 2
    override fun playGame() {
        player.playGame() // 3
    }
}

// Usage
RpgGamePlayer("monsters").playGame() // Prints: Killing monsters
WitcherPlayer("monsters").playGame() // Prints: Killing monsters
```

1. When we are talking about class delegation, there needs to be an interface that defines which methods are delegated.
2. The object that we are delegating to (delegate).
3. All methods inside the `WitcherPlayer` class should call corresponding methods on the delegate object (`player`).

This is called delegation because the `WitcherPlayer` class is delegating methods defined in the `Player` interface to an instance of type `RpgGamePlayer` (`player`). A similar result could be achieved by using inheritance instead of delegation. This would look as follows:

```
class WitcherPlayer() : RpgGamePlayer()
```

At first glance, these two approaches might look similar, but delegation and inheritance have a lot of differences. On one hand, inheritance is much more popular and more widely used. It is often used in Java, and is connected to multiple OOP patterns. On the other hand, there are sources that strongly support delegation. For example, the influential book *Design Patterns*, by the *Gang of Four*, contains the principle *favor object composition over class inheritance*. The popular book *Effective Java* also includes the rule: *favor composition over inheritance* (*Item 6*). Both of them strongly support the Delegation pattern. Here are some basic arguments that stand behind the usage of the Delegation pattern instead of inheritance:

- Often, classes are not designed for inheritance. When we override methods, we are not aware of underlying assumptions about the internal behavior of a (when methods are called, how those calls affect the objects, states, and so on). For example, when we override a method, we might not be aware that it is used by other methods, so overridden methods may be called unexpectedly by a superclass. Even if we check when the method is called, this behavior could change in a new version of the class (for example, if we extend a class from an external library), and thus break our subclass's behavior. A very small number of classes are properly designed and documented for inheritance, but nearly all non-abstract classes are designed for usage (this includes delegation).
- In Java, it is possible to delegate a class to multiple classes, but inherit only from one.
- By interface, we are specifying which methods and properties we want to delegate. This is compatible with the *interface segregation* principle (from SOLID)--we shouldn't expose unnecessary methods to the client.

- Some classes are final, so we can only delegate to them. In fact, all classes that are not designed for inheritance should be final. Kotlin designers were aware of this, and they made all classes in Kotlin final by default.
- Making a class final and providing a proper interface is good practice for public libraries. We can change the implementation of a class without worrying that it will affect library users (as long as the behavior will be the same from an interface point of view). It makes them impossible to inherit from, but they are still great candidates to delegate to.

More information on how classes should be designed to support inheritance and when delegation should be used can be found in the book *Effective Java*, in *Item 16: Favor composition over inheritance.*

Of course, there are also disadvantages to using delegation instead of inheritance. Here are the main problems:

- We need to create interfaces that specify which methods should be delegated
- We don't have access to protected methods and properties

In Java, there is one more strong argument for using inheritance: it is much easier to implement. Even when comparing code from our `WitcherPlayer` example, we can see that delegation needed a lot of extra code:

```
class WitcherPlayer(enemy: String) : Player {
    val player = RpgGamePlayer(enemy)
    override fun playGame() {
        player.playGame()
    }
}

class WitcherPlayer() : RpgGamePlayer()
```

This is especially problematic when we are dealing with interfaces with multiple methods. Fortunately, modern languages value the use of the Delegation pattern, and many of them have native class delegation support. There is strong support for the Delegation pattern in Swift and Groovy, and there is also support through other mechanisms in Ruby, Python, JavaScript, and Smalltalk. Kotlin also strongly supports class delegation, and makes using this pattern really simple, using almost zero boilerplate code. The `WitcherPlayer` class from the example could be implemented in this way in Kotlin:

```
class WitcherPlayer(enemy: String) : Player by RpgGamePlayer(enemy) {}
```

Using the `by` keyword, we inform the compiler to delegate all methods defined in the `Player` interface from `WitcherPlayer` to `RpgGamePlayer`. An instance of `RpgGamePlayer` is created during the `WitcherPlayer` construction. In simpler words `WitcherPlayer` delegates methods defined in the `Player` interface to a new `RpgGamePlayer` object.

What is really happening here is that during compilation, the Kotlin compiler generates unimplemented methods from `Player` in `WitcherPlayer` and fills them with calls to an `RpgGamePlayer` instance (the same way that we implemented them in the first example). A big improvement is that we don't need to implement those methods ourselves. Also, note that if a signature of a delegated method changes, then we don't need to change all objects that are delegated to it, so the class is easier to maintain.

There is another way to create and hold an instance of the delegate. It can be provided by a constructor, as in this example:

```
class WitcherPlayer(player: Player) : Player by player
```

We can also delegate to a property defined in the constructor:

```
class WitcherPlayer(val player: Player) : Player by player
```

Finally, we can delegate to any property accessible during class declaration:

```
val d = RpgGamePlayer(10)
class WitcherPlayer(a: Player) : Player by d
```

In addition, one object can have multiple different delegates:

```
interface Player {
    fun playGame()
}

interface GameMaker { // 1
    fun developGame()
}

class WitcherPlayer(val enemy: String) : Player {
    override fun playGame() {
        print("Killin $enemy! ")
    }
}

class WitcherCreator(val gameName: String) : GameMaker{
    override fun developGame() {
        println("Makin $gameName! ")
    }
}

class WitcherPassionate :
    Player by WitcherPlayer("monsters"),
    GameMaker by WitcherCreator("Witcher 3") {

    fun fulfillYourDestiny() {
        playGame()
        developGame()
    }
}

// Usage
WitcherPassionate().fulfillYourDestiny() // Killin monsters! Makin
Witcher 3!
```

1. The `WitcherPlayer` class delegates the `Player` interface to a new `RpgGamePlayer` object, `GameMaker` to a new `WitcherCreator` object, and also includes the `fulfillYourDestiny` function which uses functions from both delegates. Note that neither `WitcherPlayer` nor `WitcherCreator` are neither tagged as open, and without this, they cannot be extended. They can be delegated, though.

With such language support, the Delegation pattern is much more attractive than inheritance. While this pattern has both advantages and disadvantages, it is good to know when it should be used. The main cases where delegates should be used are as follows:

- When your subclass violates the *Liskov substitution principle*; for example, when we are dealing with situations where inheritance was implemented only to reuse code of the superclass, but it does not really acts like it.
- When the subclass uses only a portion of the methods of the superclass. In this case, it is only a matter of time before someone calls a superclass method that they were not supposed to call. Using delegation, we reuse only methods we choose (defined in the interface).
- When we cannot, or we should not, inherit because:
    - The class is final
    - It is not accessible and is used from behind the interface
    - It is just not designed for inheritance

Note that while classes in Kotlin are final by default, most of them will be left final. If those classes are placed in a library, then most likely we won't be able to change or open the class. Delegation will be the only option, to make a class with different behavior.

> The Liskov substitution principle is a concept in OOP stating that all subclasses should act like their superclasses. In simpler words, if unit tests pass for some class, they should be passing for its subclasses too. This principle has been popularized by Robert C. Martin, who placed it in his set of the most important OOP rules and described it in the popular book *Clean Code*.

The book *Effective Java* states that "*inheritance is appropriate only in circumstances where a subclass really is a subtype of the superclass.*" In other words, class `B` should extend a class only if an *is-a* relationship exists between the two classes. If you are tempted to have class `B` extend class `A`, ask yourself *Is every B really an A?* In the next sections, the book suggests that in every other case, composition should be used (which most common implementation is delegation).

It is also worth noting that Cocoa (the UI framework from Apple for building software programs to run on iOS) very often uses delegates instead of inheritance. This pattern is becoming more and more popular, and in Kotlin it is highly supported.

Decorator pattern

Another common case where Kotlin class delegation is really useful is when we are implementing a Decorator pattern. A Decorator pattern (also known as a Wrapper pattern) is a design pattern that makes it possible to add a behavior to an existing class without using inheritance. In contrast to extensions, where we can add a new behavior without modifying an object, we create a concrete object with a different behavior. A Decorator pattern uses delegation, but in a very specific way--a delegate is provided from outside of the class. The classic structure is presented in the following UML diagram:

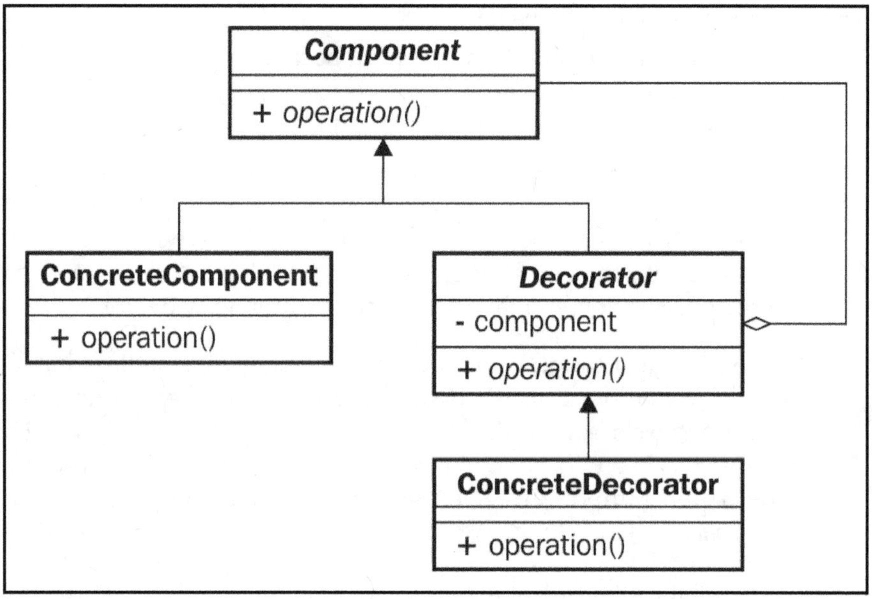

UML diagram of a classic implementation of the Decorator pattern. Source: `http://upload.wikimedia.org`

The Decorator contains the objects that it is decorating while it is implementing the same interface.

The most popular example of decorator usage from the Java world is `InputStream`. There are different kinds of types that extend `InputStream`, and a lot of decorators that can be used to add functionalities to them. This decorator can be used to add buffering, get the contents of a zipped file, or convert file content into a Java object. Let's look at the example where multiple decorators are used to read a zipped Java object:

```
// Java
FileInputStream fis = new FileInputStream("/someFile.gz"); // 1
BufferedInputStream bis = new BufferedInputStream(fis); // 2
GzipInputStream gis = new GzipInputStream(bis); // 3
ObjectInputStream ois = new ObjectInputStream(gis); // 4
SomeObject someObject = (SomeObject) ois.readObject(); // 5
```

1. Create a simple stream to read a file.
2. Make a new stream that contains buffering.
3. Make a new stream that contains functionality to read compressed data in the GZIP file format.
4. Make a new stream that adds functionality that deserializes primitive data and objects previously written using an `ObjectOutputStream`.
5. A stream is used in the `readObject` method of `ObjectInputStream`, but all objects in this example implement `InputStream` (which is what makes it possible to pack it this way) and can be read by the methods specified by this interface.

Note that this pattern is also similar to inheritance, but we can decide which decorators we want to use and in what order. This is much more flexible and offers more possibilities during usage. Some people argue that `InputStream` usage would be better if designers make one big class with all the designed functionalities, and then use methods to turn some of them on or off. This approach would violate the *single-responsibility principle* and lead to much more complicated and much less expandable code.

While the Decorator pattern is considered one of the best in practical use, it is rarely used in Java projects. This is because the implementation is not simple. Interfaces often contain multiple methods and creating a delegation to them in each decorator generates lots of boilerplate code. There is a different situation in Kotlin--we've already seen that in Kotlin class delegation is actually trivial. Let's look at some classic examples of practical class delegation usage in the Decorator pattern. Let's suppose that we want to add the first position as the *zero* element to several different `ListAdapters`. This extra position has some special properties. We couldn't implement this using inheritance, because these `ListAdapters` for different lists are of different types (which is the standard situation). In this case, we can either change the behaviors of each class (DRY rule) or we can create a decorator. Here is the short code for this decorator:

```
class ZeroElementListDecorator(val arrayAdapter: ListAdapter) :
    ListAdapter by arrayAdapter {
  override fun getCount(): Int = arrayAdapter.count + 1
  override fun getItem(position: Int): Any? = when {
      position == 0 -> null
      else -> arrayAdapter.getItem(position - 1)
  }

  override fun getView(position: Int, convertView: View?,parent:
ViewGroup): View = when {
    position == 0 -> parent.context.inflator
        .inflate(R.layout.null_element_layout, parent, false)
    else -> arrayAdapter.getView(position - 1, convertView, parent)
  }
}

override fun getItemId(position: Int): Long = when {
  position == 0 -> 0
  else -> arrayAdapter.getItemId(position - 1)
}
```

We used an inflator extension property of `Context` here, which is often included in Kotlin Android projects and should be familiar from `Chapter 7`, *Extension Functions and Properties*:

```
val Context.inflater: LayoutInflater
    get() = LayoutInflater.from(this)
```

The `ZeroElementListDecorator` class defined this way always adds a first element with a static view. Here, we can see a simple example of its use:

```
val arrayList = findViewById(R.id.list) as ListView
val list = listOf("A", "B", "C")
val arrayAdapter = ArrayAdapter(this,
      android.R.layout.simple_list_item_1, list)
arrayList.adapter = ZeroElementListDecorator(arrayAdapter)
```

In `ZeroElementListDecorator`, it might look complicated that we needed to override four methods, but in fact there are eight more of them and we didn't have to override them, thanks to Kotlin's class delegation. We can see that Kotlin class delegation is making the implementation of the Decorator pattern much easier.

The Decorator pattern is really simple to implement and is pretty intuitive. It can be used in lots of different cases to extend a class with extra functionality. It is really safe and often referred to as a good practice. These examples are just some of the possibilities provided by class delegation. I am sure that the reader will find more use cases with the presented patterns and use class delegation to make the project more clean, safe, and concise.

Property delegation

Kotlin allows not only class delegation, but also property delegation. In this section, we are going to find out what delegated properties are, review property delegates from the Kotlin standard library, and learn how to create and use custom property delegates.

What are delegated properties?

Let's start with an explanation of what property delegates are. Here is an example of the use of property delegation:

```
class User(val name: String, val surname: String)

var user: User by UserDelegate() // 1

println(user.name)
user = User("Marcin","Moskala")
```

1. We are delegating the `user` property to an instance of `UserDelegate` (which is created by the constructor).

Property delegation is similar to class delegation. We delegate to an object using the same keyword (`by`). Each call to a property (`set`/`get`) will be delegated to another object (`UserDelegate`). This way, we can reuse the same behavior for multiple properties, for example, setting a property value only when some criteria are met, or adding a log entry when a property is accessed/updated.

We know that a property doesn't really need a backing field. It might be defined just by a getter (read-only) or a getter/setter (read-write). Under the hood, property delegates are just translated to corresponding method calls (`setValue`/`getValue`). The preceding example would be compiled with the following code:

```
var p$delegate = UserDelegate()
var user: User
get() = p$delegate.getValue(this, ::user)
set(value) {
    p$delegate.setValue(this, ::user, value)
}
```

The example shows that by using the `by` keyword, we are delegating the setter and getter calls to a delegate. That is why any object that has the `getValue` and `setValue` functions with the correct parameters (this will be explained later) can be used as a delegate (for read-only properties, `getValue` is enough, because only the getter is needed). It is important that all that class needs to be able to serve as a property delegate is to have these two methods. No interface is needed. Here is an example implementation of `UserDelegate`:

```
class UserDelegate {
    operator fun getValue(thisRef: Any?, property: KProperty<*>):
          User = readUserFromFile()
    operator fun setValue(thisRef: Any?, property: KProperty<*>,
          user:User) {
        saveUserToFile(user)
    }
    //...
}
```

The `setValue` and `getValue` methods are used to set and get the value of a property (the property setter call is delegated to a `setValue` method, and the property getter delegates the value to the `getValue` method). Both functions need to be marked with the `operator` keyword. They have a special set of parameters that determine where and to which property the delegate can serve. If a property is read-only, then an object only needs to have a `getValue` method to be able to serve as its delegate:

```
class UserDelegate {

    operator fun getValue(thisRef: Any?, property: KProperty<*>):
```

```
        User = readUserFromFile()
}
```

The type returned by the `getValue` method and the type of property that the user defined in the `setValue` method determines the type of the delegated property.

The type of the first parameter of both the `getValue` and `setValue` functions (`thisRef`) is contains a reference to the context in which a delegate is used. It can be used to restrict the types that a delegate can be used for. For example, we can define delegate that might be used only inside an `Activity` class in the following way:

```
class UserDelegate {
    operator fun getValue(thisRef: Activity, property: KProperty<*>):
          User = thisRef.intent
          .getParcelableExtra("com.example.UserKey")
}
```

As you can see, there will be a reference to `this` provided in all the contexts where it is available. Only inside an extension function or on extension property, null is placed instead. Reference to `this` is used to get some data from context. If we would type it to `Activity`, then we would be able to use this delegate only inside `Activity` (in any context where `this` is of the type `Activity`).

Also, if we want to force the delegate to be used only on the top-level, we can then specify the first parameter (`thisRef`) type as `Nothing?`, because the only possible value of this type is `null`.

Another parameter in these methods is `property`. It contains a reference to a delegated property, which contains its metadata (property name, type, and so on).

Property delegation can be used for properties defined in any context (top-level properties, member properties, local variables, and so on):

```
var a by SomeDelegate() // 1

fun someTopLevelFun() {
    var b by SomeDelegate() // 2
}

class SomeClass() {
    var c by SomeDelegate() // 3

    fun someMethod() {
        val d by SomeDelegate() // 4
    }
}
```

1. At top-level property with a delegate.
2. A local variable (inside a top-level function) with a delegate.
3. A member property with a delegate.
4. A local variable (inside a method) with delegate.

In the next few sections, we will describe delegates from the Kotlin standard library. They are important not only because they are often useful, but also because they are good examples of how property delegation can be used.

Predefined delegates

The Kotlin standard library contains some property delegates that are very handy. Let's discuss how they can be used in real-life projects.

The lazy function

Sometimes we need to initialize an object, but we want to make sure that the object will be initialized only once, when it is used for the first time. In Java, we could solve this problem in the following way:

```
private var _someProperty: SomeType? = null
private val somePropertyLock = Any()
val someProperty: SomeType
get() {
    synchronized(somePropertyLock) {
        if (_someProperty == null) {
            _someProperty = SomeType()
        }
        return _someProperty!!
    }
}
```

This construction is a popular pattern in Java development. Kotlin allows us to solve this problem in a much simpler way by providing the `lazy` delegate. It is the most commonly used delegate. It works only with read-only properties (`val`) and its usage is as follows:

```
val someProperty by lazy { SomeType() }
```

The `lazy` function in the standard library function that is providing delegate:

```
public fun <T> lazy(initializer: () -> T):
      Lazy<T> =  SynchronizedLazyImpl(initializer)
```

Formally, in this example object of `SynchronizedLazyImpl`, it is used as a property delegate, although most often it is called a **lazy delegate** from its corresponding function name, the same way other delegates are named from the names of the functions that provide them.

> A lazy delegate also has a thread safety mechanism. By default, delegates are fully thread-safe, but we can change this behavior to make this function more efficient in situations where we know that there never will be more than one thread using it at the same time. To fully turn off thread-safety mechanisms, we need to place the `enum` type value `LazyThreadSafetyMode.NONE` as a first argument of the `lazy` function:
>
> ```
> val someProperty by lazy(LazyThreadSafetyMode.NONE) {
> SomeType() }
> ```

Thanks to the lazy delegate, the initialization, of the property is delayed until the value is needed. Usage of the lazy delegate provides several benefits:

- Faster class initialization leading to faster application startup time, because value initialization is delayed until they are used for the first time
- Some values may never be used for certain flows, so they will never be initialized--we save resources (memory, processor time, and battery)

Another benefit is that some objects need to be created later, after their class instance has been created. For example, in `Activity` we cannot access the resources before the layout is set using the `setContentView` method, which is typically called inside the `onCreate` method. This will be presented it in this example. Let's look at the Java class with view reference elements filled in the classic Java way:

```
//Java
public class MainActivity extends Activity {

    TextView questionLabelView
    EditText answerLabelView
    Button confirmButtonView

    @Override
    public void onCreate(Bundle savedInstanceState) {
        super.onCreate(savedInstanceState);
        setContentView(R.layout.activity_main);

        questionLabelView = findViewById<TextView>
              (R.id.main_question_label);
        answerLabelView   = findViewById<EditText>
```

```
                (R.id.main_answer_label);
            confirmButtonView = findViewById<Button>
                (R.id.main_button_confirm);
        }
    }
```

If we translate this into Kotlin one to one, it will look as follows:

```
class MainActivity : Activity() {

    var questionLabelView: TextView? = null
    var answerLabelView: TextView? = null
    var confirmButtonView: Button? = null

    override fun onCreate(savedInstanceState: Bundle) {
        super.onCreate(savedInstanceState)
        setContentView(R.layout.main_activity)

        questionLabelView = findViewById<TextView>
              (R.id.main_question_label)
        answerLabelView = findViewById<TextView>
              (R.id.main_answer_label)
        confirmButtonView = findViewById<Button>
              (R.id.main_button_confirm)
    }
}
```

Using the lazy delegate, we can implement this behavior in a simpler way:

```
class MainActivity : Activity() {

   val questionLabelView: TextView by lazy
{ findViewById(R.id.main_question_label) as TextView }
   val answerLabelView: TextView by lazy
{ findViewById(R.id.main_answer_label) as TextView }
   val confirmButtonView: Button by lazy
{ findViewById(R.id.main_button_confirm) as Button }

   override fun onCreate(savedInstanceState: Bundle) {
     super.onCreate(savedInstanceState)
     setContentView(R.layout.main_activity)
   }
}
```

The benefits of this approach are as follows:

- The property is declared and initialized in a single place, so the code is more concise.
- The properties are non-nullable instead of nullable. This prevents lots of useless nullability checks.
- The properties are read-only so, thanks to that, we have all the benefits, such as thread synchronization and smart casts.
- The lambda passed to the lazy delegate (containing `findViewById`) will be executed only when the property is accessed for the first time.
- Values will be taken later than during class creation. This will speed up the startup. If we won't use some of these views, their values won't be taken at all (`findViewById` is not really an efficient operation when the view is complex).
- Any unused property will be marked by the compiler. In the Java implementation they won't, because a set value would be recognized by the compiler as usage.

We can improve the preceding implementation by extracting the common behavior and converting it into an extension function:

```
fun <T: View> Activity.bindView(viewId: Int) = lazy { findViewById(viewId)
as T }
```

Then, we can define the view bindings in simpler, more concise code:

```
class MainActivity : Activity() {

  var questionLabelView: TextView by bindView(R.id.main_question_label)  //
1
  var answerLabelView: TextView by bindView(R.id.main_answer_label)   // 1
  var confirmButtonView: Button by bindView(R.id.main_button_confirm) // 1

  override fun onCreate(savedInstanceState: Bundle) {
    super.onCreate(savedInstanceState)
    setContentView(R.layout.main_activity)
  }
}
```

1. We don't need to set the type provided to the `bindView` function because it is inferred from the property type.

Now we have a single delegate that calls `findViewById` under the hood, when we access a particular view for the first time. This is a very concise solution.

> There is another way of dealing with this problem. The current popular one is the *Kotlin Android Extension* plugin, which generates auto-binding to views in `Activities` and `Fragments`. We will discuss the practical applications in `Chapter 9`, *Making Your Marvel Gallery Application*.

Even with such support, there are still benefits to be had from staying with bindings. One is explicit knowledge of which elements of the view we are using, and another is the separation between the name of element ID and the name of the variable in which we hold this element. Also compilation time is faster.

The same mechanism can be applied to solve other Android related problems, for example, when we pass an argument to `Activity`. The standard Java implementation looks as follows:

```
//Java
class SettingsActivity extends Activity {

  final Doctor DOCTOR_KEY = "doctorKey"
  final String TITLE_KEY = "titleKey"

  Doctor doctor
  Address address
  String title

  public static void start ( Context context, Doctor doctor,
  String title ) {
    Intent intent = new Intent(context, SettingsActivity.class )
    intent.putExtra(DOCTOR_KEY, doctor)
    intent.putExtra(TITLE_KEY, title)
    context.startActivity(intent)
  }
  @Override
  public void onCreate(Bundle savedInstanceState) {
    super.onCreate(savedInstanceState);
    setContentView(R.layout.activity_main);

    doctor = getExtras().getParcelable(DOCTOR_KEY)
    title = getExtras().getString(TITLE_KEY)

    ToastHelper.toast(this, doctor.id)
    ToastHelper.toast(this, title)
  }
}
```

We could write the same implementation in Kotlin, but we can also retrieve parameter values (`getString`/`getParcelable`) together with the variable declaration. To do this, we need the following extension functions:

```
fun <T : Parcelable> Activity.extra(key: String) = lazy
    { intent.extras.getParcelable<T>(key) }

fun Activity.extraString(key: String) = lazy
    { intent.extras.getString(key) }
```

Then we can get extra parameters by using the `extra` and `extraString` delegates:

```
class SettingsActivity : Activity() {

    private val doctor by extra<Doctor>(DOCTOR_KEY) // 1
    private val title by extraString(TITLE_KEY) // 1

    override fun onCreate(savedInstanceState: Bundle?) {
        super.onCreate(savedInstanceState)
        setContentView(R.layout.settings_activity)
        toast(doctor.id) // 2
        toast(title) // 2
    }

    companion object { // 3
        const val DOCTOR_KEY = "doctorKey"
        const val TITLE_KEY = "titleKey"

    fun start(context: Context, doctor: Doctor, title: String) { // 3
        ontext.startActivity(getIntent<SettingsActivity>().apply { // 4
            putExtra(DOCTOR_KEY, doctor) // 5
            putExtra(TITLE_KEY, title) // 5
        })
    }
  }
}
```

1. We are defining properties for which values should be retrieved from `Activity` arguments using the corresponding keys.
2. Here, we access properties from arguments within the `onCreate` method. When we ask for the property (use getter), the lazy delegate will get its value from extras and store it for later use.
3. To make a static method to start the activity, we need to use a companion object.

4. `SettingsActivity::class.java` is analous of the Java class reference `SettingsActivity.class`.
5. We are using methods defined in `Chapter 7`, *Extension Functions and Properties.*

We can also make functions to retrieve other types, which can be held by **Bundle** (for example, `Long`, and `Serializable`). This is a pretty nice alternative to argument injection libraries such as `ActivityStarter`, when we want to maintain a really fast compilation time. We can use similar functions to bind strings, colors, services, repositories, and other parts of the model and logic:

```
fun <T> Activity.bindString(@IdRes id: Int): Lazy<T> =
    lazy { getString(id) }
fun <T> Activity.bindColour(@IdRes id: Int): Lazy<T> =
    lazy { getColour(id) }
```

In `Activity`, everything that is heavy or depends on arguments should be declared using a lazy delegate (or provided asynchronously). Also, we should define as lazy all the elements that depend on elements that need to be initialized lazily. For example, `presenter` definition, which depends on the `doctor` property:

```
val presenter by lazy { MainPresenter(this, doctor) }
```

Otherwise, the attempt to construct a `MainPresenter` object will take place during class creation, when we cannot yet read values from the intent and it wouldn't be able to fill the `doctor` property, so the application would crash.

These examples are enough to convince us that the lazy delegate is really useful in Android projects. It is also a good property delegate to start with, as it is simple and elegant.

The notNull function

The `notNull` delegate is the simplest standard library delegate:

```
var someProperty: SomeType by notNull()
```

> The functions that provide most standard library delegates (including the `notNull` function) are defined in `Delegates`. To use them, we need to either refer to this object (`Delegates.notNull()`) or import it (`import kotlin.properties.Delegates.notNull`). We will assume in examples that this object has been imported, so we will omit a reference to it.

The `notNull` delegate allows us to define a variable as non-nullable, which is initialized at a later time and not during object construction. We can define a variable as non-nullable without providing a default value. This is an alternative to `lateinit:`

```
lateinit var someProperty: SomeType
```

The `notNull` delegate provides almost the same effect as `lateinit` (only the error message is different). In the case of trying to use this property before setting the value first, it will throw an `IllegalStateException` and will terminate an Android application. Therefore, it should be used only when we know that a value will be set before the first attempted use of it.

The difference between `lateinit` and the `notNull` delegate is pretty simple. `lateinit` is faster than the `notNull` delegate so it should be used instead of the `notNull` delegate as often as possible. But it has restrictions; `lateinit` cannot be used for primitives or for top-level properties, so in these cases, `notNull` is used instead.

Let's look at `notNull` delegate implementation:

```
public fun <T: Any> notNull(): ReadWriteProperty<Any?, T> =
    NotNullVar()
```

As we can see, `notNull` is actually a function returning an object that is an instance of our actual delegate hidden behind a `ReadWriteProperty` interface. Let's look at an actual delegate definition:

```
private class NotNullVar<T: Any>() : ReadWriteProperty<Any?, T> { // 1
  private var value: T? = null

  public override fun getValue(thisRef: Any?,
  property: KProperty<*>): T {
     return value ?: throw IllegalStateException("Property
            ${property.name} should be initialized before get.") // 2
  }

  public override fun setValue(thisRef: Any?,
  property: KProperty<*>, value: T) {
     this.value = value
  }
}
```

1. The class is private. It is possible because it is provided by the `notNull` function, which returns it as `ReadWriteProperty<Any?, T>`, which is a public interface.

2. Here, we see how a return value is provided. If it is null during usage, then value was not set and the method will throw an error. Otherwise, it is returning the value.

This delegate should be pretty simple to understand. The `setValue` function sets the value to a nullable field and `getValue` returns the value of this field if it is not null, and throws an exception if it is. Here is an example of such an error:

```
var name: String by.notNull()
println(name)
// Error: Property name should be initialized before get.
```

This is a really simple example of the use of delegated properties, but also a good introduction to how property delegates work. Delegated properties are very powerful constructs that have multiple applications.

The observable delegate

The observable is the most useful standard library delegate for mutable properties. Every time a value is set (the `setValue` method is called), the lambda function from the declaration is invoked. A simple example of the observable delegate is as follows:

```
var name: String by Delegates.observable("Empty"){
    property, oldValue, newValue -> // 1
    println("$oldValue -> $newValue") // 2
}

// Usage
name = "Martin" // 3
Prints: Empty -> Martin
name = "Igor" // 3
Prints: Martin -> Igor
name = "Igor" // 3, 4
Prints: Igor -> Igor
```

1. The arguments of the lambda function are as follows:
    - `property`: A reference to the delegated property. Here, it is a reference to the name. This is the same as the property from `setValue` and `getValue`, which was described earlier. It is of the `KProperty` type. In this case (and in most cases), we can put the underscore ("_" sign) instead when it is not used.

    - `oldValue`: The previous value of the property (before the change).
    - `newValue`: The new value of the property (after the change).
2. The lambda function will be invoked each time a new value is set to the property.
3. When we set the new value, then the value is updated, but at the same time the lambda method declared in the delegate is called.
4. Note that lambda is invoked each time setter is used and it doesn't matter if a new value is equal to the previous one.

It is particularly important to remember that the lambda is called each time a new value is set, and not when an object's inner state is changed. For example:

```
var list: MutableList<Int> by observable(mutableListOf())
{ _, old, new ->
    println("List changed from $old to $new")
}

// Usage
list.add(1)  // 1
list =  mutableListOf(2, 3)
// 2, prints: List changed from [1] to [2, 3]
```

1. This does not print anything, because we don't change the property (the setter is not used). We only change the property defined inside the list, but not the object itself.
2. Here, we change the value of the list, so the lambda function from the observable delegate is called and text is printed.

The observable delegate is very useful for immutable types, as opposed to mutable ones. Fortunately, all basic types in Kotlin are immutable by default (`List`, `Map`, `Set`, `Int`, and `String`). Let's look at a practical Android example:

```
class SomeActivity : Activity() {

    var list: List<String> by Delegates.observable(emptyList()) {
        prop, old, new -> if(old != new) updateListView(new)
    }
    // ...
}
```

Every time we change the list, the view is updated. Note that, while `List` is immutable, we need to use the setter when we want to apply any changes, so we can be sure the after this operation the list will be updated. It is much easier than remembering to call the `updateListView` method every time the list changes. This pattern can be used widely in the project to declare properties that edit views. It changes the way the update view mechanism can work.

Another problem that can be solved using an observable delegate is that in `ListAdapters` there was always the problem that `notifyDataSetChanged` had to be called each time elements on the list were changed. In Java, the classic solution was to encapsulate the list, and call `notifyDataSetChanged` in each function that modifies it. In Kotlin, we can simplify this using an observable property delegate:

```
var list: List<LocalDate> by observable(list) { _, old, new ->  // 1
  if(new != old) notifyDataSetChanged()
}
```

1. Note that here, the list is immutable, so there is no way to change its elements without using `notifyDataSetChanged`.

The observable delegate is used to define behavior that should happen upon the property value change. It is most frequently used when we have operations that should be done every time we change a property, or when we want to bind a property value with a view or some other values. But inside the function, we cannot decide whether a new value will be set or not. For this, the `vetoable` delegate is used instead.

The vetoable delegate

The `vetoable` function is a standard library property delegate that works in a similar way to the observable delegate, but with two main differences:

- The lambda from an argument is called before a new value is set
- It allows the lambda function from a declaration to decide if a new value should be accepted or rejected

For example, if we have an assumption that the list must always contain a larger number of items than the old one, then we will define the following `vetoable` delegate:

```
var list: List<String> by Delegates.vetoable(emptyList())
{ _, old, new ->
   new.size > old.size
}
```

If a new list does not contain a larger number of items than the old one, then the value will not change. So, we can treat `vetoable` like `observable`, which also deciding if the value should be changed or not. Let's suppose that we want to have a list bounded to view, but it needs to have three elements at least. We don't allow any change that will make it possible to have fewer elements. The implementation would look as follows:

```
var list: List<String> by Delegates.vetoable(emptyList())
{ prop, old, new ->
    if(new.size < 3) return@vetoable false // 1
    updateListView(new)
    true // 2
}
```

1. If a new list size is smaller than 3, then we do not accept it, and return `false` from lambda. This `false` value returned by return statement with label (that is used to the return from the lambda expression) is the information that the new value shouldn't be accepted.
2. This lambda function needs to return a value. This value is taken either from `return` with a label or by the last line of the lambda body. Here, the value `true` informs us that a new value should be accepted.

Here is a simple example of its usage:

```
listVetoable = listOf("A", "B", "C") // Update A, B, C
println(listVetoable) // Prints: [A, B, C]
listVetoable = listOf("A") // Nothing happens
println(listVetoable) // Prints: [A, B, C]
listVetoable = listOf("A", "B", "C", "D", "E")
// Update A, B, C, D, E
println(listVetoable) // Prints: [A, B, C, D, E]
```

We could also make it unchangeable for some other reasons, for example, we might still be loading the data. Also, the `vetoable` property delegate can be used in validators, for example:

```
var name: String by Delegates.vetoable("") { prop, old, new ->
    if (isValid(new)) {
        showNewData(new)
        true
    } else {
        showNameError()
        false
    }
}
```

This property can be changed only to a value that is correct according to the predicate `isValid(new)`.

Property delegation to the Map type

The standard library contains extensions for `Map` and `MutableMap` with the `String` key type that provides the `getValue` and `setValue` functions. Thanks to them, `map` can also be used as a property delegate:

```
class User(map: Map<String, Any>) { // 1
    val name: String by map
    val kotlinProgrammer: Boolean by map
}

// Usage
val map: Map<String, Any> = mapOf( // 2
    "name" to "Marcin",
    "kotlinProgrammer" to true
)
val user = User(map) // 3
println(user.name)  // Prints: Marcin
println(user.kotlinProgrammer)  // Prints: true
```

1. The map key type needs to be `String`, while the value type is not restricted. It is often `Any` or `Any?`.
2. This creates `Map`, which contains all the values.
3. Provides a `map` to an object.

This can be useful when we are keeping data in `Map`:

- When we want to simplify access to these values
- When we define a structure that tells us what kind of keys we should expect in this map
- When we ask for a property that is delegated to `Map`, its value will be taken from this map value for a key equal to the property name

How is it implemented? Here is the simplified code from the standard library:

```
operator fun <V, V1: V> Map<String, V>.getValue( // 1
     thisRef: Any?, // 2
     property: KProperty<*>): V1 { // 3
         val key = property.name // 4
         val value = get(key)
```

```
        if (value == null && !containsKey(key)) {
            throw NoSuchElementException("Key ${property.name}
            is missing in the map.")
        } else {
            return value as V1 // 3
        }
    }
```

1. `V` is a type of value on the list.
2. `thisRef` is of type `Any?`, so `Map` can be used as a property delegate in any context.
3. `V1` is a return type. This is often inferred from a property, but it must be a subtype of type `V`.
4. The name of the property is used as `key` on `map`.

Keep in mind that this is just an extension function. All that an object needs to be a delegate is to contain the `getValue` method (and `setValue`, for read-write properties). We can even create a delegate from an object of an anonymous class using the `object` declaration:

```
val someProperty by object { // 1
    operator fun  getValue(thisRef: Any?,
    property: KProperty<*>) = "Something"
}
println(someProperty) // prints: Something
```

1. The object does not implement an interface. It just contains the `getValue` method with a proper signature. This is enough to make it work as a read-only property delegate.

Note that in `map`, there needs to be an entry with such a name when we are asking for value of a property, otherwise an error will be thrown (making the property nullable does not change this).

Delegating fields to a `map`, can be useful, for example, when we have an object from an API with dynamic fields. We would like to treat the provided data as an object to have easier access to its fields, but we also need to keep it as a map to be able to list all the fields given by an API (even ones that we were not expecting).

In the previous example, we used `Map`, which is immutable; therefore, the object properties were read-only (`val`). If we want to make an object that can be changed, then we should use `MutableMap`, and then the properties can be defined as mutable (`var`). Here is an example:

```
class User(val map: MutableMap<String, Any>) {
    var name: String by map
```

```
    var kotlinProgrammer: Boolean by map

    override fun toString(): String = "Name: $name,
    Kotlin programmer: $kotlinProgrammer"
}

// Usage
val map = mutableMapOf( // 1
    "name" to "Marcin",
    "kotlinProgrammer" to true
)
val user = User(map)
println(user) // prints: Name: Marcin, Kotlin programmer: true
user.map.put("name", "Igor") // 1
println(user) // prints: Name: Igor, Kotlin programmer: true
user.name = "Michal" // 2
println(user) // prints: Name: Michal, Kotlin programmer: true
```

1. The property value can be changed by just changing the value of the `map`.
2. The property value can also be changed as in any other property. What is really happening there is that the value change is delegated to `setValue`, which changing `map`.

While properties here are mutable, the `setValue` function must also be provided. It is implemented as an extension function for `MutableMap`. Here is the simplified code:

```
operator fun <V> MutableMap<String, V>.setValue(
    thisRef: Any?,
    property: KProperty<*>,
    value: V
) {
    put(property.name, value)
}
```

Note how even such simple functions can allow innovative ways of using common objects. This shows the possibilities property delegates offer.

Kotlin allows us to define custom delegates. Right now, we can find many libraries that provide new property delegates that can be used for different purposes in Android. There are various ways in which property delegation can be used in Android. In the next section, we will see some examples of custom property delegates, and we will take a look at cases where this feature can be really helpful.

Custom delegates

All previous delegates came from the standard library, but we can easily implement our own property delegates. We've seen that in order to allow a class to be a delegate, we need to provide the `getValue` and `setValue` functions. They must have a concrete signature, but there is no need to extend a class or implement the interface. To use an object as a delegate, we don't even need to change its internal implementation, because we can define `getValue` and `setValue` as extension functions. However, when we are creating custom classes to be delegates, then an interface may be useful:

- It defines a function's structure, so we can generate proper methods in Android Studio.
- If we are creating libraries, then we might want to make delegate classes private or internal to prevent inappropriate use of them. We've seen this situation in the `notNull` section, where the `NotNullVar` class was private and served as a `ReadWriteProperty<Any?, T>`, which is an interface.

Interfaces that provide full functionality to allow a class to be a delegate are `ReadOnlyProperty` (for read-only properties) and `ReadWriteProperty` (for read-write properties). These interfaces are really useful, so let's look at their definitions:

```
public interface ReadOnlyProperty<in R, out T> {
    public operator fun getValue(thisRef: R,
        property: KProperty<*>): T
}

public interface ReadWriteProperty<in R, T> {
   public operator fun getValue(thisRef: R,
       property: KProperty<*>): T
   public operator fun setValue(thisRef: R,
       property: KProperty<*>, value: T)
}
```

The values of parameters have already been explained, but let's look at them again:

- `thisRef`: A reference to an object where the delegate is used. Its type defines the context in which the delegate can be used.
- `property`: A reference that contains data about a delegated property. It contains all the information about this property, such as its name or type.
- `value`: A new value to set.

> The parameters `thisRef` and `property` are not used in the following delegates: lazy, observable and vetoable. The `Map`, `MutableMap`, and `notNull` delegates use property to obtain the name of the property. But these parameters can be used in different cases.

Let's look at some short, but useful, examples of custom property delegates. We've seen the lazy property delegate for read-only properties; however, sometimes we need a lazy property that is mutable. If it is asked for the value before initialization, then it should fill its value from the initializer and return it. In other cases, it should act like a normal mutable property:

```
fun <T> mutableLazy(initializer: () -> T): ReadWriteProperty<Any?, T> =
MutableLazy<T>(initializer) //1

private class MutableLazy<T>(val initializer: () -> T) :
ReadWriteProperty<Any?, T> { //2

    private var value: T? = null //3
    private var initialized = false

    override fun getValue(thisRef: Any?, property: KProperty<*>): T {//4
        synchronized(this) { //5
            if (!initialized) {
                value = initializer()
            }
            return value as T //6
        }
    }

    override fun setValue(thisRef: Any?,
        property: KProperty<*>, value: T) { //4
        synchronized(this) {
            this.value = value
            initialized = true
        }
    }
}
```

1. The delegate is hidden behind the interface and served by a function, and as such allows us to change the implementation of `MutableLazy` without worrying whether it will affect the code that is using it.

2. We are implementing `ReadWriteProperty`. It is optional, but really useful because it imposess the correct structure of a read-write property. Its first type is `Any?`, meaning that we are allowed to use this property delegate in any context, including at the top level. Its second type is generic. Note that there are no restrictions on this type, so it might be nullable too.
3. The value of the property is stored in the `value` property, and its existence is stored in an `initialized` property. We need to do it this way because we want to allow `T` to be a nullable type. Then, `null` in the value could mean either that it has not yet been initialized or that it is just equal to `null`.
4. We don't need to use the `operator` modifier, because it has already been used in the interface.
5. If `getValue` is called before any value is set, then the value is filled using the initializer.
6. We need to cast the value to `T` because it might be not-null, and we initialized the value as nullable with `null` as an initial value.

This property delegate might be useful in different use cases in Android development; for example, when a default value of a property is stored in a file and we need to read it (which is a heavy operation):

```
var gameMode : GameMode by mutableLazy {
    getDefaultGameMode()
}

var mapConfiguration : MapConfiguration by mutableLazy {
    getSavedMapConfiguration()
}

var screenResolution : ScreenResolution by mutableLazy {
    getOptimalScreenResolutionForDevice()
}
```

This way, if a user sets a custom value for this property before its used, we won't have to calculate it ourselves. The second custom property delegate will allow us to define the property getter:

```
val a: Int get() = 1
val b: String get() = "KOKO"
val c: Int get() = 1 + 100
```

Before Kotlin 1.1, we always had to define the type of a property. To avoid this, we can define the following extension function to a functional type:

```
inline operator fun <R> (() -> R).getValue(
    thisRef: Any?,
    property: KProperty<*>
): R = invoke()
```

Then, we can define the properties with similar behavior in this way:

```
val a by { 1 }
val b by { "KOKO" }
val c by { 1 + 100 }
```

This way is not preferred because of its decreased efficiency, but it is a nice example of the possibilities that delegated properties provide us. Such a small extension function is makes a functional type be a property delegate. This is the simplified code in Kotlin after compilation (note that the extension function is marked as inline, so its calls were replaced with its body):

```
private val `a$delegate` = { 1 }
val a: Int get() = `a$delegate`()
private val `b$delegate` = {  "KOKO" }
val b: String get() = `b$delegate`()
private val `c$delegate` = { 1 + 100 }
val c: Int get() = `c$delegate`()
```

In the next section, we are going to look at some custom delegates created for real projects. They will be presented together with the problems that they solve.

View binging

When we use **Model-View-Presenter** (**MVP**) in the project, then we need to make all the changes in View using the Presenter. Thus, we are forced to create multiple functions on the View, such as:

```
override fun getName(): String {
    return nameView.text.toString()
}

override fun setName(name: String) {
    nameView.text = name
}
```

We also have to define the functions in the following `interface`:

```
interface MainView {
    fun getName(): String
    fun setName(name: String)
}
```

We may simplify the preceding code and reduce the need for setter/getter methods by using property binding. We can bind the property to `view` element. This is the result we would like to achieve:

```
override var name: String by bindToTex(R.id.textView)
```

And here is `interface`:

```
interface MainView {
    var name: String
}
```

The preceding example is more concise and easier to maintain. Note that we provide the element ID as argument. A simple class that will give us the expected result is as follows:

```
fun Activity.bindToText(
    @IdRes viewId: Int ) = object :
    ReadWriteProperty<Any?, String> {
  val textView by lazy { findViewById<TextView>(viewId) }

  override fun getValue(thisRef: Any?,
      property: KProperty<*>): String {
      return textView.text.toString()
  }

  override fun setValue(thisRef: Any?,
      property: KProperty<*>, value: String) {
      textView.text = value
  }
}
```

We could create a similar binding for different view properties and different contexts (`Fragment`, `Service`). Another really useful tool is binding to visibility, which is binding a logical property (with the type `Boolean`) to the visibility of a `view` element:

```
fun Activity.bindToVisibility(
   @IdRes viewId: Int ) = object :
   ReadWriteProperty<Any?, Boolean> {

   val view by lazy { findViewById(viewId) }
```

```
    override fun getValue(thisRef: Any?,
        property: KProperty<*>): Boolean {
        return view.visibility == View.VISIBLE
    }

    override fun setValue(thisRef: Any?,
        property: KProperty<*>, value: Boolean) {
        view.visibility = if(value) View.VISIBLE else View.GONE
    }
}
```

These implementations provide possibilities that would be really hard to achieve in Java. Similar bindings might be created for other `View` elements to make using MVP shorter and simpler. The snippets that were just presented are only simple examples, but better implementations can be found in the `KotlinAndroidViewBindings` library (`https://github.com/MarcinMoskala/KotlinAndroidViewBindings`).

Preference binding

To show more complex examples, we will present one that helps with `SharedPreferences` usage. There are better Kotlin approaches to this problem, but this examples is nice to analyze, and it is a reasonable example of property delegate usage on the extension property. As a result, we want to be able to treat the values saved in `SharedPreferences` as if they were properties of a `SharedPreferences` object. Here is an example usage:

```
preferences.canEatPie = true
if(preferences.canEatPie) {
    // Code
}
```

Here are the examples for extension property definitions:

```
var SharedPreferences.canEatPie:
Boolean by bindToPreferenceField(true) // 1
var SharedPreferences.allPieInTheWorld:
Long by bindToPreferenceField(0,"AllPieKey") //2
```

1. The property of type Boolean. When a property is non-nullable, default values have to be provided in the first argument of the function.

2. The property can have a custom key provided. It is useful in real-life projects, where we must have control over this key (for example, to not change it unintentionally during property renaming).

Let's analyze how it works through a deep investigation of the not-null property. First, let's look at the provider functions. Note that the type of the property determines the way the value is taken from `SharedPreferences` (because there are different functions, such as `getString`, `getInt`, and so on). To obtain it, we need this class type to be provided as the `reified` type of the `inline` function, or through the parameter. This is what a delegate provider function looks like:

```
inline fun <reified T : Any> bindToPreferenceField(
      default: T?,
      key: String? = null
): ReadWriteProperty<SharedPreferences, T> // 1
    = bindToPreferenceField(T::class, default, key)

fun <T : Any> bindToPreferenceField( // 2
    clazz: KClass<T>,
    default: T?,
    key: String? = null
): ReadWriteProperty<SharedPreferences, T>
      = PreferenceFieldBinder(clazz, default, key) // 1
```

1. Both functions returns an object behind the interface `ReadWriteProperty<SharedPreferences, T>`. Note that context here is set to `SharedPreferences`, so it can be used only there or in `SharedPreferences` extensions. This function is defined because the type parameter cannot be redefined, and we need to provide type as a normal parameter.
2. Note that the `bindToPreferenceField` function cannot be private or internal, because inline functions can use only functions with the same or less restricted modifiers.

Finally, let's look at the `PreferenceFieldDelegate` class, which is our delegate:

```
internal open class PreferenceFieldDelegate<T : Any>(
      private val clazz: KClass<T>,
      private val default: T?,
      private val key: String?
) : ReadWriteProperty<SharedPreferences, T> {

  override operator fun getValue(thisRef: SharedPreferences,
  property: KProperty<*>): T
    = thisRef.getLong(getValue<T>(clazz, default, getKey(property))
```

```
    override fun setValue(thisRef: SharedPreferences,
    property: KProperty<*>, value: T) {
        thisRef.edit().apply
        { putValue(clazz, value, getKey(property)) }.apply()
    }

    private fun getKey(property: KProperty<*>) =
    key ?: "${property.name}Key"
}
```

Now we know how the `thisRef` parameter is used. It is of the type `SharedPreferences`, and we can use it to get and set all the values. Here are definitions of the functions used to get and set values depending on the property type:

```
internal fun SharedPreferences.Editor.putValue(clazz: KClass<*>, value:
Any, key: String) {
    when (clazz.simpleName) {
        "Long" -> putLong(key, value as Long)
        "Int" -> putInt(key, value as Int)
        "String" -> putString(key, value as String?)
        "Boolean" -> putBoolean(key, value as Boolean)
        "Float" -> putFloat(key, value as Float)
        else -> putString(key, value.toJson())
    }
}

internal fun <T: Any> SharedPreferences.getValue(clazz: KClass<*>, default:
T?, key: String): T = when (clazz.simpleName) {
    "Long" -> getLong(key, default as Long)
    "Int" -> getInt(key, default as Int)
    "String" -> getString(key, default as? String)
    "Boolean" -> getBoolean(key, default as Boolean)
    "Float" -> getFloat(key, default as Float)
    else -> getString(key, default?.toJson()).fromJson(clazz)
} as T
```

We also need `toJson` and `fromJson` defined:

```
var preferencesGson: Gson = GsonBuilder().create()
internal fun Any.toJson() = preferencesGson.toJson(this)!!
internal fun <T : Any> String.fromJson(clazz: KClass<T>) =
preferencesGson.fromJson(this, clazz.java)
```

With such definitions, we can define additional extension properties for `SharedPreferences`:

```
var SharedPreferences.canEatPie: Boolean by bindToPreferenceField(true)
```

As we've already seen in `Chapter 7`, *Extension Functions and Properties,* we cannot really add anything to a class without modifying it. Under the hood, the extension property is compiled to getter and setter functions, and they delegates calls to a created delegate:

```
val 'canEatPie$delegate' = bindToPreferenceField(Boolean::class, true)

fun SharedPreferences.getCanEatPie(): Boolean {
  return 'canEatPie$delegate'.getValue(this,
  SharedPreferences::canEatPie)
}

fun SharedPreferences.setCanEatPie(value: Boolean) {
  'canEatPie$delegate'.setValue(this, SharedPreferences::canEatPie,
   value)
}
```

Also remember that extension functions are, in fact, just static functions with an extension on the first parameter:

```
val 'canEatPie$delegate' = bindToPreferenceField(Boolean::class, true)

fun getCanEatPie(receiver: SharedPreferences): Boolean {
   return 'canEatPie$delegate'.getValue(receiver,
   SharedPreferences::canEatPie)
}

fun setCanEatPie(receiver: SharedPreferences, value: Boolean) {
   'canEatPie$delegate'.setValue(receiver,
    SharedPreferences::canEatPie, value)
}
```

The examples presented here should be enough to understand how property delegates are working and how they can be used. Property delegates are used intensively in Kotlin open source libraries. They are used for fast and simple Dependency Injection (for example, Kodein, Injekt, and TornadoFX), binding to views (for example `KotlinAndroidViewBindings`), `SharedPreferences` (for example `PreferenceHolder`, `KotlinPreference`), binding to `Activity` arguments (for example `ActivityStarter`), to define property keys on configuration definition (for example, Konfig), or even to define a database column structure (for example, Kwery). Still, there is a broad field of usages that are waiting to be discovered.

Providing a delegate

Since Kotlin 1.1, there is an operator, `provideDelegate`, that is used to provide a delegate during class initialization. The main motivation behind `provideDelegate` was that it allows us to provide a customized delegate depending on traits of property (name, type, annotations, and so on).

The `provideDelegate` operator returns a delegate, and types that have this operator do not need to be delegates themselves in order to be used as a delegate. Here is an example:

```
class A(val i: Int) {

    operator fun provideDelegate(
        thisRef: Any?,
        prop: KProperty<*>
    ) = object: ReadOnlyProperty<Any?, Int> {

        override fun getValue(
            thisRef: Any?,
            property: KProperty<*>
        ) = i
    }
}

val a by A(1)
```

In this example, `A` is used as a delegate, while it implements neither the `getvalue` nor the `setvalue` function. This is possible because it defines a `provideDelegate` operator, which returns the delegate that will be used instead of `A`. Property delegation is compiled into the following code:

```
private val a$delegate = A().provideDelegate(this, this::prop)
val a: Int
get() = a1$delegate.getValue(this, this::prop)
```

A practical example can be found in the Kotlin supporting part of the `ActivityStarter` library (`https://github.com/MarcinMoskala/ActivityStarter`). Activity arguments are defined using annotations, but we can use property delegation to simplify usage from Kotlin and allow property definition to be defined as read-only and not `lateinit`:

```
@get:Arg(optional = true) val name: String by argExtra(defaultName)
@get:Arg(optional = true) val id: Int by argExtra(defaultId)
@get:Arg val grade: Char  by argExtra()
@get:Arg val passing: Boolean  by argExtra()
```

But there are some requirements:

- When `argExtra` is used, the property getter has to be annotated
- We need to specify a default value if an argument is optional and the type is not nullable.

To check these requirements, we need a reference to a property to get a getter annotation. We cannot have such references in the `argExtra` function, but we can implement them inside `provideDevegate`:

```
fun <T> Activity.argExtra(default: T? = null) =
ArgValueDelegateProvider(default)
fun <T> Fragment.argExtra(default: T? = null) =
ArgValueDelegateProvider(default)
fun <T> android.support.v4.app.Fragment.argExtra(default: T? = null) =
        ValueDelegateProvider(default)

class ArgValueDelegateProvider<T>(val default: T? = null) {
    operator fun provideDelegate(
        thisRef: Any?,
        prop: KProperty<*>
    ): ReadWriteProperty<Any, T> {
        val annotation = prop.getter.findAnnotation<Arg>()
        when {
            annotation == null ->
            throw Error(ErrorMessages.noAnnotation)
            annotation.optional && !prop.returnType.isMarkedNullable &&
            default == null ->
            throw Error(ErrorMessages.optionalValueNeeded)
        }
        return ArgValueDelegate(default)
    }
}

internal object ErrorMessages {
    const val noAnnotation =
     "Element getter must be annotated with Arg"
    const val optionalValueNeeded =
    "Arguments that are optional and have not-
        nullable type must have defaut value specified"
}
```

A delegate like this throws an appropriate error when a condition is not fulfilled:

```
val a: A? by ArgValueDelegateProvider()
// Throws error during initialization: Element getter must be
// annotated with Arg

@get:Arg(optional = true) val a: A by ArgValueDelegateProvider()
// Throws error during initialization: Arguments that are optional
// and have not-nullable type must have default value specified.
```

This way, unacceptable argument definitions throw appropriate errors during object initialization instead of breaking an application in unexpected situations.

Summary

In this chapter, we described class delegates, property delegates, and how they can be used to remove redundancy in code. We defined a delegate as an object to which calls from other objects or properties are delegated. We learned design patterns that class delegation is strongly connected to: the Delegate pattern and the Decorator pattern.

The delegation pattern was mentioned as an alternative to inheritance, and the Decorator pattern is a way to add functionality to different kinds of classes that implements the same interface.

We've seen how property delegation works, the Kotlin standard library property delegates `notNull`, `lazy`, `observable`, and `vetoable`, and the use of `Map` as a delegate. We learned how they work and when they should be used. We've also seen how to make a custom property delegate, together with examples of real-life usage.

Knowledge about different features and their usage is not enough--there is also a need to understand how they can be used together to build great applications. In the next chapter, we will write a demo application and explain how the various Kotlin features described throughout this book can be combined together.

9

Making Your Marvel Gallery Application

We've already seen the most important Kotlin features that allow us to make Android development easier and more productive, but it is hard to understand the whole picture just by looking at the individual pieces. This is why, in this chapter, we will build a whole Android application written in Kotlin.

It was a tough decision to choose which application should be implemented in this chapter. It needed to be short and simple, but at the same time utilize as many Kotlin features as possible. We also wanted to minimize the number of libraries used, because this is a book about Android development in Kotlin, not about Android libraries. We wanted to make it look as good as possible, but to avoid the implementation of custom graphical elements, because they are usually complex and they are not simplified so much when we move from Java to Kotlin.

We finally decided to make a Marvel Gallery application--a small app which we can use to find our favorite Marvel characters and display their details. All data is provided from the Marvel website by their API.

Marvel Gallery

Let's implement our Marvel Gallery application. This application should allow the following use cases:

- After starting the application, the user sees a gallery of characters.
- After starting the application, the user can search for a character by their name.
- When the user clicks on a character picture, there is a profile displayed. The character profile contains the character name, photo, description, and their occurrences.

These are three use cases that describe the main functionalities of the application. In the following sections, we are going to implement them one after another. If you get lost during this chapter, remember that you can always take a look at the complete application on GitHub (`https://github.com/MarcinMoskala/MarvelGallery`).

To better understand what we want to build, let's look at some screenshots from the final version of our application:

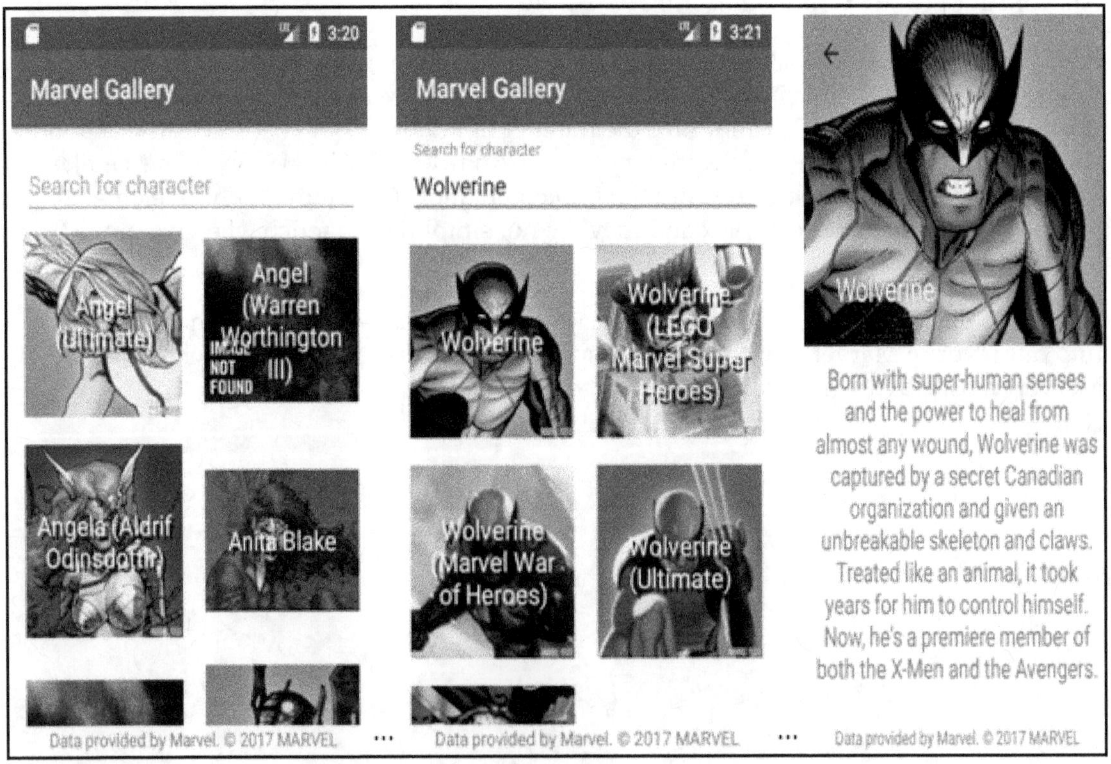

How to use this chapter

This chapter shows all the steps and code necessary to build an application. Its purpose is to show the step-by-step process of application development. As you read this chapter, concentrate on the development process and try to understand what the purpose of the presented code is. You don't need to fully understand layouts and you don't have to understand unit test definitions, as long as you understand what they are doing. Concentrate on application structure and Kotlin solutions, which make the final code simpler. Most solutions have already been described in previous chapters, so they have only a brief description. The value in this chapter is that their usage is presented in the context of a concrete application.

You can download the application code from GitHub (`https://github.com/MarcinMoskala/MarvelGallery`).

On GitHub, you can see the final code, download it, or clone it to your computer using Git:

```
git clone git@github.com:MarcinMoskala/MarvelGallery.git
```

The application also includes UI tests written in **Espresso**, but they are not presented in this chapter to make it simpler for readers who are not proficient in Espresso usage.

Each section of this chapter has a corresponding Git branch on this project, so if you want to see how the code looks at the end of the section, then you can just switch to the corresponding branch:

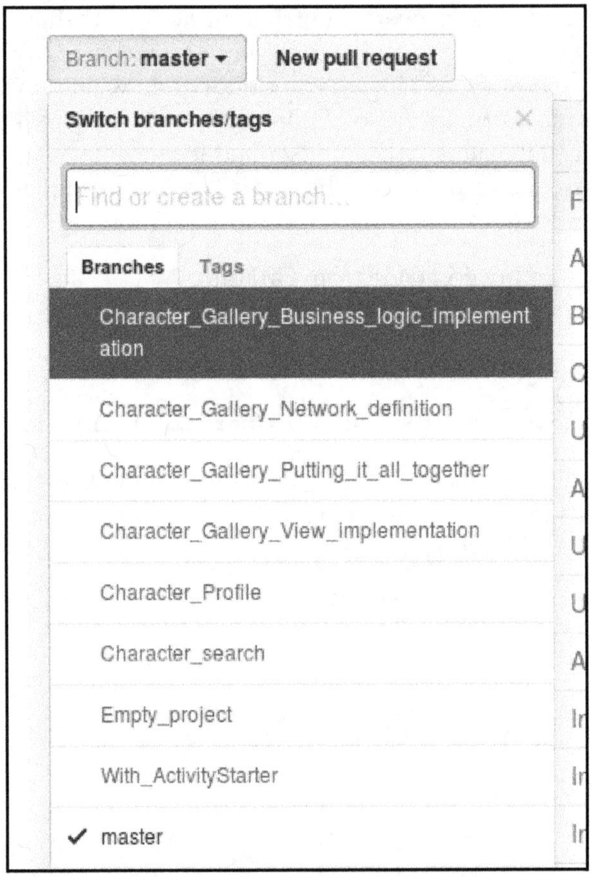

Also, locally, after you clone the repository, you can check out the corresponding branch using the following Git command:

```
git checkout Character_search
```

If you have an electronic version of this book and you want to make the whole application by copying and pasting parts of the code, then you can do so, but remember to place files in the folders corresponding to the package. That way, you will keep a clean structure in the project.

Note that if you place code from the book in another folder, there will be a warning displayed:

You can intentionally place a file in any folder, because the second fix proposition is to move the file into the path corresponding to the defined package:

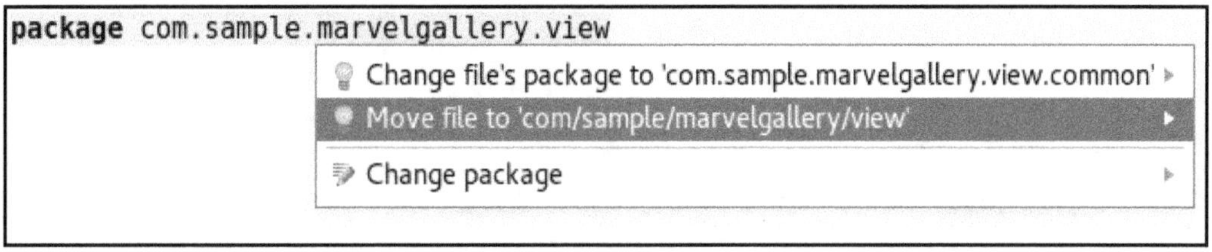

You can use this to move your file in the correct location.

Making an empty project

Before we can start implementing functionalities, we need to create an empty Kotlin Android project with a single activity, `MainActivty`. This process was described in `Chapter 1`, *Beginning Your Kotlin Adventure*. Therefore, we don't need to described in depth, but we will show what the steps are in Android Studio 3.0:

1. Set a name, package, and location for the new project. Remember to tick the **Include Kotlin support** option:

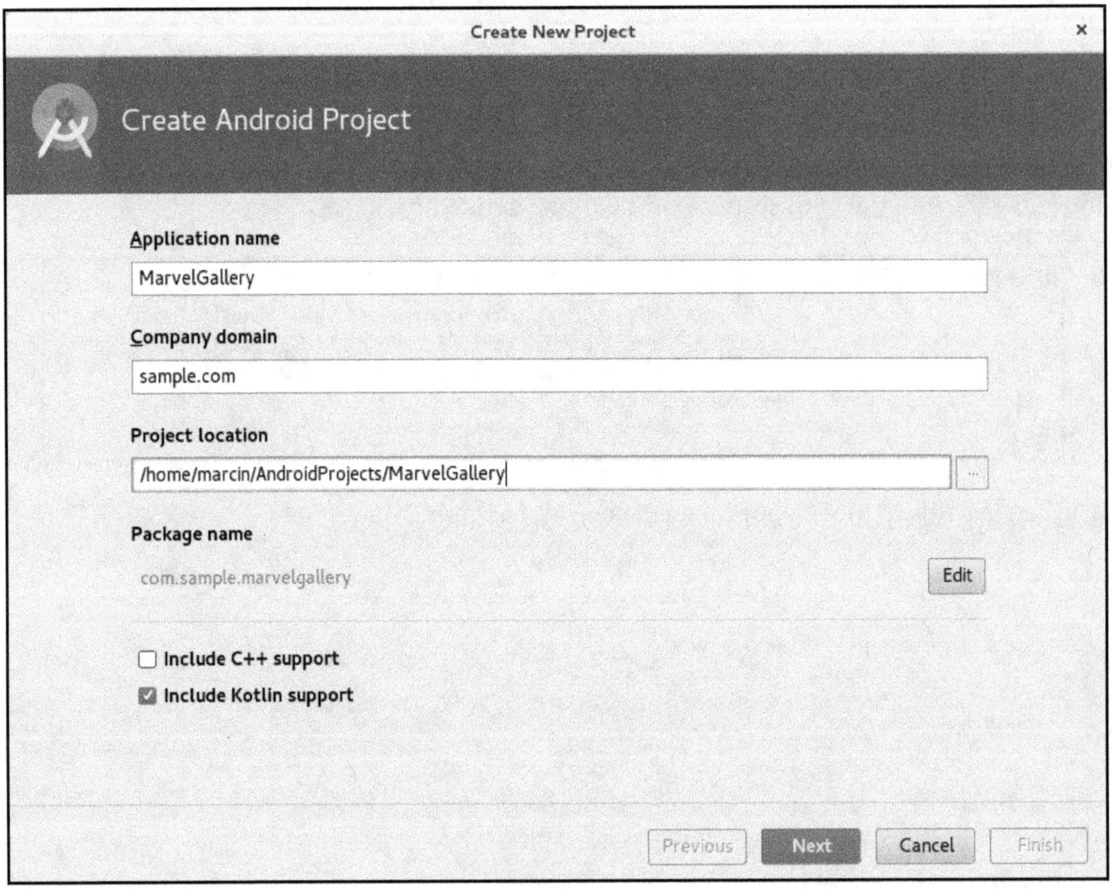

2. We can choose other minimal Android versions, but in this example, we are going to set API 16:

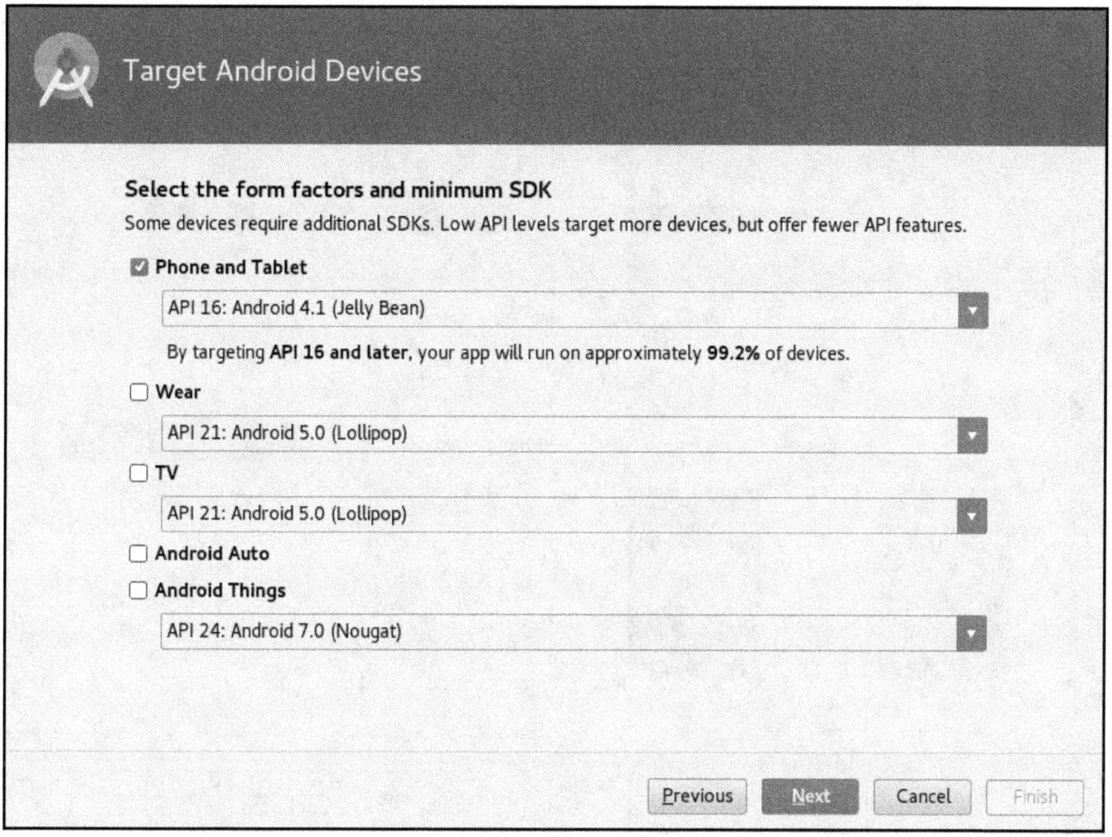

3. Choose a template. We don't need any of these templates, so we should start with **Empty Activity**:

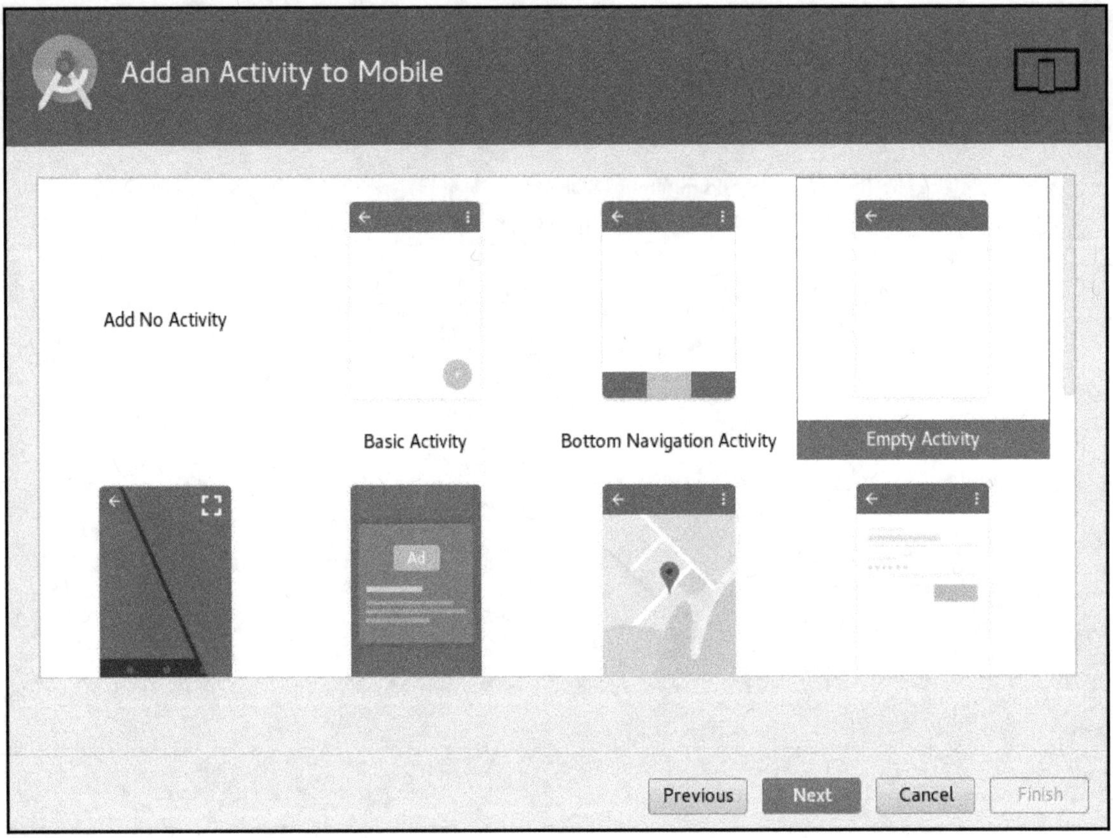

4. Name the newly created activity. We can keep the name `MainActivity`:

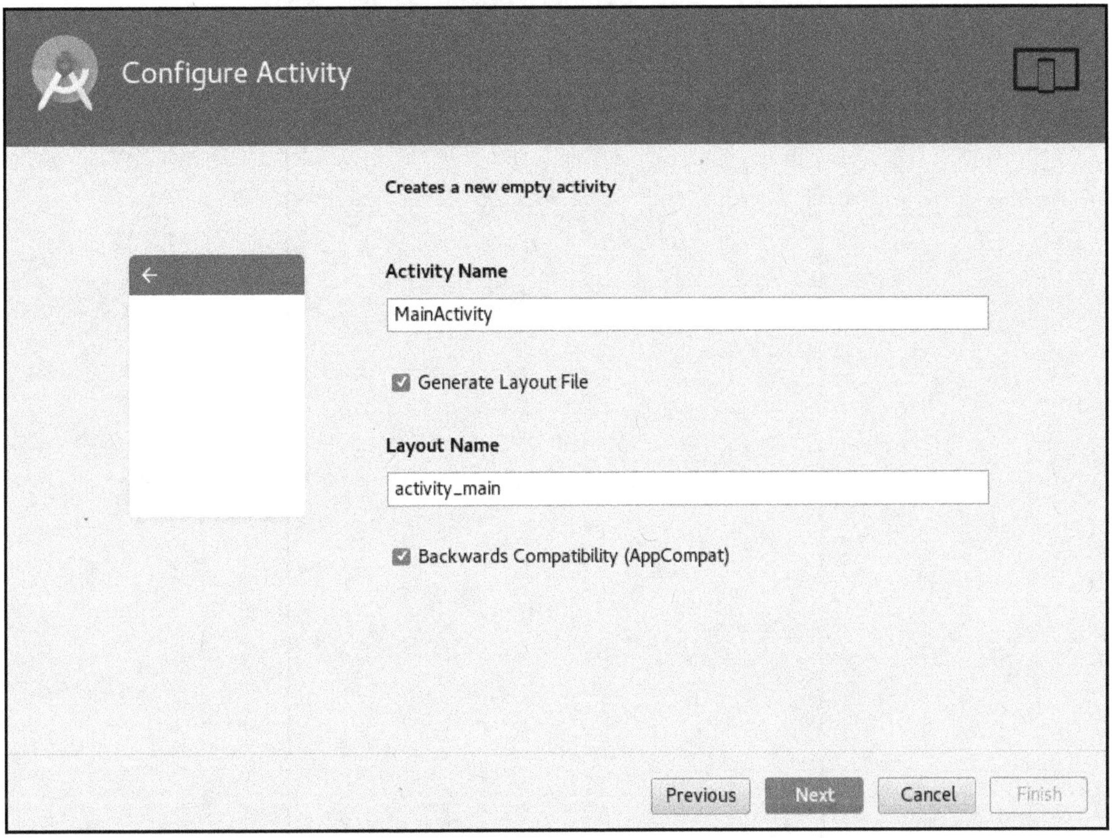

For Android Studio prior to 3.x, we need to follow slightly different steps:

1. Create a project using the template with empty Activity.

2.Configure Kotlin in the project (for example, *Ctrl/Cmd* + *Shift* + *A* and Configure Kotlin in project).

3. Convert all Java classes to Kotlin (for example, in `MainActivity` *Ctrl/Cmd* + *Shift* + *A* and Convert Java file to Kotlin file).

After these steps, we will have a Kotlin Android application with an empty activity created:

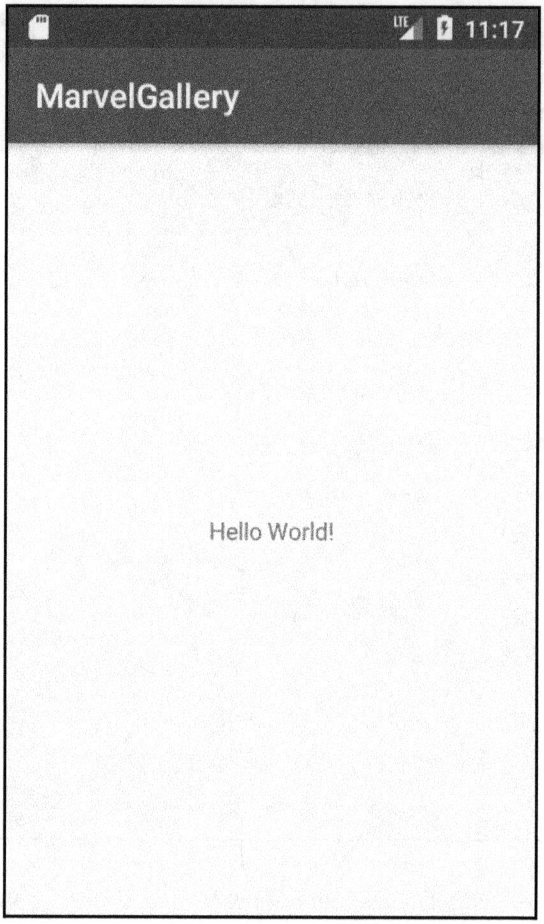

Character gallery

In this section, we will implement a single use case.

After starting the application, the user can see a gallery of characters.

This is a pretty complex use case, because it requires a view to be presented, a network connection with the API, and business rules implementation. Therefore, we will split it into the following tasks:

- View implementation
- Communication with this API
- Business logic implementation of the character display
- Putting it all together

Such tasks are much easier to implement. Let's implement them one after another.

View implementation

Let's start with the view implementation. Here, we are going to define what the list of characters will look like. For testing purposes, we are also going to define a few characters and display them.

Let's start with the `MainActivity` layout implementation. We will use `RecyclerView` to show a list of elements. The `RecyclerView` layout is distributed in a separate dependency, which we have to add to the `app` module `build.gradle` file:

```
implementation "com.android.support:recyclerview-
v7:$android_support_version"
```

The `android_support_version` instance is a variable that is not yet defined. The reason for this is that the version should be the same for all Android support libraries, and when we extract this version number as a separator variable, then it is easier to manage. This is why we should replace the hardcoded version for each of the Android support libraries with a reference to `android_support_version`:

```
implementation "com.android.support:appcompat-
    v7:$android_support_version"
implementation "com.android.support:design:$android_support_version"
implementation "com.android.support:support-
    v4:$android_support_version"
implementation "com.android.support:recyclerview-
    v7:$android_support_version"
```

And we have to set a support library version value. It is good practice to define it in the project `build.gradle` file inside `buildscript`, after the `kotlin_version` definition:

```
ext.kotlin_version = '1.1.4-2'
ext.android_support_version = "26.0.1"
```

Now we can start the implementation of the `MainActivity` layout. This is the effect that we want to achieve:

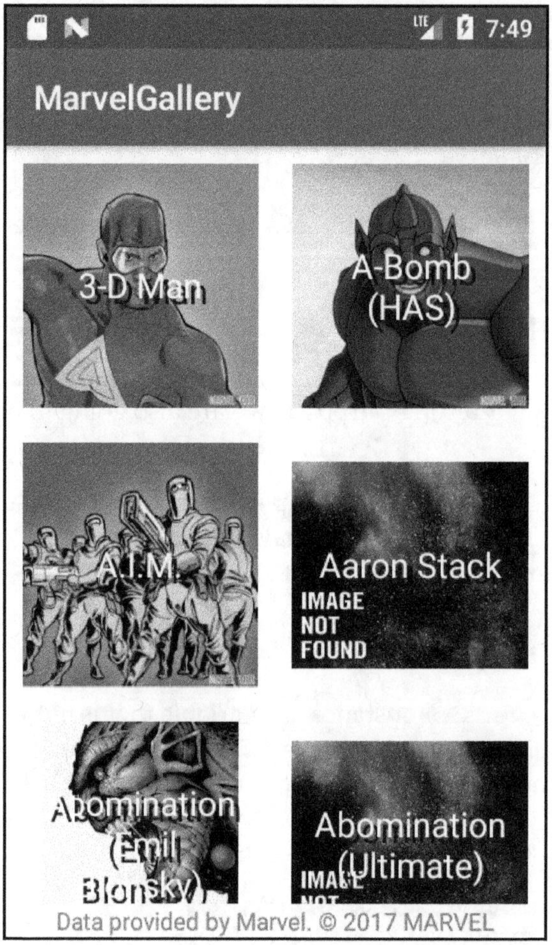

We will keep character elements on `RecyclerView` packed into `SwipeRefreshLayout` to allow swipe-refresh. Also, to comply with Marvel copyright, a label to be presented informing that the data is provided by Marvel. The layout `activity_main` (`res/layout/activity_main.xml`) should be replaced with the following definition:

```
<?xml version="1.0" encoding="utf-8"?>
<RelativeLayout xmlns:android="http://schemas.android.com/apk/res/android"
   xmlns:app="http://schemas.android.com/apk/res-auto"
   xmlns:tools="http://schemas.android.com/tools"
   android:id="@+id/charactersView"
   android:layout_width="match_parent"
   android:layout_height="match_parent"
   android:background="@android:color/white"
   android:fitsSystemWindows="true">

   <android.support.v4.widget.SwipeRefreshLayout
       xmlns:android="http://schemas.android.com/apk/res/android"
       android:id="@+id/swipeRefreshView"
       android:layout_width="match_parent"
       android:layout_height="match_parent">

       <android.support.v7.widget.RecyclerView
           android:id="@+id/recyclerView"
           android:layout_width="match_parent"
           android:layout_height="match_parent"
           android:scrollbars="vertical" />

   </android.support.v4.widget.SwipeRefreshLayout>

   <TextView
       android:layout_width="match_parent"
       android:layout_height="wrap_content"
       android:layout_alignParentBottom="true"
       android:background="@android:color/white"
       android:gravity="center"
       android:text="@string/marvel_copyright_notice" />
</RelativeLayout>
```

We need to add a copyright notice to strings (`res/values/strings.xml`):

```
<string name="marvel_copyright_notice">
    Data provided by Marvel. © 2017 MARVEL
</string>
```

Here is a preview:

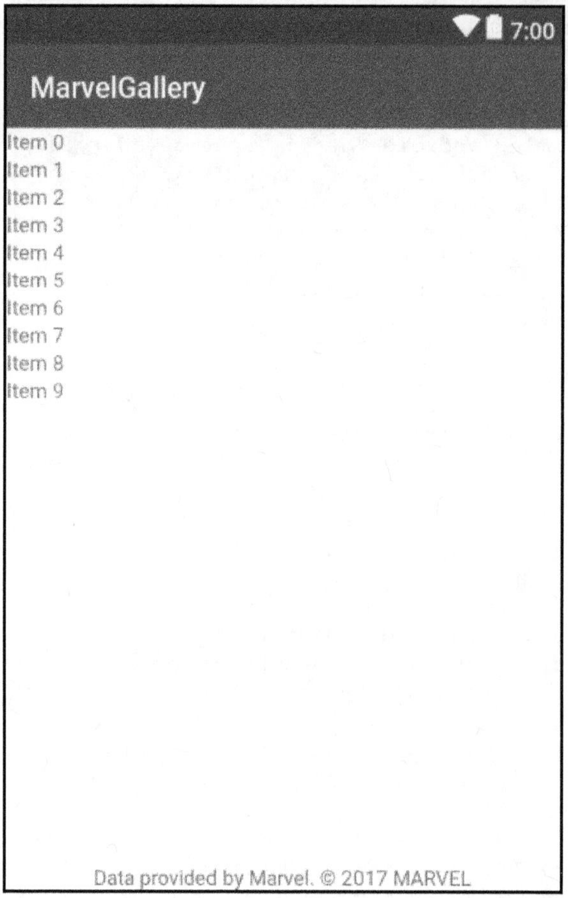

The next step is to define the item view. We would like each element to always be square. To do this, we need to define a view that will preserve the square shape (place it in `view/views`):

```
package com.sample.marvelgallery.view.views

import android.util.AttributeSet
import android.widget.FrameLayout
import android.content.Context

class SquareFrameLayout @JvmOverloads constructor( // 1
        context: Context,
        attrs: AttributeSet? = null,
```

```
        defStyleAttr: Int = 0
) : FrameLayout(context, attrs, defStyleAttr) {

    override fun onMeasure(widthMeasureSpec: Int,
    heightMeasureSpec: Int) {
        super.onMeasure(widthMeasureSpec, widthMeasureSpec) // 2
    }
}
```

1. Using `JvmOverloads` annotation, we've avoided telescoping constructors that are normally used to define a custom view in Android. This was described in `Chapter 4`, *Classes and Objects*.
2. We are forcing the element to always have the same height as width.

With `SquareFrameLayout`, we can define the layout of gallery items. This is what we want it to look like:

We need to define `ImageView` to display the character image, and `TextView` to display the character name. While `SquareFrameLayout` is actually `FrameLayout` with a fixed height, its children elements (image and text) are, by default, placed one above another. Let's add layout to the `item_character.xml` file in `res/layout`:

```
// ./res/layout/item_character.xml

<com.sample.marvelgallery.view.views.SquareFrameLayout
xmlns:android="http://schemas.android.com/apk/res/android"
    xmlns:tools="http://schemas.android.com/tools"
    android:layout_width="match_parent"
```

```
    android:layout_height="wrap_content"
    android:gravity="center_horizontal"
    android:orientation="horizontal"
    android:padding="@dimen/element_padding">

    <ImageView
        android:id="@+id/imageView"
        android:layout_width="match_parent"
        android:layout_height="match_parent"/>

    <TextView
        android:id="@+id/textView"
        android:layout_width="match_parent"
        android:layout_height="match_parent"
        android:gravity="center"
        android:paddingLeft="10dp"
        android:paddingRight="10dp"
        android:shadowColor="#111"
        android:shadowDx="5"
        android:shadowDy="5"
        android:shadowRadius="0.01"
        android:textColor="@android:color/white"
        android:textSize="@dimen/standard_text_size"
        tools:text="Some name" />
</com.sample.marvelgallery.view.views.SquareFrameLayout>
```

Note that we are also using values such as `element_padding`, defined in `dimens`. Let's add them to the `dimen.xml` file in `res/values`:

```
<?xml version="1.0" encoding="utf-8"?>
<resources>
   <dimen name="character_header_height">240dp</dimen>
   <dimen name="standard_text_size">20sp</dimen>
   <dimen name="character_description_padding">10dp</dimen>
   <dimen name="element_padding">10dp</dimen>
</resources>
```

As we can see, each element needs to display the name of the character and their image. Therefore, the model of a character needs to contain these two properties. Let's define a simple model for a character:

```
package com.sample.marvelgallery.model

data class MarvelCharacter(
       val name: String,
       val imageUrl: String
)
```

To display a list of elements using `RecyclerView`, we need to implement both a `RecyclerView` list and an item adapter. A list adapter is used to manage all elements in a list, while an item adapter is an adapter for a single item type. Here, we need only one item adapter, because we display a single type of items. It is, however, good practice to assume that in future there might be other kinds of elements on this list, for example, comics or ads. The same with the list adapter--we need only one in this example, but in most projects there is more than a single list, and it is better to extract common behavior into a single abstract class.

While this example is designed to present how Kotlin can be used in larger projects, we will define an abstract list adapter, which we will name `RecyclerListAdapter`, and an abstract item adapter, which we will name `ItemAdapter`. Here is the `ItemAdapter` definition:

```
package com.sample.marvelgallery.view.common

import android.support.v7.widget.RecyclerView
import android.support.annotation.LayoutRes
import android.view.View

abstract class ItemAdapter<T : RecyclerView.ViewHolder>
(@LayoutRes open val layoutId: Int) { // 1

   abstract fun onCreateViewHolder(itemView: View): T // 2

   @Suppress("UNCHECKED_CAST") // 1
   fun bindViewHolder(holder: RecyclerView.ViewHolder) {
       (holder as T).onBindViewHolder() // 1
   }

   abstract fun T.onBindViewHolder() // 1, 3
}
```

1. We need to pass a holder as a type parameter to allow direct operations on its fields. The holder is created in `onCreateViewHolder`, so we know that its type will always be type parameter `T`. Therefore, we can cast the holder to `T` on `bindViewHolder` and use it as a receiver object for `onBindViewHolder`. Suppression `@Suppress("UNCHECKED_CAST")` is there just to hide the warning while we know that we can securely cast in this situation.
2. A function is used to create a view holder. In most cases, it will be a single expression function that calls a constructor.
3. In the `onBin+dViewHolder` function, we will set all the values on item view.

Here is the definition of `RecyclerListAdapter`:

```
package com.sample.marvelgallery.view.common

import android.support.v7.widget.RecyclerView
import android.view.LayoutInflater
import android.view.ViewGroup

open class RecyclerListAdapter( // 1
       var items List<AnyItemAdapter> = listOf()
) : RecyclerView.Adapter<RecyclerView.ViewHolder>() {

   override final fun getItemCount() = items.size // 4

   override final fun getItemViewType(position: Int) =
       items[position].layoutId // 3, 4

   override final fun onCreateViewHolder(parent: ViewGroup,
       layoutId: Int): RecyclerView.ViewHolder { // 4
   val itemView = LayoutInflater.from(parent.context)
       .inflate(layoutId, parent, false)
       return items.first
       { it.layoutId == layoutId }.onCreateViewHolder(itemView) // 3
   }

   override final fun onBindViewHolder
   (holder: RecyclerView.ViewHolder, position: Int) { // 4
       items[position].bindViewHolder(holder)
   }
}

typealias AnyItemAdapter = ItemAdapter
    <out RecyclerView.ViewHolder> // 5
```

1. The class is `open` instead of `abstract` because it can be initialized and used without any children. We define children to allow us to define custom methods for different lists.
2. We keep items in a list.
3. We use layout to distinguish between item types. Because of this, we cannot use two item adapters with the same layout on the same list, but this solution simplifies a lot.

4. The methods are overriding methods of `RecyclerView.Adapter`, but they also use `final` modifier to restrict their override in children. All list adapters that extend `RecyclerListAdapter` should operate on items.
5. We define the type alias to simplify the definition of any `ItemAdapter`.

Using the preceding definitions, we can define `MainListAdapter` (the adapter for the character list) and `CharacterItemAdapter` (the adapter for items on the list). Here is the definition of `MainListAdapter`:

```
package com.sample.marvelgallery.view.main

import com.sample.marvelgallery.view.common.AnyItemAdapter
import com.sample.marvelgallery.view.common.RecyclerListAdapter

class MainListAdapter(items: List<AnyItemAdapter>) :
RecyclerListAdapter(items)
```

In this project, we do not need any special methods defined in `MainListAdapter`, but to show how easy it is to define them, here is `MainListAdapter` with additional methods to add and delete:

```
class MainListAdapter(items: List<AnyItemAdapter>) :
RecyclerListAdapter(items) {

   fun add(itemAdapter: AnyItemAdapter) {
       items += itemAdapter)
       val index = items.indexOf(itemAdapter)
       if (index == -1) return
       notifyItemInserted(index)
   }

   fun delete(itemAdapter: AnyItemAdapter) {
       val index = items.indexOf(itemAdapter)
       if (index == -1) return
       items -= itemAdapter
       notifyItemRemoved(index)
   }
 }
```

Here is the definition of `CharacterItemAdapter`:

```
package com.sample.marvelgallery.view.main

import android.support.v7.widget.RecyclerView
import android.view.View
import android.widget.ImageView
import android.widget.TextView
import com.sample.marvelgallery.R
import com.sample.marvelgallery.model.MarvelCharacter
import com.sample.marvelgallery.view.common.ItemAdapter
import com.sample.marvelgallery.view.common.bindView
import com.sample.marvelgallery.view.common.loadImage

class CharacterItemAdapter(
      val character: MarvelCharacter // 1
) : ItemAdapter<CharacterItemAdapter.ViewHolder>(R.layout.item_character) {

   override fun onCreateViewHolder(itemView: View) = ViewHolder(itemView)

   override fun ViewHolder.onBindViewHolder() { // 2
       textView.text = character.name
       imageView.loadImage(character.imageUrl) // 3
   }

   class ViewHolder(itemView: View) : RecyclerView.ViewHolder(itemView)
   {
       val textView by bindView<TextView>(R.id.textView) // 4
       val imageView by bindView<ImageView>(R.id.imageView) // 4
   }
}
```

1. `MarvelCharacter` is passed by the constructor.
2. The `onBindViewHolder` method is used to set up views. It was defined as an abstract member extension function in `ItemAdapter` and, thanks to that, we can now use `textView` and `imageView` explicitly inside its body.
3. The `loadImage` function is not defined yet. We will define it as an extension function a bit later.
4. In the view holder, we are binding properties to view elements using the `bindView` function that will soon be defined.

Inside, we use the functions `loadImage` and `bindView`, which are not yet defined. `bindView` is a top-level extension function to `RecyclerView.ViewHolder`, which is providing a lazy delegate that is providing a view found by its ID:

```
// ViewExt.kt
package com.sample.marvelgallery.view.common

import android.support.v7.widget.RecyclerView
import android.view.View

fun <T : View> RecyclerView.ViewHolder.bindView(viewId: Int)
      = lazy { itemView.findViewById<T>(viewId) }
```

We also need to define the `loadImage` extension function that will help us to download an image from the URL and place it in `ImageView`. Two libraries typically used for such purpose are **Picasso** and **Glide**. We will use Glide, and to do so, we need to add a dependency in `build.gradle`:

```
implementation "com.android.support:recyclerview-
v7:$android_support_version"
implementation "com.github.bumptech.glide:glide:$glide_version"
```

Specify the version in the `build.gradle` project:

```
ext.android_support_version = "26.0.0"
ext.glide_version = "3.8.0"
```

Add permission to use the internet in `AndroidManifest`:

```
<manifest xmlns:android="http://schemas.android.com/apk/res/android"
   package="com.sample.marvelgallery">
   <uses-permission android:name="android.permission.INTERNET" />
   <application
...
```

And we can finally define the `loadImage` extension function for the `ImaveView` class:

```
// ViewExt.kt
package com.sample.marvelgallery.view.common

import android.support.v7.widget.RecyclerView
import android.view.View
import android.widget.ImageView
import com.bumptech.glide.Glide

fun <T : View> RecyclerView.ViewHolder.bindView(viewId: Int)
      = lazy { itemView.findViewById<T>(viewId) }
```

```
fun ImageView.loadImage(photoUrl: String) {
   Glide.with(context)
           .load(photoUrl)
           .into(this)
}
```

It is time to define the activity that will display this list. We will use one more element, the **Kotlin Android extensions** plugin, which is used to simplify access to view elements from code. Its usage is simple--we add the `kotlin-android-extensions` plugin in the `build.gradle` module:

```
apply plugin: 'com.android.application'
apply plugin: 'kotlin-android'
apply plugin: 'kotlin-android-extensions'
```

And we have a view defined in the layout:

```
<TextView
  android:id="@+id/nameView"
  android:layout_width="wrap_content"
  android:layout_height="wrap_content" />
```

Then we can import a reference to this view inside `Activity`:

```
import kotlinx.android.synthetic.main.activity_main.*
```

And we can access a `View` element directly using its name without using the `findViewById` method or defining annotations:

```
nameView.text = "Some name"
```

We will use Kotlin Android extensions in all activities in the project. Now let's define `MainActivity` to display a list of characters with images:

```
package com.sample.marvelgallery.view.main

import android.os.Bundle
import android.support.v7.app.AppCompatActivity
import android.support.v7.widget.GridLayoutManager
import android.view.Window
import com.sample.marvelgallery.R
import com.sample.marvelgallery.model.MarvelCharacter
import kotlinx.android.synthetic.main.activity_main.*

class MainActivity : AppCompatActivity() {

   private val characters = listOf( // 1
       MarvelCharacter(name = "3-D Man", imageUrl =
```

```
"http://i.annihil.us/u/prod/marvel/i/mg/c/e0/535fecbbb9784.jpg"),
        MarvelCharacter(name = "Abomination (Emil Blonsky)", imageUrl =
"http://i.annihil.us/u/prod/marvel/i/mg/9/50/4ce18691cbf04.jpg")
    )

    override fun onCreate(savedInstanceState: Bundle?) {
        super.onCreate(savedInstanceState)
        requestWindowFeature(Window.FEATURE_NO_TITLE) // 2
        setContentView(R.layout.activity_main)
        recyclerView.layoutManager = GridLayoutManager(this, 2) // 3
        val categoryItemAdapters = characters
        .map(::CharacterItemAdapter) // 4
        recyclerView.adapter = MainListAdapter(categoryItemAdapters)
    }
}
```

1. Here, we define a temporary list of characters to display.
2. We use this window feature because we don't want to display a title.
3. We use `GridLayoutManager` as the `RecyclerView` layout manager to achieve a grid effect.
4. We are creating item adapters from characters using the `CharacterItemAdapter` constructor reference.

Now we can compile the project and we will see the following screen:

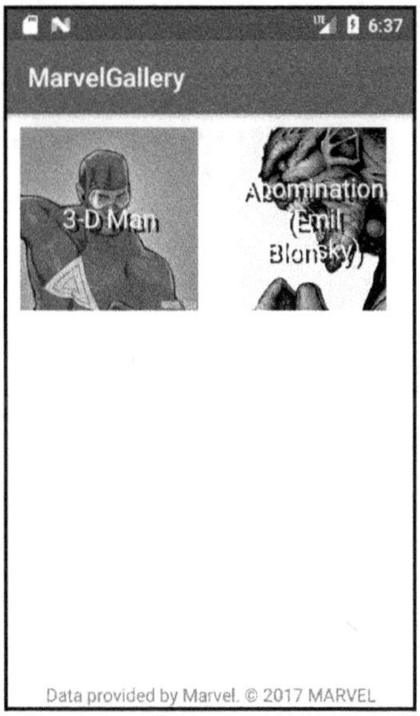

Network definition

Until now, the presented data has been hardcoded inside the application, but we want to use data from the Marvel API instead. To do this, we need to define some network mechanisms that will retrieve the data from the server. We are going to use **Retrofit**, a popular Android library used to simplify network operations, together with **RxJava**, a popular library used for reactive programming. For both libraries, we will use only basic functionalities to make their usage as simple as possible. To use them, we need to add the following dependencies in the `build.gradle` module:

```
dependencies {
   implementation "org.jetbrains.kotlin:kotlin-stdlib-jre7:
   $kotlin_version"
   implementation "com.android.support:appcompat-v7:
   $android_support_version"
   implementation "com.android.support:recyclerview-v7:
   $android_support_version"
   implementation "com.github.bumptech.glide:glide:$glide_version"

   // RxJava
   implementation "io.reactivex.rxjava2:rxjava:$rxjava_version"

   // RxAndroid
   implementation "io.reactivex.rxjava2:rxandroid:$rxandroid_version"

   // Retrofit
   implementation(["com.squareup.retrofit2:retrofit:$retrofit_version",
                   "com.squareup.retrofit2:adapter-
                    rxjava2:$retrofit_version",
                   "com.squareup.retrofit2:converter-
                    gson:$retrofit_version",
                   "com.squareup.okhttp3:okhttp:$okhttp_version",
                   "com.squareup.okhttp3:logging-
                   interceptor:$okhttp_version"])

  testImplementation 'junit:junit:4.12'
  androidTestImplementation
  'com.android.support.test:runner:1.0.0'
  androidTestImplementation
  'com.android.support.test.espresso:espresso-core:3.0.0'
}
```

And version definitions in the `build.gradle` project:

```
ext.kotlin_version = '1.1.3-2'
ext.android_support_version = "26.0.0"
ext.glide_version = "3.8.0"
```

```
ext.retrofit_version = '2.2.0'
ext.okhttp_version = '3.6.0'
ext.rxjava_version = "2.1.2"
ext.rxandroid_version = '2.0.1'
```

We already have internet permission defined on `AndroidManifest`, so we don't need to add it. A simple `Retrofit` definition might look like the following:

```
val retrofit by lazy { makeRetrofit() } // 1

private fun makeRetrofit(): Retrofit = Retrofit.Builder()
        .baseUrl("http://gateway.marvel.com/v1/public/") // 2
        .build()
```

1. We can keep the `retrofit` instance as a lazy top-level property.
2. Here, we define the `baseUrl`.

But there are some additional requirements on Retrofit that need to be matched. We need to add converters to use Retrofit together with RxJava, and to send objects serialized as JSON. We also need interceptors which will be used to provide headers and extra queries needed by the Marvel API. This is a small application, so we can define all the required elements as top-level functions. The full Retrofit definition will be the following:

```
// Retrofit.kt
package com.sample.marvelgallery.data.network.provider

import com.google.gson.Gson
import okhttp3.OkHttpClient
import retrofit2.Retrofit
import retrofit2.adapter.rxjava2.RxJava2CallAdapterFactory
import retrofit2.converter.gson.GsonConverterFactory
import java.util.concurrent.TimeUnit

val retrofit by lazy { makeRetrofit() }

private fun makeRetrofit(): Retrofit = Retrofit.Builder()
        .baseUrl("http://gateway.marvel.com/v1/public/")
        .client(makeHttpClient())
        .addConverterFactory(GsonConverterFactory.create(Gson())) // 1
        .addCallAdapterFactory(RxJava2CallAdapterFactory.create()) // 2
        .build()

private fun makeHttpClient() = OkHttpClient.Builder()
        .connectTimeout(60, TimeUnit.SECONDS) // 3
        .readTimeout(60, TimeUnit.SECONDS) // 4
        .addInterceptor(makeHeadersInterceptor()) // 5
        .addInterceptor(makeAddSecurityQueryInterceptor()) // 6
```

```
        .addInterceptor(makeLoggingInterceptor()) // 7
        .build()
```

1. Add a converter that allows object JSON serialization and deserialization using the GSON library.
2. Add a converter that will allow RxJava2 types (Observable, Single) as observables for returned values from network requests.
3. We add custom interceptors and we need to define all of them.

Let's define the necessary interceptors. `makeHeadersInterceptor` is used to add standard headers for each request:

```
// HeadersInterceptor.kt
package com.sample.marvelgallery.data.network.provider

import okhttp3.Interceptor

fun makeHeadersInterceptor() = Interceptor { chain -> // 1
   chain.proceed(chain.request().newBuilder()
           .addHeader("Accept", "application/json")
           .addHeader("Accept-Language", "en")
           .addHeader("Content-Type", "application/json")
           .build())
}
```

1. The interceptor is SAM, so we can define it using a SAM constructor.

The `makeLoggingInterceptor` function is used to display logs on the console when we are running the application in debug mode:

```
// LoggingInterceptor.kt
package com.sample.marvelgallery.data.network.provider

import com.sample.marvelgallery.BuildConfig
import okhttp3.logging.HttpLoggingInterceptor

fun makeLoggingInterceptor() = HttpLoggingInterceptor().apply {
   level = if (BuildConfig.DEBUG) HttpLoggingInterceptor.Level.BODY
           else HttpLoggingInterceptor.Level.NONE
}
```

The `makeAddRequiredQueryInterceptor` function is more complex, because it is used to provide query parameters used by the Marvel API to verify the user. These parameters need a hash calculated using the MD5 algorithm. They also need a public and private key from the Marvel API. Everyone can generate their own keys at `https://developer.marvel.com/`. Once you have generated keys, we need to place them in the `gradle.properties` file:

```
org.gradle.jvmargs=-Xmx1536m
marvelPublicKey=REPLEACE_WITH_YOUR_PUBLIC_MARVEL_KEY
marvelPrivateKey=REPLEACE_WITH_YOUR_PRIVATE_MARVEL_KEY
```

Also, add the following definitions in the `build.gradle` module in Android in the `defaultConfig` section:

```
defaultConfig {
   applicationId "com.sample.marvelgallery"
   minSdkVersion 16
   targetSdkVersion 26
   versionCode 1
   versionName "1.0"
   testInstrumentationRunner
   "android.support.test.runner.AndroidJUnitRunner"
   buildConfigField("String", "PUBLIC_KEY", "\"${marvelPublicKey}\"")
   buildConfigField("String", "PRIVATE_KEY", "\"${marvelPrivateKey}\"")
}
```

After a project rebuild, you will be able to access these values using `BuildConfig.PUBLIC_KEY` and `BuildConfig.PRIVATE_KEY`. Using these keys, we can generate the query parameters that are required by the Marvel API:

```
// QueryInterceptor.kt
package com.sample.marvelgallery.data.network.provider

import com.sample.marvelgallery.BuildConfig
import okhttp3.Interceptor

fun makeAddSecurityQueryInterceptor() = Interceptor { chain ->
   val originalRequest = chain.request()
   val timeStamp = System.currentTimeMillis()

   // Url customization: add query parameters
   val url = originalRequest.url().newBuilder()
           .addQueryParameter("apikey", BuildConfig.PUBLIC_KEY) // 1
           .addQueryParameter("ts", "$timeStamp") // 1
           .addQueryParameter("hash", calculatedMd5(timeStamp.toString() +
BuildConfig.PRIVATE_KEY + BuildConfig.PUBLIC_KEY)) // 1
           .build()
```

```
    // Request customization: set custom url
    val request = originalRequest
            .newBuilder()
            .url(url)
            .build()

    chain.proceed(request)
}
```

1. We need to provide three additional queries:
    - `apikey`: This just includes our public key.
    - `ts`: This just contains the device time in milliseconds. It is used to improve the security of the hash provided in the next query.
    - `hash`: This is calculated as an MD5 hash from the `timeStamp`, `private`, and `public` keys, one after another in a single `String`.

Here is the definition of the function used to calculate the MD5 hash:

```
// MD5.kt
package com.sample.marvelgallery.data.network.provider

import java.math.BigInteger
import java.security.MessageDigest

/**
* Calculate MD5 hash for text
* @param timeStamp Current timeStamp
* @return MD5 hash string
*/
fun calculatedMd5(text: String): String {
    val messageDigest = getMd5Digest(text)
    val md5 = BigInteger(1, messageDigest).toString(16)
    return "0" * (32 - md5.length) + md5 // 1
}

private fun getMd5Digest(str: String): ByteArray =
MessageDigest.getInstance("MD5").digest(str.toByteArray())

private operator fun String.times(i: Int) = (1..i).fold("") { acc, _ -> acc
+ this }
```

1. We use the `times` extension operator to fill the hash with zeros if it is shorter than 32.

We have interceptors defined, so we can define actual API methods. The Marvel API contains a lot of data models that represent characters, lists, and so on. We need to define them as separate classes. Such classes are called **data transfer objects** (**DTOs**). We will define the objects we will need:

```
package com.sample.marvelgallery.data.network.dto

class DataContainer<T> {
   var results: T? = null
}

package com.sample.marvelgallery.data.network.dto

class DataWrapper<T> {
   var data: DataContainer<T>? = null
}

package com.sample.marvelgallery.data.network.dto

class ImageDto {

   lateinit var path: String // 1
   lateinit var extension: String // 1

   val completeImagePath: String
       get() = "$path.$extension"
}

package com.sample.marvelgallery.data.network.dto

class CharacterMarvelDto {
   lateinit var name: String // 1
   lateinit var thumbnail: ImageDto // 1

   val imageUrl: String
       get() = thumbnail.completeImagePath
}
```

1. For values that might not be provided, we should set a default value. Values that are mandatory might be prefixed with `lateinit` instead.

Retrofit uses reflection to create an HTTP request based on the interface definition. This is how we can implement an interface that defines an HTTP request:

```
package com.sample.marvelgallery.data.network

import com.sample.marvelgallery.data.network.dto.CharacterMarvelDto
```

```
import com.sample.marvelgallery.data.network.dto.DataWrapper
import io.reactivex.Single
import retrofit2.http.GET
import retrofit2.http.Query

interface MarvelApi {

   @GET("characters")
   fun getCharacters(
           @Query("offset") offset: Int?,
           @Query("limit") limit: Int?
   ): Single<DataWrapper<List<CharacterMarvelDto>>>
}
```

With such definitions, we can finally get a list of characters:

```
retrofit.create(MarvelApi::class.java) // 1
    .getCharacters(0, 100) // 2
    .subscribe({ /* code */ }) // 3
```

1. We use a `retrofit` instance to create an object that will make HTTP requests according to the `MarvelApi` interface definition.
2. We create an observable ready to send a call to the API.
3. Using `subscribe`, we send an HTTP request and we start listening for a response. The first argument is the callback that is invoked when we successfully receive a response.

Such a network definition could be sufficient, but we could implement it better. The biggest problem is that we now need to operate on DTO objects instead of on our own data model objects. For mapping, we should define an additional layer. The repository pattern is used for this purpose. This pattern is also really helpful when we are implementing unit tests because we can mock the repository instead of the whole API definition. This is the definition of repository that we would like to have:

```
package com.sample.marvelgallery.data

import com.sample.marvelgallery.model.MarvelCharacter
import io.reactivex.Single

interface MarvelRepository {

   fun getAllCharacters(): Single<List<MarvelCharacter>>
}
```

And here is the implementation of `MarvelRepository`:

```
package com.sample.marvelgallery.data

import com.sample.marvelgallery.data.network.MarvelApi
import com.sample.marvelgallery.data.network.provider.retrofit
import com.sample.marvelgallery.model.MarvelCharacter
import io.reactivex.Single

class MarvelRepositoryImpl : MarvelRepository {

   val api = retrofit.create(MarvelApi::class.java)

   override fun getAllCharacters(): Single<List<MarvelCharacter>> =
api.getCharacters(
           offset = 0,
           limit = elementsOnListLimit
   ).map {
       it.data?.results.orEmpty().map(::MarvelCharacter) // 1
   }

   companion object {
       const val elementsOnListLimit = 50
   }
}
```

1. We get a list of DTO elements and map it into `MarvelCharacter` using a constructor reference.

To make it work, we need to define an additional constructor in `MarvelCharacter`, which takes `CharacterMarvelDto` as an argument:

```
package com.sample.marvelgallery.model

import com.sample.marvelgallery.data.network.dto.CharacterMarvelDto

class MarvelCharacter(
       val name: String,
       val imageUrl: String
) {

   constructor(dto: CharacterMarvelDto) : this(
           name = dto.name,
           imageUrl = dto.imageUrl
   )
}
```

There are different ways to provide an instance of `MarvelRepository`. In the most common implementations, a concrete instance of `MarvelRepository` is passed to `Presenter` as a constructor argument. But what about UI testing (such as Espresso tests)? We don't want to test the Marvel API and we don't want to make a UI test depending on it. The solution is to make a mechanism that will generate a standard implementation during normal runtime, but it will also allow us to set a different implementation for testing purposes. We will make the following generic implementation of such a mechanism:

```
package com.sample.marvelgallery.data

abstract class Provider<T> {

   abstract fun creator(): T

   private val instance: T by lazy { creator() }
   var testingInstance: T? = null

   fun get(): T = testingInstance ?: instance
}
```

> Instead of defining our own `Provider`, we might use some Dependency Injection libraries, such as **Dagger** or **Kodein**. The use of Dagger for such purposes is really common in Android development, but we've decided that we won't include it in this example to avoid additional complexity for developers who are not experienced with this library.

We can make the `MarvelRepository` companion object provider extending the preceding class:

```
package com.sample.marvelgallery.data

import com.sample.marvelgallery.model.MarvelCharacter
import io.reactivex.Single

interface MarvelRepository {

   fun getAllCharacters(): Single<List<MarvelCharacter>>

   companion object : Provider<MarvelRepository>() {
       override fun creator() = MarvelRepositoryImpl()
   }
}
```

Thanks to the preceding definition, we can use the `MarvelRepository` companion object to get an instance of `MarvelRepository`:

```
val marvelRepository = MarvelRepository.get()
```

It will be a lazy instance of `MarvelRepositoryImpl`, until somebody sets a non-null value of the `testingInstance` property:

```
MarvelRepository.get() // Returns instance of MarvelRepositoryImpl

MarvelRepository.testingInstance= object: MarvelRepository {
   override fun getAllCharacters(): Single<List<MarvelCharacter>>
         = Single.just(emptyList())
}

MarvelRepository.get() // returns an instance of an anonymous class in
which the returned list is always empty.
```

Such a construction is useful to allow UI tests using Espresso. Its usage for element overrides is present in the project and can be found in GitHub. It is not presented in this section to keep it easy to understand for developers who are not proficient in testing. If you are would like to see it, then you can find it at `https://github.com/MarcinMoskala/MarvelGallery/blob/master/app/src/androidTest/java/com/sample/marvelgallery/MainActivityTest.kt`.

Let's finally connect this repository to the view by implementing the business logic of the character gallery display.

Business logic implementation

We have both the view and repository parts implemented and it is time to finally implement the business logic. On this point, we need only to get the character list and display it on the list when the user enters the screen or when they refresh it. We will extract these business logic rules from the view implementation by using an architectural pattern known as **Model-View-Presenter** (**MVP**). Here are the simplified rules:

- **Model**: This is the layer responsible for managing data. The Model's responsibilities include using APIs, caching data, managing databases, and so on.
- **Presenter**: The Presenter is the middle man between Model and View, and it should include all your presentation logic. The Presenter is responsible for reacting to user interactions using and updating the Model and the View.
- **View**: This is responsible for presenting data and forwarding user interaction events to the Presenter.

In our implementation of this pattern, we will treat Activity as a View, and for each view we need to create a Presenter. It is good practice to write unit tests to check whether business logic rules are implemented correctly. To make it simple, we need to hide Activity behind an easy-to-mock interface that represents all possible Presenter interactions with View (Activity). Also, we are going to create all the dependencies (such as `MarvelRepository`) in Activity and deliver them to the Presenter via the constructor as objects hidden behind interfaces (for example, pass `MarvelRepositoryImpl` as `MarvelRepository`).

In the Presenter, we need to implement the following behaviors:

- When the Presenter is waiting for a response, the loading animation is displayed
- After the View has been created, a list of characters is loaded and displayed
- After the `refresh` method is called, a list of characters is loaded
- When the API returns a list of characters, it is displayed on the View
- When the API returns an error, it is displayed on the View

As we can see, the Presenter needs to get both View and `MarvelRepository` using constructor, and it should specify the methods that will be called when the View is created or the user request list is refreshed:

```
package com.sample.marvelgallery.presenter

import com.sample.marvelgallery.data.MarvelRepository
import com.sample.marvelgallery.view.main.MainView

class MainPresenter(val view: MainView, val repository: MarvelRepository) {

    fun onViewCreated() {
    }

    fun onRefresh() {
    }
}
```

The View needs to specify the methods used to show the list of characters, show errors, and show the progress bar when the View is refreshing (define it in `view/main` and move `MainActivity` to `view/main`):

```
package com.sample.marvelgallery.view.main.main

import com.sample.marvelgallery.model.MarvelCharacter

interface MainView {
```

```
    var refresh: Boolean
    fun show(items: List<MarvelCharacter>)
    fun showError(error: Throwable)
}
```

Before adding logic to the Presenter, let's define the first two unit tests:

```
// test source set
package com.sample.marvelgallery

import com.sample.marvelgallery.data.MarvelRepository
import com.sample.marvelgallery.model.MarvelCharacter
import com.sample.marvelgallery.presenter.MainPresenter
import com.sample.marvelgallery.view.main.MainView
import io.reactivex.Single
import org.junit.Assert.assertEquals
import org.junit.Assert.fail
import org.junit.Test

@Suppress("IllegalIdentifier") // 1
class MainPresenterTest {

   @Test
   fun `After view was created, list of characters is loaded and
displayed`() {
       assertOnAction { onViewCreated() }.thereIsSameListDisplayed()
   }

   @Test
   fun `New list is shown after view was refreshed`() {
       assertOnAction { onRefresh() }.thereIsSameListDisplayed()
   }

   private fun assertOnAction(action: MainPresenter.() -> Unit)
           = PresenterActionAssertion(action)

   private class PresenterActionAssertion
   (val actionOnPresenter: MainPresenter.() -> Unit) {

       fun thereIsSameListDisplayed() {
           // Given
           val exampleCharacterList = listOf(// 2
                   MarvelCharacter("ExampleName", "ExampleImageUrl"),
                   MarvelCharacter("Name1", "ImageUrl1"),
                   MarvelCharacter("Name2", "ImageUrl2")
           )

           var displayedList: List<MarvelCharacter>? = null
```

```
            val view = object : MainView { //3
                override var refresh: Boolean = false

                override fun show(items: List<MarvelCharacter>) {
                    displayedList = items // 4
                }

                override fun showError(error: Throwable) {
                    fail() //5
                }
            }
            val marvelRepository = object : MarvelRepository { // 3
                override fun getAllCharacters():
                 Single<List<MarvelCharacter>>
                   = Single.just(exampleCharacterList) // 6
            }

            val mainPresenter = MainPresenter(view, marvelRepository)
            // 3

            // When
            mainPresenter.actionOnPresenter() // 7

            // Then
            assertEquals(exampleCharacterList, displayedList) // 8
        }
    }
}
```

1. Descriptive names are allowed in Kotlin unit tests, but a warning will be displayed. Suppression is needed to hide this warning.
2. Define a list of example characters to display.
3. Define a view and repository and create a Presenter using them.
4. When a list of elements is shown, we should set it as a displayed list.
5. The test is failing when `showError` is called.
6. The `getAllCharacters` method just returns an example list.
7. We call a defined action on the Presenter.
8. We check whether the list returned by the repository is the same as the displayed list.

To simplify the preceding definitions, we could extract `BaseMarvelRepository` and `BaseMainView`, and keep example data in a separate class:

```
// test source set
package com.sample.marvelgallery.helpers

import com.sample.marvelgallery.data.MarvelRepository
import com.sample.marvelgallery.model.MarvelCharacter
import io.reactivex.Single

class BaseMarvelRepository(
        val onGetCharacters: () -> Single<List<MarvelCharacter>>
) : MarvelRepository {

    override fun getAllCharacters() = onGetCharacters()
}

// test source set
package com.sample.marvelgallery.helpers

import com.sample.marvelgallery.model.MarvelCharacter
import com.sample.marvelgallery.view.main.MainView

class BaseMainView(
        var onShow: (items: List<MarvelCharacter>) -> Unit = {},
        val onShowError: (error: Throwable) -> Unit = {},
        override var refresh: Boolean = false
) : MainView {

    override fun show(items: List<MarvelCharacter>) {
        onShow(items)
    }

    override fun showError(error: Throwable) {
        onShowError(error)
    }
}

// test source set
package com.sample.marvelgallery.helpers

import com.sample.marvelgallery.model.MarvelCharacter

object Example {
    val exampleCharacter = MarvelCharacter
    ("ExampleName", "ExampleImageUrl")
    val exampleCharacterList = listOf(
            exampleCharacter,
```

```
            MarvelCharacter("Name1", "ImageUrl1"),
            MarvelCharacter("Name2", "ImageUrl2")
    )
}
```

Now we can simplify the definition of `PresenterActionAssertion`:

```
package com.sample.marvelgallery

import com.sample.marvelgallery.helpers.BaseMainView
import com.sample.marvelgallery.helpers.BaseMarvelRepository
import com.sample.marvelgallery.helpers.Example
import com.sample.marvelgallery.model.MarvelCharacter
import com.sample.marvelgallery.presenter.MainPresenter
import io.reactivex.Single
import org.junit.Assert.assertEquals
import org.junit.Assert.fail
import org.junit.Test

@Suppress("IllegalIdentifier")

class MainPresenterTest {

   @Test
   fun `After view was created, list of characters is loaded and
displayed`() {
       assertOnAction { onViewCreated() }.thereIsSameListDisplayed()
   }

   @Test
   fun `New list is shown after view was refreshed`() {
       assertOnAction { onRefresh() }.thereIsSameListDisplayed()
   }

   private fun assertOnAction(action: MainPresenter.() -> Unit)
           = PresenterActionAssertion(action)

   private class PresenterActionAssertion
   (val actionOnPresenter: MainPresenter.() -> Unit) {

       fun thereIsSameListDisplayed() {
           // Given
           var displayedList: List<MarvelCharacter>? = null

           val view = BaseMainView(
                   onShow = { items -> displayedList = items },
                   onShowError = { fail() }
           )
```

```
            val marvelRepository = BaseMarvelRepository(
                    onGetCharacters =
            { Single.just(Example.exampleCharacterList) }
            )

            val mainPresenter = MainPresenter(view, marvelRepository)

            // When
            mainPresenter.actionOnPresenter()

            // Then
            assertEquals(Example.exampleCharacterList, displayedList)
        }
    }
}
```

We start the tests:

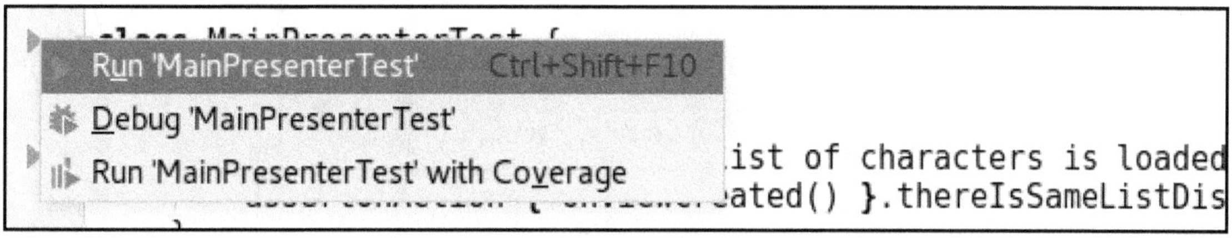

We will see that they do not pass:

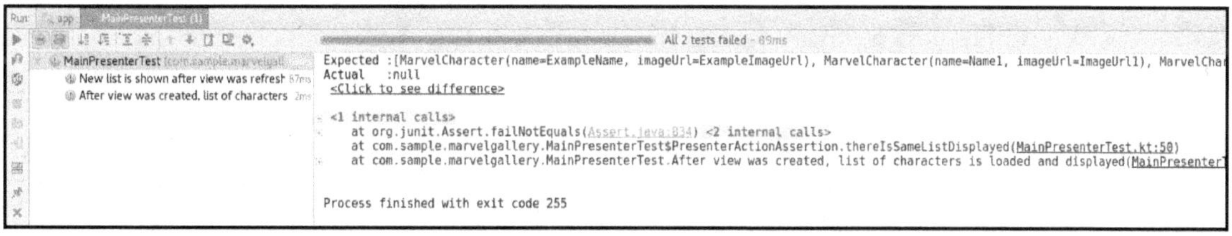

The reason is that functionalities have not been implemented yet in `MainPresenter`. The simplest code that is satisfactory to pass this unit test is the following:

```
package com.sample.marvelgallery.presenter

import com.sample.marvelgallery.data.MarvelRepository
import com.sample.marvelgallery.view.main.MainView

class MainPresenter(val view: MainView, val repository: MarvelRepository) {

    fun onViewCreated() {
```

```
        loadCharacters()
    }

    fun onRefresh() {
        loadCharacters()
    }

    private fun loadCharacters() {
        repository.getAllCharacters()
                .subscribe({ items ->
                    view.show(items)
                })
    }
}
```

Now our tests pass:

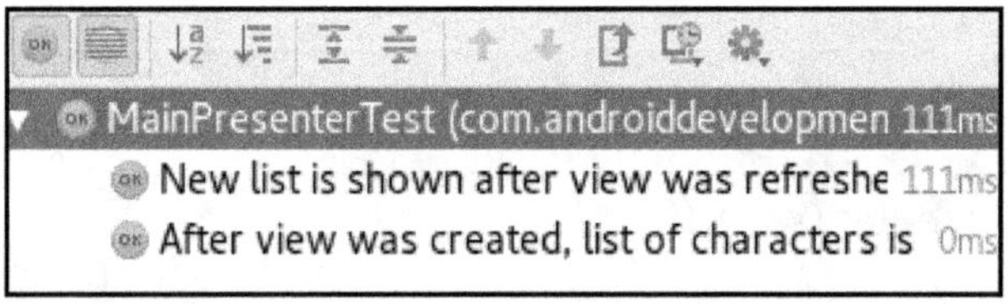

But there are two issues with this implementation:

- It won't work in Android, because `getAllCharacters` uses a network operation and it cannot run on the main thread as in this example
- We will have a memory leak if the user leaves the application before loading have finished

To resolve the first issue, we need to specify on which threads operations should run. The network request should run on the I/O thread, and we should observe on the Android main thread (because we are changing the view in the callback):

```
repository.getAllCharacters()
        .subscribeOn(Schedulers.io()) // 1
        .observeOn(AndroidSchedulers.mainThread()) // 2
        .subscribe({ items -> view.show(items) })
```

1. We specify that the network request should run in the IO thread.
2. We specify that callbacks should be started on the main thread.

While these are common schedulers to show, we can extract them in a top-level extension function:

```
// RxExt.kt
package com.sample.marvelgallery.data

import io.reactivex.Single
import io.reactivex.android.schedulers.AndroidSchedulers
import io.reactivex.schedulers.Schedulers

fun <T> Single<T>.applySchedulers(): Single<T> = this
        .subscribeOn(Schedulers.io())
        .observeOn(AndroidSchedulers.mainThread())

And use it in MainPresenter:

repository.getAllCharacters()
        .applySchedulers()
        .subscribe({ items -> view.show(items) })
```

Tests are not allowed to access the Android main thread. Therefore, our tests will not pass. Also, operations running on a new thread are not what we want in unit tests, because we would have problems with assertions synchronization. To resolve these problems, we need override schedulers before unit tests to make everything run on the same thread (add them in the `MainPresenterTest` class):

```
package com.sample.marvelgallery

import com.sample.marvelgallery.helpers.BaseMainView
import com.sample.marvelgallery.helpers.BaseMarvelRepository
import com.sample.marvelgallery.helpers.Example
import com.sample.marvelgallery.model.MarvelCharacter
import com.sample.marvelgallery.presenter.MainPresenter
import io.reactivex.Single
import io.reactivex.android.plugins.RxAndroidPlugins
import io.reactivex.plugins.RxJavaPlugins
import io.reactivex.schedulers.Schedulers
import org.junit.Assert.assertEquals
import org.junit.Assert.fail
import org.junit.Before
import org.junit.Test

@Suppress("IllegalIdentifier")

class MainPresenterTest {

   @Before
```

```
    fun setUp() {
        RxAndroidPlugins.setInitMainThreadSchedulerHandler {
            Schedulers.trampoline() }
        RxJavaPlugins.setIoSchedulerHandler { Schedulers.trampoline() }
        RxJavaPlugins.setComputationSchedulerHandler {
            Schedulers.trampoline() }
        RxJavaPlugins.setNewThreadSchedulerHandler {
            Schedulers.trampoline() }
    }

    @Test
    fun `After view was created, list of characters is loaded and
         displayed`() {
        assertOnAction { onViewCreated() }.thereIsSameListDisplayed()
    }

    @Test
    fun `New list is shown after view was refreshed`() {
        assertOnAction { onRefresh() }.thereIsSameListDisplayed()
    }
```

Now unit tests pass again:

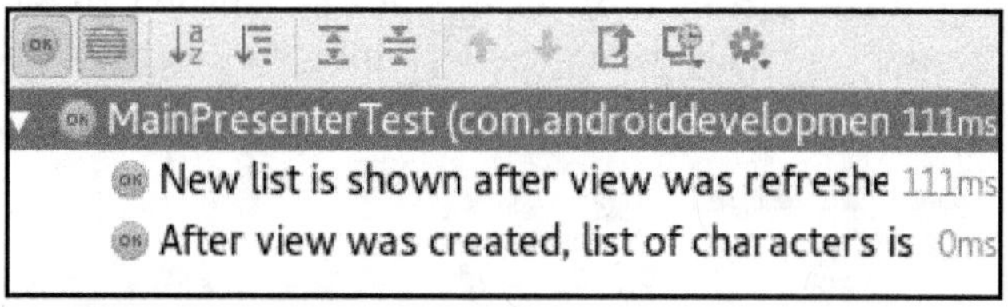

Another problem is memory leak if the user leaves the application before we get a server response. A common solution is to keep all subscriptions in composite and dispose of them all when the user leaves the application:

```
private var subscriptions = CompositeDisposable()

fun onViewDestroyed() {
   subscriptions.dispose()
}
```

In bigger applications, most presenters have some subscriptions. So, the functionality of collecting subscriptions and of disposing them when the user destroys the view can be treated as common behavior and extracted in `BasePresenter`. Also, to simplify the process, we can make a `BaseActivityWithPresenter` class that will hold the presenter behind the `Presenter` interface and call the `onViewDestroyed` method when the view is destroyed. Let's define this mechanism in our application. Here is the definition of `Presenter`:

```
package com.sample.marvelgallery.presenter

interface Presenter {
   fun onViewDestroyed()
}
```

Here is the definition of `BasePresenter`:

```
package com.sample.marvelgallery.presenter

import io.reactivex.disposables.CompositeDisposable

abstract class BasePresenter : Presenter {

   protected var subscriptions = CompositeDisposable()

   override fun onViewDestroyed() {
       subscriptions.dispose()
   }
}
```

Here is the definition of `BaseActivityWithPresenter`:

```
package com.sample.marvelgallery.view.common

import android.support.v7.app.AppCompatActivity
import com.sample.marvelgallery.presenter.Presenter

abstract class BaseActivityWithPresenter : AppCompatActivity() {

   abstract val presenter: Presenter

   override fun onDestroy() {
       super.onDestroy()
       presenter.onViewDestroyed()
   }
}
```

To simplify how a new subscription is added to subscriptions, we can define a plus assign operator:

```
// RxExt.ext
package com.sample.marvelgallery.data

import io.reactivex.Single
import io.reactivex.android.schedulers.AndroidSchedulers
import io.reactivex.disposables.CompositeDisposable
import io.reactivex.disposables.Disposable
import io.reactivex.schedulers.Schedulers

fun <T> Single<T>.applySchedulers(): Single<T> = this
        .subscribeOn(Schedulers.io())
        .observeOn(AndroidSchedulers.mainThread())

operator fun CompositeDisposable.plusAssign(disposable: Disposable) {
   add(disposable)
}
```

And we can use both solutions to make `MainPresenter` secure:

```
package com.sample.marvelgallery.presenter

import com.sample.marvelgallery.data.MarvelRepository
import com.sample.marvelgallery.data.applySchedulers
import com.sample.marvelgallery.data.plusAssign
import com.sample.marvelgallery.view.main.MainView

class MainPresenter(
        val view: MainView,
        val repository: MarvelRepository
) : BasePresenter() {

    fun onViewCreated() {
        loadCharacters()
    }

    fun onRefresh() {
        loadCharacters()
    }

    private fun loadCharacters() {
        subscriptions += repository.getAllCharacters()
                .applySchedulers()
                .subscribe({ items ->
                    view.show(items)
                })
```

```
    }
}
```

The first two `MainPresenter` behaviors have been implemented. It is time to move on to the next one--when the API returns an error, it is displayed on the view. We can add this requirement as a test in `MainPresenterTest`:

```
@Test
fun `New list is shown after view was refreshed`() {
   assertOnAction { onRefresh() }.thereIsSameListDisplayed()
}

@Test
fun `When API returns error, it is displayed on view`() {
   // Given
   val someError = Error()
   var errorDisplayed: Throwable? = null
   val view = BaseMainView(
           onShow = { _ -> fail() },
           onShowError = { errorDisplayed = it }
   )
   val marvelRepository = BaseMarvelRepository
   { Single.error(someError) }
   val mainPresenter = MainPresenter(view, marvelRepository)
   // When
   mainPresenter.onViewCreated()
   // Then
   assertEquals(someError, errorDisplayed)
}

private fun assertOnAction(action: MainPresenter.() -> Unit)
       = PresenterActionAssertion(action)
```

A simple change that will make this test pass is the error handler specification in the subscribe method in `MainPresenter`:

```
subscriptions += repository.getAllCharacters()
       .applySchedulers()
       .subscribe({ items -> // onNext
           view.show(items)
       }, { // onError
           view.showError(it)
       })
```

While `subscribe` is a Java method, we cannot use the named argument convention. Such an invocation is not really descriptive. This is why we are going to define it in the `RxExt.kt` custom subscribe method named `subscribeBy`:

```
// Ext.kt

fun <T> Single<T>.applySchedulers(): Single<T> = this
        .subscribeOn(Schedulers.io())
        .observeOn(AndroidSchedulers.mainThread())
fun <T> Single<T>.subscribeBy(
        onError: ((Throwable) -> Unit)? = null,
        onSuccess: (T) -> Unit
): Disposable = subscribe(onSuccess, { onError?.invoke(it) })
```

And we will use it instead of subscribe:

```
subscriptions += repository.getAllCharacters()
        .applySchedulers()
        .subscribeBy(
                onSuccess = view::show,
                onError = view::showError
       )
```

`subscribeBy` in the full version defined for different RxJava types (such as Observable, Flowable, and so on), together with lots of other useful Kotlin extensions to RxJava, can be found in the **RxKotlin** library (`https://github.com/ReactiveX/RxKotlin`).

To show and hide list loading, we will define additional listeners to events that always occur before and after processing:

```
subscriptions += repository.getAllCharacters()
        .applySchedulers()
        .doOnSubscribe { view.refresh = true },}
                onSuccess = view::show,
        .doFinally { view.refresh = false }
        .subscribeBy(
                onSuccess = view::show,
                onError = view::showError,
                onFinish = { view.refresh = false }
        )
```

And our tests are pass again:

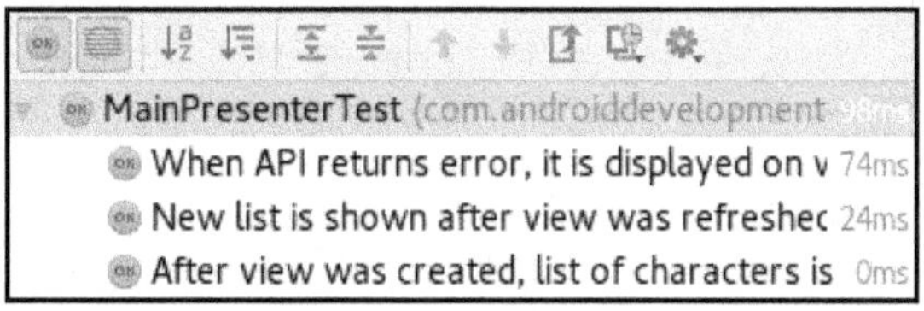

The `subscribe` method is becoming less and less readable, but we will resolve this problem together with another business rule, whose definition is the following: when the Presenter is waiting for a response, refresh is displayed. Define its unit test in `MainPresenterTest`:

```
package com.sample.marvelgallery

import com.sample.marvelgallery.helpers.BaseMainView
import com.sample.marvelgallery.helpers.BaseMarvelRepository
import com.sample.marvelgallery.helpers.Example
import com.sample.marvelgallery.model.MarvelCharacter
import com.sample.marvelgallery.presenter.MainPresenter
import io.reactivex.Single
import io.reactivex.android.plugins.RxAndroidPlugins
import io.reactivex.plugins.RxJavaPlugins
import io.reactivex.schedulers.Schedulers
import org.junit.Assert.*
import org.junit.Before
import org.junit.Test

@Suppress("IllegalIdentifier")

class MainPresenterTest {

   @Test
   fun `When presenter is waiting for response, refresh is displayed`()
   {
       // Given
       val view = BaseMainView(refresh = false)
       val marvelRepository = BaseMarvelRepository(
               onGetCharacters = {
                   Single.fromCallable {
                       // Then
                       assertTrue(view.refresh) // 1
                       Example.exampleCharacterList
                   }
               }
       )
```

```
        val mainPresenter = MainPresenter(view, marvelRepository)
        view.onShow = { _ ->
            // Then
            assertTrue(view.refresh) // 1
        }
        // When
        mainPresenter.onViewCreated()
        // Then
        assertFalse(view.refresh) // 1
    }
}
```

1. We expect refresh to be displayed during network requests and when elements are shown, but not once processing had finished.

> In the presented version on RxJava2, assertions inside callbacks do not break the test it but display an error on the execution report instead. In future versions, it will probably be possible to add a handler that allows a test to fail from inside a callback.

To show and hide list loading, we will define additional listeners to events that always occur before and after processing:

```
subscriptions += repository.getAllCharacters()
        .applySchedulers()
        .doOnSubscribe { view.refresh = true }
        .doFinally { view.refresh = false }
        .subscribeBy(
                    onSuccess = view::show,
                    onError = view::showError
        )
```

After these changes, all tests pass again:

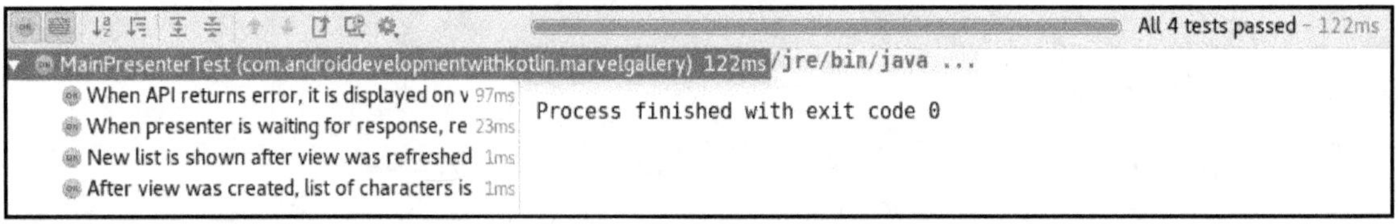

Now we have a fully functional Presenter, network, and View. Time to connect it all and finish the implementation of the first use case.

Putting it all together

We have `MainPresenter` ready to be used in the project. Now we need to use it in `MainActivity`:

```
package com.sample.marvelgallery.view.main

import android.os.Bundle
import android.support.v7.widget.GridLayoutManager
import android.view.Window
import com.sample.marvelgallery.R
import com.sample.marvelgallery.data.MarvelRepository
import com.sample.marvelgallery.model.MarvelCharacter
import com.sample.marvelgallery.presenter.MainPresenter
import com.sample.marvelgallery.view.common.BaseActivityWithPresenter
import com.sample.marvelgallery.view.common.bindToSwipeRefresh
import com.sample.marvelgallery.view.common.toast
import kotlinx.android.synthetic.main.activity_main.*

class MainActivity : BaseActivityWithPresenter(), MainView { // 1

   override var refresh by bindToSwipeRefresh(R.id.swipeRefreshView)
   // 2
   override val presenter by lazy
   { MainPresenter(this, MarvelRepository.get()) } // 3

   override fun onCreate(savedInstanceState: Bundle?) {
       super.onCreate(savedInstanceState)
       requestWindowFeature(Window.FEATURE_NO_TITLE)
       setContentView(R.layout.activity_main)
       recyclerView.layoutManager = GridLayoutManager(this, 2)
       swipeRefreshView.setOnRefreshListener
       { presenter.onRefresh() } // 4
       presenter.onViewCreated() // 4
   }

   override fun show(items: List<MarvelCharacter>) {
       val categoryItemAdapters = items.map(::CharacterItemAdapter)
       recyclerView.adapter = MainListAdapter(categoryItemAdapters)
   }

   override fun showError(error: Throwable) {
       toast("Error: ${error.message}") // 2
       error.printStackTrace()
   }
}
```

1. Activity should extend `BaseActivityWithPresenter` and implement `MainView`.
2. `bindToSwipeRefresh` and `toast` are not yet implemented.
3. We make the Presenter lazily. The first argument is a reference to the activity behind the `MainView` interface.
4. We need to pass events to the presenter using its methods.

In the preceding code, we used two functions that have already been described in the book, `toast`, used to display toast on the screen, and `bindToSwipeRefresh`, used to bind a property with the visibility of swipe refresh:

```
// ViewExt.kt
package com.sample.marvelgallery.view.common

import android.app.Activity
import android.content.Context
import android.support.annotation.IdRes
import android.support.v4.widget.SwipeRefreshLayout
import android.support.v7.widget.RecyclerView
import android.view.View
import android.widget.ImageView
import android.widget.Toast
import com.bumptech.glide.Glide
import kotlin.properties.ReadWriteProperty
import kotlin.reflect.KProperty

fun <T : View> RecyclerView.ViewHolder.bindView(viewId: Int)
       = lazy { itemView.findViewById<T>(viewId) }

fun ImageView.loadImage(photoUrl: String) {
   Glide.with(context)
           .load(photoUrl)
           .into(this)
}

fun Context.toast(text: String, length: Int = Toast.LENGTH_LONG) {
   Toast.makeText(this, text, length).show()
}

fun Activity.bindToSwipeRefresh(@IdRes swipeRefreshLayoutId: Int):
ReadWriteProperty<Any?, Boolean>
       = SwipeRefreshBinding(lazy {
findViewById<SwipeRefreshLayout>(swipeRefreshLayoutId) })

private class SwipeRefreshBinding(lazyViewProvider:
Lazy<SwipeRefreshLayout>) : ReadWriteProperty<Any?, Boolean> {
```

```
    val view by lazyViewProvider

    override fun getValue(thisRef: Any?,
    property: KProperty<*>): Boolean {
        return view.isRefreshing
    }

    override fun setValue(thisRef: Any?,
    property: KProperty<*>, value: Boolean) {
        view.isRefreshing = value
    }
}
```

Now our application should correctly show a list of characters:

Our first use case has been implemented. We can move on to the next one.

Character search

Another behavior we need to implement is character search. Here is the use case definition: *after starting the application, the user can search for a character by their name.*

To add it, we are going to add `EditText` to the `activity_main` layout:

```
<?xml version="1.0" encoding="utf-8"?>
<RelativeLayout xmlns:android="http://schemas.android.com/apk/res/android"
   xmlns:app="http://schemas.android.com/apk/res-auto"
   xmlns:tools="http://schemas.android.com/tools"
   android:id="@+id/charactersView"
   android:layout_width="match_parent"
   android:layout_height="match_parent"
   android:background="@android:color/white"
   android:fitsSystemWindows="true">

<!-- Dummy item to prevent EditText from receiving
     focus on initial load -->
   <LinearLayout
       android:layout_width="0px"
       android:layout_height="0px"
       android:focusable="true"
       android:focusableInTouchMode="true"
       tools:ignore="UselessLeaf" />

  <android.support.design.widget.TextInputLayout
     android:id="@+id/searchViewLayout"
     android:layout_width="match_parent"
     android:layout_height="wrap_content"
     android:layout_margin="@dimen/element_padding">

     <EditText
         android:id="@+id/searchView"
         android:layout_width="match_parent"
         android:layout_height="wrap_content"
         android:layout_centerHorizontal="true"
         android:hint="@string/search_hint" />
  </android.support.design.widget.TextInputLayout>

   <android.support.v4.widget.SwipeRefreshLayout
xmlns:android="http://schemas.android.com/apk/res/android"
       android:id="@+id/swipeRefreshView"
       android:layout_width="match_parent"
       android:layout_height="match_parent"
       android:layout_below="@+id/searchViewLayout"
       app:layout_behavior="@string/appbar_scrolling_view_behavior">
```

```
        <android.support.v7.widget.RecyclerView
            android:id="@+id/recyclerView"
            android:layout_width="match_parent"
            android:layout_height="match_parent"
            android:scrollbars="vertical" />

    </android.support.v4.widget.SwipeRefreshLayout>

    <TextView
        android:layout_width="match_parent"
        android:layout_height="wrap_content"
        android:layout_alignParentBottom="true"
        android:background="@android:color/white"
        android:gravity="center"
        android:text="@string/marvel_copyright_notice" />
</RelativeLayout>
```

We need to add the **Android Support Design** library dependency to allow `TextInputLayout` usage:

```
implementation "com.android.support:appcompat-v7:$android_support_version"
implementation "com.android.support:design:$android_support_version"
implementation "com.android.support:recyclerview-
v7:$android_support_version"
```

And the `search_hint` string definition in the `strings.xml` file:

```
<resources>
   <string name="app_name">MarvelGallery</string>
   <string name="search_hint">Search for character</string>
   <string name="marvel_copyright_notice">
      Data provided by Marvel. © 2017 MARVEL
   </string>
</resources>
```

Also, to keep the label with the information about Marvel's copyright when the keyboard is opened, we also need to `adjustResize` to `windowSoftInputMode` in the `activity` definition in `AndroidManifest`:

```
<activity
   android:name="com.sample.marvelgallery.view.main.MainActivity"
   android:windowSoftInputMode="adjustResize">
   <intent-filter>
       <action android:name="android.intent.action.MAIN" />
       <category android:name="android.intent.category.LAUNCHER" />
   </intent-filter>
</activity>
```

We should see the following preview:

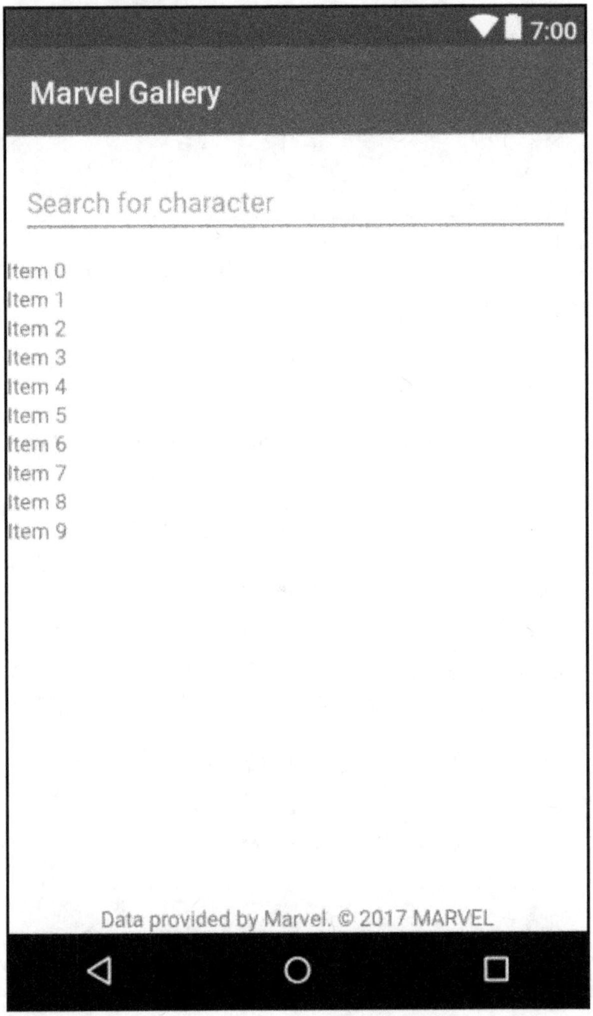

Now we have a search field added in `MainActivity`:

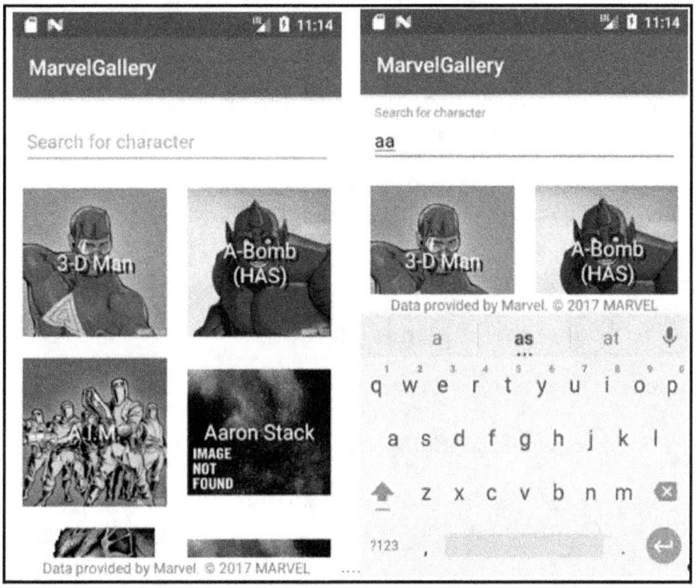

The behavior we are expecting is that whenever the user changes the text in the search field, a new list will be loaded. We need a new method in `MainPresenter`, which will be used to inform the presenter that the text has been changed. We will call it `onSearchChanged`:

```
fun onRefresh() {
   loadCharacters()
}

fun onSearchChanged(text: String) {
   // TODO
}

private fun loadCharacters() {
   subscriptions += repository.getAllCharacters()
           .applySchedulers()
           .doOnSubscribe { view.refresh = true }
           .doFinally { view.refresh = false }
           .subscribeBy(
               onSuccess = view::show,
               onError = view::showError
         )
   }
}
```

We need to change the `MarvelRepository` definition to accept a search query as a `getAllCharacters` parameter (remember to also update also `BaseMarvelRepository`):

```
interface MarvelRepository {

   fun getAllCharacters(searchQuery: String?):
   Single<List<MarvelCharacter>>

   companion object : Provider<MarvelRepository>() {
       override fun creator() = MarvelRepositoryImpl()
   }
}
```

As a result, we have to update the implementation:

```
class MarvelRepositoryImpl : MarvelRepository {

   val api = retrofit.create(MarvelApi::class.java)

   override fun getAllCharacters(searchQuery: String?):
   Single<List<MarvelCharacter>> = api.getCharacters(
           offset = 0,
           searchQuery = searchQuery,
           limit = elementsOnListLimit
   ).map { it.data?.results.orEmpty().map(::MarvelCharacter) ?:
    emptyList() }

   companion object {
       const val elementsOnListLimit = 50
   }
}
```

We also update the network request definition:

```
interface MarvelApi {

   @GET("characters")
   fun getCharacters(
           @Query("offset") offset: Int?,
           @Query("nameStartsWith") searchQuery: String?,
           @Query("limit") limit: Int?
   ): Single<DataWrapper<List<CharacterMarvelDto>>>
}
```

And to allow code compilation, we need to provide `null` as a `getAllCharacters` argument in `MainPresenter`:

```
private fun loadCharacters() {
```

```
        subscriptions += repository.getAllCharacters(null)
                .applySchedulers()
                .doOnSubscribe { view.refresh = true }
                .doFinally { view.refresh = false }
                .subscribeBy(
                        onSuccess = view::show,
                        onError = view::showError
                )
    }
}
```

And we need to update `BaseMarvelRepository`:

```
package com.sample.marvelgallery.helpers

import com.sample.marvelgallery.data.MarvelRepository
import com.sample.marvelgallery.model.MarvelCharacter
import io.reactivex.Single

class BaseMarvelRepository(
        val onGetCharacters: (String?) -> Single<List<MarvelCharacter>>
) : MarvelRepository {

    override fun getAllCharacters(searchQuery: String?)
            = onGetCharacters(searchQuery)
}
```

Now our network implementation returns a list of characters that starts from a query, or a fill list if we don't specify a query. Time to implement the presenter. Let's define the following tests:

```
@file:Suppress("IllegalIdentifier")

package com.sample.marvelgallery

import com.sample.marvelgallery.helpers.BaseMainView
import com.sample.marvelgallery.helpers.BaseMarvelRepository
import com.sample.marvelgallery.presenter.MainPresenter
import io.reactivex.Single
import org.junit.Assert.*
import org.junit.Test

class MainPresenterSearchTest {
    @Test
    fun `When view is created, then search query is null`() {
        assertOnAction { onViewCreated() } searchQueryIsEqualTo null
    }
```

```
    @Test
    fun `When text is changed, then we are searching for new query`() {
        for (text in listOf("KKO", "HJ HJ", "And so what?"))
            assertOnAction { onSearchChanged(text) }
            searchQueryIsEqualTo text
    }

    private fun assertOnAction(action: MainPresenter.() -> Unit)
          = PresenterActionAssertion(action)

    private class PresenterActionAssertion(val actionOnPresenter:
        MainPresenter.() -> Unit) {

        infix fun searchQueryIsEqualTo(expectedQuery: String?) {
            var checkApplied = false
            val view = BaseMainView(onShowError = { fail() })
            val marvelRepository = BaseMarvelRepository { searchQuery ->
                assertEquals(expectedQuery, searchQuery)
                checkApplied = true
                Single.never()
            }
            val mainPresenter = MainPresenter(view, marvelRepository)
            mainPresenter.actionOnPresenter()
            assertTrue(checkApplied)
        }
    }
}
```

To make the following test pass, we need to add a search query as a parameter with default argument to the `loadCharacters` method of `MainPresenter`:

```
fun onSearchChanged(text: String) {
    loadCharacters(text)
}

private fun loadCharacters(searchQuery: String? = null) {
    subscriptions += repository.getAllCharacters(searchQuery)
            .applySchedulers()
            .doOnSubscribe { view.refresh = true }
            .doFinally { view.refresh = false }
            .subscribeBy(
                        onSuccess = view::show,
                        onError = view::showError
        )
    }
}
```

But the tricky part is that the Marvel API does not allow only whitespaces as a search query. There should be a `null` sent instead. Therefore, if the user deletes the last character, or if they try to search with only spaces in the search field, then the application will crash. We should prevent such situations. Here is a test that checks whether the presenter changes a query with only whitespaces into `null`:

```
@Test
fun `When text is changed, then we are searching for new query`() {
   for (text in listOf("KKO", "HJ HJ", "And so what?"))
        assertOnAction { onSearchChanged(text) }
        searchQueryIsEqualTo text
}

@Test
fun `For blank text, there is request with null query`() {
   for (emptyText in listOf("", "   ", "        "))
        assertOnAction { onSearchChanged(emptyText) }
        searchQueryIsEqualTo null
}

private fun assertOnAction(action: MainPresenter.() -> Unit)
      = PresenterActionAssertion(action)
```

We can implement a security mechanism in the loadCharacters method:

```
private fun loadCharacters(searchQuery: String? = null) {
   val qualifiedSearchQuery = if (searchQuery.isNullOrBlank()) null
                              else searchQuery
   subscriptions += repository
           .getAllCharacters(qualifiedSearchQuery)
           .applySchedulers()
           .smartSubscribe(
                   onStart = { view.refresh = true },
                   onSuccess = view::show,
                   onError = view::showError,
                   onFinish = { view.refresh = false }
           )
}
```

Now all tests pass again:

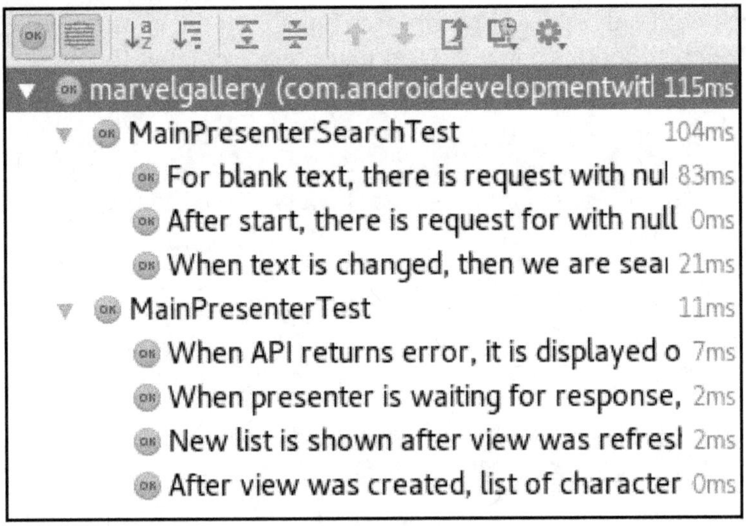

We still need to implement an `Activity` functionality that will call the presenter when text has been changed. We will do this using the optional callback class defined in `Chapter 7`, *Extension Functions and Properties*:

```
// TextChangedListener.kt
package com.sample.marvelgallery.view.common

import android.text.Editable
import android.text.TextWatcher
import android.widget.TextView

fun TextView.addOnTextChangedListener(config: TextWatcherConfiguration.()
-> Unit) {
   addTextChangedListener(TextWatcherConfiguration().apply { config() }
   addTextChangedListener(textWatcher)
}

class TextWatcherConfiguration : TextWatcher {

   private var beforeTextChangedCallback:
   (BeforeTextChangedFunction)? = null
   private var onTextChangedCallback:
   (OnTextChangedFunction)? = null
   private var afterTextChangedCallback:
   (AfterTextChangedFunction)? = null
```

```
    fun beforeTextChanged(callback: BeforeTextChangedFunction) {
        beforeTextChangedCallback = callback
    }

    fun onTextChanged(callback: OnTextChangedFunction) {
        onTextChangedCallback = callback
    }

    fun afterTextChanged(callback: AfterTextChangedFunction) {
        afterTextChangedCallback = callback
    }

    override fun beforeTextChanged(s: CharSequence,
    start: Int, count: Int, after: Int) {
        beforeTextChangedCallback?.invoke(s.toString(),
        start, count, after)
    }

    override fun onTextChanged(s: CharSequence, start: Int,
    before: Int, count: Int) {
        onTextChangedCallback?.invoke(s.toString(),
        start, before, count)
    }

    override fun afterTextChanged(s: Editable) {
        afterTextChangedCallback?.invoke(s)
    }
}

private typealias BeforeTextChangedFunction =
  (text: String, start: Int, count: Int, after: Int) -> Unit
private typealias OnTextChangedFunction =
  (text: String, start: Int, before: Int, count: Int) -> Unit
private typealias AfterTextChangedFunction =
  (s: Editable) -> Unit
```

And use it in the `onCreate` method of `MainActivity`:

```
package com.sample.marvelgallery.view.main

import android.os.Bundle
import android.support.v7.widget.GridLayoutManager
import android.view.Window
import com.sample.marvelgallery.R
import com.sample.marvelgallery.data.MarvelRepository
import com.sample.marvelgallery.model.MarvelCharacter
import com.sample.marvelgallery.presenter.MainPresenter
import com.sample.marvelgallery.view.common.BaseActivityWithPresenter
```

```
import com.sample.marvelgallery.view.common.addOnTextChangedListener
import com.sample.marvelgallery.view.common.bindToSwipeRefresh
import com.sample.marvelgallery.view.common.toast
import kotlinx.android.synthetic.main.activity_main.*

class MainActivity : BaseActivityWithPresenter(), MainView {

   override var refresh by bindToSwipeRefresh(R.id.swipeRefreshView)
   override val presenter by lazy
     { MainPresenter(this, MarvelRepository.get()) }

   override fun onCreate(savedInstanceState: Bundle?) {
       super.onCreate(savedInstanceState)
       requestWindowFeature(Window.FEATURE_NO_TITLE)
       setContentView(R.layout.activity_main)
       recyclerView.layoutManager = GridLayoutManager(this, 2)
       swipeRefreshView.setOnRefreshListener { presenter.onRefresh() }
       searchView.addOnTextChangedListener {
           onTextChanged { text, _, _, _ ->
               presenter.onSearchChanged(text)
           }
       }
       presenter.onViewCreated()
   }

   override fun show(items: List<MarvelCharacter>) {
       val categoryItemAdapters = items.map(::CharacterItemAdapter)
       recyclerView.adapter = MainListAdapter(categoryItemAdapters)
   }

   override fun showError(error: Throwable) {
       toast("Error: ${error.message}")
       error.printStackTrace()
   }
}
```

That is all we need to define the functionality of the character search. Now we can build the application and use it to find our favorite character:

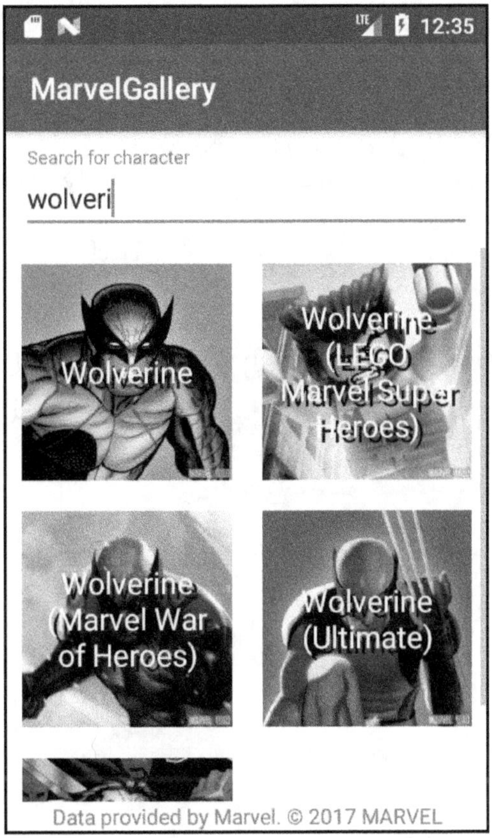

With a correctly working application, we can move on to the next use case.

Character profile display

Searching through characters is not enough. To make the app functional, we should add a character description display. Here is the use case we've defined: "when the user clicks on a character picture, there is a profile displayed. The character profile contains a character name, photo, description, and their occurrences."

To implement this use case, we need to create a new activity and layout that will define what this `Activity` looks like. To do this, create a new Activity called `CharacterProfileActivity` in the package the `com.sample.marvelgallery.view.character` package:

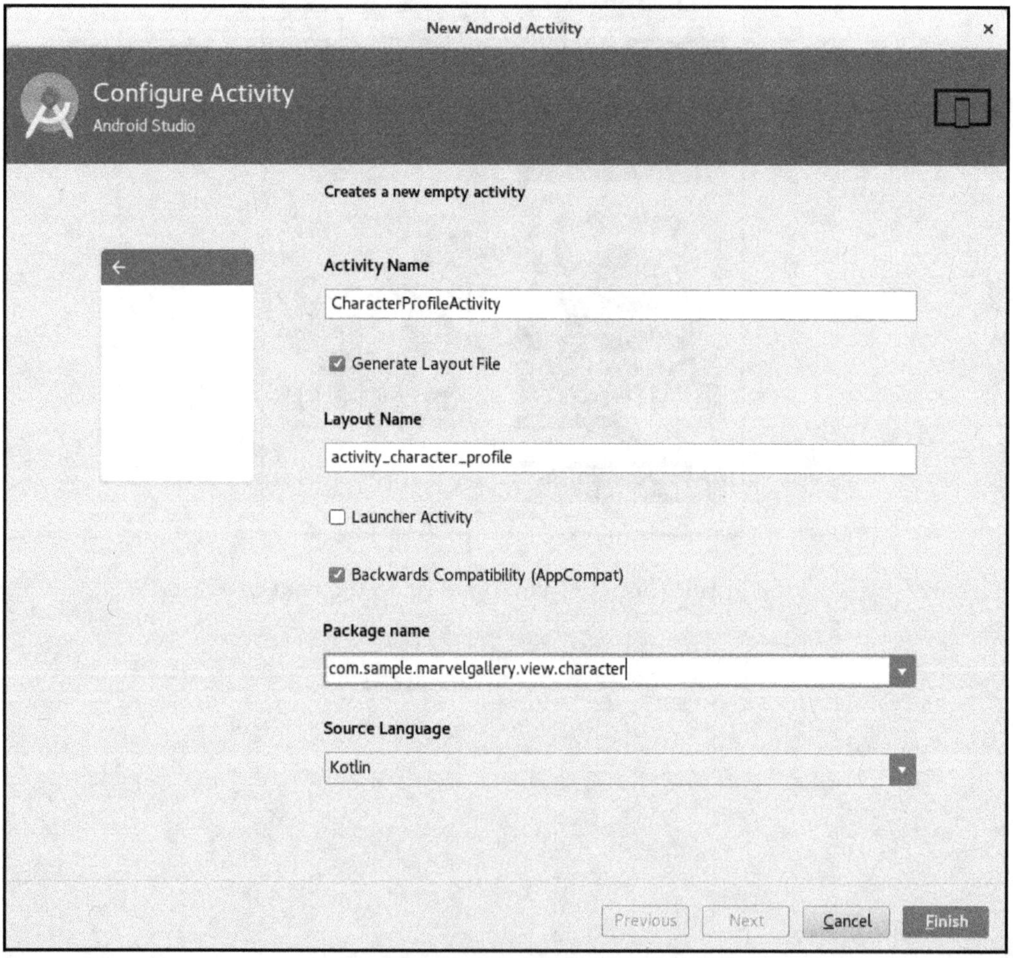

We will start its implementation from changes in the layout (in `activity_character_profile.xml`). Here is the final result we would like to achieve:

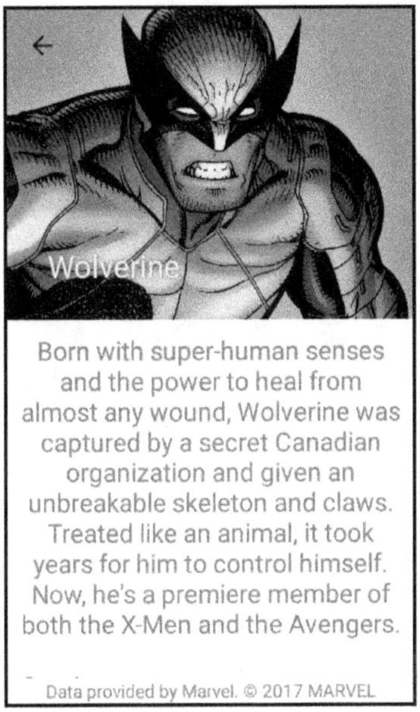

The base element is `CoordinatorLayout`, with `AppBar` and `CollapsingToolbarLayout` both used to achieve a collapsing effect known from material design:

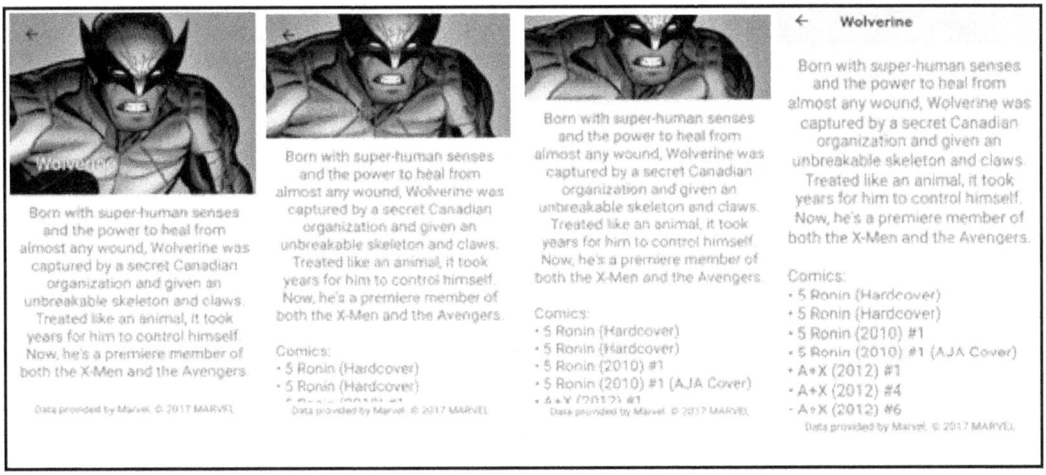

Collapsing effect step by step

We also need `TextView` for the description and occurrences, that will be filled with data in the next use case. Here is the full `activity_character_profile` layout definition:

```
<?xml version="1.0" encoding="utf-8"?>
<android.support.design.widget.CoordinatorLayout
xmlns:android="http://schemas.android.com/apk/res/android"
   xmlns:app="http://schemas.android.com/apk/res-auto"
   xmlns:tools="http://schemas.android.com/tools"
   android:id="@+id/character_detail_layout"
   android:layout_width="match_parent"
   android:layout_height="match_parent"
   android:background="@android:color/white">

   <android.support.design.widget.AppBarLayout
       android:id="@+id/appBarLayout"
       android:layout_width="match_parent"
       android:layout_height="wrap_content"
       android:theme="@style/ThemeOverlay.AppCompat.ActionBar">

       <android.support.design.widget.CollapsingToolbarLayout
           android:id="@+id/toolbarLayout"
           android:layout_width="match_parent"
           android:layout_height="match_parent"
           app:contentScrim="?attr/colorPrimary"
           app:expandedTitleTextAppearance="@style/ItemTitleName"
           app:layout_scrollFlags="scroll|exitUntilCollapsed">

           <android.support.v7.widget.AppCompatImageView
               android:id="@+id/headerView"
               android:layout_width="match_parent"
               android:layout_height="@dimen/character_header_height"
               android:background="@color/colorPrimaryDark"
               app:layout_collapseMode="parallax" />

           <android.support.v7.widget.Toolbar
               android:id="@+id/toolbar"
               android:layout_width="match_parent"
               android:layout_height="?attr/actionBarSize"
               android:background="@android:color/transparent"
               app:layout_collapseMode="pin"
               app:popupTheme="@style/ThemeOverlay.AppCompat.Light" />

       </android.support.design.widget.CollapsingToolbarLayout>
   </android.support.design.widget.AppBarLayout>

   <android.support.v4.widget.NestedScrollView
       android:layout_width="match_parent"
       android:layout_height="match_parent"
```

```
        android:overScrollMode="never"
        app:layout_behavior="@string/appbar_scrolling_view_behavior">

        <LinearLayout
            android:id="@+id/details_content_frame"
            android:layout_width="match_parent"
            android:layout_height="match_parent"
            android:focusableInTouchMode="true"
            android:orientation="vertical">

            <TextView
                android:id="@+id/descriptionView"
                android:layout_width="match_parent"
                android:layout_height="wrap_content"
                android:gravity="center"
                android:padding="@dimen/character_description_padding"
                android:textSize="@dimen/standard_text_size"
                tools:text="This is some long text that will be visible as
an character description." />

            <TextView
                android:id="@+id/occurrencesView"
                android:layout_width="match_parent"
                android:layout_height="wrap_content"
                android:padding="@dimen/character_description_padding"
                android:textSize="@dimen/standard_text_size"
                tools:text="He was in following comics:\n* KOKOKO \n* KOKOKO
\n* KOKOKO \n* KOKOKO \n* KOKOKO \n* KOKOKO \n* KOKOKO \n* KOKOKO \n*
KOKOKO \n* KOKOKO \n* KOKOKO " />
        </LinearLayout>

    </android.support.v4.widget.NestedScrollView>

    <TextView
        android:layout_width="match_parent"
        android:layout_height="wrap_content"
        android:layout_gravity="bottom"
        android:background="@android:color/white"
        android:gravity="bottom|center"
        android:text="@string/marvel_copyright_notice" />

    <ProgressBar
        android:id="@+id/progressView"
        style="?android:attr/progressBarStyleLarge"
        android:layout_width="wrap_content"
        android:layout_height="wrap_content"
        android:layout_gravity="center"
        android:visibility="gone" />
```

```
</android.support.design.widget.CoordinatorLayout>
```

We also need to add the following styles in `styles.xml`:

```
<resources>

    <!-- Base application theme. -->
    <style name="AppTheme"
           parent="Theme.AppCompat.Light.DarkActionBar">
        <!-- Customize your theme here. -->
        <item name="colorPrimary">@color/colorPrimary</item>
        <item name="colorPrimaryDark">@color/colorPrimaryDark</item>
        <item name="colorAccent">@color/colorAccent</item>
    </style>
    <style name="AppFullScreenTheme"
           parent="Theme.AppCompat.Light.NoActionBar">
        <item name="android:windowNoTitle">true</item>
        <item name="android:windowActionBar">false</item>
        <item name="android:windowFullscreen">true</item>
        <item name="android:windowContentOverlay">@null</item>
    </style>

    <style name="ItemTitleName"
           parent="TextAppearance.AppCompat.Headline">
        <item name="android:textColor">@android:color/white</item>
        <item name="android:shadowColor">@color/colorPrimaryDark</item>
        <item name="android:shadowRadius">3.0</item>
    </style>
    <style name="ItemDetailTitle"
           parent="@style/TextAppearance.AppCompat.Small">
        <item name="android:textColor">@color/colorAccent</item>
    </style>

</resources>
```

And we need to define `AppFullScreenTheme` as the theme for `CharacterProfileActivity` in `AndroidManifest`:

```
<activity android:name=".view.CharacterProfileActivity"
   android:theme="@style/AppFullScreenTheme" />
```

Here is a preview of the defined layout:

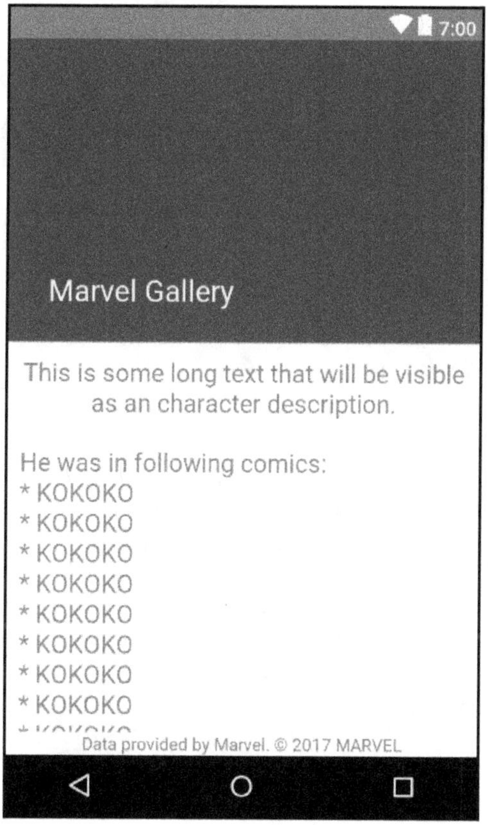

This view will be used to display data about the character, but first we need to open it from `MainActivity`. We need to set `onClickListener` in `CharacterItemAdapter`, which is calling the `clicked` callback provided by the constructor:

```
package com.sample.marvelgallery.view.main

import android.support.v7.widget.RecyclerView
import android.view.View
import android.widget.ImageView
import android.widget.TextView
import com.sample.marvelgallery.R
import com.sample.marvelgallery.model.MarvelCharacter
import com.sample.marvelgallery.view.common.ItemAdapter
import com.sample.marvelgallery.view.common.bindView
import com.sample.marvelgallery.view.common.loadImage

class CharacterItemAdapter(
       val character: MarvelCharacter,
       val clicked: (MarvelCharacter) -> Unit
) : ItemAdapter<CharacterItemAdapter.ViewHolder>(R.layout.item_character) {

   override fun onCreateViewHolder(itemView: View) =
   ViewHolder(itemView)

   override fun ViewHolder.onBindViewHolder() {
       textView.text = character.name
       imageView.loadImage(character.imageUrl)
       itemView.setOnClickListener { clicked(character) }
   }

   class ViewHolder(itemView: View) :
   RecyclerView.ViewHolder(itemView) {
       val textView by bindView<TextView>(R.id.textView)
       val imageView by bindView<ImageView>(R.id.imageView)
   }
}
```

And we need to update `MainActivity`:

```
package com.sample.marvelgallery.view.main

import android.os.Bundle
import android.support.v7.widget.GridLayoutManager
import android.view.Window
import com.sample.marvelgallery.R
import com.sample.marvelgallery.data.MarvelRepository
import com.sample.marvelgallery.model.MarvelCharacter
import com.sample.marvelgallery.presenter.MainPresenter
```

```
import com.sample.marvelgallery.view.character.CharacterProfileActivity
import com.sample.marvelgallery.view.common.BaseActivityWithPresenter
import com.sample.marvelgallery.view.common.addOnTextChangedListener
import com.sample.marvelgallery.view.common.bindToSwipeRefresh
import com.sample.marvelgallery.view.common.toast
import kotlinx.android.synthetic.main.activity_main.*

class MainActivity : BaseActivityWithPresenter(), MainView {

   override var refresh by bindToSwipeRefresh(R.id.swipeRefreshView)
   override val presenter by lazy
   { MainPresenter(this, MarvelRepository.get()) }

   override fun onCreate(savedInstanceState: Bundle?) {
       super.onCreate(savedInstanceState)
       requestWindowFeature(Window.FEATURE_NO_TITLE)
       setContentView(R.layout.activity_main)
       recyclerView.layoutManager = GridLayoutManager(this, 2)
       swipeRefreshView.setOnRefreshListener { presenter.onRefresh() }
       searchView.addOnTextChangedListener {
           onTextChanged { text, _, _, _ ->
               presenter.onSearchChanged(text)
           }
       }
       presenter.onViewCreated()
   }

   override fun show(items: List<MarvelCharacter>) {
       val categoryItemAdapters =
       items.map(this::createCategoryItemAdapter)
       recyclerView.adapter = MainListAdapter(categoryItemAdapters)
   }

   override fun showError(error: Throwable) {
       toast("Error: ${error.message}")
       error.printStackTrace()
   }

   private fun createCategoryItemAdapter(character: MarvelCharacter)
           = CharacterItemAdapter(character,
             { showHeroProfile(character) })

   private fun showHeroProfile(character: MarvelCharacter) {
       CharacterProfileActivity.start(this, character)
   }
}
```

In the preceding implementation, we are using a method from the `CharacterProfileActivity` companion object to start `CharacterProfileActivity`. We need to pass the `MarvelCharacter` object to this method. The most efficient way to pass a `MarvelCharacter` object is to pass it as *parcelable*. To allow this, `MarvelCharacter` must implement the `Parcelable` interface. This is why a useful solution is to use an annotation processing library such as **Parceler**, **PaperParcel**, or **Smuggler** that generates the necessary elements. We will use the solution from Kotlin Android Extensions we already have in the project. At the time of writing, it was still experimental, so the following definitions needs to be added in the `build.gradle` module:

```
androidExtensions {
   experimental = true
}
```

All we need to do is to add the `Parcelize` annotation before the class, and we need to make this class implement `Parcelable`. We will also add error suppression to hide the default Android warning:

```
package com.sample.marvelgallery.model

import android.annotation.SuppressLint
import android.os.Parcelable
import com.sample.marvelgallery.data.network.dto.CharacterMarvelDto

import kotlinx.android.parcel.Parcelize
@SuppressLint("ParcelCreator")
@Parcelize

   constructor(dto: CharacterMarvelDto) : this(
           name = dto.name,
           imageUrl = dto.imageUrl
   )
}
```

Now we can implement the `start` function and field `character`, which will get the argument value from Intent using the property delegate:

```
package com.sample.marvelgallery.view.character

import android.content.Context
import android.support.v7.app.AppCompatActivity
import android.os.Bundle
import android.view.MenuItem
import com.sample.marvelgallery.R
import com.sample.marvelgallery.model.MarvelCharacter
import com.sample.marvelgallery.view.common.extra
```

```
import com.sample.marvelgallery.view.common.getIntent
import com.sample.marvelgallery.view.common.loadImage
import kotlinx.android.synthetic.main.activity_character_profile.*

class CharacterProfileActivity : AppCompatActivity() {

   val character: MarvelCharacter by extra(CHARACTER_ARG) // 1

   override fun onCreate(savedInstanceState: Bundle?) {
       super.onCreate(savedInstanceState)
       setContentView(R.layout.activity_character_profile)
       setUpToolbar()
       supportActionBar?.title = character.name
       headerView.loadImage(character.imageUrl, centerCropped = true) // 1
   }

   override fun onOptionsItemSelected(item: MenuItem): Boolean = when {
       item.itemId == android.R.id.home -> onBackPressed().let { true }
       else -> super.onOptionsItemSelected(item)
   }

   private fun setUpToolbar() {
       setSupportActionBar(toolbar)
       supportActionBar?.setDisplayHomeAsUpEnabled(true)
   }

   companion object {

       private const val CHARACTER_ARG =
"com.sample.marvelgallery.view.character.CharacterProfileActivity.Character
ArgKey"

       fun start(context: Context, character: MarvelCharacter) {
           val intent = context
                   .getIntent<CharacterProfileActivity>() // 1
                   .apply { putExtra(CHARACTER_ARG, character) }
           context.startActivity(intent)
       }
   }
}
```

1. The `extra` and `getIntent` extension functions were already been presented in the book, but they have not been implemented yet in this project. Also, `loadImage` will display an error because it needs to be changed.

We need to update `loadImage`, and define `extra` and `getIntent` as top-level functions:

```
// ViewExt.kt
package com.sample.marvelgallery.view.common

import android.app.Activity
import android.content.Context
import android.content.Intent
import android.os.Parcelable
import android.support.annotation.IdRes
import android.support.v4.widget.SwipeRefreshLayout
import android.widget.ImageView
import android.widget.Toast
import com.bumptech.glide.Glide
import kotlin.properties.ReadWriteProperty
import kotlin.reflect.KProperty
import android.support.v7.widget.RecyclerView
import android.view.View

fun <T : View> RecyclerView.ViewHolder.bindView(viewId: Int)
      = lazy { itemView.findViewById<T>(viewId) }

fun ImageView.loadImage(photoUrl: String, centerCropped: Boolean = false) {
   Glide.with(context)
           .load(photoUrl)
           .apply { if (centerCropped) centerCrop() }
           .into(this)
}

fun <T : Parcelable> Activity.extra(key: String, default: T? = null):
Lazy<T>
      = lazy { intent?.extras?.getParcelable<T>(key) ?: default ?: throw
Error("No value $key in extras") }

inline fun <reified T : Activity> Context.getIntent() = Intent(this,
T::class.java)

// ...
```

Instead of defining functions to start the Activity, we might use a library that generates these methods. For example, we might use the `ActivityStarter` library. This is what `CharacterProfileActivity` would look like:

```
class CharacterProfileActivity : AppCompatActivity() {

   @get:Arg val character: MarvelCharacter by argExtra()

   override fun onCreate(savedInstanceState: Bundle?) {
       super.onCreate(savedInstanceState)
       setContentView(R.layout.activity_character_profile)
       setUpToolbar()
       supportActionBar?.title = character.name
       headerView.loadImage(character.imageUrl, centerCropped = true) // 1
   }

   override fun onOptionsItemSelected(item: MenuItem): Boolean = when {
       item.itemId == android.R.id.home -> onBackPressed().let { true }
       else -> super.onOptionsItemSelected(item)
   }

   private fun setUpToolbar() {
       setSupportActionBar(toolbar)
       supportActionBar?.setDisplayHomeAsUpEnabled(true)
   }
}
```

We should start it or get its intent using the static methods of the generated class `CharacterProfileActivityStarter`:

```
CharacterProfileActivityStarter.start(context, character)
val intent = CharacterProfileActivityStarter.getIntent(context, character)
```

To allow it, we need the **kapt** plugin in the `build.gradle` module (used to support annotation processing in Kotlin):

```
apply plugin: 'kotlin-kapt'
```

Add the `ActivityStarter` dependencies in the `build.gradle` module:

```
implementation
'com.github.marcinmoskala.activitystarter:activitystarter:1.00'
implementation 'com.github.marcinmoskala.activitystarter:activitystarter-
kotlin:1.00'
kapt 'com.github.marcinmoskala.activitystarter:activitystarter-
compiler:1.00'
```

After these changes, when we click into a character in `MainActivity`, then `CharacterProfileActivity` will be started:

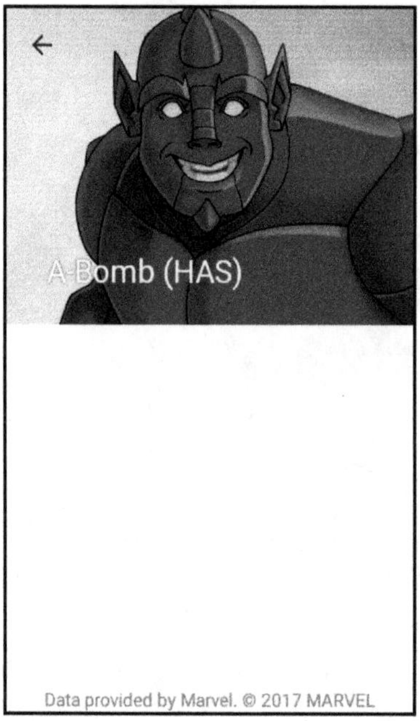

We display the name and show the character photo. The next step is to display the description and list of occurrences. The necessary data can be found in the Marvel API and we only need to extend DTO models to get it. We need to add `ListWrapper`, which is used to hold a list:

```
package com.sample.marvelgallery.data.network.dto

class ListWrapper<T> {
   var items: List<T> = listOf()
}
```

We need to define `ComicDto`, which holds the data we need about occurrences:

```
package com.sample.marvelgallery.data.network.dto

class ComicDto {
   lateinit var name: String
}
```

And we need to update `CharacterMarvelDto`:

```
package com.sample.marvelgallery.data.network.dto

class CharacterMarvelDto {

   lateinit var name: String
   lateinit var description: String
   lateinit var thumbnail: ImageDto
   var comics: ListWrapper<ComicDto> = ListWrapper()
   var series: ListWrapper<ComicDto> = ListWrapper()
   var stories: ListWrapper<ComicDto> = ListWrapper()
   var events: ListWrapper<ComicDto> = ListWrapper()

   val imageUrl: String
       get() = thumbnail.completeImagePath
}
```

Data is now read from the API and kept in DTO objects, but to use it in the project, we also need to change the `MarvelCharacter` class definition, and add a new constructor:

```
@SuppressLint("ParcelCreator")
@Parcelize

class MarvelCharacter(
        val name: String,
        val imageUrl: String,
        val description: String,
        val comics: List<String>,
```

```
        val series: List<String>,
        val stories: List<String>,
        val events: List<String>
) : Parcelable {

    constructor(dto: CharacterMarvelDto) : this(
            name = dto.name,
            imageUrl = dto.imageUrl,
            description = dto.description,
            comics = dto.comics.items.map { it.name },
            series = dto.series.items.map { it.name },
            stories = dto.stories.items.map { it.name },
            events = dto.events.items.map { it.name }
    )
}
```

Now we can update `CharacterProfileActivity` to display the description and list of occurrences:

```
class CharacterProfileActivity : AppCompatActivity() {

    val character: MarvelCharacter by extra(CHARACTER_ARG)
    override fun onCreate(savedInstanceState: Bundle?) {
        super.onCreate(savedInstanceState)
        setContentView(R.layout.activity_character_profile)
        setUpToolbar()
        supportActionBar?.title = character.name
        descriptionView.text = character.description
        occurrencesView.text = makeOccurrencesText() // 1
        headerView.loadImage(character.imageUrl, centerCropped = true)
    }

    override fun onOptionsItemSelected(item: MenuItem): Boolean = when {
        item.itemId == android.R.id.home -> onBackPressed().let { true }
        else -> super.onOptionsItemSelected(item)
    }

    private fun setUpToolbar() {
        setSupportActionBar(toolbar)
        supportActionBar?.setDisplayHomeAsUpEnabled(true)
    }

    private fun makeOccurrencesText(): String = "" // 1, 2
            .addList(R.string.occurrences_comics_list_introduction,
character.comics)
            .addList(R.string.occurrences_series_list_introduction,
character.series)
            .addList(R.string.occurrences_stories_list_introduction,
```

```
character.stories)
            .addList(R.string.occurrences_events_list_introduction,
character.events)

    private fun String.addList(introductionTextId: Int, list: List<String>):
String { // 3
        if (list.isEmpty()) return this
        val introductionText = getString(introductionTextId)
        val listText = list.joinToString(transform =
            { " $bullet $it" }, separator = "\n")
        return this + "$introductionText\n$listText\n\n"
    }

    companion object {
        private const val bullet = '\u2022' // 4
        private const val CHARACTER_ARG =
"com.naxtlevelofandroiddevelopment.marvelgallery.presentation.heroprofile.C
haracterArgKey"

        fun start(context: Context, character: MarvelCharacter) {
            val intent = context
                    .getIntent<CharacterProfileActivity>()
                    .apply { putExtra(CHARACTER_ARG, character) }
            context.startActivity(intent)
        }
    }
}
```

1. The composition of the list of occurrences is quite a complex task, so we extract it to the function `makeOccurrencesText`. There, for each occurrence type (comic, series, and so on), we want to show the introduction text and list only if there are some occurrences of this type. We also want to prefix each item with a bullet.
2. `makeOccurrencesText` is a single expression function that uses `addList` to append an initially empty string with the next lists that we want to display.
3. `addList` is a member extension function. It returns a string unchanged if the provided list is empty, or it returns a string appended with the introduction text and the list of elements with bullets.
4. This is the character that is used as a list bullet.

We also need to define strings in `strings.xml`:

```
<resources>
   <string name="app_name">Marvel Gallery</string>
   <string name="marvel_copyright_notice">
       Data provided by Marvel. © 2017 MARVEL</string>
   <string name="search_hint">Search for character</string>
   <string name="occurrences_comics_list_introduction">Comics:</string>
   <string name="occurrences_series_list_introduction">Series:</string>
   <string name="occurrences_stories_list_introduction">Stories:</string>
   <string name="occurrences_events_list_introduction">Events:</string>
</resources>
```

Now we can see the whole character profile--character name, image, description, and lists of their occurrences in comics, series, events, and stories:

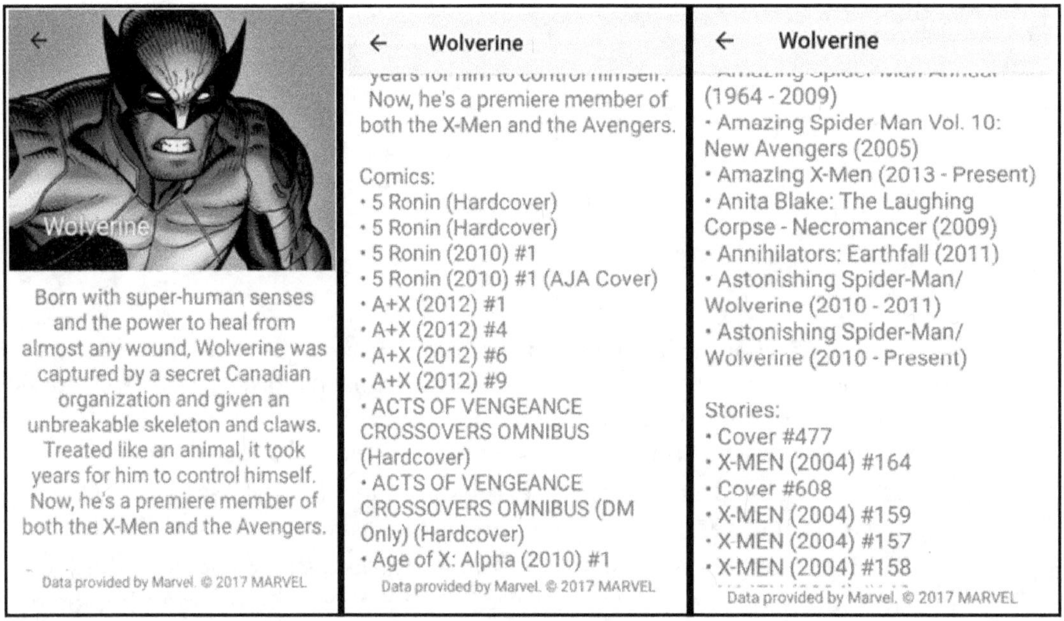

Summary

The application is complete, but there are still lots of functionalities that can be added. In this application, we've seen some examples of how Kotlin can be used to simplify Android development. But there are still a lot of solutions to discover. Kotlin simplifies Android development at any level--from common operations such as listener set or view element reference, to high-level functionalities such as functional programming or collection processing.

This book cannot cover absolutely everything about Android development with Kotlin, but it has been designed to show enough to allow everyone to start their own adventure with bags of ideas and feature understanding. The next step is to open Android Studio, create your own project, and start having fun with Kotlin. A big adventure is in front of you.

Index

A

B

C

D

E

F

G

H

I

J

K

L

M

N

O

P

Q

R

www.ingramcontent.com/pod-product-compliance
Lightning Source LLC
LaVergne TN
LVHW081511050326
832903LV00025B/1440
* 9 7 8 1 7 8 7 1 2 3 6 8 7 *